Studies at Rutgers University, and she now chairs the Department of English at Princeton University. She has lectured widely throughout the United States and England on women's writing, Victorian medical history, and literary theory. Virago publish her highly acclaimed *A Literature of Their Own: British Women Novelists from Bronte to Lessing*, *The New Feminist Criticism: Essays on Women, Literature and Theory*, *Sexual Anarchy: Gender and Culture at the Fin de Siècle* and *Daughters of Decadence: Women Writers of the Fin-de-Siècle*.

Critical acclaim for *The Female Malady: Women, Madness and English Culture 1830–1980*

'Showalter's book is bound to provoke disagreement, if only because it raises so many questions . . . a highly entertaining and original book crammed with information, very well written with an acute sensitivity to period and personality' – *Claire Tomalin, Observer*

'This beautifully written and illustrated book attempts to show how it is a consequence rather than a deviation from the traditional female role, using fiction (from Mary Wollstonecraft to Doris Lessing) as well as fact' – *Pauline Willis, Guardian*

'Elaine Showalter has written an extraordinary book – original, passionate and illuminating. . . . This intelligent and provocative analysis will surely make such neglect impossible in the future' – *Andrew T. Scull, author of Museums of Madness*

ELAINE SHOWALTER was born in Cambridge, Massachusetts in 1941, and was educated at Bryn Mawr College and the University of California. From 1969 to 1984 she taught English and Women's

The Female Malady

WOMEN, MADNESS, AND ENGLISH CULTURE, 1830–1980

Elaine Showalter

Virago

A *Virago* Book

Published by Virago Press 1987

Reprinted 1988, 1991, 1995, 1996, 1998, 2000, 2001, 2004

First published in the United States and Canada by Pantheon Books,
New York 1985
First British edition published by arrangement with Pantheon Books,
A Division of Random House, Inc.

Grateful acknowledgement is made to the following for permission to reprint previously published material:

Raritan: "R. D. Laing and the Sixties" by Elaine Showalter,
Raritan: A Quarterly Review 1, no. 2 (Fall 1981).
Reprinted by permission.

The University of Chicago Press: "Florence Nightingale's Feminist Complaint" by Elaine Showalter, *SIGNS 6* (Spring 1981). Reprinted by permission of The University of Chicago Press.

Victorian Studies: "Victorian Women and Insanity" by Elaine Showalter, *Victorian Studies* 23 (Winter 1979–80): 157–81. Reprinted by permission of Victorian Studies.

A CIP catalogue record for this book is available from the British Library

ISBN 0 86068 869 0

Printed and bound in Great Britain by Clays Ltd, St Ives plc

Virago Press
An imprint of
Time Warner Book Group UK
Brettenham House
Lancaster Place
London WC2E 7EN

www.virago.co.uk

CONTENTS

PART TWO. PSYCHIATRIC DARWINISM

PART THREE. PSYCHIATRIC MODERNISM

I L L U S T R A T I O N S

ACKNOWLEDGMENTS

I could not have written this book without the help of many institutions, scholars, and friends on both sides of the Atlantic. Thanks first to the John Simon Guggenheim Foundation, whose fellowship supported the initial research for this project, and to the National Endowment for the Humanities Summer Program and the John D. Rockefeller Foundation Humanities Fellowships for grants that allowed me further travel to London and to Paris, and then time to write. I am especially grateful for the counsel of several historians of medicine and psychiatry, who made it easier for me to find my way through the immense literature of an unfamiliar and challenging field. Gerald Grob of Rutgers University helped me get oriented in the field of psychiatric history and supplied me with comparative data from his own research on the United States. Michael J. Clark of Linacre College, Oxford, shared rich materials from his work on Henry Maudsley and late Victorian psychiatry. The faculty and staff of the Wellcome Institute for the History of Medicine in London did welcome me to their seminars and stacks. And from the earliest stages of this book, Andrew Scull's pioneering work on the social history of English psychiatry, and his friendship, encouragement, and support, gave me an intellectual model to emulate and an ideal reader for whom to write.

Many other scholars have been generous with their time and ideas during the course of my research. Robert A. Colby, Leonore Davidoff, John Reed, Dr. Alexander Walk, Angeline Goreau, Cynthia Gooding, Robert B. Martin, Cleo McNelly, Sally Mitchell, E. Ann Kaplan, Vivian Gornick, and Paul Fussell kindly provided me with information and documents about real and imaginary doctors and patients. Maxine Berry and the Honourable Mabel Smith informed me about the Octavia Wilberforce correspondence, and gave permission to publish it. Clancy Sigal talked to me about the backgrounds of his novel *Zone of the Interior* and about English psychopolitics in the 1960s. Nina Auerbach, Dr. Irwin Avery, Judith Johnston, George Levine, Alan Nadel, Roy Porter, Barry Qualls, Val Segall, Martha Vicinus, and Judith Walkowitz commented on drafts, and I am grateful for their criticism and advice. I owe special thanks to Carol Smith, who read the entire manuscript, and whose sympathy and clarity of mind helped me work through many obstacles. Thanks too to the tough and insightful responses of the Columbia University Women's Seminar, especially Gerda Lerner, Mary Parlee, and Louise Yellin. Sections of chapters 2, 3, and 9 include material from essays that originally appeared in *Victorian Studies, Raritan,* and *Signs*; thanks to these journals for permission to reprint.

Finally, I had expert help in the preparation of the manuscript from Gloria Cohn, Dorothy Tobolsky, Marilyn Walden, and especially Linda Auerbach. At Pantheon, Sara Bershtel's dedication, creativity, and editorial expertise contributed to every stage of the book. My greatest debt is to my husband, English Showalter, who listened to my ideas, processed my words, and sustained me throughout with patience, humor, and frequent glasses of Tab. This book is dedicated to him.

Elaine Showalter
Princeton, New Jersey
June 1985

Introduction

THE FEMALE MALADY

During the last year of her life, the great feminist theorist Mary Wollstonecraft worked on a novel intended as a companion piece to her political treatise *A Vindication of the Rights of Woman.* Left unfinished at her death in 1797, *Maria; or, The Wrongs of Woman* describes "the misery and oppression, peculiar to women, that arise out of the partial laws and customs of society." Wollstonecraft's heroine, Maria, has been forced into a madhouse by her abusive husband, who wants control of her fortune and liberty to pursue his sexual adventures. To Maria, the "mansion of despair" in which she is incarcerated becomes a symbol of all the man-made institutions, from marriage to the law, that confine women and drive them mad. Listening to the songs and cries of the other women in the madhouse, Maria feels her own mind giving way. Yet she can find no reason to fight for her sanity or her freedom: "Was not the world a vast prison, and women born slaves?"[1]

A French painting that depicts the same period, "Pinel Freeing the Insane," by Tony Robert-Fleury, offers a different perspective on the connections between women, madness, and confinement. In 1793,

Philippe Pinel, the doctor in charge of the Parisian madhouses during the Revolution, obtained permission from the Commune to unchain the lunatics at the Bicêtre and the Salpêtrière, a politically symbolic act like the freeing of the prisoners in the Bastille. Pinel, so the story goes, first removed the chains of several male inmates; some weeks later, he got around to the women. Yet in the painting that commemorates this historic occasion, Robert-Fleury depicts "the insane" as madwomen of different ages, from youth to senility (fig. 1). Some are crouched in melancholia, others crying out in hysterical fits, while one gratefully kisses the hand of Pinel. The representatives of sanity in the painting are all men, and this division between feminine madness and masculine rationality is further emphasized by the three figures at the center. In the foreground is a lovely, passive, and disheveled young woman, her eyes modestly cast down, upon whose exposed bosom an erect and dignified Pinel gazes with ambiguous interest. The keeper who holds

Figure 1. Tony Robert-Fleury, "Pinel Freeing the Insane," 1887.

up her arm while he unlocks her chains seems less to be releasing her than winding her up, like some huge doll; her nominal freedom, the composition suggests, exists in a complex tension with male control. In Robert-Fleury's painting, the irrationality Pinel frees from its fetters is thus visually translated into its most recognizable sign: the beautiful woman, whose disordered body and mind are exposed—and opposed—to the scrutiny of the man who has the authority to unchain her.[2]

These dual images of female insanity—madness as one of the wrongs of woman; madness as the essential feminine nature unveiling itself before scientific male rationality—suggest the two ways that the relationship between women and madness has been perceived. In the most obvious sense, madness is a female malady because it is experienced by more women than men. The statistical overrepresentation of women among the mentally ill has been well documented by historians and psychologists.[3] As early as the seventeenth century, the files of the doctor Richard Napier showed nearly twice as many cases of mental disorder among his women patients as among men.[4] By the middle of the nineteenth century, records showed that women had become the majority of patients in public lunatic asylums. In the twentieth century, too, we know that women are the majority of clients for private and public psychiatric hospitals, outpatient mental health services, and psychotherapy; in 1967 a major study found "more mental illness among women than men from every data source."[5]

But how should we interpret this statistical fact? There have always been those who argued that women's high rate of mental disorder is a product of their social situation, both their confining roles as daughters, wives, and mothers and their mistreatment by a male-dominated and possibly misogynistic psychiatric profession. Thus Richard Napier noted that, among his patients, women of all social classes complained more of stress and unhappiness in marriage, expressed more anxiety over their children, and suffered more from depression in their daily lives than their male peers.[6]

By far the more prevalent view, however, sees an equation between femininity and insanity that goes beyond statistical evidence or the social conditions of women. Contemporary feminist philosophers, literary critics, and social theorists have been the first to call attention to the existence of a fundamental alliance between "woman" and "madness." They have shown how women, within our dualistic systems of language and representation, are typically situated on the side of irrationality, silence, nature, and body, while men are situated on the side of reason, discourse, culture, and mind.[7] They have analyzed and illuminated a cultural tradition that represents "woman" *as* madness, and that uses images of the female body, as in the Pinel painting, to stand for irrationality in general. While the name of the symbolic female disorder may change from one historical period to the next, the gender asymmetry of the representational tradition remains constant. Thus madness, even when experienced by men, is metaphorically and symbolically represented as feminine: a female malady. In French, for example, the man dressed as a woman, the drag queen, is even called "the madwoman"—*la folle.* Men, on the other hand, "appear not only as the possessors, but also as the dispensers, of reason, which they can at will mete out to—or take away from—others."[8]

Given the pervasive cultural association of women and madness, it is not surprising that the madwoman has become as emblematic a figure for contemporary feminists as she was for Mary Wollstonecraft in 1797. Sandra Gilbert and Susan Gubar, in *The Madwoman in the Attic* (1979), point to the fictional character of the deranged woman who haunts the margins of nineteenth-century women writers' texts as the symbolic representation of the female author's anger against the rigidities of patriarchal tradition. The madwoman is the author's double, the incarnation of her own anxiety and rage. It is through the violence of this double that "the female author enacts her own raging desires to escape male houses and male texts."[9] Biographies and letters of gifted women who suffered mental breakdowns have suggested that madness is the price women artists have had to pay for the exercise of their creativity in a male-dominated culture. In the annals of feminist literary history, Virginia Woolf, Anne Sexton, and Sylvia Plath have become our sisters and our saints.

Feminist interest in female insanity has gone beyond artists and writers, and beyond the vision of the madwoman as victim. The psychologist Phyllis Chesler, for example, in her important study *Women and Madness* (1972), maintains that the women confined to American mental institutions are failed but heroic rebels against the constraints of a narrow femininity, pilgrims "on a doomed search for potency," whose insanity is a label applying to gender norms and violations, a penalty for "*being* 'female' as well as for desiring or daring *not* to be."[10] French feminist theory carries this identification with the madwoman to its furthest extremes. For such writers as Hélène Cixous and Xavière Gauthier, madness has been the historical label applied to female protest and revolution. They celebrate the "admirable hysterics" of the late nineteenth century, and especially Freud's famous patient "Dora," as champions of a defiant womanhood, whose opposition, expressed in physical symptoms and coded speech, subverted the linear logic of male science.[11]

It is certainly possible to see hysteria within the specific historical framework of the nineteenth century as an unconscious form of feminist protest, the counterpart of the attack on patriarchal values carried out by the women's movement of the time. In this perspective, Freud's Dora is the silent sister of Ibsen's Nora; both resist the social definitions that confine them to the doll's house of bourgeois femininity. Such claims, however, come dangerously close to romanticizing and endorsing madness as a desirable form of rebellion rather than seeing it as the desperate communication of the powerless. For madness, as Shoshana Felman has noted, is "quite the opposite of rebellion. Madness is the impasse confronting those whom cultural conditioning has deprived of the very means of protest or self-affirmation."[12] A serious historical study of the female malady should not romanticize madness as one of women's wrongs any more than it should accept an essentialist equation between femininity and insanity. Rather, it must investigate how, in a particular cultural context, notions of gender influence the definition and, consequently, the treatment of mental disorder.

This book is both a feminist history of psychiatry and a cultural history of madness as a female malady. I look at the detection and treatment of female insanity within the psychiatric profession in England over two centuries, exploring the social as well as medical contexts in which women were first defined, and then confined, as mad. I also look at the representation of the madwoman in legal, medical, and literary texts, and in painting, photography, and film. These images were not simply the reflections of medical and scientific knowledge, but part of the fundamental cultural framework in which ideas about femininity and insanity were constructed. The language of psychiatric medicine, especially in the nineteenth century, when there was scant scientific documentation for most assumptions, is as culturally determined and revealing in its metaphors as the language of fiction.

Traditionally, historians of psychiatry have paid little attention to questions of gender. The standard sources for psychiatric history, such as medical journals, psychiatric textbooks. asylum records, parliamentary minutes, court cases, and journalistic accounts, leave out, indeed silence, women's voices. Even the most radical critics of psychiatry are concerned with class rather than with gender as a determinant of the individual's psychiatric career and of the society's psychiatric institutions. Although anyone who writes about the history of madness must owe an intellectual debt to Michel Foucault, his critique of institutional power in *Madness and Civilization* (1961) does not take account of sexual difference. While he brilliantly exposed the repressive ideologies that lay behind the reform of the asylum, Foucault did not explore the possibility that the irrationality and difference the asylum silenced and confined is also the feminine.

In order to supply the gender analysis and feminist critique missing from the history of madness, we must turn to a wholly different set of cultural sources: inmate narratives, diaries, women's memoirs, and novels. These other accounts of insanity, by women from Florence Nightingale to Mary Barnes, as well as the writings of those women practitioners who commented, albeit from a marginal position, on the development of the psychiatric profession itself, offer an indispensable perspective on the diagnosis, treatment, and theory of the female malady from those who were more often the subjects of psychiatric discourse than its theorists and shapers.

I have chosen to focus on a specific national context, that of England, rather than attempt to define a general relationship between insanity and femininity, since both terms are culturally constructed. Although many fundamental English ideas about insanity were shared by the United States and Europe, the same theories had different effects within their specific national environments. Beginning in the 1830s, there was an active exchange of ideas between English, American, French, and German psychiatrists, who visited each other's asylums and eagerly read each other's publications; but by the end of the century, psychiatric attitudes and policies had become differentiated as each society established its own moral, medical, and mental boundaries. Similarly, attitudes towards femininity and sexual difference, although they shared many characteristics across national frontiers, took on special meaning within the context of a particular society.

Moreover, England is a particularly rich area for investigation because of the long-standing, cohesive, and fascinating notion of the cultural specificity of English madness. Since the eighteenth century, the links between an "English malady" and such aspects of the national experience as commerce, culture, climate, and cuisine have been the subject of both scientific treatises and literary texts.[13] The English have long regarded their country, with a mixture of complacency and sorrow, as the global headquarters of insanity. In *Reliques of Ancient English Poetry,* Percy claimed that the English had more mad-songs than any of their neighbors, and ever since its creation in 1247, Bethlem Hospital, known as "Bedlam," has been the symbol of all madhouses, holding the imaginative place in the history of asylums that the Bastille holds in the history of prisons. Ned Ward's comedy *All Men Mad; or, England a Great Bedlam* (1711) was typical of a literary tradition that satirized folly, eccentricity, and melancholy as national traits. But in 1733, the society doctor George Cheyne, in a book called *The English Malady,* claimed that madness was the by-product of English sensitivity, ambition, and intelligence. He urged his readers to take pride in the gloom, hypochondria, and spleen that were part of their national heritage, because these nervous afflictions were signs of progress and cultural superiority. "We have more nervous diseases," he explained, "since the present Age has made Efforts to go beyond former Times, in all the Arts of Ingenuity, Invention, Study, Learning, and all the Contemplative and Sedentary Professions."[14]

At the level of proverb and popular culture, if not in medical science, the connection between madness and England has persisted with remarkable tenacity. Since the antipsychiatry movement led by R. D. Laing in the 1960s, moreover, the sense of the English malady as part of the national character has enjoyed something of a revival. When I told the customs officer at Heathrow Airport in 1977 that I was planning to study madness, he cheerily assured me that I had come to the right place.

Most significantly, in England the differences in the perception of madness as it appeared in men and women stand out with particular clarity. Alongside the English malady, nineteenth-century psychiatry described a female malady. Even when both men and women had similar symptoms of mental disorder, psychiatry differentiated between an English malady, associated with the intellectual and economic pressures on highly civilized men, and a female malady, associated with the sexuality and essential nature of women. Women were believed to be more vulnerable to insanity than men, to experience it in specifically feminine ways, and to be differently affected by it in the conduct of their lives.

The Victorian psychiatrist Henry Maudsley maintained that even in violent dementia women were limited and bounded by the qualities of femininity; they did not "evince such lively exultation and energy as men, and they had quieter and less assertive delusions of grandeur conformable with their gentler natures and the quieter currents and conditions of their lives."[15]

The differentiation began at the end of the eighteenth century, when a significant shift occurred in the way that madness was viewed and treated. Whereas lunatics had formerly been regarded as unfeeling brutes, ferocious animals that needed to be kept in check with chains, whips, strait-waistcoats, barred windows, and locked cells, they were now seen instead as sick human beings, objects of pity whose sanity might be restored by kindly care. This ideological shift has been called the first psychiatric revolution. In its wake, English social reformers, including magistrates, wealthy philanthropists, and lay therapists, investigated the prevailing modes of treatment for the insane within private madhouses, workhouses, and prisons and began to create alternative institutions—asylums—in which paternal surveillance and religious ideals replaced physical coercion, fear, and force.

But it was also at this time that the dialectic of reason and unreason took on specifically sexual meanings, and that the symbolic gender of the insane person shifted from male to female. For the Augustans, the cultural imagery of the lunatic was male. In the middle of the eighteenth century, the most famous representations of madness were the two manacled male nudes sculptured by Caius Gabriel Cibber for the gates of Bethlem Hospital, then in Moorfields (figs. 2 and 3).[16] Depicting "Melancholy Madness" and "Raving Madness," these "brazen brainless brothers," as Pope called them in *The Dunciad,* marked the lunatic's entrance into the netherworld of the insane.[17] In the course of the century, however, the appealing madwoman gradually displaced the repulsive madman, both as the prototype of the confined lunatic and as a cultural icon. The lunacy-reform movement had its immediate origins in revelations of the brutal mistreatment of frail women in madhouses. In 1793, for example, after a young Quaker widow died under mysterious and ominous circumstances in the York Asylum, indignant Quaker philanthropists supported William Tuke, a wealthy local merchant, in the founding of the York Retreat, an asylum that pioneered the humane care of the insane. Over the next few decades as well, exposes of the abuse, even the rape and murder, of women patients by

Figure 2. Caius Gabriel Cibber, "Raving Madness," 1677.

Figure 3. Caius Gabriel Cibber, "Melancholy Madness," 1677.

madhouse keepers and attendants further changed the tide of opinion. While the public might be persuaded that madmen were subhuman creatures that required violent restraint, these accounts of the abuse of "delicate" women inspired a public outrage and a change of consciousness that led to a series of legislative reforms.[18]

Indeed, the correlation between madness and the wrongs of women became one of the chief fictional conventions of the age. Defoe had protested against the trade in female lunacy, the conspiracies of men and madhouse keepers to get troublesome wives or daughters out of the way. Late-eighteenth-century novelists depicted the madwoman as the victim of parental tyranny and male oppression, and as an object of enlightened sensibility; thus Henry Mackenzie's "man of feeling" weeps over a madwoman he sees in Bedlam.[19]

By 1815, Cibber's male statues had been hidden away from public view behind curtains that were drawn aside only by special request.[20] These disturbing images of wild, dark, naked men had been replaced by poetic, artistic, and theatrical images of a youthful, beautiful female insanity. The victimized madwoman became almost a cult figure for the Romantics. A typical sonnet of the period, George Dyer's "Written in Bedlam: On Seeing a Beautiful Young Female Maniac" (1801) presents the poet overcome by pity at the sight of the "sweet maid" whose "angel face" and "gentle bosom" make her madness especially enticing.[21] Yet this gentle female irrationality, so easily subjected to male reason, might also represent an unknowable and untamable sexual force. The troubling, ambiguous nature of female insanity was expressed and perpetuated by the three major Romantic images of the madwoman: the suicidal Ophelia, the sentimental Crazy Jane, and the violent Lucia. All three established female sexuality and feminine nature as the source of the female malady, but each also stood for a different interpretation of woman's madness and man's relation to it.

Virtually all of these conventions can be traced to the figure of Shakespeare's Ophelia. Laertes calls her a "document in madness," and indeed, as Sander Gilman points out, the changing representations of Ophelia over the centuries do chronicle the shifting definitions of female insanity, from the erotomania of the Elizabethans and the hysteria of the nineteenth century to the unconscious incestuous conflicts of the Freudians and the schizophrenic double bind of the Laingians.[22]

The stage conventions associated with the role have always emphasized the feminine nature of Ophelia's insanity as contrasted with Hamlet's universalized metaphysical distress. As on the Elizabethan stage, Ophelia is traditionally dressed in white, decked with "fantastical garlands" of wildflowers, and has her hair loose. She sings wistful and bawdy ballads; her speech is marked by extravagant metaphors, lyrical free associations, and explicit sexual references. She demonstrates all the classic symptoms of love melancholy.

All of these conventions carried dual messages about femininity and insanity. The woman with her hair down indicated an offense against decorum, an improper sensuality.[23] Ophelia's flowers, too, came from the Renaissance iconography of female sexuality; in giving them away, she symbolically "deflowers" herself.[24] Even her death by drowning has associations with the feminine and the irrational, since water is the organic symbol of woman's fluidity: blood, milk, tears.[25]

The Augustans were discomforted by the erotic and discordant elements in Ophelia's role. Like Samuel Johnson, they were determined to see her as an innocent victim, someone young, beautiful, harmless, and pious. Augustan objections to the shocking levity and indecency of Ophelia's speech led to censorship of the part: her lines were cut, and the part was usually assigned to a singer rather than an actress.

The Romantics, on the other hand, were captivated by the spectacle of Ophelia's sexuality and emotionality. Passionately portrayed by the Irish ingenue Harriet Smithson in a Paris production of the 1830s, Ophelia became an obsession for the century's artists. In her mad scenes, Smithson wore a long black veil, suggestive of the symbolism of female sexual mystery that permeates the Gothic novel, and scattered Bedlamish straw in her hair. Her image was widely copied in popular lithographs; French ladies of fashion adopted a "coiffure *à la folle*"; the young Hector Berlioz was so smitten that he married her; and Delacroix painted her as Ophelia in a series of intensely sexual drawings[26] (fig. 4).

Ophelia had two important auxiliary images in the Romantic imagination, each of which embodied one aspect of her character. The most popular of the wronged Romantic madwomen was Crazy Jane (sometimes called Crazy Kate or Crazy Ann), a poor servant girl who, abandoned by her lover or bereft of him through death, goes mad as a result. The original ballad of her seduction and betrayal, written by the Gothic novelist Matthew "Monk" Lewis in 1793, was quickly followed by melodramas, sequels about the death and apparition of Crazy Jane, and Sarah Wilkinson's chapbook, *The Tragical History of Miss Jane Arnold,*

Figure 4. Harriet Smithson as Ophelia in Paris, 1826.

Figure 5. George Shepheard, "Crazy Kate," 1815.

Commonly Called Crazy Jane, and Mr. Henry Perceval, Giving an Account of Their Birth, Parentage, Courtship, and Melancholy End, Founded on Facts (1813). Crazy Jane was a docile and harmless madwoman who devoted herself singlemindedly to commemorating her lost lover: "She would wander in those places where she had been used to walk with Henry. She would sing the most plaintive airs, and converse with those who addressed her about her lover. She would dress her head with willow straw, and wild flowers, disposed in a fanciful style; and this seemed to be the only amusement that soothed her mind."[27] The appeal of Crazy Jane is not hard to fathom. What activities could be more feminine and respectable, or pose less of a threat to domineering parents and false-hearted men? For Romantic writers, Crazy Jane was a touching image of feminine vulnerability and a flattering reminder of female dependence upon male affection. Romantic artists such as Thomas Barker and George Shepheard painted Crazy Jane as a wistful orphan of the storm (fig. 5).[28]

In a fascinating demonstration of the traffic between cultural images and psychiatric ideologies, her image even entered the psychiatric textbooks of the period. In the 1820s Dr. Alexander Morison, influenced by the work of the great French psychiatrist Esquirol on physiognomy, invited artists to come to the Surrey County Asylum, where he was resident superintendent of the female department. He used their drawings of patients in a series of lectures on the physiognomy of mental disease. Most of the plates show standardized female portraits in the Crazy Jane style; even when they are described as manic, these women have sweet smiles and pretty features; they are shown in elaborate caps and bonnets, like the millinery models in the ladies' annuals. Miss A. A. (fig. 6), for example, was an "erotomaniac," a domestic servant who had developed a passion for the clergyman of her parish, and who was "generally disposed to kiss."[29] Crazy Jane had become the typical inhabitant of nineteenth-century Bedlam, not only the image of madness for women but the model of insanity for men as well. In the 1850s, Richard Dadd, a Victorian artist who had murdered his father and spent most of his life in lunatic asylums, painted a male inmate of Bethlem as Crazy Jane, wearing the madwoman's patched robes and crowned with her traditional wildflowers, feathers, rags, and straw (fig. 7).

At the height of its sentimental vogue, the legend of Crazy Jane underwent a dark metamorphosis. If Crazy Jane was harmless, her dangerous counterpart, Lucy, represented female sexuality as insane violence against men. The figure came from Scott's celebrated novel *The Bride of Lammermoor* (1819). His heroine, Lucy Ashton, is prevented from marrying the man she loves and forced into a more socially acceptable alliance. But on her wedding night, the guests hear shrieks coming from the bridal chamber. Rushing to the room, they discover the bridegroom stabbed on the threshold and Lucy huddled in a corner, "her head-gear dishevelled; her night-clothes torn and dabbled with blood,—her eyes glazed, and her features convulsed into a wild paroxysm of insanity. When she saw herself discovered, she gibbered, made mouths, and pointed at them with her bloody fingers, with the frantic gestures of an exulting demoniac. . . . As they carried her over the threshold, she looked down, and uttered the only articulate words that she had yet spoken . . . 'so, you have ta'en up your bonny bridegroom?' "[30]

Women's escape from the bondage of femininity into an empowering and violent madness was a popular theme in nineteenth-century romantic opera; Scott's novel was subjected to eight operatic adaptations, including Donizetti's *Lucia di Lammermoor,* and violent sopranos reigned in one mad scene after another.[31] It has been suggested that the popularity of these operas indicates a subversive feminist sympathy in the audience; the female opera-goer could experience vicariously "the melancholia, the delirium, the suicides and murders, and the coloratura ravings of genteel male-dominated women."[32] Flaubert stresses such projection when he has Emma Bovary rapturously identify with the violent heroine of a provincial production of *Lucie de Lammermoor.*

Figure 6. "Miss A. A.," an erotomaniac, from Alexander Morison, The Physiognomy of Mental Diseases, *1843.*

Figure 7. Richard Dadd, "Sketch of an Idea for Crazy Jane," 1855.

"Oh," she asks herself, "why had not she, like this woman, resisted?"[33] But to watch these operas in performance is to realize that even the murderous madwomen do not escape male domination; they escape one specific, intolerable exercise of women's wrongs by assuming an idealized, poetic form of pure femininity as the male culture had construed it: absolutely irrational, absolutely emotional, and, once the single act is accomplished, absolutely passive.

These images of female insanity came from a cultural context that cannot be tabulated or translated into the statistics of mental health. Analyzed and objectified through the medium of psychiatric interpretation, they are nonetheless the stories that the male culture told about the female malady. Like the painting of Pinel freeing the insane, they operated as ways of controlling and mastering feminine difference itself.

As the nineteenth century went on, English psychiatry and English culture created new stories about the female malady, but the themes remained essentially the same. I have pursued these themes through three historical phases of English psychiatry: psychiatric Victorianism (1830–1870), psychiatric Darwinism (1870–1920), and psychiatric modernism (1920–1980).[34] The terms for these phases are intended to suggest the continuity between major periods of intellectual and literary culture and the psychiatric views that they produced. The advent of the Victorian era coincided with a series of significant changes in society's response to insanity and its definition of femininity. New legislation made the public asylum the primary institution for the treatment of the insane. The Lunatics Act of 1845 for the first time required all counties and principal boroughs of England and Wales to make provision for the care of lunatics, leading to an unprecedented period of asylum construction; within two years thirty-six of the fifty-two counties had built public asylums. As the inmate population of public asylums increased during the century, so too did the percentage of women; by the 1850s women were the majority of the inmate population, and the asylum rather than the attic was identified as the madwoman's appropriate space. In line with their celebration of women's domestic role, the Victorians hoped that homelike mental institutions would tame and domesticate madness and bring it into the sphere of rationality. They designed their asylums not only to house feminine irrationality but also to cure it through paternalistic therapeutic and administrative techniques. In the Victorian asylum, madness was safely managed and controlled through the arrangement of space and through daily activities and routines.

After 1870, however, it became clear that the asylum had failed to fulfill the hopes its advocates had entertained. Overcrowding, underfunding, and understaffing made the Victorian enterprise of domesticating madness a purely nominal technique. Following Darwin's theories of inheritance, evolution, and degeneration, an emerging psychiatric Darwinism viewed insanity as the product of organic defect, poor heredity, and an evil environment. Seeing the lunatic as a degenerate person of feeble will and morbid predisposition, Darwinian therapists took a dim view of the effectiveness of asylum care and paternalistic therapy; instead, they redefined their role as that of psychiatric police, patrolling the boundaries between sanity and madness and protecting society from dangerous infiltration by those of tainted stock.

The vigilance of these doctors extended not only to those tainted by class origins and moral weakness, but also to women. During the decades from 1870 to 1910, middle-class women were beginning to organize in behalf of higher education, entrance to the professions, and political rights. Simultaneously, the female nervous disorders of anorexia nervosa, hysteria, and neurasthenia became epidemic; and the Darwinian "nerve specialist" arose to dictate proper feminine behavior outside the asylum as well as in, to differentiate treatments for "nervous" women of various class backgrounds, and to oppose women's efforts to change the conditions of their lives.

At the end of the nineteenth century, hysteria, the classic female malady, became the focal point for the second psychiatric revolution, the emergence of psychoanalysis.[35] It was in dealing with hysterical women, after all, that Freud first developed his theories of the sexual origin of neurosis, and his techniques of dream analysis and free association. Yet the transition to psychiatric modernism occurred, not during the heyday of the famous female hysterics, but rather during the First World War, when the urgent necessity of treating thousands of shell-shocked soldiers—male hysterics—made the theoretical and therapeutic bankruptcy of Darwinian approaches all too clear. In coping with shell shock, psychiatrists were forced to experiment with a variety of new therapies, including psychoanalytic methods that exposed unconscious conflicts and repressions. It was men's illnesses rather than women's that made this transition possible. And although the incidence of classic hysteria in women seemed to decline after the war, the new female malady of schizophrenia soon arose to take its place. In modern literature and art, the schizophrenic woman stands for the alienation and fragmentation of the age. In medical psychiatry, which has treated schizophrenia, and which in England has taken precedence over psychoanalysis, women appear to be the prime subjects of shock treatment, psychosurgery, and psychotropic drugs.

In each of these three periods, the prevailing attitudes were shaped both by moments of social upheaval that challenged psychiatric thought, and by the careers of those individual physicians who not only dominated their generation's thinking but also transformed the social role of the psychiatrist in line with the age's cultural ideals. John Conolly in the early Victorian period, Henry Maudsley in the last decades of the nineteenth century, W. H. R. Rivers during World War I, and R. D. Laing in the 1960s are exemplary in this sense. Their lives and ideas establish the psychiatric context for the discussion of female insanity in each period and for the ways it was experienced, diagnosed, treated, and represented over two centuries of English culture.

It is significant that all these figures are men. Changes in cultural fashion, psychiatric theory, and public policy have not transformed the imbalance of gender and power that has kept madness a female malady. Despite the wide acceptance of psychotherapy, psychiatric modernism has not led to significant changes in the cultural construction of female insanity. The presence of several women among the pioneers of the British Psycho-Analytical Society did not produce a revision of Freudian ideas on female psychology and sexuality; and psychoanalysis, with its emphasis on penis envy as the main determinant of female psychosexual development, has not offered much scope for a revolutionary discourse on women and madness. Most disappointing, even the antipsychiatry movement of the 1960s, which protested against shock treatments, and which promised to analyze women's situation in the family and in society, not only failed in its theoretical effort but may well have been the most sexist of all in its practice.

In the past decade, however, we have seen the beginning of a third psychiatric revolution in the work of feminist psychologists and in the feminist therapy movement. Together these have insisted that the cultural connections between "women" and "madness" must be dismantled, that "femininity" must not be defined in terms of a male norm, and that we can expect no progress when a male-dominated profession determines the concepts of normality and deviance that women perforce must accept. This book is intended as a contribution toward the feminist revolution in psychiatric history that not only speaks for women but also allows women to speak for themselves.

PART ONE

Psychiatric Victorianism

1

DOMESTICATING INSANITY

John Conolly and Moral Management

On May 1, 1851, Queen Victoria opened the Great Exhibition at the Crystal Palace, an event, most historians agree, which also inaugurated the golden age of Victorianism, the optimistic and confident period that prevailed for the next twenty years. The Great Exhibition itself symbolized the ideals and achievements of the early Victorians. Its 100,000 exhibits honored the gospel of work and covered every aspect of art, industry, and international trade; its huge glass-and-iron building glittered in the summer sun; its splendor and ingenuity advertised the superiority of the British way of life.

Two months later, Colney Hatch Lunatic Asylum, the showcase of Victorian psychiatric reform, also opened its doors in Middlesex. The largest, most modern, and most costly asylum in England, Colney Hatch symbolized madness to the Victorians, as Bedlam had to the Augustans. It had a spectacular Italianate façade nearly a third of a mile long, with campaniles, cupolas, stone rustic quoins, cornices, and ornamental trimmings. The building was planned to hold 1,250 patients, and inside there were six miles of wards and corridors. On the grounds were a chapel, a stable, a farm, and a cemetery. With its full population of officers and attendants, it was as big as a large village, and to Dr. Andrew Wynter, the editor of the *British Medical Journal,* it presented "the appearance of a town," with wards and corridors so extensive that they were like "streets inhabited by distinct classes."[1]

Like the Crystal Palace, Colney Hatch was a wonder of modernity, an emblem of English progress, technology, and humanitarianism. Its directors underscored these similarities by preparing a special guidebook that invited English and foreign visitors at the Great Exhibition to witness the splendors of Colney Hatch's "size, elevation, and accommodation," "unrivalled . . . in this Country, or perhaps any other." To the "many men of high standing in the ranks of philanthropy, art, science, medicine, and architecture" who came to see Colney Hatch during the summer and fall of 1851, it was the model institution from which European psychiatry would take its pattern.[2]

That a lunatic asylum should be a source of national pride, a Great Exhibition of insanity, was not too surprising, for at the beginning of Victoria's reign, England, pre-eminent in art, in letters, in technology, and in trade, also led the world in madness. Both natives and foreigners agreed that as the richest and most advanced society, England necessarily had the highest incidence of insanity. After all, madness was a disease of the highly civilized and industrialized; as Dr. Andrew Halliday explained: "We seldom meet with insanity among the savage tribes of men. . . . Among the slaves in the West Indies it very rarely occurs; and . . . the contented peasantry of the Welsh mountains, the Western Hebrides, and the wilds of Ireland are almost free from this complaint."[3]

Other observers noted the same connection with a good deal less complacency, attributing the worrisome increase in insanity to the competition, financial speculation, and ambition characteristic of the age. Their anxieties peaked during the credit boom of the 1850s and 1860s. When Louise Bowater, writing her journal in the 1860s, considered the frantic pace at which most people of the age were living, she could hardly wonder at "the increase of insanity. There is a wild look in the eyes of half the men I meet on the railway."[4]

Gloomily surveying the social acceleration around him, Dr. John Hawkes of the Wiltshire County Asylum predicted an inevitable crash:

> I doubt if ever the history of the world, or the experience of past ages, could show a larger amount of insanity than that of the present day.

> It seems, indeed, as if the world was moving at an advanced rate of speed proportionate to its approaching end; as though, in this rapid pace of time, increasing with each revolving century, a higher pressure is engendered on the minds of men and with this, there appears a tendency among all classes constantly to demand higher standards of intellectual attainment, a faster speed of intellectual travelling, greater fancies, greater forces, larger means than are commensurate with health.[5]

And Andrew Wynter, reporting on lunatic asylums for the *Quarterly Review,* envisioned madness as the monstrous offspring of an advanced society: "Is it true that civilization has called to life a monster such as that which appalled Frankenstein? Is it a necessity of progress that it shall ever be accompanied by that fearful black rider which, like Despair, sits behind it?"[6]

But if Victorian England endured the stigma of epidemic insanity, it also enjoyed a reputation as the center of lunacy reform. From the 1830s to about 1870, experiments in the humane management of madness put English psychiatry in the avant-garde of Western medical practice and made English lunatic asylums a mecca for doctors and social investigators from all over the world. It was true, wrote John Charles Bucknill, the first president of the Medico-Psychological Association, and the editor of the *Asylum Journal of Mental Science,* that foreigners had for ages "jested upon the mad English, who hang themselves by scores every day, and who in November especially immolate themselves in hecatombs to the dun goddess of spleen." But by 1859, he added testily, the jest had lost its point: "At least, it may be said that if the English furnish as many madmen as their neighbours, they are somewhat better acquainted with the means of ameliorating their sad condition."[7]

The abuses of the recent past were vivid memories for many Victorian physicians specializing in the care of the insane. As John Conolly, head of Hanwell Asylum, wrote:

> In the gloomy mansions in which hands and feet were daily bound with straps or chains, and wherein chairs of restraint, and baths of surprise, and even whirling-chairs were tolerated, all was consistently bad. The patients were a defenceless flock, at the mercy of men and women who were habitually severe, often cruel, and sometimes brutal. . . . Cold apartments, beds of straw, meagre diet, scanty clothing,

> scanty bedding, darkness, pestilent air, sickness and suffering, and medical neglect—all these were common; . . . Before the appointment of commissioners, armed with power to inspect these receptacles of madness, there was so much security and concealment that the aggravations of loathsome dirt, of swarming vermin, and of the keeper's lash, were safely added. No mercy, no pity, no decent regard for affliction, for age, or for sex, existed. Old and young, men and women, the frantic and the melancholy, were treated worse, and more neglected, than the beasts of the field. The cells of an asylum resembled the dens of a squalid menagerie: the straw was raked out, and the food was thrown in through the bars; and exhibitions of madness were witnessed which are no longer to be found, because they were not the simple product of malady, but of malady aggravated by mismanagement.[8]

During Victoria's reign, however, the theory and treatment of madness in England underwent enormous, even revolutionary, change. Parliament mandated the construction of large public asylums in every county and principal borough of England and Wales. These asylums, supported by public funds and publicly administered, provided for care of the insane poor; middle-class and upper-class patients continued to be treated for a fee in private asylums and licensed hospitals. Moreover, the care of the insane, formerly an occupation for charlatans, profiteers, incompetents, or good-hearted amateurs, also came under government supervision. New laws provided that a Board of Commissioners in Lunacy would undertake the licensing and inspection of both private and public asylums. Parliament further undertook to control abuses of commitment to asylums for reasons of profit or spite. The Madhouse Act (1828) established that commitment of private patients required a certificate signed by two medical men, and commitment of pauper patients, an order signed by two magistrates, or by an overseer and a clergyman of the parish, along with a signed medical certificate.

Class remained a strong determinant of the individual's psychiatric career. The rich could avoid the stigma of certification by keeping mad relatives at home, or by seeking private care. Among the wealthier classes, bizarre behavior would be described as nervousness or eccentricity until the patient became unmanageable, suicidal, or violent.[9] For a steep price, the rich lunatic might be put to lodge with a doctor who specialized in the discreet care of a few eccentric "guests"; sent to one of the large private asylums that catered to the rich, such as Laverstock House or Ticehurst; or shipped off to be hidden away in a Continental *maison de santé.*

The middle classes regarded the public asylum as a disgrace, the "Bluebeard's cupboard of the neighbourhood," "an evil to be staved off as long as possible."[10] When institutionalization became unavoidable, they sought out the cheaper private asylums, or the registered hospitals such as Bethlem and St. Luke's, where most patients paid a small fee. But insanity was an expensive disease, especially when it struck down the family breadwinner, and thus middle-class patients too were often forced to seek public assistance.

For the poor, however, the public asylum was a welcome alternative to the workhouse or to home care; lunatics maintained in poor families had often been neglected, brutalized, or starved. Given the barely livable conditions that many working-class families had to endure, patients were materially better off in the asylum than they would have been at home. Between 1844 and 1890, the number of pauper lunatics in public asylums quadrupled. By the end of the century, they were 91 percent of all institutionalized mental patients.[11]

The vast network of newly constructed and government-supervised asylums which spread across England in the wake of lunacy reform was a source of Victorian self-congratulation. Indeed, boasted Dr. Edgar Sheppard in a moment of scriptural fervor, by the middle of the century there was

> no class of persons in the United Kingdom so well cared for as the insane. The best sites in the counties are selected for their palaces . . . an acreage per head is meted out to them in the most fertile districts; a supply of water per head is welled up for them with a profusion which alarms alike the dirty and the clean; the fat kine of our fields are laid under contribution for them; the corn and the wine is stored for them; clothing of the warmest and supervision of the best are provided for them. Every sort of indulgence within reasonable bounds is theirs.[12]

This new pride in the good treatment of the insane was reflected in a more positive terminology. By 1858, "madhouse" had become an "opprobrious epithet," replaced by "asylum" or "retreat"—"benignant refuges for the 'mentally afflicted'." "Mad-doctors" became "alienists," "asylum superintendents," or "psychiatric physicians"; "keepers" became "attendants." Madness itself became "lunacy," "mental derangement," "insanity," or "mental deficiency"; and its treatment became "mental science" or "psychiatry."[13] These polite or euphemistic terms coincided with a new respectability accorded to the profession of caring for the insane.

The most significant innovation of psychiatric Victorianism, however, was the domestication of insanity.[14] We can define this phenomenon in a variety of ways. In one sense, it involved a taming of the brutish lunatic, a reassimilation of madness into the spectrum of recognizably human experience. In another sense, it referred to Victorian efforts to bring madness into the circle of the familiar and the everyday, and to restructure the systems for its treatment in domestic terms. The public asylums were organized on the family model, with the resident medical superintendent and his wife (usually serving as the matron) playing the roles of father and mother, the attendants as elder brothers and sisters, and the patients as children. The most important feature of the asylum, one doctor wrote, was its "homishness."[15] Another noted the resemblance of a lunatic asylum to "a nursery or infant school. The patients in it have, like children, their whims and tempers, and are governed by a similar kind of discipline, the same mixture of kindness and authority which is necessary to preserve order in a family. All of them require to be managed, that is, made to feel that they are subject to a superior, who must and will be obeyed."[16] On the other side, the Victorian asylum superintendent felt an affectionate concern for his patients that filled his days with religious purpose and emotional satisfaction. A man in this position, wrote Conolly, will come to love his patients like his children: "Their cares and their joys will become his; and humanly speaking, his whole heart will be given to them."[17]

In this setting, madness itself was domesticated, purged of its fantastical properties in a decided retreat from Romantic associations of inspiration and madness. "Nothing is less like genius than insanity," wrote George Henry Lewes, who had studied Victorian insanity and cohabited with Victorian genius.[18] When an actor visited the Devon Asylum, he found the inmates "a great artistic disappointment," totally devoid of the "poetry of madness," and "as sober and respectable as a vestry meeting."[19] Instead of the thrilling lunatics of Romantic tragedy, with their flashing eyes and foaming mouths, Victorian asylums presented sedate, prosaic, even boring men and women going about their business like everyone else.

The triple cornerstones of Victorian psychiatric theory and practice were moral insanity, moral management, and moral architecture. "Moral insanity" redefined madness, not as a loss of reason, but as deviance from socially accepted behavior. "Moral management" substituted close supervision and paternal concern for physical restraint and harsh treatment, in an effort to re-educate the insane in habits of industry, self-control, moderation, and perseverance. "Moral architecture" constructed asylums planned as therapeutic environments in which lunatics could be controlled without the use of force, and in which they could be exposed to benevolent influences. While Victorian psychiatry carried on some of the ideologies and practices of bureaucratic efficiency and evangelical charity that had begun at the turn of the century, it extended and administered them in the context of its own ideals. In its optimism, paternalism, common sense, appetite for system, and especially in its fondness for domestic models of institutionalization, Victorian psychiatry reflected the character of the age.

"Moral insanity," a concept introduced by James Cowles Prichard in 1835, held madness to be "a morbid perversion of the natural feelings, affections, inclinations, temper, habits, moral dispositions, and natural impulses, without any remarkable disorder or defect of the intellect, or knowing and reasoning faculties, and particularly without any insane illusion or hallucination."[20] This definition could be stretched to take in almost any kind of behavior regarded as abnormal or disruptive by community standards.

In addition, not only moral insanity but also such traditional categories of madness as mania, dementia, and melancholia might be brought on by moral causes. By "moral causes," most doctors meant that strong emotions and psychological stresses had reduced the system, "rendering it less capable of enduring fatigue, and thus depressing the vital powers."[21] For some, the term "moral" also referred to social causes, especially poverty. According to Dr. J. C. Davey, head of the female department at Colney Hatch, "the unceasing, and in too many cases, the hopeless struggles of the poorer and middle classes for a bare existence necessarily predispose the brain to a diseased action. . . . No wonder then that . . . some accidental addition to the bitter cup of sorrow . . . should wholly unbalance the tottering mind."[22] "Speaking generally," another doctor observed, "the causation of insanity everywhere, special organic disease apart, is an affair of three W's—worry, want, and wickedness. Its cure is a matter of the three M's—method, meat, and morality."[23]

Yet Victorian theories of the causation of insanity were far from consistent. Doctors persisted in their efforts, largely futile, to establish a physical basis for insanity in lesions or inflammations of the brain and in disorders of the blood. It was assumed that organic problems, even if they could not be precisely located, were a significant contributing factor in insanity.

In practice, moral and physical causes were often hard to distinguish. Out of 411 men admitted to Colney Hatch in its first six months, for example, "physical" causes were identified for 140, including intemperance, masturbation, head injury, epilepsy, and fever. "Moral" causes were indicated for 89 cases; these included domestic grief, unemployment, loss of property, jealousy, and "over-excitement at the Great Exhibition."[24]

Whether drunkenness or excitement was the cause, Victorian doctors believed that in most cases insanity was preventable if individuals were prepared to use their willpower to fight off mental disorder and to avoid excess. Mental health was to be achieved by a life of moderation and by the energetic exercise of the will. Being sane, wrote John Barlow in *Man's Power over Himself to Prevent or Control Insanity,* depends on the individual himself:

> He who has given a proper direction to the intellectual force, and thus obtained an early command over the bodily organ [the brain] by habituating it to processes of calm reasoning, remains sane amid all the vagaries of sense; while he who has been the slave, rather than the master of his animal nature, listens to its dictates without question even when distorted by disease—and is mad.[25]

Yet even when there was brain disease, and even when madness had set in, sanity might be restored by a regime that encouraged and supported the will.

This regime—or moral management—was the second defining characteristic of Victorian psychiatry. The movement had its origins in the late eighteenth century, when William Tuke founded the York Retreat. Tuke and his grandson Samuel, who published an account of the institution in 1813, were among the first to surmise that the violence of manic patients was in large part caused by the harsh way they were treated. Treating the patient like a rational person, they suggested, was the best way to cultivate the sense of self-esteem that would lead to self-control. Moreover, all aspects of asylum life, they argued, should lead to this goal. Thus, the asylum should provide opportunities not only for social re-education but also for work, since "of all the modes by which the patients may be induced to restrain themselves, regular employment is perhaps the most generally efficacious."[26] Theories of moral management stressed the importance of enforcing good habits in patients, in an effort to teach them the steadiness and self-discipline of good citizens.

The most famous achievement of Victorian moral management was the abolition of mechanical restraint in all public asylums. At the beginning of the nineteenth century, mad-doctors still relied on mechanical restraint to carry out their task. A small but flourishing trade had long supplied madhouse keepers with appropriate instruments: manacles, chains, fetters, hobbles, gyves, leather muzzles, leather gloves, leather sleeves, handcuffs, muffs, body straps, stocks to prevent biting, strong-dresses, strait-waistcoats, coercion-chairs, strongchairs, and crib-beds (fig. 8). Noisy women were silenced with the brank, or "scold's bridle," an instrument still in use in one provincial asylum as late as 1858.[27]

Mechanical restraint obviously made the asylum keeper's job much easier. It could be applied indiscriminately to the melancholy, the manic, or the violent patient. Suicidal patients did not have to be watched; night attendance was scarcely required when patients could be strapped down to their beds. And like other aspects of asylum care, restraint could be diminished or increased in relation to the class of the patient. Moreover, mad-doctors were not cruelly inventing torments for their patients, but applying traditional methods and remedies they had been taught were reasonable and effective. John Haslam, apothecary at Bethlem, maintained that restraint and the fear of punishment established habits of self-control and that recovered lunatics credited it with their cure.[28]

During the first half of the nineteenth century, however, the idea that large numbers of lunatic patients could be handled without recourse to physical restraint won wide acceptance in England. The pioneering work of the Tukes at York, of William Ellis at Wakefield in the 1820s, and of Robert Gardiner Hill at Lincoln in the 1830s, provided examples

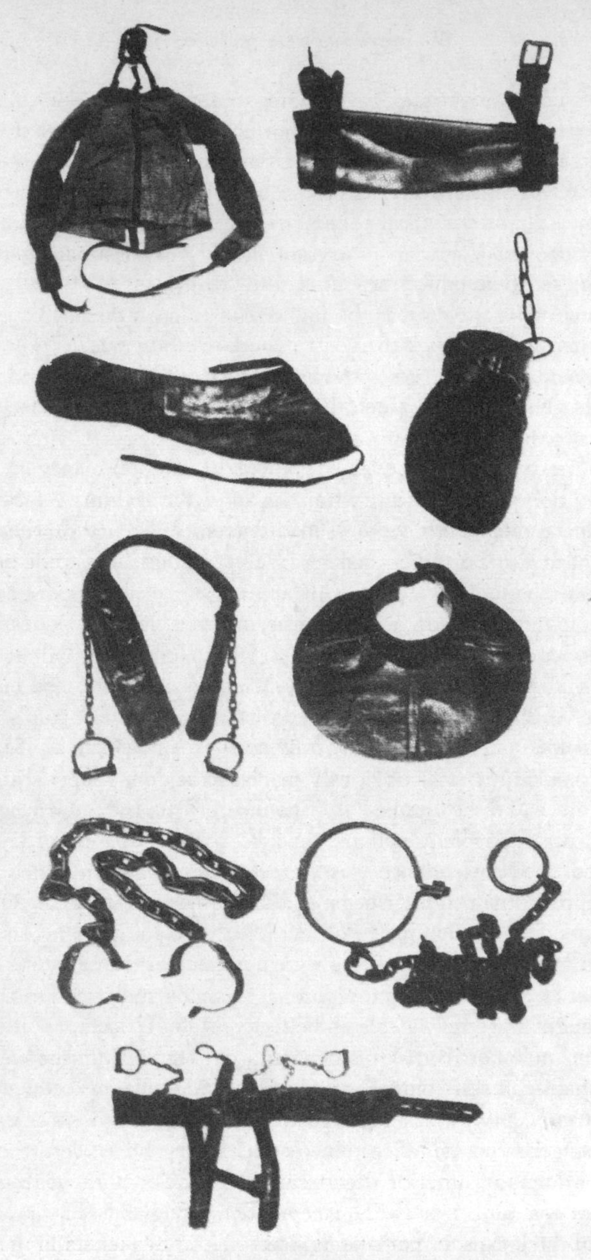

Figure 8. Mechanical restraints used at Hanwell Asylum.

of the successful application of nonrestraint.[29] In the 1830s and 1840s, the nonrestraint system was put into practice by John Conolly at Hanwell, which housed nearly a thousand patients, and it was Conolly who made it "a world-known success."[30] By 1854, twenty-seven of the thirty county asylums had adopted the new method, and nonrestraint became the symbol of Victorian psychiatric leadership. "The abolition of restraint," Sir Benjamin Ward Richardson proclaimed, ". . . has placed us first among all the nations as physicians of mental disease."[31]

Ultimately, the goal of moral management was to *cure* insanity, and the prospect of cure was the major attraction of the new asylum techniques. Conolly's vision of the reformed asylum was the most eloquent tribute to the power of moral management to bring about general social peace:

> Calmness will come; hope will revive; satisfaction will prevail. Some unmanageable tempers, some violent or sullen patients, there must always be; but much of the violence, much of the ill-humour, almost all the disposition to meditate mischievous or fatal revenge, or self-destruction, will disappear. . . . Cleanliness and decency will be maintained or restored; and despair itself will sometimes be found to give place to cheerfulness or secure tranquillity.[32]

This therapeutic optimism had clear affinities with the mid-Victorian belief in progress; in a period of British prosperity and expansion, no conquest seemed impossible.

All of the promises and expectations of Victorian psychiatry centered on the asylum. By controlling the lunatic's environment down to the last detail, doctors and administrators hoped to make the new public asylums instruments as well as places of therapy; the building itself was a "special apparatus for the cure of lunacy." Reformers dreamed of asylums that would reflect not only the best of Victorian medicine but also those domestic values celebrated in Victorian fiction and art; these "fitting receptacles" would truly be refuge, retreat, and home.[33]

The concept of moral architecture shaped the vast new enterprise of asylum construction. Victorian psychiatrists gave endless thought to asylum location, interior design, and decor. Conolly's book *The Construction and Government of Lunatic Asylums* (1847) missed no detail that might be relevant to the patients' comfort and care, describing not only the dimensions, materials, and organization of the model asylum but also suitable windows, carpets, privies, baths, furniture, linens, pianos, and gardens.[34] All these details were relevant for the full application of moral management, as Mortimer Granville explained in his survey of asylums for *The Lancet:*

> It is by domestic control, by surroundings of the daily life, by such details as the colouring of walls, the patterns on floorcloth, the furniture and decoration of rooms, by the influence of pictures, birds, and draperies, the judicious use of different kinds of clothing, suitable occupation and diversions, and, generally, by moulding and controlling the life of a lunatic, the psychologist hopes to reach, capture, and re-educate the truant mind, and perhaps reseat the dethroned intelligent will of his patient.[35]

In planning and constructing the new asylums, Victorian reformers were inevitably reproducing structures of class and gender that were "moral," that is, "normal," by their own standards. In the façades they created for the houses of madness, they defined their façades of sanity as well.

Inside the asylum, lunatics were to be classified and segregated according to the nature of their disorders, but also according to their social class and sex. Architects and lunacy reformers collaborated on buildings that carried out these intentions. Many superintendents favored buildings that stretched in a long line, which facilitated separation of the male and female sides. These asylums imitated the architecture of the English country house, with its carefully demarcated spaces for men and women, masters and servants.[36] In Scotland, some of the new asylums were built on the panoptical model advocated by Jeremy Bentham as the most efficient and economical structure for surveillance. In Bentham's version, the Panopticon, or "inspection house," was a cylindrical structure of cells with a high central tower, from which a single inspector could oversee all the inhabitants without being seen himself. According to William Stark, the architect of the Glasgow Lunatic Asylum, a star-shaped building with a central observation tower was perfectly designed for the moral management of lunatics: "In this way, each class may be formed into a society inaccessible to all others; while by a peculiar distribution of the dayrooms, galleries, and grounds, the patients, during the whole day, will be constantly in view of their keepers, and the superintendent, on his part, will have his eye both on the patients and keepers."[37] While most of the panoptical designs for asylums remained ideas rather than actual buildings, they represent the reformers' thinking not only about management but also about "proper social relations in the asylum."[38]

But whatever the model chosen, it was crucial that the asylum should not look like a prison. Private asylums were usually converted houses, or even stately homes, called Villa, Lodge, Grove, or Retreat. In public asylums, the apparatus of security—barred windows, high walls, iron gates, chains, and dungeons—which had characterized the old madhouses was disguised. At Brislington House in Somerset, inside the twelve-foot wall that surrounded the grounds, raised mounds of earth afforded inmates a pleasant view. At the York Retreat, double windows provided security without bars. Such structural innovations as the cellular unit and such disciplinary systems as regular inmate labor provided a machinery of surveillance and control that took the place of harsher techniques.[39]

The choice of an asylum's situation was influenced by Victorian ideas about nature, beauty, and *paysages moralisés*. To Conolly, the ideal site was a "gentle eminence," not too high to be remote, but high enough to provide views of "a fertile and agreeable country."[40] Gently elevated sites were more healthy, especially if they were near a stream that facilitated disposal of wastes. Although the fictional asylum of the Romantic imagination often teetered atop a sublime precipice or on the edge of a Gothic abyss, the Victorian asylum occupied the middle ground that the literary critic George Levine calls "the realist's landscape." English institutions perched on top of mild hills surrounded by the pastoral details familiar from a Constable painting or a Wordsworth poem.

> Many of them are placed on eminences which command an extensive view of the adjacent country, the field of vision embracing hill and valley, wood and water, in their most agreeable combinations; while fields of grass and tillage, divided by hedges and trees, grazing herds, cottages, and country-seats, form the nearer features of a landscape reposing in the softened light of an English sun.[41]

The grounds were carefully tended. A visiting American asylum superintendent, Dr. Isaac Ray, thought that the gardens, thickly wooded parks, and highly cultivated grounds surrounding the English asylums were peculiarly characteristic of the nation.

> Habitually accustomed as they are, to see their ordinary dwellings embellished in this manner, they cannot tolerate the nakedness of unplanted grounds; and associating all their ideas of comfort with retirement and seclusion, they implicitly require that these retreats for the afflicted and sorrowing, shall be sheltered as much as possible, from the public gaze.[42]

Hill, valley, wood, and garden were all intended to play a part in moral management. Contemplating these rural and idyllic English landscapes, lunatics were being subtly pressed towards a cultural norm. It was considered a sign of very severe psychopathology when women patients at the Fisherton Asylum for the criminally insane ripped up every flower the minute it showed its head above ground.[43]

In designing asylums, it was also necessary to find a compromise between comfort and luxury, and to avoid the overornamentation that would spoil pauper lunatics and stimulate tastes that could not be gratified in their real lives. Despite its enormous scale, the asylum was planned to imitate the virtues of the Victorian cottage rather than those of the palace.

> The hospitals for the non-affluent classes, however spacious and comfortable, should *not* be palatial; they should resemble, at many points, the homes from which their inmates have been withdrawn, because they love and have been accustomed to the very homeliness of these dwellings. . . . They should speak of early habits, former pursuits, natural proclivities, rather than the glitter and gaudiness of tinsel luxury. The pets and sights and sounds of happier days, and birds and flowers, are more health-giving and hope-inspiring to the unsophisticated heart than gorgeous vestibules, black-oak furniture, or copies of Raphael's cartoons.[44]

Inside the asylum, every detail down to the sleeping arrangements assumed a strong moral character. In France and Germany, patients slept in vast dormitories of up to fifty beds. In the United States, they had separate rooms. In England, private rooms where patients could be isolated were combined with small dormitories; at Colney Hatch, for example, the sleeping rooms held four to five patients. Differing attitudes toward class, privacy, surveillance, and the rights of the individual, as well as medical views, were reflected in these asylums. To Americans, private space seemed an essential aspect of cure: "A room which the patient may call his own, to which he may retire when desirous of being alone, in which he may store his books, papers, and the various fruits of his acquisitiveness, and which he may decorate with prints or flowers, is unquestionably a source of great satisfaction to many patients."[45]

English asylum superintendents also appreciated the positive value of privacy. Conolly in particular objected to very large dormitories and praised the healthy effect upon lunatics of having a room of their own which "becomes a kind of house to them . . . they decorate it and are made comparatively happy by its possession."[46] Female patients were encouraged to personalize their rooms with "rag dolls, bits of shell, porcelain, or bright cloth."[47] Furthermore, Conolly believed, English people, "except the merest vagrants," did not like to sleep in the company of many other people.[48] On the other hand, English asylum superintendents were wary of the opportunities privacy afforded for masturbation. Thus Granville, in his account of the accommodations at Bethlem and St. Luke's, stresses that a patient who wants to be alone for what the attendant suspects is a "prurient purpose . . . should *under no circumstances* be gratified with the solitude craved."[49] Masturbation, English alienists agreed, could be prevented only by close and constant supervision; the patient must be watched night and day. Small dormitories could be watched by a single attendant; large wards allowed too many opportunities for concealment, and privacy was risky and expensive.

The asylum's program of "suitable occupations and diversions" enforced habits of steadiness and self-discipline, even as it confirmed the impression of the mad as good citizens going about their business and pleasure as usual. A wide variety of recreations were available for asylum patients and their guests. Although the old Augustan custom of exhibiting madmen in Bedlam for a penny was officially regarded as barbaric, Victorians continued to visit public asylums. However, visitors no longer went to titter or gape; instead they went to admire, to inspect, to report, to lecture, and to participate. At Colney Hatch in July 1853, nearly two thousand visitors joined the patients for "games of a diverting nature"; in the winter the patients were amused "with dissolving views and the Chromatrope." By 1868 the recreational program included winter and summer fetes, plays, magic-lantern shows, concerts, and lectures.[50] At the Lincolnshire County Lunatic Asylum, the annual fete included "quoits, footraces, the long and high jumps, sack-races, putting the ball, throwing the hammer, Aunt-Sally, the ball-target," and in the evening, the "ascent of a fire-balloon."[51] Military drills were borrowed from Prussian asylums, where they had been more punitive than diverting and had involved sand-filled backpacks for stragglers. The English version sent both the drilling class and an "awkward squad" to parade in quick and slow time to a fife and drum.[52]

Accompanied by attendants, the more tranquil patients took walks and outings, those from Colney Hatch going first to the Crystal Palace. At the Haslar Hospital for insane sailors and naval officers, patients went on excursions in the eight-oared "madmen's boat," escorting young ladies from the neighborhood to the Isle of Wight. In the large, costly private asylums, entertainments were correspondingly lavish. At Ticehurst, for example, aristocratic patients could ride to the hounds with the asylum hunt, or enjoy the bowling green, aviary, pagoda, theater, and seahouse.[53] "The emancipation of the lunatic has come as well as of the serf!" W. A. F. Browne exclaimed. "Large parties of the insane daily take exercise in the country around every asylum, find amusement in the concert rooms and theatres of crowded cities. I have detected them copying pictures in the Louvre."[54]

Intellectual activities carefully organized to suit different classes became part of the program of self-improvement seen by many physicians as essential to the mastery of mental disease. The "better-class" patients at Murray's Royal Asylum in Perth attended a series of lectures by local experts on "The Natural History of Zoophytes" and "The Authenticity of Ossian's Poems," while the pauper patients lectured each other on such simpler topics as galvanism, the blood, time, and economic botany. (Some cultural recreations were less successful than others. At Fisherton Asylum for the criminally insane, an actor's recitation of the murder scene from *Hamlet*—not a wise choice—upset the inmates, especially one who had cut off his doctor's head and kicked it about the garden.)[55]

The most popular form of asylum recreation was the lunatics' ball, a dance held for inmates, attendants, and often visitors. Journalists went frequently, notebook in hand, to the festivities prepared to display the moral asylum at its best; Charles Dickens was one such visitor at the Christmas Ball at St. Luke's Hospital in 1851. If at first, as one writer noted, "the announcement of a ball in Bedlam seems . . . almost as much an anomaly as a fancy fair in Pentonville Penitentiary," it soon became a familiar and even conventional event, and travelers on the Great Western Railroad on winter evenings could "see the lights shining from the great hall of Hanwell and . . . hear perchance the sounds of music."[56] Katharine Drake's lithograph "Lunatics' Ball: Somerset County Asylum" (1848) captures one such occasion; the slogan "Harmony" ironically presides over a scene in which each dancer seems to keep his or her own time (fig. 9). At some asylums, dances held as frequently as once a week were "the greatest treat the poor creatures have," according to the superintendent at Fisherton Asylum, near Salisbury, where a dozen uniformed musicians played while the patients —murderers, burglars, and thieves—danced.[57] Patients concocted special costumes for the festivities; William Gilbert noted the homemade paper flowers worn by the women at Fisherton, and a journalist, astonished by the gaiety of the ball at the Morningside Asylum, wrote:

Figure 9. Katharine Drake, "Lunatics' Ball, Somerset," 1848.

> On entering the spacious and brilliantly-lighted hall, I was never more struck and interested than by the spectacle that met my gaze. . . . First comes a Scotch reel. Perhaps from forty to fifty couples wait with glistening eye the starting note, when off they go, with "life and mettle in their heels," making the walls of the stately mansion vibrate to their vigorous tread, as if sorrow and despair had never followed their footsteps, or cast a shadow over their path. Grotesque and odd enough are some of their motions; and as the "mirth and fun grow fast and furious," to watch their rapid evolutions, as I do with my mind's eye at present, seems like the phantasmagoria of a wizard dream.[58]

For most observers, the fascination of the lunatics' ball was the illusion of normality it presented. Seen at such close range and in holiday settings, madness was no longer a gross and unmistakable inversion of appropriate conduct, but a collection of slightly disquieting gestures and postures. Observers scrutinized the inmates for telling details that betrayed their true identity: "With the exception of a slovenly method of moving their feet," wrote one, "you might have fancied they were so many country people dancing at a village wake or fair."[59] At Bethlem, where most patients were educated and middle class, and where they wore their own clothes, the Monday ball was a sophisticated affair, with expert performances of such fashionable dances as the polka, waltz, and mazurka declaring the "social standing of the assembly." At Hanwell, too, Wynter saw "no disorder, nor anything that would indicate that the company were lunatics; the uniform of grey alone lends an air of incongruity to the otherwise lively scene."[60]

Moral management also extended to work. Therapeutic labor was first introduced into asylums in the 1830s at Hanwell; male patients were taught a trade or pursued their own; women patients did needlework, which was sold for them at bazaars. Asylum labor was another by-product of nonrestraint and mutual dependence. Only when patients could be trusted to walk about without trying to escape, and when kindly treatment had minimized the risk that they would turn their tools upon their keepers or each other, could they be employed. Thus the more patients an asylum could put to work, the higher its reputation for humanitarian progress. Ninety out of a hundred patients, W. A. F. Browne believed, would benefit from occupation. A melancholic "placed at a loom, and induced to produce ten or fifteen yards of cloth a day" would soon find his mind distracted from its morbid imaginings.[61] He would also contribute substantially to the finances of the asylum; and visiting committees, as John Arlidge shrewdly commented in 1856, were naturally pleased to see "a good balance from the patients' earnings, as a set-off to the cost of their maintenance."[62]

The whole economy of county asylums, like that of Dotheboys Hall, was organized on the "practical mode" of occupational therapy, with institutional self-sufficiency as the goal. The variety and amount of free labor performed by Victorian asylum patients were truly astonishing. At the North and East Riding Asylum, where most of the patients had been agricultural laborers, they grew all the vegetables consumed by the institution and sold the surplus at the asylum gates (demonstrating, according to Andrew Wynter, "that chronic cases of insanity are greatly benefitted by as much intercourse as possible with the saner part of the community").[63] Colney Hatch was conceived as "a self-supporting rural community, fed by its farm and gardens. . . . Most of the daily chores like cleaning, washing, sewing, and gardening were done for free by the patients."[64]

Dr. W. A. F. Browne stressed the bliss of universal industry in his vision of the ideal asylum:

> When you pass the lodge, it is as if you had entered the precincts of some vast emporium of manufacture. . . . You meet the gardener, the common agriculturist, the mower, the weeder, all intent on their several occupations, and loud in their merriment. The flowers are tended, and trained, and watered by one, the humbler task of preparing the vegetables for table, is committed to another. Some of the inhabitants act as domestic servants, some as artizans, some rise to the rank of overseers. The bakehouse, the laundry, the kitchen, are all well supplied with indefatigable workers. In one part of the edifice are companies of straw-plaiters, basket-makers, knitters, spinners, among the women; in another, weavers, tailors, saddlers, and shoemakers, among the men. For those who are ignorant of these gentle crafts, but are strong and steady, there are loads to carry, water to draw, wood to cut, and for those who are both ignorant and weakly, there is oakum to tease and yarn to wind. The curious thing is, that all are anxious to be engaged, toil incessantly, and in general without any other recompense then being kept from disagreeable thoughts and the pains of illness. They literally work in order to please themselves,

> and having once experienced the possibility of doing this, and of earning peace, self-applause, and the approbation of all around, sound sleep, and it may be some small remuneration, a difficulty is found in restraining their eagerness, and moderating their exertions.[65]

Browne's community of the mad is docile and harmonious, as conventional in its sexual division of labor as it is humble in its aspirations and desires. Not only is there a clear hierarchy, but also it is unquestioningly accepted by eager and grateful workers. No wonder that for many of its supporters, the asylum seemed an experiment worth emulating in the society at large. Indeed, a journalist reviewing the plans for Colney Hatch in the *Westminster Review* explicitly pointed to the social relevance of the proposed community:

> Looking back on what we have written, the thought occurs forcibly to us, that while describing what appears to us the most eligible asylum for the insane, we have really described the most eligible kind of residence for the sane. With human drudgery minimised, and human comfort maximised, with arrangements suited equally to those who are gregarious and those who are hermit-like in their habits, we have all the advantages of the old monasteries without their disadvantages.[66]

And surveying the progress that had been made by 1866, Professor G. E. Paget confidently declared that the English lunatic asylum was "the most blessed manifestation of true civilization that the world can present."[67]

Great moments of social change are brought about through the efforts of many, but succeed in part because of their identification with specific leaders whose careers come to symbolize the aspirations of the age. For Victorian psychiatry, this exemplary figure was John Conolly (1794–1866) (fig. 10). In the words of the medical historians Richard Hunter and Ida Macalpine, "It was in Conolly that the reform of the treatment of the insane, one of the finest flowerings of Victorian philanthropy, found its spokesman, the non-restraint movement its champion, and county magistrates planning and directing such institutions their guide."[68] It was Conolly who proved that the management of a large asylum could be carried out without the use of force. As the *Edinburgh*

Figure 10. John Conolly.

Review put it: "To him, hobbles and chains, handcuffs and muffs were but material impediments that merely confined the limbs; to get rid of these he spent the best years of his life; but beyond these mechanical fetters he saw there were a hundred fetters to the spirit which human sympathy, courage, and time only could remove."[69]

Conolly's colleagues and contemporaries showered him with honors and regarded him as an outstanding figure of Victorian medicine, one of the "greatest and most noble benefactors . . . that our profession and our country have ever produced," a humanitarian to whom England soon owed its pre-eminence in the treatment of mental disease."[70] Although Conolly's tenure at Hanwell Asylum lasted only from 1839 to 1843, his achievements in those four years made him the symbol of Victorian psychiatry's happiest visions of itself. Conolly's personality, too, typified a particular philanthropic mode that appealed to the age. A warm-hearted, impulsive idealist whose concern for the poor, for women, and for the mad was as emotional as it was professional, Conolly could easily have played the hero in a novel by his friend Charles Dickens.

Conolly first became fascinated by the problems of insanity as a medical student in Scotland when he visited the Royal Lunatic Asylum at Glasgow; it was a kind of conversion experience that changed his life. In his first medical practice at Stratford (where his passion for Shakespeare involved him in plans for making the town a National Trust), he pursued his interest in lunacy, working as inspecting physician to the private asylums of Warwickshire. As a member of the Society for the Diffusion of Useful Knowledge (SDUK), he wrote a number of popular articles about health and disease in a series called "The Working-Man's Companion." Handsome, sociable, and a gifted public speaker and writer, whose style was "easy, copious, elegant, and persuasive," he became active too in meetings of the local medical society.[71] Such varied activities helped him balance his dissatisfaction with the coldness, dryness, and routine of traditional medicine. When he was asked to join the medical faculty at the University of London in 1827, his reformist and literary interests continued. Conolly proposed that medical students should be trained in the care of the insane through first-hand clinical observation of asylum patients rather than through cases in books. He wrote a textbook himself, *An Inquiry Concerning the Indications of Insanity* (1830), which warned against the dangers of asylums in their present sordid and chaotic condition and argued for the potentialities of moral management.

When the London University post proved too low-paying for a married man with a family, Conolly became "seized with a restless desire" to get work as the superintendent of a lunatic asylum where he could put his theories into practice.[72] Such a position was considered so demeaning that when he applied for the job at Hanwell, one of the largest public asylums, his friends regarded his application as "the suicide of reputation and the confession of complete failure in life."[73] But Conolly persevered. His first application was rejected, he later learned, because of his "progressive politics and association with efforts to educate the working classes."[74] But within a year, the superintendency at Hanwell fell vacant again, and this time Conolly was successful. He went to Hanwell on June 1, 1839, with an intense consciousness of being initiated into an alien community, of being separated from "the ordinary ways and customs of men, and from the cheering influences of society."

> When the superintendent of such a large and peculiar institution first opens the door which leads from his own comparatively quiet apartment to the extensive wards occupied by the patients of whom he has assumed the charge, he has a strange consciousness of passing from ordinary life into a new world, to which nothing in the outside world has a resemblance.[75]

Yet he also felt a sense of contentment and belonging, and realized that he had at last found his "proper place as friend and guide to the *crazy*."[76]

Conolly's appointment as resident physician at Hanwell coincided with a political crisis in England. Chartism was approaching one of its peaks of demonstrations, rallies, and mass protest meetings. As he had supported the Society for the Diffusion of Useful Knowledge, Conolly also supported the Chartist movement for the enfranchisement of working-class men. He also approved of its major source, Owenite socialism, and invited Robert Owen himself to visit him at Hanwell. It is not surprising that Conolly should have found himself so much in sympathy with Owen, a paternal figure of socialist benevolence. Indeed, Conolly's utopian vision of the reformed asylum, a working community of the insane poor brought into loving harmony by the watchful ministrations of an enlightened and affectionate superintendent, was similar to the vision behind Owen's experimental communities, in which the working classes were to be provided with instruments of self-improvement and self-help. Only a few years after his arrival, Hanwell acquired another experimental community, the "Moreville Communitarium," founded by Goodwyn and Catherine Barmby, leaders of the Owenite Communist Church. "It thus seems," wrote the Barmbys cheerfully, "that God has decreed the first Asylum for the sane to be situated near the Asylum for the insane . . . in accordance with that Divine Law by which extremes meet."[77] Rather than extending his political activities into the outside community or taking a side in the Chartist struggle, Conolly found an outlet for his liberalism in creating the experimental community of Hanwell, working out a balance between the needs of the patients and those of attendants, solving some of the problems of power relationships on a small scale.

When he arrived at Hanwell, Conolly found extensive evidence that patients had been abused. There were 49 restraint-chairs, 78 leather-and-ticking restraint-sleeves, 353 handcuffs and leg-locks, 2 extra-strong chain leg-locks, 51 leather straps, 10 leather muffs, and 2 screw-gags. Within three months, he could claim that not one of the 850 patients was under physical restraint of any kind.[78] Yet he had a hard struggle to maintain and expand his policies. There was angry opposition from the clergy, from rival psychiatrists such as Alexander Morison, and from refractory attendants. Some insisted that restraint was an essential part of therapy. Nonetheless Conolly persisted, and also managed to raise attendants' salaries, to hire new and more carefully selected staff, and to improve conditions of diet, sanitation, and ventilation in the aging building. As part of moral management, he also made regular religious observances a significant part of asylum routine. Patients were required to attend the chapel neatly dressed, and were given prayer books, hymn books, and Bibles. Small classes were organized to teach illiterate patients how to read and write; others studied geography, drawing, and singing; and the male patients even had a class in natural history and arithmetic. Conolly noted in his 1843 Hanwell report how happy women patients in particular were when they were taught to write.

Conolly's view of the superintendent's role was idealistic and dedicated. The medical superintendent, he believed, must be fully invested in the institution and offer a steady and inexhaustible benevolence. The success of the asylum depended on the superintendent's having a "constant sense of what each hour of the day requires from him" and a minute acquaintance "with what is hourly taking place in all parts of the establishment."

> Everywhere it must be felt that his *mind,* at least, is present: he must superintend, and mingle with, and partake of, all that constitutes the daily life of his patients: so that every arrangement may be part of an harmonious system of which he is the soul; and every patient, according to the extent of his faculties, may still know that in all his afflictions and troubles, the physician is his sure and constant friend.[79]

For Conolly indeed, the asylum became his family, and vice versa: eventually all the men in his family entered asylum work: his brother, nephew, and son as proprietors of private asylums in Middlesex and Cheltenham, and his sons-in-law D. Harrington Tuke and Henry Maudsley as psychiatrists. When he retired from Hanwell, he settled in the neighborhood where every morning and evening he could hear the sound of the asylum chapel bells. If his life were to come over again, he told Maudsley, "he should like nothing better than to be at the head of a large public asylum in order to superintend its administration."[80]

Under Conolly's guidance and advocacy, the ideology of nonrestraint captured the imagination of the public. His experiments attracted powerful support from the professional and the popular press: *The Lancet,* the *Illustrated London News,* and most important, *The Times.*[81] Honors followed acclaim: over the next decade he was elected to the Royal College of Physicians, awarded an honorary degree by Oxford, and presented with his portrait and an allegorical piece of silver plate two feet high, illustrating patients with and without restraints, surmounted by the God of Healing, and flanked by figures representing Science and Mercy.

But if Conolly's achievements became the symbol of Victorian psychiatric progress, his career also suggests some of the darker sides of humanitarian reform. Gradually, Conolly's devotion to the insane poor became a kind of driven identification with them. A chronic skin irritation made him an insomniac, who prowled the wards restlessly at night, the phantom of the asylum. At the height of his fame, his conflicts with the Middlesex magistrates over the running of Hanwell by medical rather than lay administrators led him to submit his resignation. Although he briefly remained in the post of "consulting physician," Conolly was soon forced to make a living in ways he had despised in the days of youthful idealism—as the proprietor of private asylums for women, and as an expert witness in lunacy inquisitions and criminal trials. He became notorious for his willingness to certify that a wide range of behavior might be designated as insanity and require institutional treatment. While he had once protested against the indiscriminate confinement in asylums of people who were immoral or irresponsible, he now considered asylums the answer for everything. He eagerly supported "seclusion . . . and systematic treatment as can only be afforded in an asylum" for "young men, whose grossness of habits, immoderate love of drink, disregard of honesty, or general irregularity of conduct, bring disgrace and wretchedness on their relatives" and for "young women of ungovernable temper . . . sullen, wayward, malicious, defying all domestic control; or who want that restraint over the passions without which the female character is lost."[82] Conolly's legendary warmheartedness and indifference to professionalism emerged as a rather more troubling naiveté about professional ethics in a scandal in 1859, when he was found to have taken kickbacks of 15 percent of the fee for each patient he certified for a private asylum called Moorcroft House.[83] Towards the end of his career, he even became the butt of Victorian satire. Charles Reade lampooned him as Dr. Wycherley in his sensational protest novel, *Hard Cash* (1864). As Reade portrays him, Wycherley is obsessed with the mad, a pompous fountain of psychiatric double-talk, who "had so saturated himself with circumlocution, that it distilled from his very tongue." Serialized in Dickens's *Household Words,* the novel was an embarrassment to Conolly's family and friends.[84]

History too has been hard on Conolly's life and work, seeing him as a dilettante or hypocrite whose ideas on insanity changed according to his self-interest. This harsh view was initiated soon after his death, in a remarkable obituary memoir by his son-in-law Henry Maudsley. Maudsley's view of the process by which Conolly moved from provincial medical posts to a lectureship at London University and then to the direction of Hanwell Asylum, was that accident, experiment, laziness, and inadequacy in a variety of positions gradually forced him into a sphere of work despised by most of his medical colleagues, where his very "faults" of emotionalism, tenderness, and vague benevolence made him succeed. "Without conscious design of his own," Maudsley concluded, "driven by the necessities of failure arising partly out of defects of character, he is borne by the waves of a tumultuous life in which he had many times been well nigh wrecked on to a shore where the instincts of his nature had obscurely pointed, and where he finds at last a sure footing."[85]

But the contradictions and apparent hypocrisies of Conolly's life and career are best understood as representative of the contradictions of

Victorian psychiatry itself. In a sense, every vaunted innovation of moral management could be seen as a form of duplicitous control. The substitution of surveillance for physical restraint may well have imposed another and perhaps more absolute kind of restraint on the insane which implicated their whole being. An American observer, Dr. Isaac Ray, speculated that British patients could be kept in order without the use of force because of their ingrained obedience to the class system. Their deference to superior rank was a habit that persisted even in madness; "it clings to the inmate of the hospital, regulates his demeanor and exerts a restraining influence over his caprices and passions."[86] Pauper lunatics thus submitted respectfully to the will of the gentlemanly asylum superintendent as they did to the squire or the lord. Furthermore, the "therapeutic labor" of the asylum could be seen as exploitation, a way of making money out of the inmates. To radical critics of the Victorian asylum, it strongly resembled the disciplinary labor of the penitentiary or the capitalist organization of the factory.[87] In fact, the whole smoothly running organization of the asylum, as even its Victorian critics noted, could be seen as a dehumanizing "manufactory of chronic insanity," a "triumph of skill adapted to show how such unpromising materials as crazy men and women may be drilled into order and guided by rule, but not an apparatus calculated to restore their positive condition and their independent self-governing existence." Here the patient lost his or her personality and became only "a member of a machine so put together as to move with precise regularity and invariable routine."[88]

To many, the lunatics' ball was the demonstration *par excellence* of the Victorian asylum's exercise of disguised control. M. Paul Janot, who described a ball for the *Revue des Deux Mondes* in April 1857, was sensitive to the underlying melancholy of the amusement: "Certain signs sufficiently indicate that the society is not *sane.* It is not disorder—it is sadness; it is not extravagance—it is silence. The contraction of the countenance, a certain *désaccord* in the dress, the monotony of the movements, many exterior signs betray the disorder of thought, and scarcely permit a mistake to be made."[89] A reporter covering the Bedlam Ball in 1859 for the *Illustrated Times* noted a nagging sense of dissonance: "You feel in the midst of the merriment that *there is something wanting,* that the wine is corked, that the cake has a leaven of madness in it, that there is only elevenpence-halfpenny out of the shilling in the pockets of the dancers, that there is a tile off the roof of the ballroom."[90] This pervasive note of the uncanny, of a parodied ceremony, is struck in many accounts of the lunatics' ball. From beginning to end, as witnesses could not avoid noting, the dancers were obeying the commands of the keepers. Wynter observed at Hanwell: "At nine precisely, although in the midst of a dance, a shrill note is blown, and the entire assembly, like so many Cinderellas, breaks up at once and the company hurry off to their dormitories."[91]

The utopian vision of social harmony which ennobled the Victorian asylum seemed as much a beautiful fantasy as the joyful lunatics' ball. In fact, the ceremonials of worship, work, and play all functioned to help a community divided between the needs and values of its working-class inmates and its bourgeois superintendents achieve a tenuous fiction of familial interdependence. Like other Victorian institutions—the penitentiary, the workhouse, and the factory—the reformed asylum was part of a paternalist tradition in which "humanitarianism was inextricably linked to the practice of domination."[92] Eating, sleeping, dressing, working, even dancing, the lunatic was surrendered to a system of benign control.

Conolly's benevolence, too, was rooted in a firm belief in paternal authority. Part of the generation of reformers that flourished in the 1830s and 1840s, Conolly put his faith in hierarchy and order, in "ruling, guiding, and helping."[93] As long as the asylum remained small and homelike, Conolly's ideals of a community in which inmates, staff, and superintendents were bound together by personal relations and "reciprocal bonds of authority and deference" could succeed.[94] But as asylums grew to be mammoth institutions, benevolent ideals gave way to management techniques. Conolly's experience of power at Hanwell had convinced him of his own authority to determine and to dispense reason. Despite his youthful political sympathies for the poor, unprotected, disenfranchised, and abused, Conolly gradually became the spokesman for more conservative and coercive policies towards the insane. Mirroring the patriarchal character of the Victorian age, the asylum became increasingly like the family, ruled by the father, and subject to his values and his law.

2

THE RISE OF THE VICTORIAN MADWOMAN

Within the ideology and practice of Victorian psychiatry, women occupied a special place. Like most visitors to the Victorian asylum, Charles Dickens was particularly struck by the female lunatics. When he went to St. Luke's Hospital in 1851 for the Christmas Ball, Dickens looked with special interest at the madwomen who attended the ball: "There was the brisk, vain, pippin-faced little old lady, in a fantastic cap—proud of her foot and ankle; there was the old-young woman, with the dishevelled long light hair, spare figure, and weird gentility; there was the vacantly-laughing girl, requiring now and then a warning finger to admonish her; there was the quiet young woman, almost well, and soon going out." Dickens particularly noted the sex ratio in the hospital: "The experience of this asylum did not differ, I found, from that of similar establishments, in proving that insanity is more prevalent among women than among men. Of the eighteen thousand seven hundred and fifty-nine inmates St. Luke's Hospital has received in the century of its existence, eleven thousand one hundred and sixty-two have been women."[1]

It is notable that the domestication of insanity and its assimilation by the Victorian institution coincide with its feminization. Although individual doctors such as Richard Napier had seen large numbers of unhappy and mentally disturbed women in their private practice as far back as the seventeenth century, the mid-nineteenth century is the period when the predominance of women among the institutionalized insane first becomes a statistically verifiable phenomenon. Before the middle of the century, in fact, records showed that men were far more likely to be confined as insane. In 1845, a study by John Thurnam, medical superintendent of the York Retreat, had indicated that male asylum patients outnumbered women by about 30 percent.[2] But within a few years after the passage of the Lunatics Act, the situation had changed. Gradually the percentages of women in Victorian asylums increased, and by the 1850s there were more women than men in public institutions. As the asylum population expanded throughout the century, the greater proportion of women remained constant. According to the census of 1871, there were 1,182 female lunatics for every 1,000 male lunatics, and 1,242 female pauper lunatics for every 1,000 male pauper lunatics. By 1872, out of 58,640 certified lunatics in England and Wales, 31,822 were women.[3] There were more female pauper lunatics in county and borough asylums, in licensed houses, in workhouses, and in single care. Men still made up the majority of middle- and upper-class patients in private asylums, but by the 1890s, the predominance of women had spread to include all classes of patients and all types of institutions; female paupers and female private patients were in the majority in licensed houses, registered hospitals, and the county asylums.[4] The only remaining institutions with a majority of male patients were asylums for the criminally insane, military hospitals, and idiot schools. Outside the asylums, too, women were the primary clientele at the surgical clinics, water-cure establishments, and rest-cure homes; they flocked to the new specialists in the "female illnesses" of hysteria and neurasthenia, and to the new marginal therapies such as mesmeric healing. Even in the novel, the madwoman, who started out confined to the Gothic subplot—to the narrative and domestic space that Charlotte Brontë calls "the third story"—by the *fin de siècle* had taken up residence in the front room. Thus, by the end of the century, women had decisively taken the lead as psychiatric patients, a lead they have retained ever since, and in ever increasing numbers.

As the number of women patients in Victorian asylums increased, moreover, the number of women caring for the insane as madhouse proprietors declined. In the eighteenth century and up to the 1840s, women had often been the licensed proprietors of private madhouses, where they provided care primarily for female patients. Their services were often preferred to those of the large asylums. Thus Mary Lamb, who suffered manic attacks throughout her life, was brought by her brother Charles to a private hospital, where "the good lady of the Madhouse, and her daughter, an elegant sweet behaved young lady, love her and are taken with her amazingly."[5] William Thackeray, whose wife Isabella had developed a postpartum psychosis and attempted suicide after the birth of her third child, was unable to find an English asylum where he could bear to leave her; even the York Retreat seemed too cold and brutalizing. He finally left her in the care of a kindly woman in Camberwell, where she remained until her death.[6]

Between 1854 and 1870, about one out of five provincial licensed houses and one out of four metropolitan licensed houses still had female proprietors, but the claims of the medical profession that, despite the apparent commonsensical nature of moral management, only doctors were qualified to treat the insane, gradually forced women into marginal, secondary, or volunteer roles, much as the rising profession of obstetrics demoted midwifery. Medical men protested against the common practice of transferring private asylum licenses to the wives or daughters of proprietors. "If insanity is a disease requiring medical treatment," Bucknill insisted in 1857, "ladies cannot legally or properly undertake the treatment. . . . If private interests . . . are to override public ones, the widow of a clergyman ought on the same principle to hold the rectory of her departed husband, and manage the parochial duties by means of curates."[7] Such arguments led the Commissioners in Lunacy to announce in their 1859 report that they considered granting new licenses for private asylums only to medical men, and women applicants were thereafter discouraged, though not always refused.[8] As the number of private licensed houses run by lay proprietors diminished, women played an even smaller role in the treatment of the insane.

Public asylums had always had male superintendents, but by the middle of the century, vigorous campaigning by doctors had led to a series of legislative reforms that placed control in the hands of the medical profession. The Madhouse Act of 1828 stipulated that a resident medical superintendent had to be employed when an asylum held more than a hundred patients. In all asylums, moreover, a doctor had to visit the patients at least once a week, and sign a weekly register. The Lunatics Act of 1845 required that asylums keep records of medical visits and treatments.[9] At the same time as doctors established a monopoly on the treatment of the insane, women were denied access to medical education. Furthermore, in their effort to upgrade the status of the psychiatric profession, some doctors denigrated the supportive work done by women in public administration. In the early part of the century, the wives of asylum superintendents had also acted as matrons, with responsibility for the women's side. Conolly's wife, however, did not accompany him to Hanwell, and Bucknill campaigned to have the position of matron in the county asylums abolished. His sarcastic suggestion that matrons, if absolutely required, should be selected by weight, was a thinly veiled insult to the stout Charlotte Walker, whose maternal concern for patients had been praised by Dickens at St. Luke's. In the end, Bucknill was forced to apologize in the *Journal of Mental Science.*[10] Matrons, female nurses, and attendants were paid on a much lower scale than male workers, were regarded as less reliable, and were subject to more rules and restrictions.[11] Any effort to equalize their status encountered intense opposition, as when John Arlidge indignantly protested that in one asylum the matron was as well paid as the doctors. Conolly maintained that matrons often tried to "usurp authority" from the medical superintendent.[12] Victorian psychiatry thus established lunatic asylums increasingly populated by women but supervised by men.

The reasons for the increase in female insanity were the subject of fierce debate among Victorian reformers and asylum superintendents. Some doctors denied that any real gender differences in the insane population existed. In their view the larger number of women in the asylum was not a proof that the incidence of mental disease was higher among women, but rather reflected the fact that women patients outlived men and were less likely to be discharged as cured.[13] Others argued that the shift reflected the "feminization" of Victorian poverty. Poverty was, after all, one of the moral causes of insanity. Women were the majority of recipients of poor-law relief, and poor people were more likely to be committed to institutions than people from the middle or upper class.[14] Furthermore, diseases caused by poverty could lead to madness. "Lactational insanity," for example, was the name given to the delirium of poor mothers who nursed their babies for long periods in order to save money and to prevent conception; it was caused by malnutrition and anemia. A third point of view held that not all women in asylums were actually insane; asylum populations also included many women who were senile, tubercular, epileptic, physically handicapped, mentally retarded, or otherwise unable to care for themselves. The medical superintendent at Colney Hatch in 1869 declared that he "could discharge more than 100 of the females without the slightest hesitation and at once if I could ensure for them outside the most reasonable consideration for their condition and infirmity."[15]

Of course, doctors' expectations may also have determined patient supply. St. Luke's had remodeled its dormitories in the 1830s on the assumption that the number of women patients would always exceed the number of men; and W. A. F. Browne recommended "that in the case of a public asylum, a larger portion of the building should be allotted to females, as their numbers almost always predominate."[16] Throughout the century, more dormitory spaces were planned for female than for male patients, and more private asylums limited their clientele to women. The availability of institutional space, as Andrew Scull has argued, made the option of confining helpless, troublesome, or destitute family members a realistic alternative to home care and thus encouraged institutionalization of marginal cases.[17] Finally, the rise of the Victorian madwoman may have been linked to the rise of the psychiatric profession, with its attitudes towards women and its monopoly by men. As one female lunatic sardonically remarked to her asylum physician: "Well, Sir A——, since I have had the pleasure of seeing you last, I have been benighted and you have been knighted."[18]

For despite their awareness of poverty, dependency, and illness as factors, the prevailing view among Victorian psychiatrists was that the statistics proved what they had suspected all along: that women were more vulnerable to insanity than men because the instability of their reproductive systems interfered with their sexual, emotional, and rational control. In contrast to the rather vague and uncertain concepts of insanity in general which Victorian psychiatry produced, theories of female insanity were specifically and confidently linked to the biological crises of the female life-cycle—puberty, pregnancy, childbirth, menopause—during which the mind would be weakened and the symptoms of insanity might emerge. This connection between the female reproductive and nervous systems led to the condition nineteenth-century physicians called "reflex insanity in women." The "special law" that made women "the victim of periodicity" led to a distinct set of mental illnesses that had "neither homologue nor analogue in man."[19]

According to G. Fielding Blandford, "Women become insane during pregnancy, after parturition, during lactation; at the age when the catamenia [menses] first appear and when they disappear. . . . The sympathetic connection existing between the brain and the uterus is plainly seen by the most casual observer."[20] And George Man Burrows wrote: "The functions of the brain are so intimately connected with the uterine system, that the interruption of any one process which the latter has to perform in the human economy may implicate the former."[21] Given so shaky a constitution, it seemed a wonder that any woman could hope for a lifetime of sanity, and psychiatric experts often expressed their surprise that female insanity was not even more frequent.

Although a relatively small percentage of women patients were admitted to asylums during their adolescent years, doctors regarded puberty as one of the most psychologically dangerous periods of the female life-cycle. Doctors argued that the menstrual discharge in itself predisposed women to insanity. Either an abnormal quantity or quality of the blood, according to this theory, could affect the brain; thus psychiatric physicians attempted to control the blood by diet and venesection. Late, irregular, or "suppressed" menstruation was regarded as a dangerous condition and was treated with purgatives, forcing medicines, hip baths, and leeches applied to the thighs.[22]

The proper establishment of the menstrual function was viewed as essential to female mental health, not only for the adolescent years but for the woman's entire life-span. Menarche was the first stage of mental danger, requiring anxious supervision from mothers if daughters were to emerge unscathed. Doctors warned that moral insanity could easily begin at adolescence, when "the pet of the family" became inexplicably "irreligious, selfish, slanderous, false, malicious, devoid of affection . . . self-willed and quarrelsome."[23] Dr. Edward Tilt described female adolescence as indeed a state of "miniature insanity," when previously well-behaved girls turned "snappish, fretful . . . full of deceit and mischief."[24]

Obviously, puberty was a turbulent period for Victorian girls, a potentially traumatic transition from the freedom of androgynous childhood to the confines of the adult feminine role. Prudery and embarrassment prevented many mothers from preparing their daughters for menarche, so that the unsuspecting girls were "left in culpable innocence . . . terrified at what they could only construe as vaginal hemmorrhaging."[25] Tilt reported that 25 percent of his female patients had been left totally ignorant of the menstrual cycle. When their first menstruation occurred, many were frightened, screamed, or even went into fits. Some thought themselves wounded and frantically tried to wash the blood away.[26]

There were other psychological problems faced by Victorian girls at the onset of menses. Up until this point, their lives were not too radically unlike those of their brothers. But menstruation sharply marked the beginning of a different and more limited existence. Simply to manage the hygiene of menstruation in a household where it could not be acknowledged or revealed created a sense of anxiety and shame. Physical activities, traveling, exercise, and study were curtailed or forbidden. While their brothers went away to school, most middle-class girls were educated at home, their social life outside the home restricted to a few safe contacts with other girls, clergymen, or local philanthropies.[27] No wonder that, as one Victorian doctor observed, "puberty, which gives man the knowledge of greater power, gives to woman the conviction of her dependence."[28]

A girl's growing awareness of this social dependence and constraint, the realization of her immobility and disadvantage as compared with her brothers, and other boys, may well have precipitated an emotional crisis. Case histories of mental breakdown attributed to the biological stresses of puberty suggest both gender conflict and protest against sexual repression. "Miss J. V.," for example, described herself as "a mixture of a nymph and a half-man, half-woman and a boy." "Miss C. G.," seventeen years old, was committed to the Royal Edinburgh Asylum because "without showing any previous sign of insanity, except conduct that was called wayward and disobedient, she left her home, wandered to where some workmen lived, a lonely place many miles off, and spent the night with them."[29]

Threatening as such delusions and behaviors were to families and physicians who expected that the "pet of the family" would remain docile, the anger, manifest sexuality, and violence of puerperal insanity were worse. Ranging from the mild and short-term symptoms of postpartum depression to incurable psychosis, puerperal insanity accounted for 7 to 10 percent of female asylum admissions. By 1850, puerperal insanity generally was taken to mean mental disorder occurring within the month after confinement. It could take a number of disturbing forms. According to Bucknill and Tuke, the woman suffering from puerperal madness evinced "a total negligence of, and often very strong aversion to, her child and husband . . . explosions of anger occur, with vociferations and violent gesticulations; and, although the patient may have been remarkable previously for her correct, modest demeanor, and attention to her religious duties, most awful oaths and imprecations are now uttered, and language used which astonishes her friends."[30]

Cases of puerperal insanity seemed to violate all of Victorian culture's most deeply cherished ideals of feminine propriety and maternal love. Women with puerperal mania were indifferent to the usual conventions of politeness and decorum in speech, dress, and behavior; their deviance covered a wide spectrum from eccentricity to infanticide. In a typical mild case, Conolly explained, the young mother might show a "great degree of excitement . . . with a lively propensity to every kind of mischief."[31] More severe cases, according to Henry Maudsley, displayed "much moral perversion" in craving stimulants.[32] Whereas maternity was viewed by the Victorians as a pure and almost sacred state, violent puerperal maniacs flaunted their sexuality in ways that shocked physicians. As Bucknill and Tuke noted, "Every medical man has observed the extraordinary amount of obscenity, in thought and language, which breaks forth from the most modest and well-nurtured woman under the influence of puerperal mania."[33] Masturbation was also common in these patients, and psychiatrists wondered whether these manifestations were the pathological result of organic disturbance or the revelations of a salacity natural to women but kept under control in daily life. Most agreed that "religion and moral principles alone give strength to the female mind; and that, when these are weakened or removed by disease, the subterranean fires become active, and the crater gives forth smoke and flame."[34]

Women suffering from puerperal insanity also acted out their misery in severe depression, and psychiatrists observed that "in no form of insanity is the suicidal tendency so well-marked."[35] Conolly described a case in which a young working-class woman, after a long postpartum depression in which she had "repudiated her infant," jumped out of a window.[36] But the most terrible act of the puerperal maniac was child murder. It was during the nineteenth century that the infanticidal woman first became the subject of psychiatric as well as legal discourse. Her crime was the worst that could be imagined by a society that exalted maternity; medical theory struggled to account for it in a way that maintained the mythology of motherhood and the maternal instinct. The psychiatric explanation of puerperal insanity was that after childbirth a woman's mind was abnormally weak, her constitution depleted, and her control over her behavior diminished. In fact, infanticide did not appear randomly in the population; in middle-class households, where there were nurses and servants to help with child care, puerperal insanity rarely ended in infanticide. As we would expect, child murder was much more likely to occur in conjunction with illegitimacy, poverty, and brutality. These factors, whether or not they were considered by medical specialists, were certainly taken into account by Victorian judges and juries, who were reluctant to sentence infanticidal women to death, and who responded compassionately to the insanity defense generally used in their behalf. Infanticidal women who were committed for life to Bethlem or Broadmoor were also more likely to be released by order of the home secretary than any other group of the criminally insane.[37]

Humanitarian in its legal effects, the psychiatric definition of puerperal violence nonetheless ignored both the social problems of unmarried, abused, and destitute mothers and the shocks, adjustments, and psychological traumas of the maternal role. Rather than looking at the social meaning of infanticide and at its contexts, doctors, lawyers, and judges categorized it as an isolated and biologically determined phenomenon, an unfortunate product of woman's "nature."

Similarly, psychiatrists ignored the psychological and social impact of aging, and stressed feminine biology to explain insanity in older women. They claimed that the end of women's reproductive life was as profound a mental upheaval as the beginning. "The death of the reproductive faculty," wrote one physician, "is accompanied . . . by struggles which implicate every organ and every function of the body."[38] Doctors spoke in violent metaphors of "revolution" in the female economy and of "climacteric paroxysms" creating a "distinct shock to the brain."[39] When insanity occurred, it took the form of extreme delusions "that the world is in flames, that it is turned upside down, that everything is changed, or that some very dreadful but undefined calamity has happened or is about to happen."[40] Whereas we might interpret such "delusions" as metaphoric female communications about the terrors of a drastically altered and diminished sexual status,[41] Victorian psychiatrists were indifferent to the psychological messages of their patients' symptoms, and to the social contexts in which these physical crises took place.

A few of the moral managers did recognize that the intellectual and vocational limitations of the female role, especially in the middle classes, were as maddening as its biological characteristics. They lamented the absence of serious and absorbing mental exercise for "females of the middle and higher ranks," who, according to the Reverend William Moseley, "have no strong motives to exertion . . . no interests that call forth their mental energies."[42] While he agreed that feminine vulnerability to insanity was caused by constitutional weaknesses, W. A. F. Browne also felt that women's "imperfect and vicious" education deserved some of the blame:

> It tends to arrest the development of the body; it overtasks certain mental powers, it leaves others untouched and untaught; so far as it is moral it is directed to sordid and selfish feelings, and substitutes a vapid sentimentalism for a knowledge of the realities and duties of life. From such a perversion of the means of training, what can be expected to flow but sickly refinement, weak insipidity, or absolute disease?[43]

Conolly too found "the condition of the female mind" deplorable, even in the highest classes; "the few accomplishments possessed by them have been taught for display in society, and not for solace in quieter hours."[44] Since their education provided them with so little of the self-discipline and inner resources psychiatrists deemed essential for the individual's struggle against moral insanity, women were seen as poor mental risks.

But if some of the moral managers paid heed to the circumstances of women's lives, they nevertheless saw the problems as failures of training and will. They were no more sensitive than others to the way that madness expressed conflicts in the feminine role itself, or to how women experienced their condition. How did women, rather than doctors, feel about menarche or menopause? How did the asylum and its medical superintendents look to female patients? What did women working in asylums as nurses or matrons think about the causes of puerperal mania? Such direct witnessing is almost impossible to recover. Women did not have access to the pages of the professional journals that discussed the statistics and the theories of insanity. There were no female medical officers to speak about the psychology of women, and the few women who seem to have had significant careers as matrons or proprietors of private asylums have not left records.

We do not hear the voices of female lunatic patients, either. Early-nineteenth-century asylum case histories are not, by and large, revealing documents; they rarely provide much information about the patients' lives, let alone their words. Indeed, following the advice of moral managers like Samuel Tuke, who insisted that it was unwise to allow lunatics to speak ("No advantage has been found to arise from reasoning with them on their particular hallucinations. . . . In regard to melancholics, conversation on the subject of their despondency is found to be highly injudicious"), Victorian asylum superintendents were reluctant to listen to their patients, or to find out how they felt and why. However benevolent their physical care of the patients, moral therapists, Roy Porter reminds us, "were no more interested in entering into the witness of the mad, in negotiating with their testimony, even in exploring and decoding its meanings, than the advocates of mechanical and medical treatment had been."[45] Their cure involved refusing to discuss the lunatic's feelings, ignoring her demands and observations, and instead, diverting her mind from its "delusions" through physical activity and communal recreation.

To find the female perspective on insanity, we must turn to Victorian women's diaries and novels. Although this literature deals exclusively with the experience of middle-class and aristocratic women, the letters and journals of Florence Nightingale, the psychological fiction of Charlotte Brontë, and the sensation novels of Mary E. Braddon give us a more subtle and complex way of understanding the crises of the female life-cycle than the explanations of Victorian psychiatric medicine.

These texts present female insanity in its social contexts, and as a reaction to the limitations of the feminine role itself. Unmarried middle-class women, for example, were widely considered a social problem by the Victorians. Stigmatized by terms like "redundant," "superfluous," and "odd," they were also regarded as peculiarly subject to mental disorders. But while doctors blamed menstrual problems or sexual abnormality, women writers suggested that it was the lack of meaningful work, hope, or companionship that led to depression or breakdown. Dinah Mulock Craik argued that the Anglican religious sisterhoods would be a salvation for the unmarried woman. Better a convent than a madhouse, she urged, for

> what does not society suffer from these helpless excrescences upon it —women with no ties, no duties, no ambition—who drone away a hopeless, selfish existence, generally ending in confirmed invalidism,

> or hypochondria, or actual insanity!—for diseased self-absorption is the very root of madness. It is a strange thing to say—yet I dare to say it, for I believe it to be true—that entering a Sisterhood, almost any sort of sisterhood where there was work to be done, authority to compel the doing of it, and companionship to sweeten the same, would have saved many a woman from a lunatic asylum.[46]

In a work that explores many of these issues, Florence Nightingale compared the confinement of women in the family to the circumstances of the lunatic in the asylum:

> It is almost invariable that, when one of a family is decidedly in advance of all the others, he or she is tyrannized over by the rest, and declared "quite incapable of doing anything reasonable." A man runs away from this—a woman cannot. . . . It is not only against those esteemed physically insane that commissions of lunacy are taken out. Others have been kept unjustly in confinement by their well-intentioned relations, as unfit to be trusted with liberty. In fact, in almost every family, one sees a keeper, or two or three keepers, and a lunatic.[47]

She was writing about her own experience. Madness, she believed, could be the result of mental atrophy and moral starvation within the most benevolent home; "there are quite as many who have lost their reason *out of* as *in* a lunatic asylum."[48] Before she made the final break with her family to become a nurse, Nightingale herself had suffered from years of agonizing mental depression in which she experienced dreamlike trances, religious hallucinations, and moments of suicidal despair.

In a private autobiographical note, Nightingale had recorded "that as a very young child she had an obsession that she was not like other people. She was a monster; that was her secret which might at any moment be found out."[49] In Nightingale's case, as in so many lives described in women's literature and memoirs, the image of monstrosity was related to her anger and discontent and to the necessity of concealing her drives for independence, work, and power. Early in her life, she learned to cope with family tensions by playing the expected domestic role and keeping silent about her real feelings and wishes. But by adolescence the cleavage between the acceptable public image of the dutiful daughter and the secret, aspiring "monstrous" self, which seemed to her so much the more essential and creative identity, led to a series of disabling psychic disorders.

In the late 1840s, having refused an offer of marriage from an eligible and attractive man in order to pursue her vocation, but prevented by her mother's opposition from training as a nurse, Nightingale came close to a breakdown. She fainted frequently, could not concentrate, felt weak and ill. She fell into trances in which she lost all sense of time and place. In daily life she moved like an automaton, unable to remember what had been said or even where she had been. Her agonies of guilt and self-reproach were intensified by the conviction that she was going insane. "My present life is suicide," she wrote on New Year's Eve, 1850. "I have no desire but to die."[50]

Unable to defy her family's wishes, and confined to the domestic routines of her home, Nightingale channeled all her immense energy, thwarted ambition, anger, and despair into a vast literary project, drawing heavily on her own experience to describe a society in which both mothers and daughters were confined in "the prison which is called a family."[51] Part of this three-volume work of philosophical and theological critique was an autobiographical novel, which by stages became an essay called *Cassandra.*

Cassandra is a scathing analysis of the stresses and conventions that drove Victorian middle-class women to silence, depression, illness, even lunatic asylums and death. At the age of thirty, Cassandra realizes that her passion, intellect, and moral energy have been destroyed by the petty obligations, genteel rituals, and religious cant of a mindless social code. Inspired by a divine vision, she tries to emulate the life of Christ, to become the savior whose suffering will awaken other women from their thrall. But society calls her mad and will not listen to her prophecies, and she dies unregarded.

Nightingale's appropriation of the Cassandra story is revealing. In Greek mythology the Trojan princess Cassandra is cursed by Apollo for having rejected his love: her prophecies, though true, are fated never to be believed. The myth suggests that women who reject sexuality and marriage (the two were synonymous for Victorian women) are muted or even driven mad by social disapproval. Nightingale had once referred to herself as "poor Cassandra." Feared and scorned, Cassandra stands for Nightingale's long-hidden monstrosity, her carefully concealed and troubling difference from "normal" women.

The essay begins with a description of Cassandra's insomnia, "the night-walk of one prematurely awake."[52] Cassandra cannot sleep, both because of her personal wretchedness and because she is conscious of the desires that other women in their "sleeping ignorance" refuse to acknowledge. Mothers pretend they have no passion, and teach their daughters that women feel no sexual desire, because, "in the conventional society, which men have made for women, and women have accepted, they *must* have none, they *must* act the farce of hypocrisy." Nonetheless women's lives are eaten up in fantasy, the product of repressed sexuality, boredom, and vacuity. Their time is at the service of the family, so that they cannot pursue any serious education or vocation. Instead they "play through life" at "sketchy benevolence" and ladylike accomplishments. Although marriage is "the only chance offered to women for escape from this death," it too is cheapened by women's economic dependence and intellectual restrictions; a true marriage of equals does not exist.

The suffocation of family life, boredom, and patriarchal protectivism gradually destroys women's capacity to dream, to work, or to act. Nightingale brilliantly analyzes the psychological effects of constant small frustrations, of social restraint, and of inertia. Eventually passivity breeds exhaustion, enervation, and illness: "The accumulation of nervous energy, which has had nothing to do during the day, makes them feel every night, when they go to bed, as if they were going mad; and they are obliged to lie long in bed in the morning to let it evaporate and keep it down." Deprived of significant spheres of action and forced to define themselves only in personal relationships, women become more and more dependent on their inner lives, more prone to depression and breakdown. Sickness presents a tempting escape from the contingency of the feminine role; it offers a respectable reason to be alone, and real, if perverse, opportunities for self-development.

The ending of *Cassandra* dramatizes the despair Nightingale could imagine as her own fate: Cassandra dies at the age of thirty, "withered, paralyzed, extinguished." In her youth she had "dreamed of Institutions to show women their work & to train them how to do it" and had "sacrificed my individual future" of marriage for "glimpses of a great general future." But:

> My people were like children playing on the shore of the eighteenth century. I was their hobby-horse, their plaything; and they drove me

> to and fro, dear souls! never weary of the play themselves, till I, who had grown to woman's estate and to the ideas of the nineteenth century, lay down exhausted, my mind closed to hope, my heart to strength.

Death comes to Cassandra as a welcome release.

Cassandra is not a brief for invalidism, although it makes Nightingale's own strategic sickness explicit. Depression, illness, withdrawal, and complaint, she understood, were feminine forms of protest far less effective than rebellion and action. What terrified Nightingale was that middle-class Victorian women were Cassandras rendered so crazy and powerless by their society that they could rail and rave but never act. In a brilliant insight, she observed that passivity transforms even altruism into hate: "The great reformers of the world turn into the great misanthropists, if circumstances of organization do not permit them to act. Christ, if he had been a woman, might have been nothing but a great complainer."

If women are to be saved, Nightingale argues, they must first be awakened from their infantile unconsciousness. Women must be able to suffer if they are to grow. Experiencing frustration and discontent to its fullest, suffering all its pangs, is the price of adulthood, a "privilege" that may lead to action. To deny, suppress, and stupefy these emotions leads to madness, the hysteria and mental deterioration Nightingale saw everywhere in the lives of well-to-do English women. Out of her conviction came the most powerful and original passage of *Cassandra,* the defiant invocation that demands on women's behalf, not money or votes or even work, but the restoration of pain: "Give us back our suffering, we cry to heaven in our hearts—suffering rather than indifferentism; for out of nothing comes nothing. But out of suffering may come the cure. Better have pain than paralysis! A hundred may struggle and drown in the breakers. One discovers the new world. But rather, ten times rather, die in the surf, heralding the way to that new world, than stand idly on the shore!" Not just private suffering, but contact with "the practical reality of life—sickness, and crime, and poverty in masses," were antidotes to the mental paralysis in women's lives.

Writing *Cassandra* may have helped Nightingale clarify her own feelings and needs and strengthened her own resolve to break free. Soon after writing it, she left home to direct an institution for sick gentlewomen, the first step of her real career as a nurse and administrator.

Within a year, she was on her way to the Crimea to take up the responsibilities that would make her a legend.

After her return in 1858, Nightingale sent her three-volume work called *Suggestions for Thought to Searchers After Religious Truth* to several of the most distinguished male intellectuals of her day, including the Oxford Regius Professor of Classics Benjamin Jowett and John Stuart Mill. Mill recommended publication, but few Victorian readers would have been less likely than Jowett to sympathize with Nightingale's explicit angry feminism. His advice was all in terms of modifying, subduing, and muting her message: "The book appears to me full of antagonisms," he wrote; "perhaps these could be softened."[53] Nightingale made extensive revisions in her manuscript in an effort to soften its antagonisms. In *Cassandra* she conscientiously eliminated personal details, dramatic scenes, and first-person statements. Vital pieces of her argument were ruthlessly cut because they were too revealing, too forceful, or too "crazy." To move through the multiple strata of the manuscript of *Cassandra* in the British Library is thus to observe a sad paradigm of Victorian female self-censorship. The gutted final work, with its mysterious allusions and abrupt transitions, was privately printed in 1860, and *Cassandra* was formally published for the first time in 1928 as the appendix to Ray Strachey's history of the English women's movement, *The Cause.* It is still not available in a complete and accurate text. In its history of thwarted publication, as well as in its account of women's confinement in the family and the psychic costs of that confinement, *Cassandra* is one of the most striking examples of the Victorian silencing of female protest.

Another important analysis of female mental disorder came from Charlotte Brontë. Out of her own "buried life" and her own psychosomatic afflictions, she generated a symbolic lexicon that sometimes borrows from earlier conventions but always reinvests these conventions with authenticity, immediacy, and imaginative force. Her work shows an evolution from Romantic stereotypes of female insanity to a brilliant interrogation of the meaning of madness in women's daily lives.

The most famous of Brontë's madwomen is Bertha Mason, Rochester's mad wife in *Jane Eyre* (1847). Bertha is a violent and hideous predator on men. Confined to a windowless room in the attic of Thornfield Hall, she is a "clothed hyena," "corpulent," with "shaggy locks" and "bloated features," a "demon," a "wild beast," the wreckage of a woman who once was "tall, dark, and majestic" (chaps. 26, 27).

Brontë offers several explanations for Bertha's madness, all taken from the discourse of Victorian psychiatry. As Rochester tells the story, Bertha is a victim of diseased maternal heredity, "the true daughter of an infamous mother" who was "both a madwoman and a drunkard." After their marriage, Bertha too becomes "intemperate and unchaste," a monster of sexual appetite who finally is pronounced mad by "medical men." Brontë's account echoes the beliefs of Victorian psychiatry about the transmission of madness: since the reproductive system was the source of mental illness in women, women were the prime carriers of madness, twice as likely to transmit it as were fathers. Furthermore, "it is agreed by all alienist physicians," wrote one doctor, "that girls are far more likely to inherit insanity from their mothers than from the other parent."[54]

Bertha's madness is also linked to female sexuality and the periodicity of the menstrual cycle. Her worst attacks come when the moon is "blood-red" (chap. 25), or "broad and red" (chap. 27); at these moments she is vicious and destructive, although at other times she is lucid and calm. Still a prisoner of her reproductive cycle (we can calculate from the novel that she is forty-two years old), Bertha suffers from the "moral insanity" associated with women's sexual desires. In a letter to her editor, Brontë described Bertha's disease as "a phase of insanity . . . in which all that is good or even human seems to disappear from the mind, and a fiend-nature replaces it."[55]

The portrait of Bertha Mason depicts a time before moral management, when it was common for crazy women to be kept hidden in homes (there were numerous legends of such women in Brontë's native Yorkshire), or to behave and be treated like wild beasts in cruel asylums. When Rochester takes Jane to see his mad wife, she is absolutely the brutalized animal.

> In the deep shade, at the farther end of the room, a figure ran backwards and forwards. What it was, whether beast or human being, one could not, at first sight tell: it grovelled, seemingly, on all fours; it snatched and growled like some strange wild animal: but it was covered with clothing, and a quantity of dark, grizzled hair, wild as a mane, hid its head and face. [Chap. 26]

When Bertha sees the intruders she springs on her husband, tries to choke him, and bites his cheek. Rochester and Grace Poole quickly subdue her, first by tying her hands behind her back, and then by tying her to a chair. Bertha must be kept in restraints, Rochester insists, because she is subject to paroxysms when her familiar prompts her "to burn people in their beds at night, to stab them, to bite their flesh from their bones" (chap. 27). He plans to keep her even more closely confined than in the past, shutting up Thornfield, boarding up its windows, and completing its transformation into a madhouse by hiring Grace Poole's son, the keeper at the "Grimsby Retreat," to guard his wife.

Bertha's violence, dangerousness, and rage, her regression to an inhuman condition and her sequestration became such a powerful model for Victorian readers, including psychiatrists, that it influenced even medical accounts of female insanity. The image of Bertha Mason haunts Conolly's book *Treatment of the Insane Without Mechanical Restraints* (1856), and supports his argument that insane women should be treated in asylums rather than at home. Lady patients at home, Conolly writes, are "quite estranged" from all their relatives; "all their conduct has been fierce and unnatural" and the house itself is rendered

> awful by the presence of a deranged creature under the same roof: her voice; her sudden and violent efforts to destroy things or persons; her vehement rushings to fire and window; her very tread and stamp in her dark and disordered and remote chamber, have seemed to penetrate the whole house; and, assailed by her wild energy, the very walls and roof have appeared unsafe, and capable of partial demolition.[56]

Surely it is Brontë's Bertha Mason that Conolly describes and her final successful effort to burn down Thornfield that is hinted at in his imagery of conflagration and destruction.

To contemporary feminist critics, Bertha Mason has become a paradigmatic figure. Sandra Gilbert and Susan Gubar make her the quintessential "Madwoman in the Attic," the dark double who stands for the heroine's anger and desire, as well as for all the repressed creative anxiety of the nineteenth-century woman writer. They point out that Bertha not only acts *for* Jane in expressing her rage towards Rochester's mastery but also acts *like* her, paralleling Jane's childhood outbursts of violent rebellion against injustice and confinement.[57] What is most notable about Brontë's first representation of female insanity, however, is that Jane, unlike the contemporary feminist critics who have interpreted the novel, never sees her kinship with the confined and monstrous double, and that Brontë has no sympathy for her mad creature. Before Jane Eyre can reach her happy ending, the madwoman must be purged from the plot, and passion must be purged from Jane herself.

In her last novel, *Villette,* however, Brontë made use of more current ideas about insanity to explore the psychological contradictions in nineteenth-century women's lives. The metaphor she chose for this novel was "solitary confinement." During the 1840s, the punishment of solitary confinement had been widely publicized as an effective and "humane" form of penal discipline at model prisons in England and the United States, and as a useful technique for quieting patients in "moral" lunatic asylums. In the Eastern State Penitentiary near Philadelphia, and at Pentonville in London, convicts sometimes spent their entire sentences alone, unable to speak to each other or to the outside world. Prison officials praised the method as a nonviolent, efficient form of control, one that had the additional benefit of breaking down the prisoner's psychological resistance to repentance by making him tremulous, emotional, and dependent. As one prison chaplain proudly explained, "A few months in the solitary cell renders a prisoner strangely impressible. The chaplain can then make the brawny navvy cry like a child; he can work on his feelings in almost any way he pleases; he can, so to speak, photograph his thoughts, wishes, and opinions on his patient's mind, and fill his mouth with his own phrases and language."[58]

But this mind control struck other observers as a most vicious perversion of the ideology of reform. By the 1850s it had become evident that solitary confinement had unintended and extreme effects on the sanity of convicts. In prisons where it was practiced, the incidence of mental illness was ten times higher than in other penal systems. Prisoners in solitary confinement suffered from nightmares and hallucinations; suicide attempts were frequent. Upon release, many had bouts of hysterical crying, or else sat in listless torpor.[59]

In 1853, Brontë had visited both Pentonville prison and Bethlem, and she had seen how frighteningly effective solitary confinement could be.

> The world can understand well enough the process of perishing for want of food; perhaps few persons can enter into or follow out that of going mad from solitary confinement. They see the long-buried prisoner disinterred, a maniac or an idiot!—how his senses left him —how his nerves, first inflamed, underwent nameless agony, and

> then sunk to palsy—is a subject too intricate for examination, too abstract for popular comprehension. [Chap. 24]

In *Villette* (1853), she explored the impact of a more metaphoric solitary confinement. Lucy Snowe, the heroine of *Villette,* is not a prisoner. She has a good job as a governess and teacher in a respectable school for girls in "Labassecour" (Belgium); no scheming parents coerce her into unwanted matrimony; no wicked uncle tricks her into a madhouse. She is only alone, only unloved, only "superfluous" and "odd," an "inoffensive shadow" in the background of other people's lives.

Yet in a society that ostracizes the spinster, Lucy too comes close to madness. She is tormented by attacks of agonizing depression, loneliness, and anxiety, leading to hallucinations and breakdown; she is surrounded by monitory figures of female confinement, with whom she explicitly identifies. Her first employer, Miss Marchmont, is a hysterical cripple, whose affliction began when her fiancé died in an accident. In Miss Marchmont's service, Lucy too begins to go mad in her solitude: "Two hot, close rooms thus became my world . . . I forgot that there were fields, woods, rivers, seas, an everchanging sky outside the steam-dimmed lattice of this sick chamber. . . . All within me became narrowed to my lot" (chap. 4). Breaking out of this narrow cell when her employer dies, she takes a position at a girls' school in Villette, where in the enclosed garden or "vast solitary garret" she is repeatedly haunted by the apparition of a faceless nun. The nun appears whenever Lucy is struggling to keep her sexual desires in check, and represents the cloistered celibacy her life is coming to resemble. Her physician, Dr. John Bretton, is sure that the nun is "a case of spectral illusion . . . resulting from long-continued mental conflict." According to the best Victorian moral system, he recommends happiness and a cheerful mind; but as Lucy skeptically responds, "No mockery in this world ever sounds to me so hollow as that of being told to *cultivate* happiness" (chap. 21).

Finally, Lucy is left alone in her school for six weeks during the summer holiday to care for a deformed cretin.

> The hapless creature had been at times a heavy charge; I could not take her out beyond the garden, and I could not leave her a minute alone; for her poor mind, like her body, was warped; its propensity was to evil. A vague bent to mischief, an aimless malevolence made constant vigilance indispensable. As she very rarely spoke, and would

> sit for hours together moping and mowing and distorting her features, with indescribable grimaces, it was more like being prisoned with some strange tameless animal, than associating with a human being. [Chap. 18]

Like the nun, the cretin is an externalized representation of Lucy's own primal but now stunted desires; she is the hungering, restless, untamed part of the self that Lucy has tried unsuccessfully to cage and starve. After this episode, Lucy finally loses control; she cannot eat or sleep, begins to have hallucinations, goes out in the storm to make a desperate confession to a Catholic priest, and finally collapses in the street.

The elements of her symbolism are as romantic in *Villette* as in *Jane Eyre,* but Brontë sets them in the realistic context of her heroine's life. Lucy's intense Protestantism will not permit religious ecstasy or the refuge of a sisterhood, as Dinah Craik had recommended. Although her nervous breakdown brings Lucy a brief respite from solitude, her need to support herself makes it impossible for her to rely on invalidism as a long-term emotional solution. Neither does Dr. John, whom she secretly loves, find her craziness seductive or attractive and weep over her like the Romantic sonneteer in Bedlam. Unlike Cassandra, Lucy's torment comes from within as well as from outside, and Brontë cannot resolve her heroine's suffering with either a conflagration or a martyr's death. Her solitary confinement is partly self-imposed; it is the price of her decision to work and to support herself, and it cannot be cut away from her full experience. Brontë goes beyond Nightingale in her refusal to blame women's madness on external wrongs alone. Granted the rights to mobility, work, and autonomy that Victorian feminists like Nightingale were beginning to demand, Lucy still finds herself racked "by a cruel sense of desolation." Only when she finds the assurance that she is loved—along with rewarding work—is Lucy no longer sick. In this novel, then, Brontë provides the sophisticated understanding of women's complex emotional needs that the more sensational *Jane Eyre* lacks.

In a very different register, Mary Elizabeth Braddon's sensational best-seller *Lady Audley's Secret* (1861) presents a subversive feminist view of puerperal mania and its murderous results. The plot of her novel echoes one of Conolly's case studies of a woman with puerperal insanity. This "sensitive woman, whose mother had been insane, became deranged and melancholic almost as soon as her poor little child came into the world of want." Before her confinement, her husband had "left her, and his home, and his country, to seek employment in Australia."[60] A similar abandonment befalls Braddon's heroine, Lucy; but rather than becoming deranged, she leaves her child with her father, changes her last name, and goes out as a governess. When her wealthy employer Sir Michael Audley proposes, she readily accepts. In marrying him, she does not mean to commit bigamy but to free herself from the confinement of drudgery, maternity, and poverty. When her first husband returns to claim her, she tries to kill him; later she attempts to blackmail and murder other men who threaten her.[61] Like Scott's Lucy Ashton, she defends herself through violent attacks on men.

When she is confronted with the evidence of her crimes, Lady Audley makes use of the insanity defense popularized in cases of puerperal mania. As she dramatically announces to the man who comes to arrest her, "You have conquered—A MAD WOMAN!" Furthermore, she explains, her puerperal insanity is a hereditary disease in the maternal line handed down from her grandmother to her mother, who was a patient in a lunatic asylum, and to herself. "My mother had been, or had appeared sane, up to the hour of my birth . . . the only inheritance I had to expect from my mother was—insanity!" She argues that she became mad after childbirth, when her husband left her to seek his future: "I looked upon this as desertion, and I resented it bitterly. . . . I did not love the child, for he had been left a burden upon my hands. The hereditary taint that was in my blood had never until this time showed itself by any one sign or token; but at this time I became subject to fits of violence and despair . . . for the first time I crossed that invisible line which separates reason from madness" (chap. 34).

The psychiatrist Sir Alwyn Mosgrave accepts her story; and instead of being tried for her crimes, Lady Audley is committed to a private madhouse in "Villebrumeuse," near Brussels, echoing the confinement of Lucy Snowe in *Villette*. But like Brontë's novel, *Lady Audley's Secret* suggests that the psychiatric discourse on female insanity obscured many more profound tensions in women's lives. Is Lady Audley's secret that she carries hereditary insanity? Or is the secret that "insanity" is simply the label society attaches to female assertion, ambition, self-interest, and outrage?

The accounts of female insanity by Nightingale, Brontë, and Braddon are psychologically much richer than the descriptions by Victorian doctors. They also suggest that the rise of the Victorian madwoman was one of history's self-fulfilling prophecies. In a society that not only perceived women as childlike, irrational, and sexually unstable but also rendered them legally powerless and economically marginal, it is not surprising that they should have formed the greater part of the residual categories of deviance from which doctors drew a lucrative practice and the asylums much of their population. Moreover, the medical belief that the instability of the female nervous and reproductive systems made women more vulnerable to derangement than men had extensive consequences for social policy. It was used as a reason to keep women out of the professions, to deny them political rights, and to keep them under male control in the family and the state. Thus medical and political policies were mutually reinforcing. As women's demands became increasingly problematic for Victorian society as a whole, the achievements of the psychiatric profession in managing women's minds would offer both a mirror of cultural attitudes and a model for other institutions.

3

MANAGING WOMEN'S MINDS

Victorian psychiatry defined its task with respect to women as the preservation of brain stability in the face of almost overwhelming physical odds. First of all, this entailed the management and regulation, insofar as possible, of women's periodic physical cycles and sexuality. Secondly, it meant the enforcement in the asylum of those qualities of self-government and industriousness that would help a woman resist the stresses of her body and the weaknesses of her female nature.

Nineteenth-century medical treatments designed to control the reproductive system strongly suggest male psychiatrists' fears of female sexuality. Indeed, uncontrolled sexuality seemed the major, almost defining symptom of insanity in women. Both asylum doctors and male patients reported being shocked by the obscenity of female patients. At one private asylum, a gentlemanly inmate returned dazed to his room when a woman patient accosted him in the public road "with one of the worst words in the English language."[1] Psychiatrists wrote frequently about the problem of nymphomania. John Millar, the medical superintendent at Bethnal House Asylum in London, observed that nymphomanic symptoms were "constantly present" when young women were insane.[2] "We have . . . to note and bear in mind," another psychiatrist warned his colleagues, "how often sexual ideas and feelings arise and display themselves in all sorts of insanity . . . so that it seems inexplicable that a virtuous person should ever have learnt, as it is distressing that she should manifest, so much obscenity of thought and feeling."[3]

The regulation of women's cycles in Victorian psychiatry often seems like an effort to postpone or extirpate female sexuality. Dr. Edward Tilt argued that menstruation was so disruptive to the female brain that it should not be hastened but rather be retarded as long as possible, and he advised mothers to prevent menarche by ensuring that their teen-age daughters remained in the nursery, took cold shower baths, avoided feather beds and novels, eliminated meat from their diets, and wore drawers. Delayed menstruation, he insisted, was "the principal cause of the pre-eminence of English women, in vigour of constitution, soundness of judgement, and . . . rectitude of moral principle."[4]

Menopausal women were more harshly discussed, more openly ridiculed, and more punitively treated than any other female group, particularly if they were unmarried. In this age group, expressions of sexual desire were considered ludicrous or tragic, and husbands of menopausal women were advised to withhold the desired "sexual stimulus." Treatments suggested for the erotic and nervous symptoms of menopause were so unpleasant that one can easily imagine their deterrent effectiveness. W. Tyler Smith, for example, recommended a course of injections of ice water into the rectum, introduction of ice into the vagina, and leeching of the labia and the cervix. "The suddenness with which leeches applied to this part fill themselves," he wrote admiringly, "considerably increases the good effects of their application, and for some hours after their removal there is an oozing of blood from the leech-bites."[5]

The most extreme and nightmarish effort to manage women's minds by regulating their bodies was Dr. Isaac Baker Brown's surgical practice of clitoridectomy as a cure for female insanity. Brown was a member of the Obstetrical Society of London who became convinced that madness was caused by masturbation and that surgical removal of the clitoris, by helping women to govern themselves, could halt a disease that would otherwise proceed inexorably from hysteria to spinal irritation and thence to idiocy, mania, and death. The first symptoms of the disease, he thought, manifested themselves at puberty, when girls became "restless and excited . . . and indifferent to the social influences of domestic life." There might be depression, loss of appetite, "a quivering of the eyelids, and an inability to look one in the face."[6] One clue was that such girls often wanted to work, to escape from home and become nurses or sisters of charity; we can easily imagine how he would have reacted to Florence Nightingale.

Brown carried out his sexual surgery in his private clinic in London for seven years, between 1859 and 1866. In the 1860s, he went beyond clitoridectomy to the removal of the labia. As he became more confident, he operated on patients as young as ten, on idiots, epileptics, paralytics, even on women with eye problems. He operated five times on women whose madness consisted of their wish to take advantage of the new Divorce Act of 1857, and found in each case that his patient returned humbly to her husband. In no case, Brown claimed, was he so certain of a cure as in nymphomania, for he had never seen a recurrence of the disease after surgery.[7]

We can only speculate on the depths of shame, misery, pain, self-hatred, and fear that Brown's patients experienced. The surgery they endured at his hands was a ceremony of stigmatization that frightened most of them into submission, or at least into greater secrecy and concealment of their discontent. His patients seem to have been unusually sensitive to the hypocrisy and repressiveness of Victorian social codes, and his case studies are almost poetically expressive of perceptions that Brown himself was too literal-minded to grasp. He was very proud, for example, of his successful treatment of "Miss E.R.," who at thirty-four had never had an offer of marriage. She would not be polite to callers, took long solitary walks, was "forward and open" to gentlemen, and said "people's faces were masks." This angry and despairing woman called her mother "monsieur le diable" and her father "God." She said of herself that she was "lost," "dead," and "buried." After the operation, she was kept heavily drugged for a week with opium and chloroform. Thereafter, Brown reported, she recovered, "moved in high society," and was "universally admired."[8] The mutilation, sedation, and psychological intimidation of Miss E.R. and other deviant and unladylike women seems to have been an efficient, if brutal, form of reprogramming.

Although Brown did not treat a great number of patients, clitoridectomy has a symbolic meaning that makes it central to our understanding of sexual difference in the Victorian treatment of insanity. Clitoridectomy is the surgical enforcement of an ideology that restricts female sexuality to reproduction. The removal of the clitoris eliminates the woman's sexual pleasure, and it is indeed this autonomous sexual pleasure that Brown defined as the symptom, perhaps the essence, of female insanity. Many of his successful case histories ended with the woman's pregnancy. One twenty-year-old girl was brought to him because she had suffered "great irregularities of temper," had been "disobedient to her mother's wishes," was sexually assertive in sending her visiting cards to men she liked, and spent "much time in serious reading." Within two years of the operation, she was married, the mother of a son, and pregnant again. "Mrs. S.M.," a thirty-year-old mother of three children, sent to Brown because of her "great distaste" for cohabitation with her husband, "soon became pregnant . . . and became a happy and healthy wife and mother."[9] With their sexuality excised, his patients gave up their independent desires and protests, and became docile child-bearers.

In 1867, Brown was expelled from the Obstetrical Society, not so much because his colleagues disagreed with his method as because patients had complained of being tricked and coerced into the treatment. Some had been threatened that if they refused to have surgery, their condition would worsen and they would become hopelessly insane. In his defense, Brown argued that many other members of the society had also performed the operation. Indeed, Dr. Charles Routh, an eminent gynecologist, was particularly impressed with the case of an idiot girl who after clitoridectomy improved so much that she was able to read the Bible, converse, and go into domestic service. Dr. T. Hawkes Tanner, however, who had performed three such operations, testified that he had been disappointed in his results; and both Henry Maudsley and Forbes Winslow testified that in their experience, female masturbation was, "not a cause, but a consequence of insanity." Others granted the grave danger of masturbation, but wondered if less extreme remedies could be found. Among those who opposed clitoridectomy was Dr. Wynn Williams, who "thought that the clitoris was not the offending member, but the arms and hands. These, then, were the members that should be cut off." Williams explained that while he was not seriously recommending amputation of the arms, he saw "no reason why they should not be put back by restraint behind the back."[10]

The final decision to expel Brown was made after a speech by Seymour Haden, secretary of the society, who appealed to the honor of his brother physicians. As Haden explained to them, the issues of the case had to do with misuse of male authority. As "a body who practise among women," he declared to applause,

> we have constituted ourselves, as it were, the guardians of their interests, and in many cases, . . . the custodians of their honor (*hear, hear*). We are, in fact, the stronger, and they the weaker. They are obliged to believe all that we tell them. They are not in a position to dispute anything we say to them, and we, therefore, may be said to have them at our mercy. . . . Under these circumstances, if we should depart from the strictest principles of honour, if we should cheat or victimize them in any shape or way, we would be unworthy of the profession of which we are members. (*Loud cheers.*)[11]

Haden's remarks were a forceful, if unintentional, description of the sexual power relationships in Victorian medicine. Within the lunatic asylums, the management of women's minds was carried out much more subtly than in Brown's clinic, but nonetheless it too expressed the power of male psychiatrists over definitions of femininity and insanity. Instead of the surgical knife, moral management looked to the physical design and domestic routines of the asylum to regulate even the most deviant female behaviors. While there can be no question that women were better off in Victorian asylums than in the days before moral management, they were nonetheless subject to ubiquitous male authority. Furthermore, women's training to revere such authority in the family often made them devoted and grateful patients of fatherly asylum superintendents.

In his work at Hanwell Asylum, Conolly had claimed that the "most striking instances" of the efficacy of moral management could be found in the women's side. A "young and delicate" widow, for example, was brought to the asylum in *two* straitjackets, with her ankles chained together. When she realized that her chains would be removed, "she broke out into the liveliest expressions of joyful gratitude, and from that time, although still for a while maniacal, and often excited, her confidence in those about her remained unshaken." After three months, she left the asylum "perfectly rational." A poor tailor's wife "was a kind of mad skeleton. Looking as if she might at any moment drop down and die, she still danced and sang, and ran to and fro, and tore her clothes, and all ordinary bedding to rags." She was given remnants to rip up instead; soon "she employed herself in making dresses instead of tearing them," and a happy recovery was achieved. Deeply depressed young women, emaciated, mute, feeble, sickly, who cowered against the walls, "the very personification of despair," were converted by means of good diet, kindly attention, and sympathetic words into "cheerful hopeful creatures, full of health and spirits, and unfeignedly grateful to those who had been their friends in the asylum."[12] Conolly was proudest of his success with prostitutes and fallen women,

> whose lives had been a sort of troubled romance. Profligate, intemperate, violent, regardless of domestic ties, their children abandoned to all the evils of homeless poverty, themselves by degrees given up to utter recklessness—they had been the cause of ruin and shame to their families, and the history of their wild life had closed with madness. Others, and not a few, were the victims of the vices of those of a station superior to them, and left at length to struggle with difficulties and mortifications and remorse, beneath which reason gave way.

Even these wretched outcasts, he boasted, could be tamed by patience and kindliness, so that eventually they became almost ladylike: "quiet, decorous in manners and language, attentive to their dress, disposed to useful activity, and able to preserve their good behaviour in the chapel."[13]

The ladylike values of silence, decorum, taste, service, piety, and gratitude, which Conolly successfully imposed on even the wildest and most recalcitrant female maniacs, were made an integral part of the program of moral management of women in Victorian asylums. Within the asylums the experience of women would not be identical with that of men. The sexes were always kept separate, to the point that some asylums even had separate kitchens and mortuaries. Women's dietary allotments, furthermore, were substantially lower. And though all asylum patients were subject to surveillance, or "careful watching," as the Victorians called it, women were more closely and carefully watched than men. At the 1859 hearings of the House of Commons Select Committee on Lunatics, representatives of the Alleged Lunatics' Friend Society protested against the censorship of patients' mail, but conceded that ladies needed to be protected in this way against possibly shameful self-revelation.[14] Women patients also had to be protected against rape and seduction. Before 1845, Gardiner Hill reported, there were many "instances on record of the female patients being with child by the keepers and the male patients."[15] After 1845, therefore, the commissioners took particular notice of security arrangements for women. At Colney Hatch, for instance, only doctors and the chaplain had keys to the female ward. When, despite all these precautions, an unmarried woman bore a child in the asylum, the infant was turned over to the guardians of the mother's home parish, or, in the case of vagrants, to the local workhouse.[16]

Furthermore, the institutions into which Victorian madwomen were moving were places in which women seemed strangely at home, and in their proper sphere. Female patients at Bethlem, in one journalist's description, might almost be a family of sisters spending an evening with their elderly mother: "Every conceivable kind of needlework is dividing their attention with the young lady who reads aloud 'David Copperfield' or 'Dred'; while beside the fire, perhaps, an old lady with silver locks gives a touch of domesticity to the scene."[17] A drawing of

Figure 11. Women's ward, Bethlem Hospital, in the 1860s.

the women's ward of Bethlem, reproduced in *Illustrated London News* in 1860 (fig. 11), shows a long gallery in which the women patients are as evenly distributed as the decorative statues spaced in niches. There are ferns hanging in the windows, paintings and birdcages on the walls, books and flowers on the tables. But the women are oddly frozen in their domestic environment, like figures in a museum. These artifacts of the feminine role were less for the patients' pleasure than for their training in the discipline of femininity. In the foreground, one young woman, carrying a box, seems to be running, as if attempting to escape from the tableau.

Since women were accustomed to being ordered to submit to the authority of their fathers, brothers, and husbands, doctors anticipated few problems in managing female lunatics. Yet rebellion was in fact frequent. Victorian madwomen were not easily silenced, and one often has the impression that their talkativeness, violation of conventions of feminine speech, and insistence on self-expression was the kind of behavior that had led to their being labeled "mad" to begin with. Conolly noted that it was the female side of the asylum "where the greatest daily amount of excitement and refractoriness was to be met and managed." Mortimer Granville was concerned that female lunatics were always "chattering about their grievances" or else involved in "an excess of vehement declaration and quarreling." He recommended that the women be set to work that would keep them too busy to talk.[18] The commissioners visiting Colney Hatch "regularly remarked that the female department, as is usually the case in all asylums, was the most noisy." And even a male patient at the Glasgow Royal Asylum felt qualified to complain that "female lunatics are less susceptible to control than males. They are more troublesome, more noisy, and more abusive in their language."[19]

Women's deviations from ladylike behavior were severely punished. At Bethlem, for example, women patients were put in solitary confinement in the basement "on account of being violent, mischievous, dirty, and using bad language." At Colney Hatch, they were sedated, given cold baths, and secluded in padded cells, up to five times as frequently as male patients.[20]

The excessive confinement that replicated the feminine role outside the asylum may have contributed to the excitability and restlessness of asylum women. They simply had fewer opportunities than male patients for outdoor activity, physical recreation, or even movement within the building. While physical exercise and manual labor seemed more necessary therapies for male patients, social activities and social decorum were regarded as more important for women. In one large asylum in 1862, only 50 out of 866 female patients ever went from their ward to the day room. At Colney Hatch, women left the asylum for fewer walks or excursions than male patients. Although Dr. D. F. Tyerman, who headed the male department, believed physical exercise was essential to mental health and so had a "properly prepared and level Cricket-ground" constructed in the 1850s where male patients could play, women were only allowed to watch the games from a "specially fenced-off enclosure."[21] Ideally, women patients contented themselves with genteel, improving, and passive activities, as in Bethlem, where they might admire the Landseer prints on the walls, feed the birds in the aviaries, sew, and make use of the library.

Women's work within the asylum was also more rigidly circumscribed than that of men. Women's occupations were intended to reinforce conventional sex-role behavior; in Conolly's scheme for a model asylum, the domestic traits he thought healthy for women patients were reflected in his optimistic vision of their happy hours making puddings in the asylum's "busy and cheerful and scrupulously clean kitchen."[22] While male patients worked at a variety of jobs in workshops and on the asylum farms, women patients had little choice in their employment, which took place indoors and in some cases was meaningless fancywork or make-work, such as sorting colored beans into separate piles that were dumped together again at night.[23] That task uncannily resembles the mythic labors of Psyche, who was ordered by Aphrodite to sort a huge pile of barley, millet, poppy seeds, peas, lentils, and beans. This motif, echoed in many fairy tales and folk tales, has been interpreted by Erich Neumann to mean that the woman is being assigned to bring order into the "disordered welter of fruitful predispositions . . . that are present in the feminine nature."[24]

A more prosaic view of feminine nature was suggested by the primary tasks of women in the asylum: cleaning, laundry, and sewing. Female patients supplied the asylum with thousands of dresses, shirts, aprons, chemises, petticoats, and caps. Isaac Ray, a visiting asylum superintendent from Rhode Island, noted that the piles of fancy clothing produced by female patients at Wakefield and Hanwell were enough "to set up a respectable shop on Broadway."[25] The women's work most highly touted by the Victorians for its therapeutic effects was laundry. Andrew Wynter proudly noted as a sign of progress that in Bethlem the old manacles had been converted into stands for flatirons, an ironically efficient transformation of restraint into domestic work.[26] Apparently laundry had been recommended as a therapy for female lunatics in England for some time; Thomas Rowlandson's etching of St. Luke's shows women ironing huge piles of clothes. Visiting Hanwell in 1834, Harriet Martineau had been impressed by the women busy in the washhouse and the laundry, "who would be tearing their clothes to pieces if there was not the mangle to be turned."[27] Presumably the aggressive activity of pounding the wet clothes, wringing them out, hanging them, and ironing them was thought to be a useful and effective outlet for the superfluous nervous energy (or the anger) of women patients. Conolly believed that only the salutary activity of the laundry prevented asylum washerwomen from becoming violent.

> In the laundries of our large asylums near London, such cases abound. You see a number of active women, busy at the washing-tub, or dexterous in mangling and folding, but whose air and manner, and somewhat fiery countenance, show that they are not always so composed; and indeed, the nerves of visitors are generally more likely to be shaken in the crowd of these useful but eccentric laundresses than elsewhere; for it is the custom of many of them, on some sudden impulse, to break off from work at once, and exhibit much violence of voice and gesture.[28]

Asylum laundresses at Hanwell and Colney Hatch worked from six-thirty in the morning until late afternoon, six days a week. In order to provide the most time-and-energy-consuming amount of mangling and folding, asylum superintendents were urged to avoid the purchase and "the use in the washing-house of all machinery which diminished the amount of hand labour."[29] If the asylum linen alone was insufficient to occupy its women patients, washing for the neighborhood could also be taken in.

The relationship of madwomen and laundry filled one journalist, Francis Scott, with enthusiasm for the possibilities of moral management. In France, he informed his readers, laundry had even been divided into categories assigned to women patients according to the nature of their madness: the delirious washed, the imbeciles carried the linen to dry, the melancholy ironed it, and the monomaniacs folded it and put it away. No activity could be more proper and salubrious for crazy English women, he thought, than a day with the suds and the tubs; doing laundry might interest them in their surroundings and "bring back that vital activity which they so often lack."[30] Although Granville pointed out that "women's world cannot, even among paupers, be successfully limited to the washtub," the lunatic laundress, whose work not only paid for her treatment but also symbolized her purgation, was considered by many to be the perfect solution to two dirty problems.[31]

Because male employment was considered psychologically more important, and because jobs for men were harder to find, male inmates were sometimes assigned domestic tasks, much to the disgust of asylum visitors. Isaac Ray was shocked to find men "demurely knitting stockings" at Surrey County Asylum, and Francis Scott deplored the laxity of English arrangements whereby "a large proportion even of the men act principally as male housemaids—an arrangement neither manly, healthful, nor useful." He much preferred the traditional division of labor in Scottish asylums, where women did "all the women's work, such as ward-cleaning and bed-making, leaving the males to the extent of 75 per cent free to engage in work more suited to their sex and habits."[32]

Finally, but most tellingly, Victorian madwomen became subject to the moral management of their appearance. Victorian psychiatrists had strong views about the way their women patients should look. Female lunatics were expected to care more about their appearance than males, and indeed, their sanity was often judged according to their compliance with middle-class standards of fashion. Conolly worried about bareheaded female patients, believing that "it is not *natural* to the woman to neglect the dress of her head." This natural tendency could be encouraged or restored, he thought, by presenting each female inmate with "a neat or even pretty cap" for Sunday wear. In his own biweekly rounds of Hanwell Asylum, he noticed and commended women who had "hair more carefully arranged, a neater cap, a new riband."[33] Inmates who wished to impress the staff with their improvement could do so by conforming to the notion of appropriate feminine grooming. Asylum superintendents were especially urged to use clothing as a weapon in managing women patients: "Dress is women's weakness, and in the treatment of lunacy it should be an instrument of control, and therefore of recovery."[34]

Yet too much attention to dress and appearance was a sign of madness as well. James Crichton Browne, medical director of the West Riding Asylum at Wakefield, photographed a woman patient who suffered from "Intense Vanity" (fig. 12). Not content with the plain asylum

Figure 12. James Crichton Browne's photograph of a woman in West Riding Lunatic Asylum manifesting "Intense Vanity."

dress, she had chosen a ruffled shirtwaist decorated with jewelry, leaves, wide sleeves, and a wide belt, a costume too girlish for her years and unflattering to her heavy features, but hardly, it would seem, so tasteless as to demand sequestration.[35] "Sane" dress obviously had to coincide with male superintendents' views of suitability for class and age.

As the photographs of madwomen in medical texts reveal, moreover, Victorian doctors imposed cultural stereotypes of feminity and female insanity on women who defied their gender roles. The advent of photography provided a valuable aid in the management of women. Dr. Hugh Welch Diamond, who succeeded Alexander Morison as physician to the female department at the Surrey Asylum in 1848, was the pioneer of psychiatric photography in England. During the ten years of his residence at Surrey, Diamond photographed many of his women patients. He argued that photography had a significant function in the asylum, not only as a record of patients and a diagnostic guide to insane physiognomy, but also as a therapeutic tool. For women patients especially, he maintained, it was salutary to have this reminder of personal appearance, and to have the natural feminine vanity, dulled by disease, stimulated by a photographic portrait. T. N. Brushfield, superintendent of the Chester County Lunatic Asylum, who had heard Diamond lecture on asylum photography at the Royal Society in 1852, wrote that "patients are very much gratified at seeing their own portraits. . . . In our worst female ward I have had a positive (on glass) framed and hung up for nearly eighteen months, and it has never yet been touched by any of the patients." At Bethlem, Sir William Charles Hood noted that "the taking of portraits has become one of the pleasures of which the patients cheerfully partake in our lunatic asylums; and helps . . . to diversify and cheer the days spent in necessary seclusion from the busier, but scarcely happier world, without." He gave the case of a woman patient who had worried about the portrait because she thought her dress was unbecoming, but whose "sense of propriety" was satisfied by being "represented with a book in her hand."[36]

Diamond particularly valued photography for its objectivity: psychiatric photographs, he believed, provided permanently valid records of types of insanity, "free altogether from that painful caricaturing which so disfigures almost all the published pictures of the Insane as to render them nearly valueless either for purposes of art or of science."[37] Indeed, looking at Diamond's photographs, we seem at first to be voyeurs of the inner world of madness. The women have lank, dirty curls, or strange knots and twists of hair, or bald patches. They do not wear flowing white gowns but dark bunchy dresses, too large or too tight, obviously from the hospital store. Even in "mania" they look gloomy and still, sad rather than mad.

Yet of course these photographic representations were no more objective or scientific than Morison's sketches, but simply made use of another set of visual and psychiatric conventions. Diamond's subjects, for example, are shown in chiaroscuro, posed against draperies; in some plates, they are sitting in front of windows, which ironically emphasize the viewer's sense of their confinement. The calotype process that he used for asylum work required a long sitting, and produced a rough, shadowy, and painterly print rather than the sharp, clear image of the daguerreotype. Some of the younger women, with their heavy hair and distracted gaze, resemble the well-known studies of women artistically photographed by Diamond's contemporaries, especially Julia Margaret Cameron or Henry Peach Robinson.

Literary and aesthetic models of femininity influenced Diamond's choice of subjects and affected the way he asked them to pose. Women were given props that symbolized, often with pathetic futility, the asylum superintendent's hope of making them conform to Victorian ideals of feminine decorum. Even the craziest women have some small emblem of respectable attire—a kerchief, a battered bonnet, a huddled shawl, even a blanket draped around the shoulders. The cretin sits next to a table with books on it (fig. 13); the alcoholic and the depressive have clasped their hands as if in prayer. The woman going through four stages of puerperal mania, from dementia to recovery, Victorianizes Hogarthian conventions of the "progress." Her madness is represented by untidy hair; her return to sanity, primarily by appropriate feminine costume—a matronly bonnet and a nice paisley shawl (fig. 14).

In choosing his subjects, moreover, Diamond was drawn to those women who seemed to be acting out the very fantasies that their society recommended as appropriate for them. He was struck, for example, by the great number of female lunatics who claimed to be queens, and attempted to photograph all of them together as a mad court. In Victoria's reign, the delusion of being a queen was perhaps an obvious one; it is easy to see why Lewis Carroll, a good friend of Diamond's, picked

Figure 13. A cretin in Surrey Asylum, photographed by Hugh W. Diamond.

Figure 14. Four stages of puerperal mania.

it for *Through the Looking-Glass,* where the White Queen is also a mad-woman whose clothes are twisted, whose shawl is awry, and whose brush is tangled in her hair. The metamorphosis of madwoman into queen had a kind of female logic as well. In his famous lecture "Of Queens' Gardens" (1864), Ruskin rapturously addressed all the women in his audience as "queens" and implored them to seek the womanly power "to heal, to redeem, to guide and to guard." Coveting this power rather than the coarse economic leverage or intellectual prowess of men, they would become "no more housewives, but queens."[38] Diamond's regal inmates—many of them the worn-out wives of poor clerks—took this invitation to transcend their powerless lives to heart.

But an even more popular image than the queen for women in Victorian asylums was that of Ophelia. For a variety of reasons, Ophelia was a compelling figure for many Victorian artists, writers, and doctors seeking to represent the madwoman. The English Pre-Raphaelites returned again and again to the subject of the drowning Ophelia.[39] In the Royal Academy show of 1852, Arthur Hughes's entry shows a tiny waiflike creature—a sort of Tinker-Bell Ophelia—in a filmy white gown, perched on a tree trunk by a stream. The over-all effect is softened, sexless, and hazy, although the straw in her hair resembles a crown of thorns (fig. 15). Hughes's juxtaposition of childlike femininity and Christian martyrdom, however, was overpowered by John Everett Millais's strong painting of Ophelia in the same show (fig. 16). Millais's Ophelia is a sensuous siren as well as a victim.

A model for the mad Miss Havisham in Dickens's *Great Expectations,* for Tennyson's "Maud," for Wilkie Collins's "Woman in White," Ophelia became the prototype not only of the deranged woman in Victorian literature and art but also of the young female asylum patient.[40] Victorian psychiatrists and superintendents of lunatic asylums were often enthusiasts of Shakespeare. They turned to his plays for models of mental aberration that could be applied to their clinical practice, and the case of Ophelia was one that seemed particularly apt. As J. C. Bucknill remarked in 1859, "Ophelia is the very type of a class of cases by no means uncommon. Every mental physician of moderately extensive experience must have seen many Ophelias. It is a copy from nature, after the fashion of the Pre-Raphaelite school."[41] Conolly concurred. In his *Study of Hamlet* in 1863 he noted that even casual visitors to mental institutions could recognize an Ophelia in the wards: "The same young years, the same faded beauty, the same fantastic dress and interrupted song."[42] Medical textbooks sometimes illustrated their discussions of female patients with sketches of Ophelia-like maidens; as one historian notes, the descriptions of these "Ophelias whose delicate and refined sensibilities had been wounded . . . and maddened by a disappointment in love" were often "affectingly drawn."[43] And when

Figure 15. Arthur Hughes, "Ophelia," 1852.

Figure 16. John Everett Millais, "Ophelia," 1852

young women in lunatic asylums did not willingly throw themselves into Ophelia-like poses, asylum superintendents with cameras imposed the conventional Ophelia costume, gesture, props, and expression upon them. Diamond dressed one young woman in a black shawl and placed a garland of wildflowers in her hair (fig. 17).

The figure of Ophelia eventually set the Victorian style for female insanity. In the 1860s Conolly urged actresses playing Ophelia to come to the asylum and study real madwomen. "It seems to be supposed," he protested, "that it is an easy task to play the part of a crazy girl, and that it is chiefly composed of singing and prettiness. The habitual courtesy, the partial rudeness of mental disorder, are things to be witnessed. . . . An actress, ambitious of something beyond cold imitation, might find the contemplation of such cases a not unprofitable study."[44] In the 1870s, Ellen Terry took up his challenge. Yet when she visited a London asylum to get ideas for her role, she found the madwomen much "too *theatrical*" to teach her anything.[45]

Just as they were accustomed to moralizing about the images of women in Academy paintings or the heroines of popular novels, Victorian psychiatrists drew moral lessons from asylum photographs of women. Diamond himself found a comforting message in his series of photographs of the patient with puerperal mania:

> I feel that I shall be supported by the Chaplain to our Asylum if I show a moral truth from these portraits, which, if I apprehend it rightly amounts to this—that religion can win its way to hearts barred against every other influence, that it can soften and conquer dispositions which would else remain intractable and savage; and that hereby in addition to all its other and higher merits, it establishes a title to be considered the great humanizer of Mankind.[46]

John Conolly's essays on the physiognomy of insanity, which appeared in the *Medical Times and Gazette* in 1858, contained similar passages of emotional projection. Using lithographs made of Diamond's photographs, Conolly argued that these were "true pictures of what is effected by mental malady." In fact, the lithographic copies made for the medical journal were even more simplified and conventionalized versions of Diamond's photographs, often with changes in pose, dress, or gesture; and Conolly's case studies were speculative, high-

Figure 17. A Victorian Ophelia in Surrey Asylum.

ly colored accounts, unlike anything we would recognize as scientific analysis.

In the picture of one elderly woman, Conolly could see the history of a wasted life, a "lamentable tale of long mental vexation . . . when carelessness, unheeded or untended, a giddy mind uneducated, wild manners and irregular habits, unrestrained by any care or protection, opened a wide way to disturbance." In the face of an alcoholic, he detected the signs of inner conflict, "the painful questioning of a woman not forgetful of her former life, nor unconscious of the comfortless change that has come over her . . . we might almost fancy the poor patient breaking out, in this suffering mood, into expressive words . . . relative to her earlier life now gone, and happier thoughts long dispersed, and to remembrances of having once been esteemed and even admired in the modest circle in which she moved." In another alcoholic, however, "the bloated face . . . the large lips . . . the disordered, uncombed, capriciously cut hair [and] the indolent position of the body" told Conolly he was looking at a "woman of low and degraded life, into whose mind, even before madness supervened, no thoughts except gross thoughts were wont to enter"[47] (fig. 18).

Conolly was especially fascinated by the photograph of a young woman diagnosed as melancholic who had converted to Catholicism, but then became guilt-ridden and anxious about her beliefs (fig. 19). She was tormented by the sense of her own sins, and had punished herself by fasting. This patient had become weak and emaciated; her menstrual periods had stopped, and she thought often of suicide. Yet Conolly found her wasting despair oddly feminine and attractive; he was moved by her pallor and sensitivity, and noted especially her "womanly figure . . . ample chest and pelvis." In the asylum she was cured with tonics and shower baths; her "mental perplexities . . . gradually died away," but along with them died the meditative and romantic qualities that had made her appealing to Conolly. He saw a second photograph of her after she was cured, and felt disappointed: "The ample forehead, of course, remained, and the deep orbits; but the eyes, when open, were small and inexpressive, and the mouth seemed to have become commonplace. Her whole appearance was, indeed, so simply that of an uneducated Irish girl, that the very neat gown, cloak, and bonnet, in which she was dressed by the kindness of those about her, seemed incongruous and peculiar." She had declined in class status as well as in sexual magnetism.[48]

Figure 18. An alcoholic, photographed by Hugh W. Diamond.

Figure 19. A melancholic asylum patient.

Hugh Diamond's photographs of female lunatics were recycled in the twentieth century as authenticating period decor in the asylum set for the film of *The French Lieutenant's Woman,* and used as models for the way Victorian madwomen "really" looked. In John Fowles's novel about Victorian England, the melancholic heroine—"Tragedy," as she is named by the community—acts out the traditional role of the Ophelia-like madwoman, abandoned by her lover, haunting the farthest point of the sea wall "like a living memorial to the drowned." Writing in 1969, Fowles is fully aware of the way this heroine, like the melancholic subject of Conolly's analysis, is appropriated by men; her "madness" is the accumulated projection of male fantasy and male guilt. For Conolly and his mid-Victorian contemporaries, too, the brooding images of the helpless women they treated in the asylums often evoked their own unconscious erotic reveries, their own displaced melancholia, aggression, and discontent.

That we should have so many remarkable pictures of Victorian madwomen, and so few of their words, reminds us how strongly the power of definition rested with the male observer. In the photographs of Victorian madwomen by Diamond and others, we are made to *see* the moral management of female insanity, as well as its reduction, in Victorian terms, to visual conventions. The act of photographing itself is a form of appropriation: a capture of the subject. Some of the women looked frightened; others, lost in their own fantasies, seem unaware of the presence of the camera. All sit at the doctor's bidding; they surrender to his lens; they are at his service. Susan Sontag has pointed out that nineteenth-century photography very quickly became a "useful tool of . . . surveillance and control," especially in institutions that needed records to identify inmates, such as prisons and orphan asylums, and in the "typological sciences" of criminology, eugenics, and psychiatry.[49]

Of course, the rhetoric of moral management obscured its power. In his essay about the Christmas Ball at St. Luke's, Dickens praised the progressive Victorian spirit that had brought the asylum out of barbarism and into civilization. The wicked old days when, as he recalled, "nothing was too wildly extravagant, nothing too monstrously cruel to be prescribed by mad-doctors," had been succeeded by an age sympathetic to the sufferings and misfortunes of the mad. "Chains, straw, filthy solitude," the cruel restraints of Bedlam, had been replaced by the patterned steps of a dance and by the colorful costumes of the dancers: "The only chain that made any clatter was Ladies' Chain, and there was no straiter waistcoat in company than the polka-garment of the old-young woman with the weird gentility."[50] It is a charming image, but Dickens fails to see the irony in his own account. What confined women in the Victorian asylum was precisely the ladies' chain of feminine propriety and the straitjacket of a weird but mandatory feminine gentility. Dickens could not perceive that both the social circumstances and the social services available to women might be maddening, and that despite its humanitarianism, Victorian psychiatry silenced women as effectively through its ideology as the scold's bridle had muzzled noisy women in Bedlam before reform.

And yet, one of the most appalling ironies of women's treatment in the Victorian asylum was that despite its limitations, asylum superintendents thought it offered a more tolerant, comfortable, interesting life than some women could expect outside. Conolly claimed that women patients at Hanwell shed more tears upon leaving the asylum than on entering it, and often returned to visit their former companions and attendants.[51] T. S. Clouston advised medical superintendents not to keep hysterical cases in the asylum too long after convalescence, because "they sometimes get too fond of the place, preferring the dances, amusements, and general liveliness of asylum life . . . to the humdrum and hard work of poor homes."[52] The success of moral management for women may have had less to do with the humanity of the asylum than with the dreariness of life beyond the walls.

PART TWO

Psychiatric Darwinism

4

ON THE BORDERLAND

Henry Maudsley and Psychiatric Darwinism

The ideal asylum of which Victorian psychiatry had been so proud could not be sustained for long. The buildings themselves, emblems of the new era of reform, disintegrated with alarming rapidity. By 1857, only six years after its dedication, Colney Hatch was literally falling apart; sections of its walls, ceilings, and roof had cracked or collapsed, and additional funds had to be hastily allotted for repairs. In 1859, the Middlesex directors tried unsuccessfully to sue the architect-builder.[1] By the mid-1870s, investigating conditions in the metropolitan asylums on behalf of *The Lancet,* Mortimer Granville reserved his sharpest comments for Colney Hatch. The asylum, he declared, "is a colossal mistake. . . . It combines and illustrates more faults in construction and errors of arrangement than it might have been supposed possible in a single effort of bewildered or misdirected ingenuity."[2]

Conolly's ideology, the ideology of psychiatric Victorianism, had also run its course. Within a decade of his death in 1866, it became clear that the system for which he had been so effective an advocate was moribund—overcrowded, inefficient, and demoralized. "There are epochs in all institutions," wrote Andrew Wynter in 1875, "at which a paralysis seems to seize upon those conducting them. With regard to our present superintendents as a body . . . we unhesitatingly assert the spirit of Conolly is dead. A miserable spirit of routine, without resources, spring, or energy, is sapping and destroying asylum life."[3]

Why did this period of therapeutic pessimism succeed the hopeful era of Victorian psychiatric reform? First of all, the utopian claims of the moral managers could not be sustained in huge institutions where personalized care was impossible. Between 1867 and 1877, the asylum population was increasing by 1,775 a year. When asylums built to hold four hundred swelled into "lunatic colonies of eight or nine hundred, or even a thousand or more inhabitants," any pretenses to genuine therapy evaporated; what prevailed was regimentation. By 1874, Colney Hatch had more than two thousand patients, and only two directing physicians. "If lunacy continues to increase as at present," *The Times* editorialized in April 1877, "the insane will be in the majority, and freeing themselves, will put the sane in asylums."[4]

The need to control large numbers of often unruly patients meant that the invisible restraints of moral management had to be replaced by disciplinary techniques closer to those of the workhouse or prison: elaborate timetables and schedules for every activity; systems of reward and punishment; the use of opiates; and the practice of keeping inmates on a near-starvation diet.[5]

Critics of the asylum increasingly charged that the domestic façades and homely activities of the mammoth institutions were simply deceits. The exterior of Colney Hatch might be palatial, wrote one journalist, but inside, the darkness and low ceilings gave "a stifling feeling and a sense of detention as in a prison."[6] An inmate, commenting on the "sedative influence which an asylum has on its patients," attributed it in part to the "feeling of protection and security which an asylum affords," but much more to the sense "of a power and authority which it would be useless to resist."[7]

This cynical sense that the asylum was a prison masquerading as a retreat becomes prominent in the sensation fiction of the 1860s and 1870s. In Charles Reade's *Hard Cash* (1864), the hero, Alfred Hardie, is tricked with a forged letter into entering a private lunatic asylum. He is first conducted to a spacious drawing-room, but from there he is led to "a very long room, as plain or even sordid as the drawing-room was inviting; the unpapered walls were a cold drab, and wanted washing; there was a thick cobweb in one corner . . . that side of the room they had entered by was all books." Alfred discovers where he is when, reaching for a book, he finds that it is "a piece of iron, admirably painted"; when he tries to open the door, he finds only a knob: "the door was blocked up." Similarly, in Sheridan LeFanu's *The Rose and the Key* (1871), the heroine, Maud Vernon, thinks she is at a party at a country house when she is actually a patient in Dr. Antomarchi's lunatic asylum. Although she is somewhat puzzled by her fellow guests ("Some of these people, foreigners she supposed, were very demonstrative in their talk and gestures. And a dozen or so . . . were dressed extremely oddly, not to say grotesquely"), she does not realize where she is until a patient she has taken for a duchess is put into a straitjacket, and she herself has been subjected to a cold shower. Cases of wrongful confinement in lunatic asylums that received public attention in the 1860s and 1870s further fostered distrust of the domestic imagery that the early Victorians had promoted.

In this discouraging climate, asylum superintendents could no longer find even the personal satisfactions and professional opportunities that had motivated the moral managers. Despite Conolly's success, asylum superintendents' status as a group had remained low within medicine as a whole, in large part because it did not seem that *medical* treatments were an important or efficacious part of their jobs. Their personal interactions with patients were impeded by the ever-growing burden of administration in a large institution. As the superintendent withdrew to concentrate on administrative concerns, the routine medical care of patients was gradually delegated to assistant physicians; the assistants in their turn passed on "the dirty work of dealing with the patients on a day-to-day, hour-by-hour basis" to the attendants, "who in return for long hours spent in close, defiling contact with the insane, received suitably low status and financial rewards."[8]

For the most ambitious men in this generation, then, the asylum seemed a less and less promising base for a career in psychiatric medicine. Moreover, while the moral managers had found emotional gratification in a familial relationship with inmates, the Darwinians felt that their social positions were compromised by too close a relationship with the insane. By the 1870s, it was considered inappropriate for the superintendent's wife to play the traditional role of matron. As Granville observed:

> The circumstances of the superintendent's wife acting as matron involves a sacrifice of social position injurious, if not fatal, to success. It

> is above all things indispensable that medical superintendents of asylums should be educated gentlemen; and if that is to be the case, their wives cannot be matrons. Indeed, it is inconceivable that a man of position and culture would allow his family to have any connection with an asylum.[9]

In a climate that looked for scientific answers to all questions, their medical reputations, too, might be undermined by the environmental emphasis of moral management. Although advocates of moral management had insisted that it was a total therapy that only doctors were qualified to supervise, asylum superintendents' contention that madness was a physical disorder had little empirical proof. And if merely spiritual or psychological problems were at the root of physical disorder, the clergyman, the philanthropist, even the novelist, might be a better therapist than the physician.

Thus the second generation of nineteenth-century psychiatrists, inspired by Darwinian theories of evolution in geology, biology, and the social sciences, sought to apply rigorous scientific methods to the study of insanity rather than rely any longer on the vague humanitarian sympathies and administrative reforms of their predecessors. They insisted that insanity had a physical cause that could be discovered by a sophisticated medical practice. As G. Fielding Blandford writes in *Insanity and Its Treatment* (1871), "disorder of the mind means disorder of the brain, and . . . the latter is an organ liable to disease and disturbance, like other organs of the body, to be investigated by the same methods and subject to the same laws."[10] "Lunatics and criminals," Henry Maudsley asserts, "are as much manufactured articles as are steam-engines and calico-printing machines. . . . They are neither accidents nor anomalies in the universe, but come by law and testify to causality; and it is the business of science to find out what the causes are and by what laws they work."[11]

Their focus was on laws of selection and survival, which they believed operated as strongly in the mental as in the social world. Darwinism emphasized the hereditary disposition to madness and the congenital inferiority of the insane—madness as the mark of the impotent and unfit, the sign of social, intellectual, and moral decline. Whereas at least some early Victorian reformers deplored the social problems that had brought so many wretched people to the asylums, Darwinian psychiatrists sternly maintained that hereditary organic taint compounded by vicious habits caused madness.

Darwinian, determinist, or evolutionist psychiatry dominated the English scene from about 1870 to the First World War, and brought with it changes in the view of the psychiatrist's role and of the proper conduct of treatment, as well as in the definition of madness itself. Claiming a new social authority as experts on the laws of heredity and the operations of the mind, Darwinian psychiatrists extended their professional role far beyond the asylum walls. They sought to capture a wide sphere of power in late nineteenth-century society: in the courtroom, where they made pronouncements on the family and the education of youth; in the bedroom, where they defined acceptable sexual behavior; and in the state, where they proposed mental hygiene as the model of social discipline.[12]

In defining insanity, they also moved beyond the large and simple categories of aberrant behavior the Victorians used to classify lunatics —moral insanity, melancholy, mania, and so on—to the more ambiguous manifestations of eccentricity and deviance which they hoped to annex. The most characteristic and revealing metaphor of Darwinian psychiatry was that of the "borderland," the shadowy territory between sanity and madness which sheltered "latent brain disease" and the "seeds of nervous disorders." On this terrain, as one physician explained, lurked "many persons who, without being insane, exhibit peculiarities of thought, feeling, and character which render them unlike ordinary beings and make them objects of remark among their fellows." Only a trained specialist, psychiatrists insisted, was qualified to patrol this mental and sexual frontier, watching for the "incipient lunatics" who "pass about the world with a clean bill of mental health," and thus saving society from their dangerous infiltration.[13]

As Andrew Wynter described it, the borderland was a kind of perilous no man's land, where every now and then "a passenger is . . . missed from the ever-ebbing stream of life, and none but the physician notes that he has dropped through the pitfall on the bridge and will never mix in the busy haunts of men again."[14] Mortimer Granville divided the borderland into subterritories called Mazeland, Dazeland, and Driftland, where the degenerate lower classes and the effeminate upper classes filled an increasingly populous district. Driftland was specifically the limbo of rich young men, who, "as the nation prospers and the exigencies of life for the sons of rich people decrease," let their mental and masculine faculties "first stiffen from disuse and then rot."[15] The imagery of the borderland reflected the anxieties of late Victorian psychiatrists, who felt that they were in a temporal and sexual limbo where the traditional boundaries of gender, labor, and behavior were being challenged by New Women and decadent men.

To explain what would drive someone into the borderland, the Darwinian posited a hierarchy of mental, intellectual, and emotional faculties ranging from the instincts of the savage to the refined perceptions of the civilized elite. In the development of the individual as well as in the evolution of the race, there was ascendancy from "sensation, passion, emotion, reason, to the highest phase of mental force, a well-fashioned will."[16] Will, self-restraint, and self-control were still considered the ultimate development of mental health, an ordering that also governed late Victorian sexual codes and economic policies. Daniel Hack Tuke called this faculty "inhibitory power" and named its absence "inhibitory insanity." Either because of hereditary taint or diseased cerebral development, he maintained, some individuals could not control their lower nature and emotions.[17] Then they might cross the borderland into madness.

In Darwinian terms, insanity thus represented an evolutionary reversal, a regression to a lower nature. As Charles Mercier explained: "Insanity is a dissolution; it is a retrogression; it is a traversing of the path of development in the reverse direction. It is a peeling off of those superimposed layers of development which have been laboriously deposited by the process of evolution."[18]

Mental regression revealed itself, doctors believed, in physical defects, often subtle or slight, which the trained specialist could recognize. For Darwinian psychiatrists, the set of an ear, the shape of a brow, even the quiver of an eyebrow, were "stigmata of degeneration" to which others might be blind.[19] In Henry Maudsley's writing, this mystique of visible vice and mental degeneracy found its most pungent expression. In *Body and Mind* he wrote: "It would scarcely be an exaggeration to say that few persons go mad . . . who do not show more or less plainly by their gait, manner, gestures, habits of thought, feeling, or action, that they have a sort of predestination to madness." The "insane temperament" could be recognized by such "bodily and mental marks" as "an irregular and unsymmetrical conformation of the head, a want of regularity and harmony of the features . . . malformations of the external ear . . . tics, grimaces . . . stammering and defects of pronunciation . . . peculiarities of the eyes," or a predilection for puns.[20]

In women, physical signs of mental disorder were thought to be especially striking, and it was during this period that European criminologists such as C. S. Lombroso published their photographic studies of the female criminal-degenerate face. In England Maudsley urged prospective husbands to scrutinize their future wives for "physical signs . . . which betray degeneracy of stock . . . any malformations of the head, face, mouth, teeth, and ears. Outward defects and deformities are the visible signs of inward and invisible faults which will have their influence in breeding."[21] Dr. L. Forbes Winslow went even further to argue that "the abnormal criminal woman is far more vindictive and cruel than the male" and that she usually goads the male criminal into his acts. These deadly females, however, could be readily detected by their large jaws, short arms, "badly shaped heads . . . large projecting ears and flat foreheads." Worst of all were the women of the Paris Commune, whom he had examined in 1871. Winslow was horrified by their peculiar craniums, broad cheekbones, and inexpressive faces; these women seemed to him so deficient in "every moral feeling . . . we are accustomed to find in the sex" that he classed tham as "acutely maniacal lunatics."[22] (During the furor that seized London in 1889 after the Jack the Ripper murders, Winslow volunteered his services to the police as one who might identify the killer by scientific analysis of physiognomies. Ironically, his eagerness made him a prime suspect.[23])

The search for hereditary physical traits hinting at the female's predisposition to insanity and her power to drive men mad reached its *reductio ad absurdum* in Furneaux Jordan's analysis of battered wives. Jordan, a surgeon at Queens College, Birmingham, suggested that certain women had the unfortunate hereditary combination of delicate skin, thin eyebrows, convex spine, and sharp tongue that made men unable to resist hitting them. In considering the "bodily conformation" and "congenital impulses of character" in these women, he noted fine distinctions of complexion, spinal curve, and personality between those who were merely assaulted and those who were actually murdered. For Jordan, these biological and psychiatric determinants of character far outweighed any differences of class or marital circumstance; "the unimpassioned tradeswoman who entreats a magistrate to protect her from a brutal husband, and the delicately born but erring (impassioned) lady who is summoned to the Divorce Court resemble in organisation and proclivity their humbler sisters who were brought into hospitals with bruised bodies or with fatal wounds."[24]

Discovering physical signs provided doctors with "scientific" confirmation of the hypothesis that lunatics were actually degenerates. Contempt for the insane as evolutionary failures characterized the discourse of psychiatric Darwinism. The rhetoric of heredity, inheritance, and degeneracy which appears obsessively in the medical literature of the time is also closely linked to class prejudice and to ideas of race superiority. The rich and the well educated, although they were increasingly vulnerable to the neuroses of modern civilization—to wit, the denizens of Driftland—were essentially seen as a reservoir of mental health, while the poor and disreputable were the breeding ground of madness. While the moral managers had hoped that the insane poor could be cured, the Darwinians thought that they could only be segregated; in the long run, physicians hinted, their numbers could be reduced through stricter immigration laws and selective breeding.

The circumstances of poverty and deprivation, of hopelessness and fear, moreover, were no longer held accountable for the incidence of insanity. That the poor went mad proved that they were inadequate persons, who demonstrated their inferiority by being poor and crazy in the first place. As Charles Mercier declared:

> Insanity does not occur in people who are of sound mental constitution. It does not, like smallpox and malaria, attack indifferently the weak and the strong. It occurs chiefly in those whose mental constitution is originally defective, and whose defect is manifested in a lack of the power of self-control and of forgoing immediate indulgence.[25]

Some statisticians argued that the highest percentage of lunatics came from the agricultural counties. "The dull swain with clouted shoon too frequently finds his way into the asylum," wrote Hack Tuke in a jocular mood, not "merely because his mind is in an uncultivated condition," but also "because his habits . . . and the brain he inherited from his parents" cause mental derangement.[26] Not urban stress but isolation and ignorance produced mental disorder, Wynter argued: "The Hodges of England, who know nothing of the march of intellect . . . contribute far more inmates to the public lunatic asylums than the toil-worn artisans of Manchester or Liverpool, who live in the great eye of the world, and keep step with the march of civilisation, even if they do but bring up its rear."[27] Others, employing the same logic, maintained that the cities with their fetid corners of alcoholism and sexual promiscuity contributed the most lunacy. In neither case was refinement or sensitivity the cause of madness, as an earlier generation had believed. On the contrary, wrote Maudsley, "There is most madness where there are the fewest ideas, the simplest feelings, and the coarsest desires and ways."[28] Criminals, too, were part of the tainted hereditary pool. Whereas Charlotte Brontë had protested against the psychological dangers of solitary confinement in prisons like Millbank and Pentonville, psychiatrists now suggested that the rate of mental breakdown among convicts proved that criminals were crazy to begin with. With his customary cheery urbanity, Dr. George Savage commented on the evidence that prisoners went mad in their solitary cells: "It is not astonishing that a good many prisoners should become mad. Prisoners differ among themselves in their insanities, but I believe that in them there is a great tendency to organized delusions, such as that of persecution."[29]

The physiological obsessions of late Victorian psychiatry were in perfect conformity with the body metaphors of late Victorian social analysis. Although such exponents of an organic social view as Herbert Spencer described the body politic in terms of the governing male as the Head, the workers as Hands, and middle-class women as the Heart, prudery generally kept the lower parts of the body from inclusion in such explicit analogies. Nonetheless Victorians identified the nether regions with the pauper, criminal, or mendicant classes, a social underworld associated with sexuality, filth, and contagion.[30] Edwin Chadwick's Sanitary Report of 1842 had showed that the laboring classes lived in rubbish, offal, and excrement; Mayhew's *London Labour and the London Poor* described the bizarre variety of scavengers and street people who lived off this refuse, trading in rags, bones, dust, and "pure," or dog excrement. Social investigators used a "cloacal imagery" of "moral refuse," and even the term "residuum" referred to both the sanitary and the human condition: it was "the offal, excrement, and other waste that constituted the sanitary problem; and it was also the name applied to the lowest layer of society, the class that was thought to constitute the major social problem."[31]

The Darwinian rhetoric of censure and disgust is also related to the political anxieties of the 1870s and 1880s, when severe economic depression, industrial unemployment, and socialist organizing presented the threat of class revolution. For a brief period after the Second Reform Bill of 1867, it had been hoped that housing reform, moralizing philanthropies, and the forces of social and industrial progress would reduce the problem of poverty as moral management was reducing the problem of lunacy. But the investigations of journalists and the social surveys of Charles Booth and others in the early 1880s revealed the existence of a vast population of casual laborers, paupers, and criminals in London's East End. Discussions of "Outcast London" in the press and explorations of the abyss of urban poverty by sensational reporters became urgent and alarmist; "the discovery of a huge and swelling residuum and the growing uncertainty about the mood of the respectable working class portended the threat of revolution."[32] In the mid-1880s, demonstrations and riots by the East End unemployed confirmed middle-class fears of a menacing underclass, a nether world "that could be readily mobilized into the revolutionary ranks of the new socialist movement."[33]

Pauperism, it was feared, could not be eliminated by social policies; moreover, it would reproduce itself in further generations of the ugly, feeble, idle, ignorant, and immoral. The only remedy was to exterminate the brutes—not by murder, but by studied neglect and population control. "Let them die out by leaving them alone," suggested one observer. "Keep such people from coming into existence," advised another. "Persons in any rank of life who are not in good physical or mental health have no moral right to have children."[34]

These fears of social degeneration have their counterpart in psychiatric literature in the new emphasis on state intervention, eugenics, and selective breeding. If, as Savage maintained, "the transmission of insanity leads gradually to the abasement and ultimate extinction of the race," then control over reproduction and immigration is essential for the benefit of the state.[35] Within a few decades, even such relatively moderate eugenicists as Dr. F. W. Mott deplored the "neuropathic taint" carried by the children born "to the feeble-minded, to the pauper, to the alien Jew, to the Irish Roman Catholic, to the thriftless casual laborers, to the criminals and . . . the denizens of one-roomed tenements of our great cities."[36] As late as 1924, in his book *The Borderland,* Dr. T. B. Hyslop saw further threats in the unchecked immigration that made Great Britain "a dumping-ground for the unfit . . . it is a strange irony that once a lunatic is on the sea his only landing-place appears to be England, which has thus become the asylum of the world."[37]

For all their claims to scientific validity, the Darwinians were no more successful than their Victorian counterparts in pinpointing an organic cause for madness—except in one instance. In the 1890s, research in medical science and cellular pathology proved what had been only partly suspected: that general paralysis of the insane, a form of insanity that affected a substantial percentage of male asylum patients, was actually the terminal form of syphilis. General paralysis of the insane (usually called GPI) had been recognized as a disease since the 1820s; its symptoms were "grandiose delusions, dramatic personality changes, failing memory, facial tremor, slurred speech, and unsteady gait"; within three years, the dementia progressed to helplessness and death. It affected ten times as many men as women.[38]

The male paralytic had his own cultural mythology, established by medical texts, quack advertisements, and sensational literature. Many accounts emphasized his violence. According to Thomas Austin, "extreme and sudden violence" was the most usual immediate cause of the paralytic's admission to the lunatic asylum, and in most cases his wife was the injured victim. Within the asylum, furious maniacal attacks might come on at night, in which "noise, restlessness, dirty, destructive habits, and . . . raving, are all carried to an extreme pitch. I have seen no mania comparable with paralytic furor."[39]

In the popular mind, the most salient symptom of general paralysis was the "failure or perversion of moral sense." The paralytic might begin with euphoria or with violent fits, but in any case his acts soon ceased "to be guided, as formerly, by religion, altruism, sense of morality, or duty, patriotism, love of family, of truth, of friendship, of beauty."[40] The personality changes of GPI could transform a solid citizen into a criminal: "A man who has been hitherto temperate in all his habits, prudent and industrious in business, and exemplary in the relations of life, undergoes a great change of character, gives way to dissipation of all sorts, launches into reckless speculations in business, and becomes indifferent to his wife, his family, the obligations of his position."[41] The paralytic was a favorite villain, or rather antihero, of the late nineteenth century: the reprobate whose descent into vice paralleled the decline of the prostitute. Indeed, the syphilitic and the whore, the fallen man and the fallen woman, are frequently coupled in literature of the period.

General paralysis of the insane was the perfect Darwinian disease because it linked immoral behavior to hereditary causes. Many Darwinian psychiatrists initially described GPI as a degenerative disease caused by a hereditary disposition to vice. In 1877, Krafft-Ebing blamed such diverse causes as heredity, alcoholism, and smoking.[42] By 1894 Fournier established that general paralytics, far more than any other mental patients, had a history of syphilitic infection. By 1913, the discovery of the spirochete conclusively demonstrated the relationship between syphilis and general paralysis of the insane.

This understanding of general paralysis confirmed Darwinian psychiatrists' belief in scientific medicine and hereditary predisposition. They hoped that the discovery of the etiology of general paralysis was the beginning of a breakthrough in which other forms of insanity would also be traced to indisputable organic causes, and that the physical basis of all mental disease would soon be firmly established.[43]

As psychiatric Victorianism found its champion and laureate in John Conolly, so Darwinian psychiatry found a spokesman and advocate in Henry Maudsley (1835-1918), editor of the *Journal of Mental Science,* benefactor and founder of the Maudsley Hospital, and prolific writer on mental medicine[44] (fig. 20). A precociously brilliant, caustic individualist, Maudsley dominated English psychiatry of the *fin de siècle* as forcefully as Conolly had dominated in the days of reform, a succession that seemed all the more appropriate because Maudsley was Conolly's son-in-law.

Yet no two men could have been more different in personality, in ideology, and in style of work. Maudsley was a prodigy, Conolly a late bloomer. Where Conolly was genial, gregarious, and popular, Maudsley's acquaintances noted his "difficult personality, his tart replies, and scathing judgments." Conolly beams jovially from his official portrait; Maudsley sits, grim, unsmiling, and heavily bearded, in his faculty photograph. Conolly's buoyant optimism led him to envision asylums that would comfort and cure the mentally afflicted: Maudsley spent only a few years in asylum work, and regarded optimism as "the practical expression of unthinking feeling," while pessimism was "the stern conclusion of thinking reason."[45] Conolly saw asylum reforms as the beginning of social reform and utopian harmony. Maudsley saw nervous debility as the first step in a chain of grim necessity spiraling downward to distemper, insanity, idiocy, and sterility. And while Conolly's labors in Hanwell brought him only modest prosperity, Maudsley was one of the first English psychiatrists to make a fortune in the consulting room.

Two themes dominate Maudsley's work: the physical basis of all mental illness, and the hereditary origins of mental weakness and defect. A classical education nourished his sense of cosmic despair; the scientific method formed his faith that future discoveries would provide

Figure 20. Henry Maudsley, 1881.

the organic evidence for the laws of devolution that reason posited. This combination of Greek tragedy, Hebraic resignation, and positivist philosophy gave Maudsley's writing its peculiarly sonorous and lugubrious tone:

> There is a destiny made for each one by his inheritance; he is the necessary organic consequent of certain organic antecedents; and it is impossible he should escape the tyranny of his organization. All nations in all ages have virtually confessed this truth, which has affected in an important manner systems of religion, social and political institutions. . . . The dread, inexorable destiny which played so grand and terrible a part in Grecian tragedy, and which Grecian heroes are represented as struggling manfully against, knowing all the while that their struggles were foredoomed to be futile, embodied an instinctive perception of the law by which the sins of the father are visited upon the children unto the third and fourth generations.[46]

Maudsley's personal background perhaps offers some explanation of his gloomy philosophy. In an unpublished autobiographical fragment, he described himself as a divided spirit torn between skeptical reason and altruistic emotion. Like many Victorian intellectuals, Maudsley associated these extremes with his masculine and feminine psychic inheritance: "I have always thought and said that the paternal and maternal were never vitally *welded* in me, but only *riveted.*" His mother was warmly religious; his father, a Yorkshire farmer, was taciturn, cold, obstinate, "a stolid Tory . . . quietly fixed to old ways of thinking and doing."[47]

But Maudsley's mother died when he was a child, and his father became even more withdrawn, and rarely spoke to his sons. Maudsley's education offered no escape from his dreary home; he was a day boy at a public school, walking two miles each way for the standard rote education in Latin and mathematics. He was rescued from this miserable life by the intervention of his mother's sister, Elizabeth Bateson, a teacher who taught him poetry. Maudsley recalled that having memorized a poem, he would "rush into the kitchen and declaim it to the servant. To that early and useful instruction I owe, I believe, any quality of style in my writings."[48] Besides giving him affection and encouraging his imagination, his aunt arranged for him to be sent to a first-rate tutor, and then—over his father's objections—to University College Hospital to study medicine.

Maudsley was a rebellious and strong-minded student who antagonized his professors. Early on he demonstrated the arrogance and the intellectual impatience that would later make him so tough a critic of his contemporaries. Annoyed by his abrasiveness, one professor wrote: "Maudsley has great abilities, but he has chosen to throw them into the gutter."[49] Nonetheless he completed his studies successfully, and after a relatively brief phase of apprenticeship in asylums at Wakefield and Brentwood, he was appointed at the age of twenty-four as medical superintendent of the Cheadle Royal Hospital for the Insane at Manchester, a registered hospital like Bethlem and St. Luke's which took both paying and pauper patients.

Under Maudsley's administration, the hospital prospered: the number of paying patients increased, the salaries of the asylum officers were raised, and new land was purchased.[50] But he had no intention of remaining an asylum administrator. He was certain that asylums had little to offer most of their patients, and that "future progress in the improvement of the treatment of the insane lies in the direction of lessening the sequestration and increasing the liberty of them."[51] An early advocate of decarceration, Maudsley believed that many chronic, incurable, and harmless lunatics would be better off at home than in institutions. He was also ambitious and impatient; having had no personal experience of parental benevolence, he seemed to lack the paternal emotions for his patients that are so prominent a feature in the preceding generation. Despite his own unhappy childhood, he did not cherish a Dickensian sympathy for unhappy or neglected others. Life, he felt, was "not a gay walk through a pleasure garden" but rather a "stern duty," and the manly behavior was to adjust to its "inevitable harshness."[52] The insane had not made this adjustment, but were weak, mistaken, and unfit social beings whose deficiencies threatened society as well as themselves. In his early books, Maudsley's case histories of his patients are judgmental and snobbish; he describes "a conceited Cockney . . . with offensive dissenting zeal"; "the daughter of a common labourer, who had become very rich in the colliery business . . . very vulgar, and spent the greater part of her time in drinking gin and reading sensational novels"; a Primitive Methodist with "boundless conceit of self."[53] It was not among such lowly folk that he planned to spend his life; as he wrote in a later book, "Village Hampdens, mute inglorious Miltons, and bloodless Cromwells do *not* sleep in the graves of the rude forefathers of the hamlet."[54]

In January 1862, after only three years, Maudsley resigned his post at Cheadle, moved to London, and became the editor of the *Journal of Mental Science.* He had already begun to publish essays on metaphysics, positivism, and literary genius. As editor he had an excellent forum for his views on the genesis of mind, brain disorder, faulty heredity, and cerebral development, and the opportunity to meet important men like Conolly. He assisted Conolly at his residence and private asylum for women, Lawn House, and in 1866 married his youngest daughter, Anne Caroline. She was five years his senior, and the marriage was childless —a sad detail in the life of a man who wrote incessantly about breeding, descent, and "proper" sexual expression. The marriage, one suspects, was not a love match but rather a professional alliance.

Two months after the wedding, Conolly died. His new son-in-law, as the editor of the major professional journal, was called upon to write an official memoir on behalf of the Medico-Psychological Association. The memoir Maudsley produced only a short time after his father-in-law's death is an extraordinary document, scathing in its judgments of Conolly's weaknesses and cold in its estimates of his strengths. Maudsley found his distinguished father-in-law an intellectual lightweight, and something of a Skimpole in his lack of ambition, his improvidence, and his naive indifference to economic realities. Over all, in Maudsley's stern late Victorian retrospect, there was something self-indulgent and unsound about Conolly, something sentimental and almost unmanly.

> He had a great sensibility of character; but his feelings were quick and volatile rather than deep and abiding. In some respects, I think, his mind seemed to be of a feminine type; capable of a momentary lively sympathy, which might even express itself in tears, such as enemies, forgetful of his character, might be apt to deem hypocritical; and prone to shrink from the disagreeable occasions of life, if it were possible, rather than encounter them with deliberate foresight and settled resolution.

The feminine side of Conolly's character was unfortunate, for "a character most graceful and beautiful in a woman is no gift of fortune to a man having to meet the adverse circumstances and pressing occasions of a tumultuous life."[55]

Maudsley's analogy to gender is a revealing one. In comparison to the domestic and devoted asylum doctors of Conolly's generation, Maudsley and his cohorts were conspicuously and aggressively masculine in their interests, attitudes, and goals. They sought success in private consulting rather than in service to the asylum. They were athletic rather than literary; sportsmen and clubmen rather than stay-at-home fathers of a lunatic *famille nombreuse.* Maudsley won ten gold medals in sports at the university; John Charles Bucknill was an ardent sportsman, proficient in fishing, hunting, sailing, coursing, and riflery; G. Fielding Blandford developed his taste for sports at Rugby; Lyttleton Winslow was a fanatical cricketer; George Savage was a passionate golfer, fisherman, and Alpine climber. Even Charles Mercier, although he was physically disabled at the end of his life, valued the ability to play games so highly that he carped at the poor sportsmanship of the insane, who neglect "those little offices which oil the wheels of social intercourse. . . . Others may collect the balls for them at tennis; may spot the red at billiards; may shuffle the cards and mark the points at whist; but when their turn comes, they do not reciprocate."[56] In their practice too, healthy physical exercise, in the form of "manly sport and games," was fervently recommended as an antidote to idleness and morbid introspection.[57]

The mind of a masculine type, one deduces from Maudsley, lacks superficial charm but is profoundly just, reliable, and strong. In literature, its tastes are for Goethe and German philosophy rather than for French authors and French style. In psychiatric medicine, it aims for exact scientific investigation rather than eloquent and pathetic portrayal of the external features of the disease. It is rational, not emotional; deliberate rather than impulsive.

Maudsley's contempt for Conolly, which he prudently concealed out of ambition, emerges clearly in these pages. The memoir's transgressions of filial piety and professional decorum tell us more about Maudsley than about Conolly. In his unsparing dissection of Conolly's limitations, he systematically defined the direction and values of his own professional life. Conolly's death was his coming of age. In memorializing Conolly's achievement, Maudsley thus annihilated it, and cleared the way for his own very different career.

Within a year of Conolly's death, Maudsley had begun to publish the ambitious and contentious studies that made him famous. His first book, *The Physiology and Pathology of Mind* (1867), was, according to Aubrey

Lewis, "a turning-point in English psychiatry; it presaged the end of a period in which psychiatry rested on a magma of empirical observations and windy philosophizing, and it embodied a critical synthesis of biological and other scientific advances so far as they had an evident bearing on mental activity, in health and disease." The book went through four editions, each extensively revised, and was widely read in Europe as well as in England. To Lewis, Maudsley, if not quite "a giant among the English pygmies," was superior to all of his contemporaries in "the grasp, the acumen, and the faculty of expression which make his work outstanding and potent."[58] This work, along with *Body and Mind* (1870), *Responsibility in Mental Disease* (1874), and *Natural Causes and Supernatural Seemings* (1886), certainly established him as the intellectual leader of his psychiatric generation. Furthermore, Maudsley's vivid accounts of how it must feel to experience delusions, dementia, or suicidal anxiety are unparalleled in nineteenth-century psychiatric writing.

Yet his literary insights, his great gifts of expression, and his wide-ranging intellectual powers were overwhelmed by the depths of his misanthropy. Much as he prided himself on reason, Maudsley's unacknowledged emotions and bitterness often led him into excess. *Responsibility in Mental Disease,* for example, is very much a work of the 1870s, with its sections on "The Borderland," on law and insanity, and on eugenic control; but it also reflects Maudsley's personal pessimism. The theme of the book, as in all of Maudsley's work, is the inescapable destiny of hereditary influence: "No one can elude, were he able to attempt it, the tyranny of his organization." Maudsley makes his case for psychological determinism, a case that grimly refutes the consoling sentimentalities of Victorian social reform, with rhetoric and literary allusions rather than with scientific evidence. The wicked, he maintains, are not social victims but people with a natural affinity for evil and a low intelligence; thus "the most sober and experienced prison officials are driven sooner or later to a conviction of the hopelessness of reforming habitual criminals." Maudsley goes even further to claim that members of the criminal class are physically deformed as well as morally corrupt, recognizable by their "badly formed angular heads" and, in the case of women, by their ugliness and gracelessness. Crime is a disease like insanity and epilepsy, "the physical result of physiological laws of production and evolution."[59]

Maudsley's view of degeneration exaggerated the already bleak pessimism of the *fin de siècle.* He saw signs of degeneration everywhere—

in the irreversibility of mental decline and the genetic multiplication of crime, vice, and mental defect. From his extreme perspective, even the genius of his age seemed decadent, narrow, and intense, an "expiring flash" that "sparkles in its ashes."[60] And evolution by itself held little hope for improvement. Survival of the fittest, he reminded his readers, "does not always mean survival of the best . . . it means only the survival of that which is best suited to the circumstances, good or bad, in which it is placed—the survival of a savage in a savage social medium, of a rogue among rogues, of a parasite where a parasite alone can live."[61]

Maudsley's bitterness infected his professional relations. His career is a record of intellectual contradictions, professional quarrels, and personal conflicts. He disparaged the work of his contemporaries, especially in academic psychology, and finally "became so detached from the main body of the profession that the Medico-Psychological Association was forced to create a special category of Honorary Members to maintain even a nominal connection with him."[62] His arrogance alienated most of his colleagues, and despite considerable financial success and professional influence, he was an unhappy and lonely man. At the height of his fame, he was regarded by his peers as "a bitter recluse, given over to mordant nihilism."[63] Furthermore, while his acquaintance with the latest British and Continental research in neuroanatomy, physiology, histology, pathology, and abnormal psychology put him at the forefront of scientific thought in the 1870s, he never developed beyond his early evolutionist views and "lived to become an outstanding intellectual anachronism."[64] Towards the end of his career, Maudsley himself admitted that the concept of degeneracy had gone too far and had become an ideological weapon, a "metaphysical something" stretched to "cover all sorts and degrees of deviations from an ideal standard of feeling and thinking, deviations that range actually from wrong habits of thought and feeling to the worst idiocy, and some of . . . which are no more serious marks of morbid degeneracy than long legs or short legs, long noses or short noses."[65]

But without it, Maudsley had nothing to fall back on. By 1895, at the age of sixty, he recorded a gloomy and disillusioned appraisal of his life's work:

> A physician who had spent his life in ministering to diseased minds might be excused if, asking at the end of it whether he had spent his life well, he accused the fortune of an evil hour which threw him on

> that track of work. He could not well help feeling something of bitterness in the certitude that one-half the diseased he had dealt with never could get well, and something of misgiving in the reflection whether he had done real service to his kind by restoring the other half to do reproductive work. Nor would the scientific interest of his studies compensate entirely for the practical uncertainties, since their revelation of the structure of human nature might inspire a doubt whether, notwithstanding impassioned aims, paeans of progress, endless pageants of self-illusions, its capacity of degeneration did not equal, and might someday exceed, its capacity of development.[66]

It is a very different kind of self-evaluation from that which Conolly had composed in *his* retirement when he listened nostalgically to the sound of Hanwell bells. Blaming the victims to the last, Maudsley could not bring himself to admit the possibility that his own character, rather than evil fortune, incurable lunatics, or unregenerate humanity, had robbed him of the satisfactions of his career.

Whatever the particularities of Maudsley's character, he nonetheless set the model for the psychiatrists of his age. The psychiatrist's role would no longer be to provide an example of kindness, but rather one of manliness, maturity, and responsibility. Stern guardians of the health of future as well as present generations, the "nerve specialists," as they were called, presided over the vast and uncertain territory George Savage called "the kingdom of disease."[67] As it turned out, its most alarming inhabitants would not be criminals, syphilitics, immigrants, or the unemployed, but rather more familiar figures: middle-class women, who refused to adjust to the "inevitable" conditions of their lives, and whose rebellion against their sex roles led to an unprecedented wave of nervous disorders.

5

NERVOUS WOMEN

Sex Roles and Sick Roles

The appearance of the New Woman, with her demands for education, work, and personal freedom, presented Darwinian psychiatry with a direct challenge to its social gospel. At the same time that new opportunities for self-cultivation and self-fulfillment in education and work were offered to women, doctors warned them that pursuit of such opportunities would lead to sickness, sterility, and race suicide. They explicitly linked the epidemic of nervous disorders—anorexia nervosa, hysteria, and neurasthenia—which marked the *fin de siècle* to women's ambition. As T. Clifford Allbutt noted, "the stir in neurotic problems first began with the womankind"; by the 1890s, he continued, "daily we see neurotics, neurasthenics, hysterics, and the like . . . every large city [is] filled with nerve-specialists and their chambers with patients."[1]

From a feminist perspective, Darwinian psychiatry posed especially serious problems for women, and not only because it was carried out by such a moralistic, domineering, and masculinist generation of doctors. Theories of biological sexual difference generated by Darwin and his disciples gave the full weight of scientific confirmation to narrow

Victorian ideals of femininity. Female intellectual inferiority could be understood as the result of reproductive specialization, and the "womanly" traits of self-sacrifice and service so convenient for the comfort of a patriarchal society could be defended in evolutionary terms as essential for the survival and improvement of the race. In 1871 Darwin himself had confidently defined the "natural" differences in the mental powers of the sexes in *The Descent of Man.* Through natural selection, he explained, man had become superior to woman in courage, energy, intellect, and inventive genius, and thus would inevitably excel in art, science, and philosophy. Even those faculties in which women had the edge—intuition, perception, and imitation—were actually signs of inferiority, "characteristic of the lower races, and therefore of a past and lower state of civilisation."[2]

Darwin's ideas were further developed in Herbert Spencer's widely read treatises on social evolution, and in work by the Scottish biologists Patrick Geddes and J. Arthur Thompson on the biology of sex differences. In *Principles of Sociology* (1876), Spencer argued that human development depended on the expenditure of a fixed fund of energy. Since women depleted, or sacrificed, their energy in the reproductive process, they were heavily handicapped, even developmentally arrested, in intellectual competition. *The Evolution of Sex* (1889) by Geddes and Thompson put forward a theory of sexual differentiation based on cell metabolism. Male cells, they explained, were *katabolic,* or active and energetic; female cells were *anabolic,* or energy-conserving, passive, and life-supporting. Moving from simple to complex forms of life, Geddes and Thompson argued that men, like the flagellate sperm, were aggressive, competitive, and inventive, while women, like the ovum, were placid, altruistic, and nurturant.[3]

The theories of sexual difference adumbrated by Darwinian science were incorporated into a highly prescriptive late Victorian psychology of women. From the 1870s onward, this generation of doctors, and especially Henry Maudsley and T. S. Clouston, presented a constellation of rigid views on gender roles. While the fundamental differences between the sexes were, of course, physical, Darwinian psychiatrists insisted that (in Maudsley's words), "there is sex in mind as distinctly as there is sex in body." Clearly, they agreed, female physiology marked women "for very different offices in life from those of men."[4] But because the brain responded to the operation of the reproductive organs (as it did to the other organs of the body), the *mentalities* of the sexes differed as well. It was the totality of the physical and the mental differences that made up the essence doctors confidently called woman's "nature."

By *nature,* then, woman was constituted to be "the helpmate and companion of man"; her innate qualities of mind were formed to make her man's complement rather than his equal. Among these qualities, Clouston believed, were the cheerfulness, vivacity, and powers of endurance that made woman capable "not only of bearing her own share of ills, but helping to bear those of others."[5]

Furthermore, women were mentally constituted to take care of children, as well as physically constituted to give birth. While women, Maudsley explained, "are manifestly endowed with qualities of mind which specially fit them to stimulate and foster the first growths of intelligence in children," men had much less mental capacity for patience, attachment, and sympathy. Thus, "if the nursing of babies were given over to men for a generation or two, they would abandon the task in despair or in disgust, and conclude it to be not worth while that mankind continue on earth."[6]

The sexual division of labor advocated by psychiatrists followed on these beliefs. Woman's work was clearly motherhood, which fulfilled and exercised her nature as it also served the needs of society and the race. "Man's chief work," as Clouston put it, was "more related to the present"; woman's chief work, however, was related "to the future of the world."[7] And women's "foreordained work as mothers and nurses of children," even if it might be seen as less noble than man's work as father of ideas, had to be done in a serious and dedicated way.[8]

Mental breakdown, then, would come when women defied their "nature," attempted to compete with men instead of serving them, or sought alternatives or even additions to their maternal functions. And once it appeared, mental disorder might be passed on to the next female generation, endangering future mothers. All Darwinian psychiatrists agreed that "the greater tendency of mothers to transmit insanity to their female children" was among the chief causes for the predominance of women among asylum patients.[9]

It is clear to a twentieth-century reader that these theories were convenient ramifications of existing social relations between the sexes. Despite his pious words about the importance of the maternal function in essays written for a general audience, Maudsley revealed in his professional texts how disgusting he found childbirth and how degrading he found childcare:

> Looking at the matter objectively in the dry light of reason, could anything be more ridiculous than all this affectionate fuss about what is essentially an excretory product and comes into the world by excretory ways? Moreover, there is nothing nice in the process of parturition nor in the base services which the child exacts.[10]

If half the population was to be consigned to these lowly activities, it was reassuring to know that their nature made pleasant to them what would have been boring, repellent, and maddening to men. The counterarguments of feminists fell upon deaf Darwinian ears. Maudsley dismissed John Stuart Mill's *The Subjection of Women* (1869) as an absurdity, especially Mill's claim that "what is now called the nature of women is an eminently artificial thing." That a women's movement seemed actually to be under way in the 1870s, Maudsley explained, owed less to widespread female discontent than to the "awakened moral sense and . . . more enlightened views of men," who magnanimously assisted a handful of feminists instead of suppressing their efforts.[11]

In the decades from 1870 to World War I, psychiatrists and feminists battled over the question of what women should be. These battles were waged on many fronts: in journals, where a few women doctors at last had access; in courts of law, where there were protests over wrongful confinement of wives and daughters; and in fiction, where the nerve specialist and his hysteric became a familiar couple. There were also contests fought on more private terrain—in the sickroom and the consulting room, where nervous women communicated their malaise in a variety of baffling symptoms, and where doctors strove for mastery and domination.[12]

Feminist reformers and Darwinian doctors clashed first and most dramatically over the issue of higher education for women. In a famous essay, "Sex in Mind and Education," published in the *Fortnightly Review* in 1874, Maudsley argued that the intellectual training of adolescent girls could produce permanent injury to their reproductive systems and their brains. The occasion of Maudsley's essay was the publication of a book by an American doctor, Edward Clarke, called *Sex in Education,* which purported to describe the disastrous effect of coeducation upon the health of American women. Were the English reformers who were most eager to improve the education and social status of woman giving "proper consideration to the nature of her organization, and to the demands which its special functions make upon its strength"? Maudsley felt that the "extraordinary expenditure of vital energy" made through the establishment of menstruation during the critical years of puberty (and after) left "little vitality to spare" for other functions.

Drawing on the new theories of conservation of energy, Maudsley maintained that the demands of intellectual work and physiological change were antagonistic: "The energy of a human body being a definite and not inexhaustible quantity, can it bear, without injury, an excessive mental drain as well as the natural physical drain which is so great at that time? . . . Nor does it matter greatly by what channel the energy be expended; if it be used in one it is not available for use in another. What Nature spends in one direction, she must economise in another direction."

He painted a dire picture of the results of this overexpenditure of vital energy. The stimulus of competition, healthy and even necessary to bring out the best in boys, would act powerfully and disastrously to upset the more unstable nerve centers of girls, who could then become seriously deranged. Menstrual functions could be made irregular or even arrested by sustained mental effort; headache, lassitude, and insomnia might ensue. In the long run, the girl would become a "delicate and ailing woman, whose future life is one of more or less suffering." The injuries to the menstrual cycle might never be corrected, and in some cases might even lead to epilepsy, chorea, or mental breakdown.

The most horrible outcome of such a calamitous chain of events was the degeneration of the reproductive capacity, beginning with the atrophy of the breasts and ending with a total loss of "pelvic power," or sexless sterility. Feminine vanity, Maudsley warned, would conceal the early physical defects from the physician's watchful eye. "Those in whom the organs are wasted invoke the dressmaker's aid in order to gain the appearance of them; they are not satisfied unless they wear the show of perfect womanhood." If these imperfect women were not quite lunatics, they were nonetheless freaks and monstrosities, "something which having ceased to be woman is yet not man." If women continued to unsex themselves in study, race suicide must follow. Maudsley could foresee the day when "a race of sexless beings . . . undistracted and unharassed by the ignoble troubles of reproduction, shall carry on the intellectual work of the world, not otherwise than as the sexless ants do the work and fighting of the community."[13]

Similarly, Hack Tuke reported cases of "complete prostration of brain" in girls cramming for examinations, and George Savage, concerned about "the danger of solitary work" for girls "of nervous family" studying at home, forbade the fifteen-year-old Virginia Woolf to continue with her lessons, and ordered her to spend four hours a day gardening. T. S. Clouston foresaw an even darker prospect: that soon "all the [female] brain energy would be used up in cramming a knowledge of the sciences, and there would be none left at all for . . . reproductive purposes." When this catastrophe left England exhausted and barren, it would be necessary for men to look to other nations for more docile and fecund wives, to make "an incursion into lands where educational theories were unknown, and where another rape of the Sabines was possible."[14]

Women fought back in a variety of ways. Maudsley's and Clarke's attacks on the dangers of female higher education were vigorously refuted by women doctors—Mary Putnam Jacobi and Elizabeth Garrett Anderson. The 1870s also initiated a period of legal and journalistic agitation over the wrongful confinement of women in lunatic asylums. Georgiana Weldon's *How I Escaped the Mad-Doctors* (1878) and Rosina Bulwer-Lytton's *A Blighted Life* (1880) were essentially protests against the power that could be exerted by vengeful husbands over rebellious or difficult wives. At least one of these narratives, Louisa Lowe's *The Bastilles of England; or, The Lunacy Laws at Work* (1883), went further in developing a feminist critique of the whole structure of Victorian psychiatry. An energetic campaigner against the lunacy laws, Lowe also attacked the male monopoly over the asylum system and the absence of highly trained and well-paid female professionals within its ranks. Lowe was the first to suggest that women's feelings would be better understood by women doctors, attendants, and inspectors.

> Too much stress can scarcely be laid on the appointment of *inspectresses* for female patients. The rapid growth of medical studies among women affords hope that at no distant period there will be sufficient female doctors to obviate entirely the cruel necessity of placing female lunatics in the charge of men at all; meanwhile, few things would tend more to be their comfort, and, in some cases, hasten their cure, than inspection by persons of their own sex, who, *ceteris paribus,* would, in the nature of things, be better able to enter into their feelings, and detect the border-line between sanity and insanity than those of an opposite sex, and consequently, different habit of mind.

> And, moreover, it surely needs but little reflection to convince all thoughtful persons that there is most unseemly moral cruelty in subjecting woman in her hour of weakness and humiliation to the inspection of man, in forcing her to lay bare to him perhaps the most secret sorrows of her life, possibly the vagaries of a diseased mind, or of morbid and polluted affections. From personal observation, I am convinced that many a sane and pure-minded woman has passed with the commissioners as the reverse, simply through the confusion and pain occasioned by interrogatories, which, coming from an inspectress, would have been calmly and satisfactorily answered. Except as occasional consultants, the less men-doctors have to do with female lunatics the better.[15]

Not until 1894, and after much debate, however, did the Medico-Psychological Association admit women to membership; by 1898 there were still only eight women working as medical officers in British state, private, and charitable hospitals.[16]

But the most dramatic battle took place within the doctor-patient relationship, as nervous women and nerve specialists clashed over the relationship of sex roles to sick roles. The first of the female nervous disorders to be labeled during this period was anorexia nervosa, which was identified in 1873 as a new clinical syndrome among adolescent girls in both England and France. In a report to the Clinical Society of London read in October 1873, Dr. William Witney Gull, a prominent physician who treated members of the royal family, discussed cases of the disorder among young girls between the ages of fifteen and twenty. He described its major symptoms as extreme emaciation, loss of appetite, amenorrhea, and restless activity. Gull attributed "the want of appetite . . . to a morbid mental state. I have not observed in these cases any gastric disorder to which the want of appetite could be referred. I believe, therefore, that its origin is central and not peripheral. That mental states may destroy appetite is notorious, and it will be admitted that young women at the ages named are specially obnoxious to mental perversity."[17] E. C. Lasegue, a Parisian doctor who reported on eight cases of the disorder in the same year, viewed anorexia as characterized by the patient's "truly pathological" contentment: "Not only does she not sigh for recovery, but she is not ill-pleased with her condition, notwithstanding all the unpleasantness it is attended with."[18]

During the years when Gull and Lasegue were seeing their first anorexic patients, celebrated cases of "fasting girls," who seemingly lived without nourishment of any kind, attracted popular attention on both sides of the Atlantic. Such cases, taken up by the press and treated as miraculous, had also occurred previously; Ann Moore, the fasting woman of Tutbury, was a notorious early-nineteenth-century case. While many of these women were exposed as impostors, their fasting behavior could be seen as a form of female cultural protest.[19] This is how Florence Nightingale interpreted it in a vehement passage in *Cassandra*:

> To have no food for our heads, no food for our hearts, no food for our activity, is that nothing? If we have no food for the body, how we do cry out, how all the world hears of it, how all the newspapers talk of it, with a paragraph headed in great capital letters, DEATH FROM STARVATION! But suppose one were to put a paragraph in the "Times," *Death of Thought from Starvation,* or *Death of Moral Activity from Starvation,* how people would stare, how they would laugh and wonder! One would think we had no heads or hearts, by the indifference of the public towards them. Our bodies are the only things of any consequence.[20]

What Nightingale had said about fasting girls could also be applied to anorexia. When only the body was regarded as important, anorexic girls paraded physical starvation as a way of drawing attention to the starvation of their mental and moral faculties. The portrait of the anorexic painted by Darwinian psychiatry is paradoxically that of the self-sacrificing Victorian heroine. Refusing to eat, she acted out the most extreme manifestation of the feminine rôle, flaunting her martyrdom, literally turning herself into a "little" woman. In his essay on anorexia as a "neurosis of the stomach," T. Clifford Allbutt described the typical anorexic as a young woman of "ardent and self-forgetful nature," and he noted that "happily there are many such." Despite the fact that at the limits of self-starvation her clothes were hanging on her body, her pulse was slow, her menstrual periods had stopped, her hair was "like that of a corpse dry and lustreless, her face and limbs ashy and cold, [and] her hollow eyes the only vivid thing about her," the ardent anorexic continued her hectic round of feminine duties, attending "mother's meetings," sewing dresses for her little sisters, and persisting in various activities that Allbutt praised as "unselfish effort."[21]

In her attempt to become the incorporeal Victorian angel, unaffected by earthly appetite, the anorexic particularly renounced meat; "meat, even the smell of it, makes them sick," Allbutt reported. Meat, the "roast beef of old England," was not only the traditional food of warriors and aggressors but also believed to be the fuel of anger and lust. Disgust with meat was a common phenomenon among Victorian girls; a carnivorous diet was associated with sexual precocity, expecially with an abundant menstrual flow, and even with nymphomania.[22] Earlier in the century, Victorian physicians such as Edward J. Tilt had recommended low-protein diets as a way to retard menarche. In late Victorian women's literature, feminism, chastity, and vegetarianism often appear together as connected values; in feminist utopias such as Charlotte Perkins Gilman's *Herland* (1915), the virginal heroines abstain from the "heating diet" of red meat. Thus, in the rigid control of her eating, the anorexic both expressed her fear of adult sexual desire and enacted an exaggerated form of the deadening life of the dutiful daughter.

Some physicians regarded anorexia as one of the manifold forms of hysteria, a disorder whose symptoms and cultural meaning changed from era to era. For centuries, hysteria had been the quintessential female malady, the very name of which derived from the Greek *hysteron,* or womb; but between 1870 and World War I—the "golden age" of hysteria—it assumed a peculiarly central role in psychiatric discourse, and in definitions of femininity and female sexuality.[23] By the end of the century, "hysterical" had become almost interchangeable with "feminine" in literature, where it stood for all extremes of emotionality.[24] Not only did the analysis and management of hysterical women occupy a major place in the work of leading English, American, French, and German physicians of the period, and become the starting point for psychoanalysis, but also cases of classic hysteria peaked in frequency; by the twentieth century, the clinical incidence of the dramatic episodes had greatly declined. "Hysteria" was linked with the essence of the "feminine" in a number of ways. Its vast, unstable repertoire of emotional and physical symptoms—fits, fainting, vomiting, choking, sobbing, laughing, paralysis—and the rapid passage from one to another suggested the lability and capriciousness traditionally associated with the feminine nature. As Dr. Edward J. Tilt noted in his textbook on female diseases, "mutability is characteristic of hysteria, because it is characteristic of women—'*La donna è mobile.*' "[25] Like other aspects of the feminine, it seemed elusive and enigmatic, resistant to the powers of masculine rationality. Thus Weir Mitchell calls hysteria "the nosological limbo of all unnamed female maladies" and protests that it might just as well be called "mysteria."[26]

Classic hysteria, as it had been described by doctors in the early nineteenth century, had many symptoms, but two defining characteristics: the seizure, and the *globus hystericus*, or sensation of choking. The hysterical attack generally began with pain in the uterine region, and with a sense of obstruction in the chest and throat. At its height, the victim alternately sobbed and laughed; she might have convulsive movements of the body, heart palpitations, impaired hearing and vision, or unconsciousness. The fits were followed by exhaustion, and usually by rapid recovery, although occasionally the effects lasted for days. A striking aspect of the seizure was the *globus hystericus,* the sensation that a ball was rising in the esophagus, producing a feeling of choking or suffocation. Indeed, the ancients had believed that this feeling was caused by the rising of the womb itself within the body.

The basic explanatory model of hysteria generated by Darwinian psychiatry, however, related it to faulty heredity exacerbated by the biological and social crisis of puberty. While these explanations emphasized the physical element, they were not blind to the significance of the particular constraints—restricted activity and sexual repression—placed on women. In 1879 Maudsley summed up the problem of female adolescence thus:

> Girls are more liable to suffer at this period, I think, than youths; and it is not difficult to understand why. In the first place, the affective life is more developed in proportion to the intellect in the female than in the male sex, and the influence of the reproductive organs upon the mind more powerful; secondly, the range of activity of women is so limited, and their available paths of work in life so few, compared with those which men have in the present social arrangements, that they have not, like men, vicarious outlets for feelings in a variety of healthy aims and pursuits; in the third place, social feelings sanction tacitly for the one sex an illicit indulgence which is utterly forbidden to the other; and lastly, the function of menstruation, which begins at puberty in women, brings with it periodical disturbances of the mental tone which border closely on disease in some cases, while the irregularities and suppressing to which it is liable from a variety of mental and bodily causes may affect the mind seriously at any time.[27]

These views were echoed by Charles Mercier in his treatise *Sanity and Insanity*. Mercier noted that women did not share the masculine "safety-valve" of physical exercise to work off nervous and sexual energy. Partly as a result, he believed, adolescent hysteria was the norm rather than the exception: "few women pass through this period of their development without manifesting signs of disorder . . . at this period, more or less decided manifestations of hysteria are the rule."[28]

The neurologist Horatio Bryan Donkin, who wrote the essay on hysteria for the *Dictionary of Psychological Medicine* (1892), went further in pointing to the sexual inhibition and enforced passivity of girls as factors of nervous disorders. Unlike Maudsley and Mercier, Donkin was a progressive thinker, accepted not only in the medical and club worlds (he was on the Committee of the Savile Club) but also in radical and socialist circles. He had been an active participant in the Men and Women's Club, a London-based group of intellectuals and feminists who met in the late 1880s to discuss the relations between the sexes. He was the friend and admirer of several New Women whose prolonged struggles to integrate their radical beliefs about marriage and independence with traditional injunctions about femininity had led to a variety of nervous afflictions. In 1881 he had treated Eleanor Marx, who was suffering from physical symptoms of anorexia, trembling, and convulsive spasms, as well as depression and exhaustion. He had also been the physician and even the suitor of Olive Schreiner. Thus he was unusually familiar with, and sympathetic to, the stresses experienced by intellectual and ambitious women.[29]

In his essay for the *Dictionary,* Donkin described the "typical subject of hysteria" as "the young woman" and related the disease not only to "her organism" but also to "her social conditions." Like his contemporaries, he saw puberty as a risky period in female development, the stress of which was "more sudden and intense in the female" than in the male, but he also condemned the education and social repression that impeded female development: "All kinds of . . . barriers to the free play of her power are set up by ordinary social and ethical customs. 'Thou shalt not' meets a girl at every turn."[30]

Yet even Donkin preferred the biological argument that female hysteria comes from unsatisfied sexual and maternal drives to the cultural argument that women were unsatisfied and thwarted in other aspects of their lives. In discussing the case of Olive Schreiner, he concluded that her "nerve-storms," asthma attacks and recurring breakdowns were caused by her efforts to stifle and deny her sexual desires; he did not go further to question the pressures of her public role as a writer, feminist, or political activist. It was much simpler to blame sexual frustration, to continue to see hysterical women as lovelorn Ophelias, than to investigate women's intellectual frustration, lack of mobility, or needs for autonomy and control.

The idea that sexual frustration was a significant cause of hysteria was a traditional one, which had been strongly revived in the mid-nineteenth century by Dr. Robert Brudenell Carter. In an influential study of hysteria written in 1852 when he was only twenty-five, Carter had observed:

> It is reasonable to expect that an emotion, which is strongly felt by great numbers of people but whose natural manifestations are constantly repressed in compliance with the usages of society, will be the one whose morbid effects are most frequently witnessed. This anticipation is abundantly borne out by facts; the sexual passion in women being that which most accurately fulfills the prescribed conditions, and whose injurious influence upon the organism is most common and familiar.

Women were more liable to hysteria than men because "the woman is more often under the necessity of endeavouring to conceal her feelings."[31]

What Carter does *not* go on to suggest is that sexual feelings were not the only ones women endeavored to conceal; and indeed, as some historians argue, there may have been much more leeway within nineteenth-century bourgeois marriage for female sexual expression than we have realized. But longings for independence and for mastery were socially unacceptable at every phase of the female life-cycle. Even when doctors observed these longings in their female patients, and noted the women's powerless position in their families, they did not make the obvious connections.

F. C. Skey, for example, who delivered an important series of lectures on hysteria to the students of St. Bartholomew's Hospital in 1866, noticed that hysterical girls were typically energetic and passionate, "exhibiting more than usual force and decision of character, of strong resolution, fearless of danger, bold riders, having plenty of what is termed *nerve.*" He noticed, too, that the parents of these girls were unusually interfering and controlling. In one case a patient had been treated unsuccessfully for pain under the ribs by her own father, a physician who had applied leeches by the hundred and "blisters, the sum of which might be calculated by the square yard." In another case, an eighteen-year-old girl complained of acute pain in eating. At the interview her mother insisted on answering all the questions, and Skey had to ask her to leave. Yet he does not wonder whether the mother's interference might have been a source of the girl's pain.[32]

But it is precisely in a reaction against this kind of supervision that hysterical women were led to violate the expectations of the female domestic role. When the hysterical woman became sick, she no longer played the role of the self-sacrificing daughter or wife, as did the anorexic. Instead, she demanded service and attention from others. The families of hysterics found themselves reorganized around the patient, who had to be constantly nursed, indulged with special delicacies, and excused from ordinary duties. Carroll Smith-Rosenberg has speculated that such behavior threatened the male physician by placing him in a position of conflict. As a doctor, he certified and confirmed the hysteric in her sick role, one that legitimated her withdrawal from the accepted sex role in the belief that she was ill and trying to get well. But as a result, he was made to side with the woman against male family members, fathers and husbands. Physicians were concerned that hysterical women were indeed enjoying their freedom from domestic and conjugal duties, as well as their power over the family and the doctor himself. They did not wish to become "accomplices in her deviant role."[33]

Thus physicians perceived hysterical women as their powerful antagonists. Despite a certain sympathy for women's restricted lives, English doctors found their hysterical patients personally and morally repulsive, idle, intractable, and manipulative. Like pauper lunatics, hysterical women were the products of bad heredity and bad habits. "Exceeding selfishness," wrote Donkin, "delight in annoying others, groundless suspicion, and unprovoked quarrelsomeness are of very common occurrence; and the instances of self-mutilation and wondrous filthy habits are numerous."[34] Maudsley roundly denounced the "moral perversion" of hysterical young women who, "believing or pretending that they cannot stand or walk, lie in bed . . . all day . . . objects of attentive sympathy on the part of their anxious relatives, when all the while their only paralysis is a paralysis of will." The "immoral vagaries" and the "moral degeneration" of some of these women, he thought, would make them perfect case studies of systematic moral insanity: "nowhere more perfect examples of the subtlest deceit, the most ingenious lying, the most diabolic cunning, in the service of vicious impulses."[35]

Hysterics also expressed "unnatural" desires for privacy and independence. "The cardinal fact in the psychopathy of hysteria," wrote Donkin, "is an exaggerated self-consciousness . . . the hysteric is preeminently an individualist, an unsocial unit."[36] Darwinian psychiatry generally held that "asociality," the avoidance of company and withdrawal from society into morbid introspection and solitary habits, was "perhaps the most distinguishing feature of the insane."[37] G. Fielding Blandford maintained that the ideal treatment should redirect the patient's feelings from "morbid self-contemplation" to a more normal "care and concern for others."[38] Not surprisingly, since altruistic care and concern for others was regarded as especially natural in women, its absence struck doctors as unhealthy or insane egoism.

Neurasthenia, the third disorder of the 1870s, was a more prestigious and attractive form of female nervousness than hysteria, although it shared so many of hysteria's symptoms that even specialists could not always distinguish between the two. Like hysteria, neurasthenia encompassed a wide range of symptoms from blushing, vertigo, headaches, and neuralgia to insomnia, depression, and uterine irritability. Dr. George Savage's description of the neurasthenic, for example, incorporated some of the sexual stereotypes of the hysteric:

> A woman, generally single, or in some way not in a condition for performing her reproductive function, having suffered from some real or imagined trouble, or having passed through a phase of hypochondriasis of sexual character, and often being of a highly nervous stock, becomes the interesting invalid. She is surrounded by good and generally religious and sympathetic friends. She is pampered in every way. She may have lost her voice or the power of a limb. These temporary paralyses often pass off suddenly with a new doctor or a new drug; but, as a rule, they are replaced by some new neurosis. In the end, the patient becomes bedridden, often refuses her food, or is capricious about it, taking strange things at odd times, or pretending to starve. Masturbation is not uncommon. The body wastes, and the face has a thin anxious look, not unlike that represented by Rossetti in many of his pictures of women. There is a hungry look about them which is striking.[39]

Unlike the disagreeable and disliked hysterics, however, neurasthenics were thought to be cooperative, ladylike, and well-bred, "just the kind of women one likes to meet with," one doctor declared, "sensible, not over sensitive or emotional, exhibiting a proper amount of illness . . . and a willingness to perform their share of work quietly and to the best of their ability." Physicians often contrasted the hysteric's *belle indifférence* and moral turpitude with the neurasthenic's "refined and unselfish nature."[40]

Originally, neurasthenia was an American disorder, described as "American nervousness" by the neurologist George Miller Beard in the late 1860s. Beard saw a significant correlation between modern social organization and nervous illness. A deficiency in nervous energy was the price exacted by industrialized urban societies, competitive business and social environments, and the luxuries, vices, and excesses of modern life. Five characteristic features of nineteenth-century progress—the periodical press, steam power, the telegraph, the sciences, and especially the increased mental activity of women—could be held to blame for the sapping of American nervous strength.[41]

American nervousness was alarmingly frequent "among the well-to-do and the intellectual, and especially among those in the professions and in the higher walks of business life, who are in deadly earnest in the race for place and power." The labors of domestic servants, the harshness of rural existence, the brutalities of savage tribes, were nowhere near as mentally wearing and exhausting as the refinements of civilization. Masturbation, for example, could rapidly deplete the nervous force of the refined, but "strong, phlegmatic Irish servant-girls may begin early the habit of abusing themselves and keep it up for years, with but little apparent harm." And the Indian squaw enjoyed her "slow and easy drudgery . . . in the open air," spared the "exhausting sentiment of love," while the sensitive white woman had the more demanding anxieties of romance to handle. It was absurd to expect that a Southern black should suffer from nervous diseases, or that insanity, epilepsy, and neurasthenia should flourish on the banks of the Amazon or the Nile.[42]

In the United States, neurasthenia was seen as an acceptable and even an impressive illness for men, ideally suited to a capitalistic society and to the identification of masculinity with money and property. Many American nerve specialists, including Beard himself, had experienced crises of nervous exhaustion in their own careers, and they were highly sympathetic to other middle-class male intellectuals and professionals tormented by vocational indecision, sexual frustration, internalized cultural pressure to succeed, and severely repressed emotional needs.

When Herbert Spencer visited the United States in 1882, he was struck by the widespread ill-health of male intellectuals and businessmen: "In every circle I have met men who had themselves suffered from nervous collapses, due to stress of business, or named friends who had crippled themselves by overwork."[43] An elaborate system of cures, including nerve tonics, galvanic belts, electric faradization, health spas, and retreats catered to the prosperous neurasthenic seeking help for his sexual problems or nervous exhaustion.

The majority of American neurasthenic patients, however, were female, often educated, urban, and middle-class. In such essays as "Neurasthenia and Its Relation to Diseases of Women" (1886), Dr. Margaret Cleaves, herself a sufferer who would describe her experience in the anonymously published *Autobiography of a Neurasthene,* attributed female neurasthenia not simply to overwork but to women's ambitions for intellectual, social, and financial success, ambitions that could not be accommodated within the structures of late-nineteenth-century society. She herself was the daughter of a doctor who had encouraged her to pursue a medical career. Nonetheless, she felt, "women, more than men, are handicapped at the outset, not necessarily because they are women, but because, suddenly and without the previous preparations that men for generations have had, they attempt to fulfill certain conditions and are expected to qualify themselves for certain work and distinctions." It may be true, she conceded, "that girls and women are unfit to bear the continued labor of mind because of the disqualifications existing in their physiological life." Beard, too, had felt that women were more at risk than men in trying to follow careers, since they were accustomed to using their brains "but little and in trivial matters." At several points in her life, Cleaves suffered what she called a "sprained brain," and had to take a leave of absence from her work to recuperate.[44]

English psychiatrists quickly picked up the neurasthenia diagnosis as an apt description of English nervousness. They maintained that neurasthenia was "neither a modern nor an American disease only" but simply a new name for what they had long called spinal irritation, neuralgic disease, or nervous weakness.[45] Neurasthenics were viewed as borderers, denizens of Driftland and Mazeland whose mental organization was weakened by hereditary predisposition. Furthermore, in its passage from America to England, neurasthenia was mainly associated with young women. "Inasmuch as neurasthenia is mainly congenital," wrote a late Victorian expert, "and always associated with chlorosis . . . it is natural that the female sex, being more sensitive, should be more subject to it."[46] For many late Victorian female intellectuals, especially those in the first generation to attend college, nervous illness marked the transition from domestic to professional roles. Similar to the fears and depressions described by Nightingale, Brontë, and Craik in the 1850s, these protracted and vaguely understood illnesses were now subsumed under the label of "neurasthenia." From the pioneering doctor Sophia Jex-Blake to the social worker Beatrice Webb, New Women and nervous illness seemed to go together.[47]

Whether the disorder was anorexia, hysteria, or neurasthenia, English psychiatric treatment of nervous women was ruthless, a microcosm of the sex war intended to establish the male doctor's total authority. It could be compared to "a game of chess . . . a complex sequence of offensive and defensive maneuvers requiring elaborate strategic planning. . . . And the medical ideal of a full and radical cure took the form of a kind of moral checkmate—the complete submission of the patient to the physician's authority, with a full confession of moral wretchedness and the various tricks and artifices involved in the presentation of the 'symptoms.' "[48] The goal was to isolate the patient from her family support systems, unmask her deceitful stratagems, coerce her into surrendering her symptoms, and finally overcome her self-centeredness.

In the case of anorexia, doctors had noted that fasting girls exercised an unusual degree of control over their families. At mealtimes, Allbutt observed, "her mother may cry, her father may storm"; Lasegue's patients became the center of family concern, "the sole object of preoccupation and conversation."[49] Approved medical attitudes towards the anorexic girl are described in Sarah Grand's best-selling novel *The Heavenly Twins* (1893), where the London nerve specialist Sir Shadwell Rock treats an anorexic patient as if he were taming a shrew; he sends her away from her family with "a perfect stranger, a hard, cold, unsympathetic person who would irritate her, if possible; and she was not to be allowed luxuries of any kind. . . . When she fainted she was left just where she fell to recover as best she could, and when any particular food disagreed with her, it was served to her incessantly." The girl at last confesses to Dr. Rock that she had been "shamming from beginning to end."[50]

The assumption that the patient was shamming also dictated the psychiatric treatment of hysteria. With hardened actresses, Allbut suggested, the only remedy was to stop paying attention—to empty the theater and take away the audience. Physicians agreed on the benefits of "observant neglect" in which indifference to the patient's expectations of sympathy established the physician's lofty authority.[51] Some went beyond mere indifference to intimidation, blackmail, and threats. The treatments suggested for hysterical fits included "the sudden production of some painful impression": pouring water on the head, compressing the supraorbital nerve, stopping the patient's breathing, slapping the face and neck with wet towels, and exercising pressure "on some tender area."[52] In his lectures on hysteria, Skey advised his audience that "ridicule to a woman of sensitive mind, is a powerful weapon . . . but there is no emotion equal to fear and the threat of personal chastisement."[53]

In late Victorian literature, too, representations of the hysterical woman as a malingerer support punitive treatment. Charles Reade, for example, gives a full account of a faked hysterical seizure in *A Terrible Temptation* (1870). Rhoda Somerset falls to the floor, grinding her teeth, banging her head, and waving her arms, and revives only when the page is about to fling water on her. This traditional remedy for female hysteria was also employed at the Cheltenham Ladies College in 1889. When the school first opened, the addiction of some of the pupils to fainting fits in chapel or study hall had a bad effect on academic discipline. The matron solved the problem, however, by calling for cold water to pour over the victim; those who recovered before the water arrived were dosed with laxative powders.[54]

The standard treatment for neurasthenia was Silas Weir Mitchell's rest cure, a technique that this distinguished American neurologist had developed after the Civil War. Mitchell's rest cure, which he first described in 1873, depended upon seclusion, massage, electricity, immobility, and diet. When his neurasthenic subjects, among them such prominent American women intellectuals as Jane Addams, Winifred Howells (daughter of William Dean Howells), and Edith Wharton, became thin, tense, fretful, and depressed, Mitchell ordered them to enter a clinic for "a combination of entire rest and of excessive feeding, made possible by passive exercise obtained through steady use of massage and electricity." For six weeks the patient was isolated from her family and friends, confined to bed, forbidden to sit up, sew, read, write, or to do any intellectual work, visited daily by the physician, and fed and massaged by the nurse. She was expected to gain as much as fifty pounds on a diet that began with milk and gradually built up to several substantial meals a day. Mitchell was well aware that the sheer boredom and sensory deprivation of the rest cure made it a kindly punishment for neurasthenia, the psychological equivalent of the hysteric's bucket of water: "When they are bidden to stay in bed a month, and neither to read, write, nor sew, and have one nurse—who is not a relative—then rest becomes for some women a rather bitter medicine, and they are glad enough to accept the order to rise and go about when the doctor issues a mandate which has become pleasantly welcome and eagerly looked for."[55]

Although it had the medical rationale of building up the patient's depleted supply of fat and blood, the rest cure had striking psychological effects. Mitchell insisted on isolation both as a way of removing the patient from the sympathetic collusion of her family and as a way of maximizing his own semimagical influence over her, an influence he believed essential to a cure. The misogynistic implications of the rest cure have been the subject of controversy among contemporary feminist historians. Barbara Sicherman points out the similarities between the enforced dependency of the rest cure and infancy, and suggests that such a temporary yielding up of the will in childlike obedience to a charismatic physician may actually have been restorative for some women who were unable to accept their own emotions and dependencies.[56] But other feminist historians see Mitchell in a harsher light, not as the benignly paternal guardian, but as a man unaware of his own hostility to women who "cured" them by "restoring them to their femininity or . . . by subordinating them to an enlightened but dictatorial male will." Forced back into "womblike dependence," the patient was reborn, re-educated by the parental team of subservient female nurse and godlike male doctor, and "returned to her menfolk's management, recycled and taught to make the will of the male her own."[57]

Yet another aspect of the rest cure emerges in the practice of W. S. Playfair, professor of obstetric medicine at King's College, who introduced Mitchell's rest cure to England in the 1880s. Playfair suggested the adoption of Mitchell's method for women suffering from neurasthenia associated with pregnancy problems, and for "the worn and wasted, often bedridden woman, who had broken down, either from some sudden shock, such as grief, or money losses, or excessive mental or bodily strain."[58]

Whereas Playfair resented the "fat, well-feeding hysterics who thoroughly enjoy their life of inert self-indulgence," he felt an intuitive sympathy for the neurasthenic invalids, who were often emaciated and enfeebled, who were "of high culture and refinement," and "who heartily long for good health if they only knew how to obtain it."[59] The neurasthenic woman was already a model of ladylike deportment and hyperfemininity, a paradigm of that wasting beauty that the late Victorians found so compelling. Like the consumptive, the neurasthenic woman was spiritualized, incorporeal, and pure. Playfair treated a woman so "fine and cultivated" that she had spent most of her married life lying in a dark room at the back of the house, unable to bear the slightest noise, light, or physical contact. This exquisite invalid, who also had no appetite and fainted frequently, had to be totally anaesthetized before she could be conveyed from her house in the country to Playfair's London clinic. In encouraging her to eat, acclimating her to vigorous massage, and moving her to a bright room, Playfair ended her bondage to a debilitating ideal of angelic womanhood. The rest cure made women who were denying their bodies, their appetites, and their sensations confront nothing but the body, the appetite, and the senses for a prolonged period. This cannot have been entirely a bad thing.

In fact, Playfair used the rest cure successfully in many cases where women had been total invalids of many years' duration, and he was able to restore his patients to lives that were much more active and satisfying than the ones they had been leading. Most of his clients were women reacting to traumatic miscarriages, stillbirths, or painful deliveries that had left them physically and emotionally scarred. In case after case, their immobility, sensitivity, loss of appetite, and depression seem to be forms of sexual withdrawal, the body protecting itself against further invasion. Playfair was able to get these women physically fit, and less fearful of the future.

It would seem that the practice of the rest cure had different implications in the United States and England, and two fictional studies by American and English feminist writers suggest how differently this controversial therapy could be experienced and perceived. The more famous of the two accounts is the short story "The Yellow Wallpaper" (1892) by the American socialist and feminist Charlotte Perkins Gilman. Gilman explained the genesis of the story in her journal *The Forerunner.* In 1887, suffering from chronic acute depression, she had consulted Weir Mitchell, who applied the rest cure for a month and then sent her home with advice to lead a thoroughly domestic life, to limit her reading to two hours a day, and to give up writing altogether. "I went home," Gilman told her readers,

> and obeyed these directions for some three months, and came so near the borderline of utter mental ruin that I could see over.
>
> Then, using the remnants of intelligence that remained . . . I cast the noted specialist's advice to the winds and went to work again—work, the normal life of every human being . . . ultimately recovering some measure of power.
>
> Being naturally moved to rejoicing by this narrow escape, I wrote "The Yellow Wallpaper" . . . and sent a copy to the physician who so nearly drove me mad. He never acknowledged it. . . . [But] many years later I was told that the great specialist had admitted to friends of his that he had altered his treatment of neurasthenia since reading "The Yellow Wallpaper."[60]

Her story is a powerful polemic against Mitchell's methods. The woman narrator of "The Yellow Wallpaper" is a writer being treated for postpartum depression by her doctor-husband in an isolated country house. Although she thinks that "congenial work," variety, stimulation, excitement, the company of friends, and the advice and support of other writers would restore her spirits, her husband thinks otherwise. He insists on total passivity, isolation, mental blankness, and provides her with an hourly schedule of phosphates, tonics, food, naps, and exercise. Most of the time he is away on business, leaving her in the watchful care of his sister.

The room in which she spends most of her time is also her husband's choice. They call it "the nursery at the top of the house," and it is certainly related to her enforced infantilism and regression. But it also has all marks of a cell for the solitary confinement of a raving lunatic: the windows are barred, there are rings in the wall, the wallpaper is torn, the floor is scratched, the plaster is dug out, the bed is nailed down, and the bedposts have been gnawed. The sinuous lines and oscillating abstractions of the sulphurous yellow wallpaper torment her, and she pleads with her husband to let her leave the house or at least move to another room. But he blandly assures her that he knows what is best, and threatens that if she does not improve he will send her to Weir Mitchell.

As the days go by, depression, repressed anger towards her husband,

and inactivity make the woman less able to assert her own needs without breaking down in tears, which would only confirm her "sickness"; and even when she escapes the dual surveillance of husband and sister-in-law to try to write, she finds herself too tired to make the effort. All her blocked imaginative power gradually fixes on the wallpaper, which in the story becomes the correlative of her mental disintegration. She first sees "bulbous eyes" in the pattern staring at her, and then "a strange, provoking, formless sort of figure that seems to skulk about behind that silly and conspicuous front design." Soon the faint figure has become a woman, trapped in the encircling arabesque, who makes the pattern quiver and shake in her desperate efforts to escape its strangling curves. Finally the narrator, completely mad, rips all the paper off the wall to release her double. She has lost the sense of ego boundaries; the wallpaper woman is at once the other, herself, and many women, creeping away into "the open country, creeping as fast as a cloud shadow in the wind." Frantic to escape, yet bound in one direction by the dim memories of wifely propriety, and in the other by injunctions against suicide, she escapes into madness, making the room her refuge, creeping around its margins, and locking the door against her husband. When he breaks it down, he finds her on her hands and knees. Her triumph over the rest cure and its complacent guardians comes at the price of her mind.

Gilman's haunting and passionate protest against the rest cure has become a modern feminist classic, a paradigmatic text for critics and historians looking at the relation between sex roles, madness, and creativity. Like Nightingale's *Cassandra,* it shows how solitary confinement within the bourgeois family could be maddening for intelligent women. Because Gilman's story deals specifically with a woman writer who is denied any legitimate outlet for her imagination and craft, it has also been interpreted as a parable of female *literary* confinement, "*the* story that all literary women would tell if they could speak their 'speechless woe.'"[61] And the loving destruction of the woman in the rest cure which Gilman so chillingly portrays has been taken as symbolic of the effects of marriage on women, a bold attack on "the sexual politics of the male-female, husband-wife relationship."[62] When the husband forces his way into the room, Ann Douglas suggests, he enacts the sexual violence that some nineteenth-century American feminists saw reproduced in the relations of male doctors and female patients.[63]

The English version of the rest cure, however, turns Gilman's story inside out. In Elizabeth Robins's novel *A Dark Lantern* (1905), the rest cure is a rescue from an impoverished life, and the doctor-lover is a savior. Robins too was a feminist, an American-born actress who moved to England in 1889 and became an activist in the suffrage movement. Her heroine, Katharine Dereham, is a young poet who becomes neurasthenic from overwork, anxiety about her family, and sexual pressure. After a variety of doctors have been unable to help her, she turns to Garth Vincent, a glamorous nerve specialist who has become celebrated for his successful rest cures. Dr. Vincent's demands are as rigid, his manner as brusque, as Mitchell's. He orders her to bed, cuts off her visitors and her mail, regulates her diet, hires her nurses, restricts her reading, and prescribes vigorous massage. Katharine resists the massage most of all; "to be touched by strange hands was an offence to the spirit, a positive hurt to the nerves."

However, the English doctor allows his patient to write; Katharine grows stronger, and during the few hours Vincent allows her to work each day she composes the most powerful poems of her career. The final step in her cure comes when in a startling turnabout she herself goes to his country estate to ask the doctor to become her lover. Robins stresses love rather than mere lust, but obviously the physical element is the great transformer: "Spring! What would it bring to her? What was to be *her* awakening? For she too, in a fashion, had slept, had been quiescent as the bare brown fields, not looking before or after; lulled; yes, yes, she had slept, and must awake."

Spring brings her sexual fulfillment, physical strength, and glowing reviews for her book of sonnets. And summer brings marriage to the high-handed but adoring physician. At the end of *A Dark Lantern,* when the doctor-husband breaks down Katharine's door after she locks him out in a quarrel, he is clearly meant to represent life-giving passion breaking in upon her neurotic withdrawal, and not rape or violation of her spirit. Although Robins's novel is lurid and sentimental, it shows that even for feminists, the rest cure might have had creative and sexual advantages.

Not long after her first rest cure in 1904, Virginia Woolf read and reviewed *A Dark Lantern*: "I have been reading Miss Robin's *[sic]* book all the evening, till the last pages. It explains how you fall in love with your doctor, if you have a rest cure. She is a clever woman, if she weren't so brutal."[64] Although Woolf's doctor was George Savage, by then a stout clubman in his sixties, she did not make fun of Robins's plot as we might expect. Even Gilman, linking the husband with the physician in "The Yellow Wallpaper," acknowledged a kind of eroticism in the rest cure. For Woolf as for Gilman, however, the romantic implications of this quasi-courtship were overshadowed by its intrusions. She resisted even the mild rest cure that Savage imposed upon her after her father's death. Under his orders she was sent to stay with an aunt in the country. "I have never spent such a wretched 8 months in my life," she wrote to Violet Dickinson, "and yet that tyrannical and as I think, shortsighted Savage wants yet another two. . . . Really a doctor is worse than a husband."[65] Alice James, too, found the condescension of her doctors to be one of the worst burdens of her neurasthenia: "I suppose one has a greater sense of intellectual degradation after an interview with a doctor than from any human experience," she confided to her diary in 1890.[66]

Surely the "hungry look" that Savage saw in the faces of his neurasthenic female patients was a craving for more than food. The nervous women of the *fin de siècle* were ravenous for a fuller life than their society offered them, famished for the freedom to act and to make real choices. Their nervous disorders expressed the insoluble conflict between their desires to act as individuals and the internalized obligations to submit to the needs of the family, and to conform to the model of self-sacrificing "womanly" behavior. As the feminist novelist "George Egerton" wrote in 1894, "When we shall have larger and freer lives, we shall be better balanced than we are now."[67] There were important differences between the phenomena of hysteria, anorexia, and neurasthenia, even if diagnostic categories were far from precise. But in England, these terms became three labels for the same unhappy woman, three faces of Eve.

6

FEMINISM AND HYSTERIA

The Daughter's Disease

During an era when patriarchal culture felt itself to be under attack by its rebellious daughters, one obvious defense was to label women campaigning for access to the universities, the professions, and the vote as mentally disturbed, and of all the nervous disorders of the *fin de siècle,* hysteria was the most strongly identified with the feminist movement.

Both clinical observation and sexual prejudice contributed to this association. First of all, doctors had noticed that hysteria was apt to appear in young women who were especially rebellious. F. C. Skey, for example, had observed that his hysterical patients were likely to be *more* independent and assertive than "normal" women, "exhibiting more than usual force and decision of character, of strong resolution, fearless of danger."[1] Donkin too had seen among his patients a high percentage of unconventional women—artists and writers. From these observations, it was a quick jump to conclude that rebelliousness could produce nervous disorder and its attendant pathologies.

Darwinian psychiatrists wrote in an ominous way about the psychological and physical consequences of feminist rebellion:

> In this matter the small minority of women who have other aims and pant for other careers, cannot be accepted as the spokeswomen of their sex. Experience may be left to teach them, as it will not fail to do, whether they are right or wrong in the ends which they pursue and in the means by which they pursue them; if they are right, they will have deserved well the success which will reward their faith and works; if they are wrong, the error will avenge itself upon them and their children, if they should ever have any. In the worst even they will not have been without their use as failures; for they will have furnished experiments to aid us in arriving at correct judgments concerning the capacities of women and their right functions in the universe.[2]

In literature, too, the women who aspired to professional independence and sexual freedom were denounced as case studies in hysteria and degeneration. "The masculine tone is passing out of the world," wrote Henry James; "it is a feminine, nervous, hysterical, chattering, canting age." *Hedda Gabler*, wrote the critic of *The Times* in an obvious allusion to Maudsley, is "a demonstration of the pathology of mind, such as may be found in the pages of the *Journal of Mental Science* or in the reports of the medical superintendents of lunatic asylums." And Thomas Hardy's feminist Sue Bridehead in *Jude the Obscure* (1895) was attacked as a "poor maimed 'degenerate' ignorant of herself and of the perversion of her instincts."[3]

In a few celebrated cases, radical women who challenged the norms of feminine conduct were actually committed to lunatic asylums. One such case concerned Edith Lanchester, the daughter of a prosperous London architect. She had been an honors student at London University and Cambridge, and was working as a speaker for the Social Democratic Federation and Independent Labour Party and as secretary to Eleanor Marx. Through her political activities she had met a handsome young Irish railway clerk, James Sullivan, and in 1895 they started living together in Battersea. But Lanchester's father and three brothers kidnapped her and had her committed to the Priory, a private asylum in Roehampton Lane, on an "urgency order" signed by Dr. G. Fielding Blandford, who gave the supposed cause of her insanity as "over-education." Blandford later explained that he had judged her insane because "he believed that her opposition to conventional matrimony made her unfit to take care of herself." Members of the SDF held a vigil outside the asylum, and Lanchester was released five days later through the intervention of the Commissioners in Lunacy. Subsequently the Social Democratic Federation fought to have Blandford censured, but *The Lancet* and the *British Medical Journal* supported him, although they questioned his involvement in the kidnapping.[4]

In the aftermath of this scandal, Edith Lanchester stayed with Sullivan, bearing him several children (including the actress Elsa Lanchester) and maintaining her vigorous commitment to radical politics and the women's suffrage movement for the rest of her life. But Darwinian psychiatry undoubtedly intimidated many feminists with its prophecies of hysterical breakdown for women who transgressed their destined roles.

And yet, staying within the roles offered women no protection against hysteria either. For a feminist analysis, we have to turn the question around. Instead of asking if rebellion was mental pathology, we must ask whether mental pathology was suppressed rebellion. Was the hysterical woman a feminist heroine, fighting back against confinement in the bourgeois home? Was hysteria—the "daughter's disease" —a mode of protest for women deprived of other social or intellectual outlets or expressive options? In order to sort out the historical relationship between hysteria and feminism, we must turn to a different cultural context: the European clinics and consulting rooms in which the symbolic systems of female hysteria were first decoded, and in which psychoanalysis—"the child of the hysterical woman"—was born.[5] Here the manifestations of hysteria were most fully documented, and the case histories of hysterical women were most fully preserved.

The first of the great European theorists of hysteria was Jean-Martin Charcot (1825–1893), who carried out his work in the Paris clinic at the Salpêtrière. Charcot had begun his work on hysteria in 1870. While he believed that hysterics suffered from a hereditary taint that weakened their nervous system, he also developed a theory that hysteria had psychological origins. Experimenting with hypnosis, Charcot demonstrated that hysterical symptoms such as paralysis could be produced and relieved by hypnotic suggestion. Through careful observation, physical examination, and the use of hypnosis, Charcot was able to prove that hysterical symptoms, while produced by emotions rather than by physical injury, were genuine, and not under the conscious control of the patient. Freud, who studied at the Salpêtrière from October 1885 to February 1886, gave Charcot the credit for establishing the legitimacy of hysteria as a disorder. According to Freud, "Charcot's work restored dignity to the subject; gradually the sneering attitude which the hysteric could reckon meeting with when she told her story, was given up; she was no longer a malingerer, since Charcot had thrown the whole weight of his authority on the side of the reality and objectivity of hysterical phenomena." Furthermore, Charcot demonstrated that hysterical symptoms also occurred in men, and were not simply related to the vagaries of the female reproductive system. At the Salpêtrière there was even a special wing for male hysterics, who were frequently the victims of trauma from railway accidents. In restoring the credibility of the hysteric, Freud believed, Charcot had joined other psychiatric saviors of women and had "repeated on a small scale the act of liberation commemorated in the picture of Pinel which adorned the lecture hall of the Salpêtrière."[6]

Yet for Charcot, too, hysteria remained symbolically, if not medically, a female malady. By far the majority of his hysterical patients were women, and several, such as Blanche Wittmann, known as the "Queen of the Hysterics," became celebrities who were regularly featured in his books, the main attractions at the Salpêtrière's Bal des Folles, and hypnotized and exhibited at his popular public lectures. Axel Munthe, a doctor practicing in Paris, wrote a vivid description of Charcot's Tuesday lectures at the Salpêtrière: "The huge amphitheatre was filled to the last place with a multicoloured audience drawn from tout Paris, authors, journalists, leading actors and actresses, fashionable demimondaines." The hypnotized women patients put on a spectacular show before this crowd of curiosity seekers.

> Some of them smelt with delight a bottle of ammonia when told it was rose water, others would eat a piece of charcoal when presented to them as chocolate. Another would crawl on all fours on the floor, barking furiously when told she was a dog, flap her arms as if trying to fly when turned into a pigeon, lift her skirts with a shriek of terror when a glove was thrown at her feet with a suggestion of being a snake. Another would walk with a top hat in her arms rocking it to and fro and kissing it tenderly when she was told it was her baby.[7]

The grand finale would be the performance of a full hysterical seizure.

Furthermore, the representation of female hysteria was a central aspect of Charcot's work. His hysterical women patients were surrounded by images of female hysteria. In the lecture hall, as Freud noted, was Robert-Fleury's painting of Pinel freeing the madwomen. On the opposite wall was a famous lithograph of Charcot, holding and lecturing about a swooning and half-undressed young woman before a room of sober and attentive men, yet another representation that seemed to be instructing the hysterical woman in her act (fig. 21).

Finally, Charcot's use of photography was the most extensive in nineteenth-century psychiatric practice. As one of his admirers remarked, "The camera was as crucial to the study of hysteria as the microscope was to histology."[8] In 1875 one of his assistants, Paul Régnard, had assembled an album of photographs of female nervous patients. The pictures of women exhibiting various phases of hysterical attacks were deemed so interesting that a photographic workshop or atelier was installed within the hospital. By the 1880s a professional photographer, Albert Londe, had been brought in to take charge of a full-fledged photographic service. Its methods included not only the most advanced technology and apparatus, such as laboratories, a studio

Figure 21. Charcot lecturing on hysteria at the Salpêtrière.

with platforms, a bed, screens, black, dark-gray, and light-gray background curtains, headrests, and an iron support for feeble patients, but also elaborate administrative techniques of observation, selection of models, and record-keeping.[9] The photographs of women were published in three volumes called *Iconographie photographique de la Salpêtrière.* Thus Charcot's hospital became an environment in which female hysteria was perpetually presented, represented, and reproduced.

Such techniques appealed to Charcot because his approach to psychiatric analysis was strongly visual and imagistic. As Freud has explained, Charcot "had an artistically gifted temperament—as he said himself, he was a '*visuel,*' a seer. . . . He was accustomed to look again and again at things that were incomprehensible to him, to deepen his impression of them day by day until suddenly understanding of them dawned upon him."[10] Charcot's public lectures were among the first to use visual aids—pictures, graphs, statues, models, and illustrations that he drew on the blackboard in colored chalk—as well as the presence of the patients as models.

The specialty of the house at the Salpêtrière was *grande hystérie,* or "hystero-epilepsy," a prolonged and elaborate convulsive seizure that occurred in women. A complete seizure involved three phases: the epileptoid phase, in which the woman lost consciousness and foamed at the mouth; the phase of clownism, involving eccentric physical contortions; and the phase of *attitudes passionnelles,* a miming of incidents and emotions from the patient's life. In the *iconographies,* photographs of this last phase were given subtitles that suggested Charcot's interpretation of hysteria as linked to female sexuality, despite his disclaimers: "amorous supplication," "ecstasy," "eroticism" (figs. 22, 23, 24). This interpretation of hysterical gestures as sexual was reinforced by Charcot's efforts to pinpoint areas of the body that might induce convulsions when pressed. The ovarian region, he concluded, was a particularly sensitive hysterogenic zone.

Because the behavior of Charcot's hysterical stars was so theatrical, and because it was rarely observed outside of the Parisian clinical setting, many of his contemporaries, as well as subsequent medical historians, have suspected that the women's performances were the result of suggestion, imitation, or even fraud. In Charcot's own lifetime, one of his assistants admitted that some of the women had been coached in order to produce attacks that would please the *maître.*[11] Furthermore, there was a dramatic increase in the incidence of hysteria during Char-

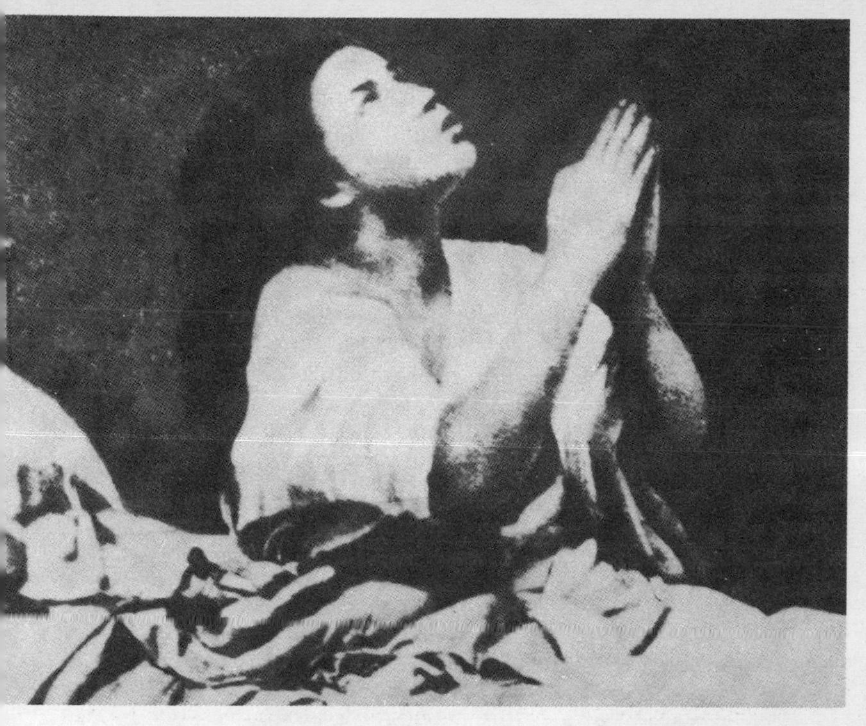

Figure 22. Augustine, "Supplication amoureuse," 1878.

cot's tenure at the Salpêtrière. From only 1 percent in 1845, it rose to 17.3 percent of all diagnoses in 1883, at the height of his experimentation with hysterical patients.[12]

When challenged about the legitimacy of hystero-epilepsy, however, Charcot vigorously defended the objectivity of his vision. "It seems that hystero-epilepsy only exists in France," he declared in a lecture of 1887, "and I could even say, as it has sometimes been said, that it only exists at the Salpêtrière, as if I had created it by the force of my will. It would be truly marvelous if I were thus able to create illnesses at the pleasure of my whim and my caprice. But as for the truth, I am absolutely only the photographer; I register what I see."[13] Like Hugh Diamond at the Surrey Asylum, Charcot and his followers had absolute faith in the scientific neutrality of the photographic image; Londe boasted: "La plaque photographique est la vraie rétine du savant."[14]

But Charcot's photographs were even more elaborately framed and staged than Diamond's Victorian asylum pictures. Women were not simply photographed once, but again and again, so that they became used to the camera and to the special status they received as photogenic subjects. Some made a sort of career out of modeling for the *iconographies*. Among the most frequently photographed was a fifteen-year-old girl named Augustine, who had entered the hospital in 1875.[15] Her hysterical attacks had begun at the age of thirteen when, according to her testimony, she had been raped by her employer, a man who was also her mother's lover. Intelligent, coquettish, and eager to please, Augustine was an apt pupil of the atelier. All of her poses suggest the

Figure 23. Augustine, "Extase," 1878.

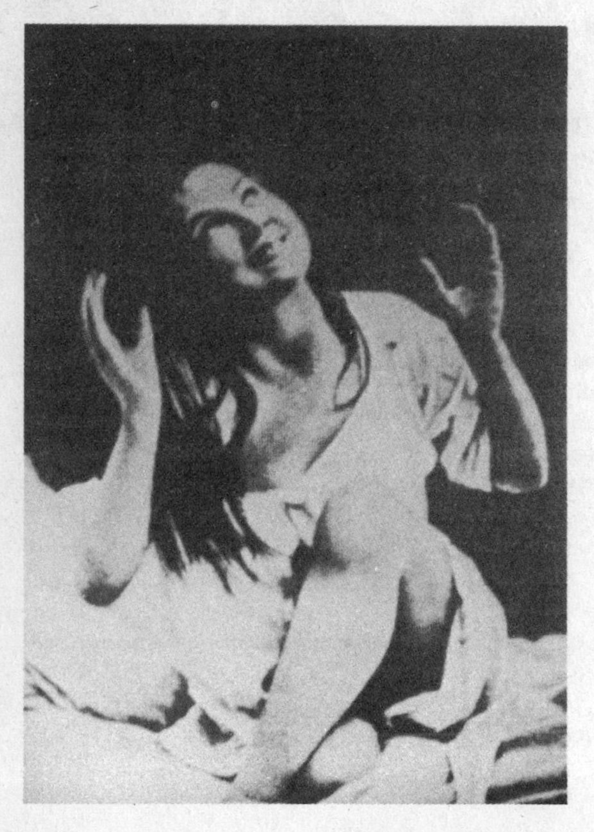

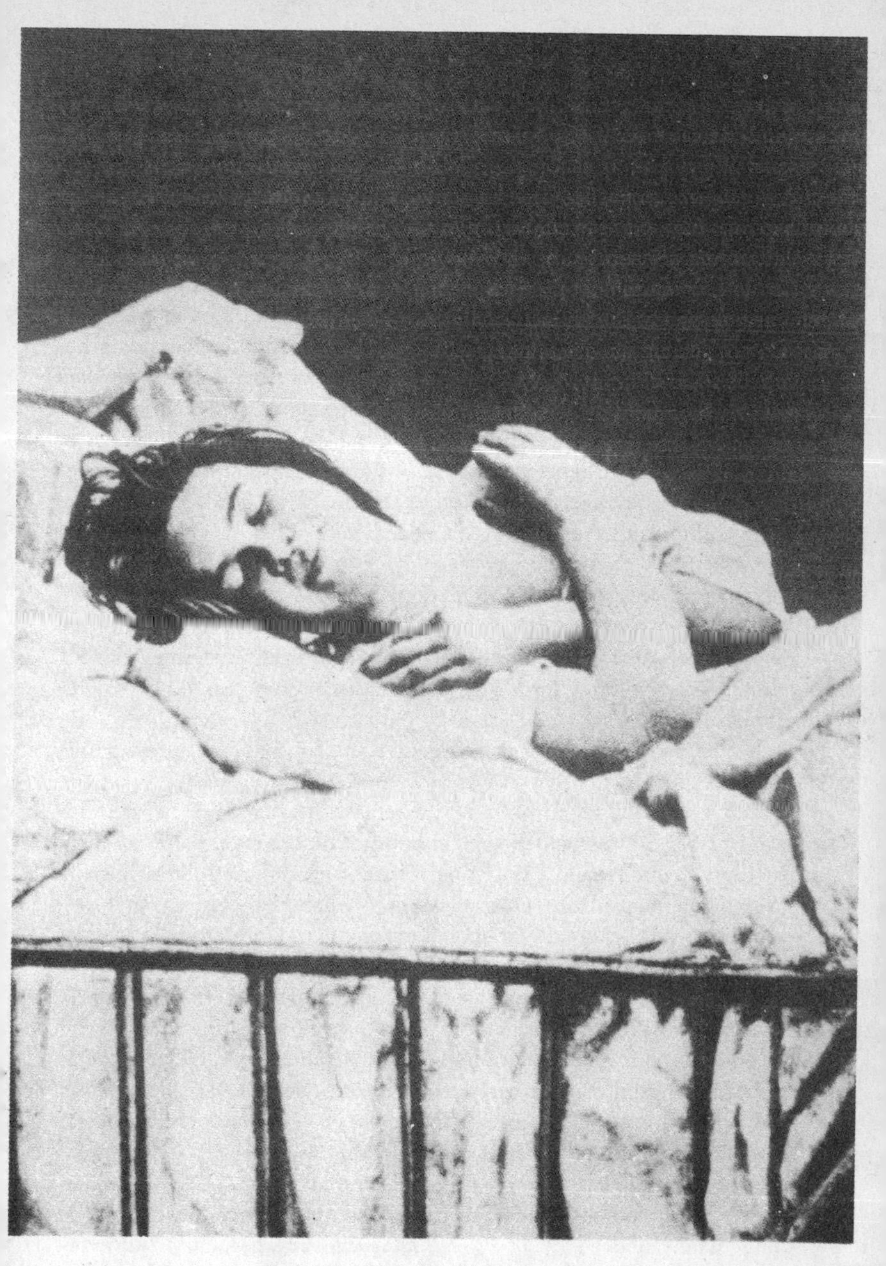

Figure 24. Augustine, "Erotisme," 1878.

exaggerated gestures of the French classical acting style, or stills from silent movies. Some photographs of Augustine with flowing locks and white hospital gown also seem to imitate poses in nineteenth-century paintings, as Stephen Heath points out: "a young girl composed on her bed, something of the Pre-Raphaelite Millais's painting *Ophelia.*"[16] Among her gifts was her ability to time and divide her hysterical performances into scenes, acts, tableaux, and intermissions, to perform on cue and on schedule with the click of the camera.

But Augustine's cheerful willingness to assume whatever poses her audience desired took its toll on her psyche. During the period when she was being repeatedly photographed, she developed a curious hysterical symptom: she began to see everything in black and white. In 1880, she began to rebel against the hospital regime; she had periods of violence in which she tore her clothes and broke windows. During these angry outbreaks she was anaesthetized with ether or chloroform. In June of that year, the doctors gave up their efforts with her case, and she was put in a locked cell. But Augustine was able to use in her own behalf the histrionic abilities that for a time had made her a star of the asylum. Disguising herself as a man, she managed to escape from the Salpêtrière. Nothing further was ever discovered about her whereabouts.[17]

If Charcot and his staff had listened as closely to Augustine's words as they had watched her gestures, they might have predicted that she would eventually try to run away. The case study records her descriptions of her dreams, which were about fire, blood, rape, hatred of men, revolution, and escape.[18] But while Charcot looked carefully at hysterical women, he paid very little attention to what they were saying. "You see how hysterics shout," he noted on one occasion; "much ado about nothing."[19] As we have seen, the traditions of English psychiatric medicine during the nineteenth century had also tended to silence the female patient, to make her the object of techniques of moral management, or of photographic representation and interpretation. In England, psychiatrists believed that their therapeutic authority depended on domination over the patient's language. "If a patient . . . interrupts the speaker," Robert Carter admonished his fellow doctors, "she must be told to keep silence and to listen; and must be told, moreover . . . in such a manner as to convey the speaker's full conviction that the command will be immediately obeyed."[20] The *globus hystericus,* which doctors had interpreted as the rising of the womb, may have been a physical manifestation of this choked-off speech.

While we have a full pictorial record of Charcot's hysterical patients, but only a few fragments of their words, with the case studies of Josef Breuer and Sigmund Freud, women's voices, stories, memories, dreams, and fantasies enter the medical record. Psychoanalysis begins with intimate conversations between hysterical women and male psychiatrists, dialogues rather than exhibitions.

From a feminist perspective, the most important of these newly audible voices may be that of Bertha Pappenheim, a twenty-one-year-old Viennese woman whom Breuer treated for hysteria from 1880 to 1882. Under the pseudonym of "Anna O.," she figures as the first case history in Breuer and Freud's ground-breaking *Studies on Hysteria* (1895). (Breuer never explained why he had picked the name "Anna O." for Bertha Pappenheim, but the palindromic form of "Anna" suggests the divided feminine psyche, while the "O" suggests the letter of the mad Ophelia, the symbolic circle or cipher of feminine sexual mystery.) Anna O., in fact, was the inventor of the "talking cure" of psychoanalysis, Breuer's partner in a remarkably shared and egalitarian therapeutic exchange. In her later life, she became prominent as a social worker, reformer, and feminist activist; she translated Mary Wollstonecraft's *Vindication of the Rights of Woman,* wrote a play called *Women's Rights,* and helped to found the German League of Jewish Women. The issues of feminism, language, creativity, and power are all illuminated in the story of her analysis.[21]

Anna O. was very much like the frustrated intellectuals and rebellious New Women seen by English nerve specialists. Although Breuer noted that she had a "powerful intellect," "great poetic and imaginative gifts," and "sharp and critical common sense," she had no outlet for her mental talents. At sixteen, she had finished all the schooling available to her as the daughter of a wealthy Jewish family. While her less brilliant younger brother, Willhelm, went off first to the university and then to law school, Anna "led an extremely monotonous existence" at home, carrying out routine domestic duties, which did not occupy her mind. She devoted her energies to charity work, reading (she knew four languages), and nursing her tubercular father. After his death in 1880, her complex hysterical symptoms began. When Breuer saw her, she was suffering from anorexia, paralyses, and hallucinations, as well as an elaborate sequence of speech disorders, culminating in mutism. As Breuer describes her disorganization of language, Anna was first "at a loss to find words. . . . Later she lost her command of grammar and syntax . . . [and] in the process of time she became almost completely deprived of words. She put them together laboriously out of four or five languages and became almost unintelligible. . . . For two weeks she became completely dumb and in spite of making great and continued efforts to speak she was unable to say a syllable." During the course of her analysis, Anna O. also suffered brief periodic interruptions of her speech, which Breuer called "absences." Breuer hypothesized that her mutism was a form of psychical inhibition; "she had felt very much offended over something and had determined not to speak about it."[22] When, after hypnosis, Anna's powers of speech returned, she was still unable to speak her native German, and instead spoke and read English, French, and Italian; she was able to produce instantaneous translations of texts in these three languages.

In Breuer's analysis of the case, Anna O. was offended and silenced by the very conditions of her role as the dutiful daughter in an Orthodox Jewish family; her hysteria was a "creative" escape from the boredom and futility of her daily life. Daydreams were a substitute for the intellectual nourishment she craved; the symptoms of hysteria were the outcome of "an unemployed surplus of mental liveliness and energy." Breuer's treatment consisted of spending many hours a day listening to Anna O.'s "stories," the "stock of imaginative products" which incorporated both her fantasies and her creativity.[23] Evening after evening, like the sultan with Scheherazade, Breuer made Anna tell him stories. This was the origin of what she called the "talking cure" and what others have called the "listening treatment."[24] Under hypnosis, too, Anna brought numerous repressed memories to the surface, and with them, her symptoms disappeared one by one. Breuer thus concluded that repressed emotion could cause hysteria. But the treatment itself played a large part in her emotional life. Through her illness, Anna temporarily won Breuer's intellectual companionship (he saw her virtually every day), and in some degree compensated for the aridity of her family life. Although the phenomenon of analytic transference was poorly understood at this early stage of psychoanalysis, she fell in love with Breuer. The analysis ended abruptly when Anna O. had a hysterical pregnancy in which she imagined giving birth to his child. Breuer fled both from the awkward situation and also, as many therapists now believe, from his own emotional involvement with Anna O.

In another sense, though, this "child" may have been the psychoanalytic method that they evolved together. A contemporary critic, Dianne Hunter, has offered an important interpretation of Anna O.'s hysterical "language," her feminism, and her role in the creation of psychoanalysis. Like Breuer, Hunter connects Anna O.'s linguistic disorders with her rejection of the partriarchal orthodoxy of her father, a cultural order articulated through the organization of language; but she gives this interpretation a specifically feminist slant. Using the theories of Jacques Lacan, Hunter argues: "In patriarchal socialization, the power to formulate sentences coincides developmentally with a recognition of the power of the father," the discovery of "the father's role in the primal scene and . . . male dominance in the social world."[25] On the unconscious level, therefore, Anna O.'s rejection of the patriarchal order became her rejection of the father's language.

Anna O.'s loss of words followed her recognition that she had lost her place in the world of the fathers. We might say that *words failed her,* as her father had failed her in consigning her to a subordinate role in the family, and as the patriarchal organization of Orthodox Judaism had failed her. In the process of her hysteria she also "lost" the grammar and syntax of German, but gained in their place a mother tongue, a female language akin to the pre-Oedipal "semiotic babble that exists between an infant and its mother," a language partly of the body and partly a pastiche of foreign words, gestures, and neologisms.[26] Breuer at first found this language alien and "unintelligible," but he made the effort to understand it; and in using Anna O.'s linguistic codes to start up her speech after an "absence," he entered a female world of consciousness repressed by the patriarchal structure, the world of the unconscious.

Hunter concludes that Anna O.'s hysteria was "a discourse of femininity addressed to patriarchal thought," signifying through the body, and particularly through speech, the protest that social conditions made unspeakable in words.[27] Because Breuer respected the intelligence of his hysterical female patient, encouraged her to speak, and then listened carefully to what she said, he was able to translate the body language and the female antilanguage of hysteria into a psychoanalytic theory of the unconscious.

In strong contrast to the hostile portraits of hysterical women produced by most English and French physicians of the period, Freud and Breuer's *Studies on Hysteria* presented a sympathetic and even admiring view. They maintained that hysterics were neither weak nor mentally deficient, as Charcot and Pierre Janet had said, but included "people of the clearest intellect, strongest will, greatest character and highest critical power." Based on his experiences with Anna O., Breuer argued that the hysterical predisposition lay in an excess, rather than in a lack, of energy, drive, and talent.

> Adolescents who are later to become hysterical are for the most part lively, gifted and full of intellectual interests before they fall ill. Their energy of will is often remarkable. They include girls who get out of bed at night so as secretly to carry on some study that their parents have forbidden for fear of their overworking. The capacity for forming sound judgments is certainly not more abundant in them than in other people; but it is rare to find in them simple, dull intellectual inertia and stupidity. The overflowing productivity of their minds has led one of my friends to assert that hysterics are the flower of mankind, as sterile, no doubt, but as beautiful as double flowers.[28]

Among the case studies Freud discussed were many intellectual women, such as "Elizabeth von R.," whom he described as gifted, ambitious, and independent; "Emmy von N.," whose intelligence and energy were "no less than a man's"; and "Frau Cäcilie M.," who possessed "quite unusual" artistic gifts, who had written poems "of great perfection," and whose powers of symbolization surpassed those of any other patient.[29]

While English psychiatrists believed that a rebellion against domesticity was itself pathological, Freud and Breuer saw the repetitious domestic routines, including needlework, knitting, playing scales, and sickbed nursing, to which bright women were frequently confined, as the causes of hysterical sickness. For people of a lively disposition, Breuer believed, such monotonous and uninteresting occupations were a torture, and they had to amuse themselves by fantasizing. Freud modified the Weir Mitchell rest cure by adding the work of psychoanalysis to it, because the passivity of the cure itself produced an exquisite boredom that led to more daydreaming. *Studies on Hysteria* thus seemed to lay the groundwork for a culturally aware therapy that took women's words and women's lives seriously, that respected the aspirations of New Women, and that allowed women a say in the management of hysterical symptoms.

By the turn of the century, however, some of the openness to women's words and feelings displayed in *Studies on Hysteria* had become codified in the interests of Freud's emerging psychoanalytic system. We can see this increased rigidity in Freud's "Fragment of an Analysis of a Case of Hysteria," his case history of an eighteen-year-old girl, whom he renamed "Dora." Like Anna O., Dora (whose real name was Ida Bauer) was an attractive, "sharp-sighted" girl whose father had taken great pride in the "early growth of her intelligence." Freud believed that Dora's "critical powers" and her "intellectual precocity" came from her father, since her mother was "an uncultivated woman" who "was occupied all day long in cleaning the house with its furniture and utensils." Dora's position was similar to that of many New Women. Although she felt contempt for her mother's monotonous domestic life, it was the life she too was destined for as a woman. Her mother was "bent upon drawing her into taking a share in the work of the house." Dora could find no support for her intellectual aspirations. Although she had a governess who was "well-read and of advanced views," Dora believed that the governess was neglecting her and was really in love with her father.[30] She arranged to have the woman dismissed. Afterwards, she struggled alone with the effort to keep up her serious reading, and she attended lectures specially given for women. Her older brother, however, went off to the university.

Moreover, Dora was treated like a pawn or a possession by her father and denied the rights to privacy or personal freedom. Her father was having an affair with the wife of a friend, Herr K., who had attempted to seduce Dora when she was only fourteen, and she felt that "she had been handed over to Herr K." by her father in exchange for his complicity in the adultery. A private note she wrote about her despair with her life was discovered by her father, although Dora claimed that it had been shut up in her desk. Professing to be anxious about her depressive state of mind, but really, Dora believed, afraid that she would betray his sexual secrets, her father then "handed her over" to Freud for psychotherapeutic treatment. He wanted Freud to persuade Dora that her perceptions were simply adolescent fantasies. He hired Freud hoping for an advocate to "bring her to reason."[31]

Dora's "most troublesome symptom," like Anna O.'s, was "a complete loss of voice." But while Breuer's chief concern was to listen to his patient, Freud was eager to penetrate the sexual mysteries of Dora's hysterical symptoms and to dictate their meanings to her. In spite of his earlier commitment to understanding the hysteric's plight, he ignored the social circumstances of Dora's life. In his view, her hysteria came from masturbatory fantasies, incestuous desires for her father, and possible homosexual or bisexual wishes. Dora responded to these insistent interpretations first with denials and finally by breaking off the analysis. Her story did not end as happily as Anna O.'s; while Dora's brother, Otto, entered politics and had a prestigious career as one of the leaders of the Austrian Socialist Party, she herself made an unhappy marriage and remained a neurotic patient for the rest of her life.[32] Freud failed Dora because he was too quick to impose his own language on her mute communications. His insistence on the sexual origins of hysteria blinded him to the social factors contributing to it.

As virtually all who have commented on this intriguing case have noted, Freud's tone with Dora is that of an antagonist. Like the Victorian nerve-doctors who saw themselves locked into combat with their hysterical patients in a contest for mastery, Freud wanted to demolish Dora's intellectual defenses. He was particularly piqued by her cleverness, her "independent judgment," and especially her habit of laughing at the efforts of doctors.[33] In his case history of Dora, if not in the actual treatment, Freud is determined to have the last word—he even has a postscript—in constructing his own "intelligible, consistent, and unbroken" account of her hysteria. He asserts his intellectual superiority to this bright but rebellious young woman. He uses his text to demonstrate his power to bring a woman to reason, and to bring reason to the mysteries of woman.

Dora's case has been the most compelling one of all of Freud's case histories for modern feminists, who, in Claire Kahane's words, have seen in it "a melodrama of sexual politics" and a "paradigmatic text of patriarchal assumptions about female desire."[34] Some feminists take particular satisfaction in Dora's termination of the power struggle by walking out on Freud. Others see feminist elements in Dora. In the view of one theorist, Jane Gallop, "feminists' attraction to the case of Dora may be an attraction to hysteria itself. Freud links hysteria to bisexuality; the hysteric identifies with members of both sexes, cannot choose one sexual identity. . . . If feminism is the calling into question of constraining sexual identities, then the hysteric may be a proto-feminist."[35]

For the French feminist theorist Hélène Cixous, Dora's hysteria is a powerful form of rebellion against the rationality of the patriarchal order, the "reason" which the father hires the doctor to bestow upon his daughter. To Cixous, who has written a play about Dora, hysteria is a kind of female language that opposes the rigid structures of male discourse and thought. "Silence: silence is the mark of hysteria. The great hysterics have lost speech . . . their tongues are cut off and what talks isn't heard because it's the body that talks and man doesn't hear the body."[36] The hysteric is the "woman-type in all her power: a power which was turned back against Dora, but which, if women begin to speak the language of their own desire, would be a force capable of demolishing the structures of the family and society."[37] To Catherine Clément, however, the hysteric's deviance and rebellion are carefully programmed and delimited by the social order. Hysteria is tolerated because in fact it has no power to effect cultural change; it is much safer for the patriarchal order to encourage and allow discontented women to express their wrongs through psychosomatic illness than to have them agitating for economic and legal rights.[38]

It is difficult to escape this sobering view. In its historical contexts in the late nineteenth century, hysteria was at best a private, ineffectual response to the frustrations of women's lives. Its immediate gratifications—the sympathy of the family, the attention of the physician—were slight in relation to its costs in powerlessness and silence.

Dora's triumph over Freud was minor and short-lived; according to Felix Deutsch's account, having been a famous psychiatric case study was the high point of a life she spent going from doctor to doctor in search of a remedy for various psychosomatic complaints.

But hysteria and feminism do exist on a kind of continuum, as the career of Bertha Pappenheim illustrates. The availability of a women's movement in which the "protofeminism" of hysterical protest could be articulated and put to work, offered a potent alternative to the self-destructive and self-enclosed strategies of hysteria, and a genuine form of resistance to the patriarchal order. If we see the hysterical woman as one end of the spectrum of a female avant-garde struggling to redefine women's place in the social order, then we can also see feminism as the other end of the spectrum, the alternative to hysterical silence, and the determination to speak and act for women in the public world.

The feminist critique of Freud should not obscure the fact that the early years of psychoanalysis offered a considerable advance over the biological determinism and moralism of Darwinian psychiatry. In the Freudian model, masculinity and femininity were not simply biological imperatives that naturally shaped male and female personalities, but rather cultural constructs. In principle, although not always in practice, psychoanalysis was not moralistic; it did not judge the hysteric as weak or bad, but saw hysterical symptoms as the product of unconscious conflicts beyond the person's control. Finally, psychoanalysis was attentive to the process of therapy, recognizing the fantasies that therapist and patient might project upon each other. The patient became an active, although not an equal, partner in the cure.

In England, however, the medical responses to the "talking cure" of psychoanalysis and the official responses to the militant voices of feminists and suffragists were very similar, suggesting that the resistance to listening to women's complaints was widespread across a range of male-dominated institutions. *Studies on Hysteria* was received with skepticism or derision. In his essay on hysteria for the authoritative textbook *System of Medicine,* J. A. Ormerod gave a thorough review of Freud and Breuer's theories on the psychogenesis of hysteria, but he also expressed distress at their quasi-religious powers of "inquisition and confessional."[39] T. Clifford Allbutt was even more indignantly outspoken about the risks of stimulating the worst impulses of hysterical patients—egotism, deceit, shamelessness, volubility—through the doctor's invitation to discuss sexual problems. He was particularly disgusted that "these medical penitents are mostly women; in a recent work on Psychoneuroses the self-revelations of two morbid women occupy one third of its wearisome pages."[40] "This method of psychoanalysis," the *British Medical Journal* declared in 1908, "is in most cases incorrect, in many hazardous, and in all dispensable."[41] When David Eder presented a psychoanalytic paper on hysteria to the British Medical Association in 1911, the audience rose and walked out in silent protest.[42]

In a sense, the elements of hunger, rebellion, and rage latent in the phenomenon of female nervous disorder became explicit and externalized in the tactics of the suffrage campaigns. The hunger strikes of militant women prisoners brilliantly put the symptomatology of anorexia nervosa to work in the service of a feminist cause. In 1912 the nation was confronted with the spectacle of women deliberately starving themselves in Holloway Gaol. The government responded by treating these women as hysterical; they behaved towards them as Darwinian nerve specialists had behaved in asserting dominance over their female patients. In fact, the home secretary Reginald McKenna acknowledged that he had frequently brought psychiatrists to Holloway to examine the suffragette prisoners, but that "in no case have they been willing to certify them as lunatics."[43] Ridicule, shaming, and physical abuse culminated in forcible feeding (fig. 25), a technique which had been employed with lunatics in the old madhouses. The represen-

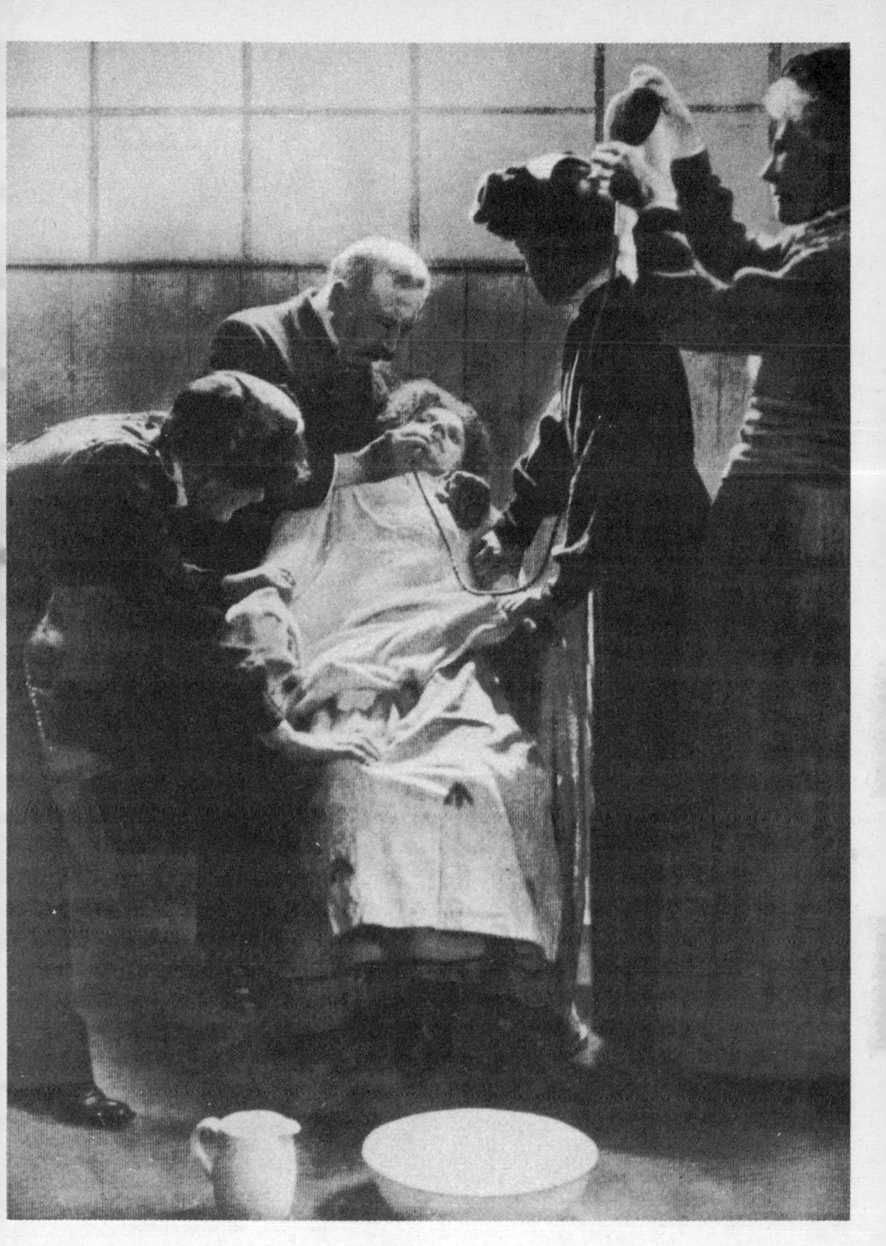

Figure 25. A suffragette being forcibly fed in Holloway Gaol, 1912.

tation of the forcible feeding of suffragettes in the press, with a struggling woman held down by nurses while an elegantly dressed male doctor assaults her with funnels and tubes, echoes the sexual iconography of Charcot's hysterics, and anticipates the clinical photographs of electric-shock treatment in the twentieth century.

Resistant to Freudian theories and hostile to feminist protests, English psychiatry, on the eve of the war, seemed to have reached an intellectual impasse. Only a few doctors were experimenting with psychotherapeutic or psychoanalytic techniques. In its efforts to deal with mental disorders, psychiatric Darwinism had little beyond the Wassermann test to offer either women or men. In 1913, Leonard Woolf consulted five leading London mental specialists—George Savage, Henry Head, Maurice Craig, Maurice Wright, and T. B. Hyslop—about his wife's disturbing condition. Despite their high professional standing, Woolf felt that "what they knew amounted to practically nothing. They had not the slightest idea of the nature or the cause of Virginia's mental state . . . no real or scientific knowledge of how to cure her." English medical knowledge of insanity in 1913, Woolf concluded, was "desperately meagre," "primitive and chaotic."[44] The English dominance of psychiatry dwindled away as the centers of research and innovation shifted from London to Vienna, Paris, and New York.

What would finally change the direction of English psychiatry was not the *fin de siècle* epidemic of female nervous disorder, to which Virginia Woolf fell victim, but the experience of the Great War. Only when hysteria, under the new name it was given during the war, became a widespread malady of men did the talking cure enter English psychiatric practice. Not feminism but shell shock initiated the era of psychiatric modernism.

PART THREE

Psychiatric Modernism

7

MALE HYSTERIA

W. H. R. Rivers and the Lessons of Shell Shock

In November 1914, Dr. Charles S. Myers, a Cambridge University laboratory psychologist who had volunteered for the Royal Army Military Corps in France, saw a number of cases of mental breakdown among men being treated in a temporary hospital in Le Touquet. In one case three shells had burst near a soldier while he was trying to disentangle himself from barbed wire; he was suffering from impairment of vision and had lost the sense of taste and smell. Two other men arriving at Le Touquet who had survived a shell explosion in their trench did not seem to have physical injuries, but they had similar symptoms, and had lost their memories as well. In an article for *The Lancet* in February 1915 describing his treatment of the functional nervous disorders in these men, Myers assumed that the physical force or chemical effects of a shell bursting at close range had caused these symptoms, which he termed "shell shock." In fact they were cases of male hysteria, and within the years of the war as well as its aftermath they would force a reconsideration of all the basic concepts of English psychiatric practice. Built on an ideology of absolute and natural difference between women and men, English psychiatry found its categories undermined by the evidence of male war neurosis.

Although he immediately noted the "close relation of these cases to those of hysteria," Myers first believed that the physical symptoms of mental impairment had to be traced to an organic cause. But carrying out clinical tests, he soon concluded that neither concussion, nor carbon-monoxide poisoning, nor changes in atmospheric pressure, nor internal secretions, nor "an invisibly fine molecular commotion in the brain" could be held responsible for the vast number of nervous disorders he saw. Some of these men had indeed been buried in shell explosions, but others were "remote from the exploding missile," and there were some who had never been near an exploding shell, had not been under fire for months, or had never come under fire at all. So shells were not to blame; and in men who were already exhausted or convalescing, the breakdown could be so gradual that the term "shock" too was a misnomer. For these reasons, Myers confessed in his memoir, shell shock was medically "a singularly ill-chosen term," and it became highly controversial, denounced by some medical authorities as a "bungling" and "quasi-legal" diagnosis, and ultimately banned during the final stages of the war. Nonetheless, "shell shock" was a singularly memorable and popular term that stuck, winning out over such alternatives as "anxiety neurosis," "war strain," and "soldier's heart."[1]

It also became an epidemic. By the winter of 1914, there were indications of a high percentage of mental breakdown among hospitalized men and officers. By 1916 one observer reported that shell-shock cases accounted for as much as 40 percent of the casualties in the fighting zones. And by the end of the war, 80,000 cases had passed through army medical facilities.[2]

In terms of treatment, the government was unprepared to handle the startling numbers of soldiers with hysterical symptoms. In the early months of the war, many soldiers suffering from shell shock were diagnosed as insane and sent back from base hospitals to civilian hospitals in the United Kingdom. By 1915 the shortage of hospital beds for the "wounded in mind" created an emergency, and thus a group of county lunatic asylums, private mental institutions, and disused spas were taken over and designated as war hospitals for mental diseases and war neuroses. The medical superintendents of the asylums were given temporary commissions in the Royal Army Medical Corps, employees became noncommissioned officers, and the female attendants became probationers in the nursing corps.[3] By 1918 there were over twenty army hospitals for shell-shock casualties in the United Kingdom.

This parade of emotionally incapacitated men was in itself a shocking contrast to the heroic visions and masculinist fantasies that had preceded it. The public image of the Great War was one of strong unreflective masculinity, embodied in the square, solid untroubled figure of Douglas Haig, the British commander-in-chief. Most brilliantly evoked in Paul Fussell's *The Great War and Modern Memory,* this image was prepared by the boys' books of G. R. Henty, by Rider Haggard's male adventure stories, by the romantic military poems of Tennyson and Robert Bridges. For the public-school boys, the university aesthetes and athletes, victory seemed assured to those who played the game. Generals wrote in all seriousness about the English military advantages of prior training in football, and it was considered plucky and spirited for platoons to kick a football through No Man's Land on the way to attacking an enemy trench. Chief among the values promoted within the male community of the war was the ability to tolerate the appalling filth and stink of the trenches, the relentless noise, and the constant threat of death with stoic good humor, and to allude to it in phlegmatic understatement. Indeed, emotional repression was an essential aspect of the British masculine ideal. As Fussell notes in his glossary of the feudal vocabulary of the prewar English literature of combat, "not to complain" is to be "manly."[4]

Even a sophisticated Freudian like Ernest Jones was sufficiently swept up in the cult of manliness to write in 1915 that war "brings a man a little closer to the realities of existence, destroying shams and remoulding values. It forces him to discover what are the things that really matter in the end, what are the things for which he is willing to risk life itself. It can make life as a whole greater, richer, fuller, stronger, and sometimes nobler."[5] Jones's paean to the virtues of war was not far from the jingoistic language of the recruiting poster.

The psychiatric theories which developed around shell shock reflect the ambivalence of the medical establishment upon being faced with the unexpected phenomenon of wholesale mental breakdown among men. Military physicians first tried to assimilate shell shock to the explanatory categories of Darwinian psychiatry. Early theories, as we have seen, maintained that it was caused by physical injury to the brain or the central nervous system. When confronted with hysterical soldiers who displayed unmanly emotions or fears—such as a private who cried so continuously that he could not handle his rifle (diagnosed as "excessive action of the lachrymal glands"), or a soldier who would not budge from a fetal position, or a gunner who had "terrible dreams of falling, and war dreams in which faces and parts of dead bodies seemed to come towards him"—psychiatrists desperately sought explanations for their condition in food poisoning, noise, or "toxic conditions of the blood."[6]

Another way to explain the prevalence of shell shock was to blame it on hereditary taint, and on careless recruiting procedures that had not weeded out unsuitables. André Léri described soldiers who suffered hysterical disorders in combat as "moral invalids," predisposed by their biological weakness to collapse in the face of the enemy.[7] Charles Myers too believed that shell shock was dependent on a psychoneurotic history, and that it was highly contagious, more frequent among the nervous, weakly, and maladjusted, and among undisciplined units: "There can be no doubt that, other things being equal, the frequency of 'shell shock' in any unit is an index of its lack of discipline and loyalty."[8] The idea that the shell shock of individuals reflected on the performance of the group as a whole obviously made the burden of guilt even worse for those who succumbed to it.

But gradually most military psychologists and medical personnel, if not generals, came to agree that the real cause of shell shock was the emotional disturbance produced by warfare itself, by chronic conditions of fear, tension, horror, disgust, and grief; and that war neurosis was "an escape from an intolerable situation," a compromise negotiated by the psyche between the instinct of self-preservation and the prohibitions against deception or flight, which were "rendered impossible by ideals of duty, patriotism, and honor."[9] Shell shock then was so obviously a retreat from the war that the British military initially tried to keep it from the public; when Myers requested permission in 1916 to publish a book on the features and causation of shell shock, he was told that the General Staff strongly opposed any such publication.[10] When they realized that shell shock did not have an organic cause, many military authorities refused to treat victims as disabled and maintained that they should not be given pensions or honorable discharges. Some went so far as to argue that shell-shock cases should be shot for malingering or cowardice. Insensitive though these responses may be, they show how accurately male hysteria was perceived as a form of resistance to the war. "The real source of wonder," wrote Dr. Thomas Salmon, was not that neurosis "should play such an important part in military life, but that so many men should find a satisfactory adjustment without its intervention."[11]

We can also see now that shell shock was related to social expectations of the masculine role in war. The Great War was a crisis of masculinity and a trial of the Victorian masculine ideal. In a sense, the long-term repression of signs of fear that led to shell shock in war was only an exaggeration of the male sex-role expectations, the self-control and emotional disguise of civilian life. As Elliott Smith and T. H. Pear suggested in their important book, *Shell-Shock and Its Lessons* (1917), "the suppression of fear and other strong emotions is not demanded only of men in the trenches. It is constantly expected in ordinary society."[12] Both men and officers had internalized these expectations as thoroughly as any Victorian woman had internalized her lesson about feminine nature. When all signs of physical fear were judged as weakness and where alternatives to combat—pacifism, conscientious objection, desertion, even suicide—were viewed as unmanly, men were silenced and immobilized and forced, like women, to express their conflicts through the body. Placed in intolerable circumstances of stress, and expected to react with unnatural "courage," thousands of soldiers reacted instead with the symptoms of hysteria.

For some, the experience of combat and loss may have brought to the surface powerful and disturbing feelings of love for other men. At the same time that it advocated a forceful and unassailable manliness, the atmosphere of the war was intensely, if unconsciously, homoerotic. Jones noted that the motives impelling men to enlist might well include "the homosexual desire to be in close relation with masses of men."[13] In his chapter "Soldier Boys," Paul Fussell discusses the multiple links between the environments of warfare and sexuality: the thrill of exposure, the sublimated passion of officers for vulnerable young soldiers, the worship by young soldiers of dashing officers. For the officers, the male relationships of the army, as J. R. Ackerley observed in his autobiography, were "simply an extension of my public school"—chaste, intense, platonic, unacknowledged. J. B. Priestley agreed that the emotional training of all-male public schools prepared many officers to hail "with relief . . . a wholly masculine way of life uncomplicated by Woman."[14] Witnessing the death of beloved male companions was a traumatic event that triggered much of the memorable poetry of the trenches, and Richard Fein has said, "War poetry has the subversive tendency to be our age's love poetry."[15]

Certainly a number of the best-known shell-shock cases—Wilfred

Owen, Siegfried Sassoon, Ivor Gurney, Beverly Nichols, to mention a few—were also homosexual. For most, however, the anguish of shell shock included more general but intense anxieties about masculinity, fears of acting effeminate, even a refusal to continue the bluff of stoic male behavior. If the essence of manliness was not to complain, then shell shock was the body language of masculine complaint, a disguised male protest not only against the war but against the concept of "manliness" itself. While epidemic female hysteria in late Victorian England had been a form of protest against a patriarchal society that enforced confinement to a narrowly defined femininity, epidemic male hysteria in World War I was a protest against the politicians, generals, and psychiatrists. The heightened code of masculinity that dominated in wartime was intolerable to surprisingly large numbers of men.

The efficacy of the term "shell shock" lay in its power to provide a masculine-sounding substitute for the effeminate associations of "hysteria" and to disguise the troubling parallels between male war neurosis and the female nervous disorders epidemic before the war. As I have noted earlier, psychiatrists knew that men were not immune to hysteria.[16] As early as 1828, George Burrows had discussed male hysterics in his *Commentaries on Insanity,* explaining that the masculine form often appeared as mania. Robert Brudenell Carter had attributed hysteria to sexual repression and frustration, and noted that male hysterics were often celibate, "a circumstance which may have assimilated the effects of emotiveness upon them to those which are constantly witnessed in the female."[17] In his essay for the *Dictionary of Psychological Medicine* in 1892, Charcot had declared that hysterical men were indifferent to sex, or suffered from spermatorrhea, or were impotent.

All these accounts of male hysteria—a rare phenomenon—suggest that it is a feminine kind of behavior in male subjects. And this feminine aspect is a recurrent theme in the discussions of war neuroses. When military doctors and psychiatrists dismissed shell-shock patients as cowards, they were often hinting at effeminacy or homosexuality. Karl Abraham, a hard-line Freudian, was one who argued that war neurotics were passive, narcissistic, and impotent men to begin with, whose latent homosexuality was brought to the surface by the all-male environment.[18]

On a subtler level, the men themselves experienced their anxiety as emasculating. Sexual impotence was a widespread symptom.[19] And, as Sandra Gilbert has brilliantly illustrated, impotence was a central image of psychic anxiety in postwar literature, a major trope of literary Modernism: "From Lawrence's paralyzed Clifford Chatterley to Hemingway's sadly emasculated Jake Barnes to Eliot's mysteriously sterile Fisher King . . . the gloomily bruised modernist anti-heroes churned out by the war suffer specifically from sexual wounds, as if, having traveled literally or figuratively through No Man's Land, all have become not just No Men, nobodies, but *not* men, *un*men."[20]

Clearly many combatants felt themselves rendered powerless, unmanned, by the barrage of horror to which they were subjected, and by their uncontrollable physical and emotional responses to it. In *Death of a Hero,* one of the many novels about the war, Richard Aldington's protagonist, George Winterbourne, is "amazed and distressed and ashamed to find how much his flesh shrank when a shell dropped close at hand, how great an effort he now needed to refrain from ducking or cowering. He railed at himself, called himself coward, poltroon, sissy, anything abusive he could think of. But still his body instinctively shrank."[21] McKechnie, in Ford Madox Ford's *Parade's End* (1925), makes the male gender anxiety even more explicit: "Why isn't one a beastly girl and privileged to shriek?"[22]

Not surprisingly, hostility towards "beastly" women who were allowed to scream or cry, and whose hysteria had been an accepted form of feminine expression before the war, became the theme of much war literature. Men's quarrels with the feminine element in their own psyches became externalized as quarrels with women, and hysteria expressed itself in part as fear or anger towards the neurotic woman, an anger we see in the war poetry of Owen and Sassoon, in the novels of Aldington and Ford, and in texts such as T. S. Eliot's prose-poem "Hysteria" (1917), where male anxiety is projected onto the devouring female: "As she laughed I was aware of becoming involved in her laughter and being part of it. . . . I was drawn in by short gasps, inhaled at each momentary recovery, lost finally in the dark caverns of her throat, bruised by the ripple of unseen muscles."[23]

It is not to be wondered at that the conditions of war should have inspired an identification with the female role in men who had to endure them. As the sociologist Erving Goffman has noted, with regard to lack of autonomy and powerlessness the soldier is in an analogous position to women.[24] That most masculine of enterprises, the Great War, the "apocalypse of masculinism," feminized its conscripts by taking away their sense of control. The constriction of the trenches, Sandra Gilbert suggests, was analogous to the tight domestic, vocational, and sexual spaces allowed to nineteenth-century women: "paradoxically, in fact, the war to which so many men had gone in hope of becoming heroes, ended up emasculating them . . . confining them as closely as any Victorian woman had been confined."[25]

Doctors noted that war neurosis took different forms in officers and regular soldiers. Symptoms of hysteria—paralysis, blindness, deafness, contracture of a limb, mutism, limping—appeared primarily among the regular soldiers, while neurasthenic symptoms, such as nightmares, insomnia, heart palpitations, dizziness, depression, or disorientation, were more common among officers. This extraordinarily tidy distribution of symptoms and diagnoses is consistent with late Victorian moralistic and class-oriented attitudes to hysteria and neurasthenia in women. Military doctors may have been reluctant to attach the stigmatizing feminine label of hysteria to men of their own social class. But in fact, the rate of war neurosis was four times higher among officers than among the men. For officers in particular, the pressures to conform to British ideals of manly stoicism were extreme. A 1917 brochure of instruction for officers describes the platoon commander as one who is "well turned out, punctual, and cheery, even in adverse circumstances," looks "after his men's comfort before his own and never spares himself," and is "blood-thirsty and forever thinking how to kill the enemy."[26] Some doctors had commented that when officers imagined their fear was visible to the men, they took unnecessary risks to show they were not afraid. Smith and Pear noticed that the most severe cases of shell shock occurred in officers who had made a reputation as daredevils, who had unnecessarily risked their lives as snipers and dispatch riders on the firing line.

Charles Myers, however, thought that the officers' social training and more active and responsible role in the trenches made them better prepared to deal with stress and to avoid hysteria: "The forces of education, tradition, and example make for greater control in the case of the Officer. He, moreover, is busy throughout a bombardment, issuing orders and subject to worry over his responsibilities, whereas his men can do nothing during the shelling, but watch and wait until the order is received for an advance."[27] W. H. R. Rivers, one of the leading psychiatrists of the period, also saw male hysteria as an inferior kind of psychic response to conflict. Faced with the long-term and unrelenting stresses of combat, the private, because of his "simpler mental training," his heightened suggestibility, and his dependence, is more likely "to be content with the crude solution of the conflict between instinct and duty which is provided by such disabilities as dumbness or the helplessness of a limb." The officer, on the other hand, has a more "complex and varied" mental life, the benefit of a public-school education, which has taught him "successfully to repress, not only expressions of fear, but also the emotion itself." Furthermore, his position requires him to continue to repress emotion in order to set an example for his men. Responsibility for others and the difficulty of keeping up appearances under continual strain or shock produce "a state of persistent anxiety." Neurasthenia, then, can be interpreted as selfless and noble. Indeed, Rivers concludes, the victims of neurasthenia suffer mainly from excessive zeal and "too heavy a sense of responsibility, and are likely to be the most valuable officers."[28]

Just as social classes differed in their susceptibility to hysteria and neurasthenia, so did races and ethnic groups. According to W. N. Maxwell, in his *Retrospect of the Great War,* the gregarious, emotional, and thoughtless Mediterranean type met crises by becoming hysterical, while the ideal British male was rational, reserved, and introspective: "Habitually he adapts himself through thought rather than feeling, and . . . should he break down under strain his neurotic symptoms take the form of fear-tinged thought about himself, strange obsessions, reluctance to perform certain acts, but never complete inability to accomplish them, doubts about certain things that have been done or should have been done, but never complete forgetfulness of them."[29]

In sum, then, the hysterical soldier was seen as simple, emotional, unthinking, passive, suggestible, dependent, and weak—very much the same constellation of traits associated with the hysterical woman—while the complex and overworked neurasthenic officer was much closer to an acceptable, even heroic male ideal. Interestingly, mutism, which was the most common shell-shock symptom among soldiers and noncommissioned officers, was very rare among officers. To be reduced to a feminine state of powerlessness, frustration, and dependency led to a deprivation of speech as well, just as it had for Anna O. Ernst Simmel argued that mutism was a symptom of the soldier's repressed aggression towards his superior officers, a censorship of anger and hostility by turning it in upon the self.[30] Thus shell shock may actually have served the same kind of functional purpose in military life—defusing mutiny—that female hysteria served in civilian society.

Attitudes towards hysteria and neurasthenia also influenced treatment. Disciplinary therapy provided for soldiers took a harsh moral view of hysteria as within the conscious control of the patient; they stressed quick cures, shaming, and physical re-education, which often involved the infliction of pain. Therapeutic treatments provided for officers took a situational view of neurasthenia, saw its source in unconscious conflict beyond the patient's control, and stressed the examination of repressed traumatic experience through conversation, hypnosis, or psychoanalysis. But although they were strategically different, both of these treatments were essentially coercive. The goal of wartime psychiatry was primarily to keep men fighting, and thus the handling of male hysterics and neurasthenics was more urgently purposeful than the treatments Harley Street specialists had offered their nervous women patients. Nevertheless, the two kinds of treatment suggest parallels to the hostile therapies and silencings that English doctors had recommended for hysterical women, on the one hand, and the talking cures developed in Europe, on the other. The two psychiatrists most identified with each treatment, Lewis Yealland and W. H. R. Rivers, represent the two poles of psychiatric modernism.

At the most punitive end of the treatment spectrum was electric faradization. In *Hysterical Disorders of Warfare,* Dr. Lewis Yealland described with complacent pride his clinic at Queen's Square, London. In 1917, for example, he had treated an unnamed twenty-four-year-old private who had fought in the worst campaigns of the war—the Mons retreat, the battle of the Marne, Ypres, Hill 60, Neuve Chapelle, Loos, and Armentières. Sent to Salonica, the soldier had collapsed, as he believed, on account of the heat. For nine months he had been mute and had resisted all efforts at cure, including hypnotism, electric shocks to his neck and throat, "hot plates" in his mouth, and cigarette burns on the tip of the tongue.

Yealland was determined to make this man speak, though, as with all his patients, he had no intention of *listening* when the words came back. In their first consultation, he simply ordered the soldier to get well:

> You are a young man with a wife and child at home; you owe it to them if not to yourself to make every effort to restore yourself. You appear to me to be very indifferent, but that will not do in such times as these. . . . You must recover your speech at once.

But instead of speaking, the soldier understandably only "became somewhat depressed." Later that evening the treatment got under way.

It was conducted in the locked and darkened electrical room in the hospital basement, illuminated only by the resistance bulbs of the electric battery. The soldier was fastened down in a chair, his mouth was propped open with a tongue depressor, and strong electric currents were applied to his pharynx, causing him to start backwards so that the wires pulled out of the battery. At this point Yealland explicitly reminded his patient of the obligations of masculinity: "Remember, you must behave as becomes the hero I expect you to be. . . . A man who has gone through so many battles should have better control of himself." For four hours the shocks continued. After the first hour the patient could whisper "ah," but soon after, he became tired and frustrated and tried to leave the room. Yealland prevented him: "You will leave me when you are cured, remember, not before." In an effort to accelerate the treatment the soldier pointed to the electrical apparatus and to his throat, but Yealland refused to let him dictate the timing of the shocks, or to exercise any power in the treatment.

> "No," I said, "the time for more electrical treatment has not come; if it had I should give it to you. Suggestions are not wanted from you; they are not needed. When the time comes for more electricity you will be given it, whether you wish it or not." I had intended at that time to resort to electricity, but, owing to his attitude, I postponed its use and instead made him walk up and down the room repeating "ah, ah, ah," merely to keep him awake and to show him that his suggestion regarding the electricity would not be accepted.

Eventually he returned to the battery, administering shocks until the patient began to stammer and to cry. Even then Yealland was not satisfied, and "very strong faradic shocks were applied" until this young man spoke without stutter or tremor. He was required to say "thank you" at the end.[31]

Most of Yealland's patients came from the ranks, and his blatant use of power and authority was part of the therapy. Usually he began by demanding a statement from the patient that he wished to be treated and cured. If the soldier was cynical, depressed, resistant, argumentative, or otherwise showed what Yealland called "the hideous enemy . . . of negativism," he was threatened with court-martial. Another important aspect of disciplinary treatment was to refuse all conversation that was not a direct response to a command: "When he did not make satisfactory progress, I increased the strength of the current, refusing to listen to anything he had to say." Symptoms of emotional disturbance—nightmares, terrible memories, anxieties, depression—were harshly rejected as irrelevant, and Yealland would not listen to any description of them. One of his patients, a twenty-three-year-old who had spent six months in the trenches near the Somme, choked and twitched continually, and dreamed of blood and being near an exploding mine. "It makes very little difference to me what you think of your condition," Yealland told him. "I do not want to hear about your views on the subject." After ten minutes of strong electric shocks he had stopped what Yealland called his "silly noises." That night he dreamed no more of blood and mines. He "dreamt that he was having electrical treatment in the trenches."[32] Yealland considered the therapy a success.

Yealland was probably the most extreme advocate of disciplinary treatment among the English doctors. The Orwellian scenes of mind control over which he presided are so brutally direct in their power tactics as to seem painfully embarrassing to contemporary readers. Yet it is easy to see how a wartime society accustomed to harsh treatment of hysterical women would become much more violent when confronting soldiers apparently unmanned by the experience of the front. Male hysteria elicited angry responses because men were not supposed to show weakness. When regimental medical officers regarded shell shock as an escape clause for malingerers, cowards, and "dirty sneaks," a strong element of scorn in the treatment of male hysteria satisfied the dual needs of therapy and punishment.

Let us turn now to another therapeutic scenario, which also took place in 1917. In this case the diagnosis was neurasthenia, the setting was Craiglockhart Military Hospital near Edinburgh, the therapist was Dr. W. H. R. Rivers, and the patient was Second Lieutenant Siegfried Sassoon. This time the patient and the doctor were friends; the therapy was kindly and gentle; the hospital was luxurious; the most advanced Freudian ideas came into play. Yet the reprogramming of the patient's consciousness was more profound and longer-lasting than in Yealland's electrical laboratory.

Sassoon's experience was particularly striking because he was not in fact shell-shocked at all, and class privilege accounted for his categorization as neurasthenic rather than insubordinate. His assignment to Craiglockhart had been engineered by Robert Graves when it appeared in July 1917 that Sassoon's defiant "Soldier's Declaration" (a fierce protest against the continuation of the war, sent as a letter to his commanding officer) would get him court-martialed and imprisoned. When Graves read the "Declaration," he decided at once that it was a futile and self-destructive gesture, that Sassoon was being cruelly manipulated by the pacifists, and that he should be saved from the consequences of his act by being declared mentally ill by a military medical board. Graves believed with considerable justification that Sassoon's psychological stability was shaky. Like the daredevil officers seen by military psychiatrists, Sassoon dealt with fear by reckless acts of combat, which had won him the nickname "Mad Jack." Recuperating from a wound in London, he hallucinated corpses on the pavement; he contemplated assassinating General Haig in protest, but feared that if he did he would be shut up in a madhouse, like Richard Dadd. (Dadd's great-nephews were comrades of Graves and Sassoon.) Although Graves knew that Sassoon was angry and rebellious rather than sick, he saw that a plausible case of shell shock could be made, one that would benefit both sides.

Graves proceeded to contact his friends in the government and to rig the medical board. The most difficult step was persuading Sassoon to go along. As Sassoon recalls the episode in his fictionalized *Memoirs of an Infantry Officer,* Graves convinced him that the authorities were determined not make a martyr of him by taking his "Declaration" seriously: "He said that the Colonel at Clitherland had told him to tell me that if I continued to refuse to be 'medically boarded' they would shut me up in a lunatic asylum for the rest of the War. Nothing would induce them to court-martial me. It had all been arranged with some big bug in the War Office in the last day or two."[33]

This was a bluff, but Sassoon accepted it and allowed himself to be described as someone with a nervous breakdown, something he would later regret. Before the board, too, Graves performed magnificently as a witness. He carefully pitched his story to suit the different personalities of the three doctors, and cried repeatedly during his own testimony. If Graves was a healthy man, the doctors must have thought, Sassoon must be a desperate case. (Some shell-shock experts would have regarded Sassoon as a likely candidate for breakdown anyway since there was a theory that "strange first names" were symptomatic of latent family degeneracy.)[34] Sassoon says understandably little about the board in the *Memoirs* or in his diary; it is perhaps the only shaming occasion of his military career. But he admits that when it was over, and he had been diagnosed as suffering from shell shock and ordered into a hospital, he felt gratitude and relief: "At that moment, it seemed as though I had finished with the war."[35] He was wrong.

Craiglockhart Military Hospital, or "Dottyville," as it was called by Sassoon and Graves, had been built in the 1870s as a hydropathic establishment. Situated in "a charming position," as a 1913 brochure boasted, the Italianate building "from its elevated site" commanded "a magnificent panoramic view of the valley of the Forth and adjacent counties, with the Ochils and Grampians in the distance."[36] Sir Walter Scott had described the prospect in *Marmion.* In 1916 the Red Cross had taken it over as a military hospital for shell-shocked officers. At first, according to the thinly disguised satirical portrait of the hospital in A. G. Macdonnell's *England, Their England* (1933), the military commandant in charge of this "monster hydropathic" was an expert on the drainage system of Leith, who did not believe in the legitimacy of shell shock, and whose universal remedy for it "consisted of finding out the main likes and dislikes of each patient, and then ordering them to abstain from the former and apply themselves diligently to the latter."

> For example, those of the so-called patients . . . who disliked noise were allotted rooms on the main road. Those who had been, in happier times, parsons, schoolmasters, journalists, and poets, were forbidden the use of the library and driven off in batches to physical drill, lawn tennis, golf, and badminton. Those who wished to be alone were paired with horse-racing, girl-hunting subalterns. Those who were terrified of solitude had special rooms by themselves behind green-baize doors at the end of remote corridors. By means of this admirable system, the three hundred separate psychological problems were soon reduced to the uniform level of the Leith drainage and sewerage, and by the time that a visiting commission of busybodies, arriving unexpectedly and armed with an absurd technical knowledge and jargon, insisted upon the immediate sack of the Commandant and his replacement by a civilian professor of psychology, it was estimated that the mental condition of as many as two per cent of the patients had definitely improved for the better since admission to the hospital.[37]

When Sassoon arrived, however, therapeutic conditions and policies at Craiglockhart had been much improved. There was an asylum journal, a fortnightly rather ominously named *The Hydra* and edited by

Wilfred Owen, another patient. Agricultural and athletic occupations were encouraged for those who liked them, and there were excellent facilities for gardening, tennis, bowls, cricket, swimming, or water polo in the indoor heated pool, and for Sassoon's especial passion, golf. He had his clubs sent up from London, and played every day. Meals were stodgy—steamed pudding appeared too often to be welcome—but Sassoon, for one, was an honorary member of an Edinburgh club where better food and "noble Burgundy" could be obtained. At first, he was irritated by his roommate—a "prosy Theosophist"—but by October he was given a private room where he could write uninterrupted.[38]

The contrast to both the treatment of hysterical soldiers and the rest cure of neurasthenic women is significant. Many military psychiatrists had criticized the usefulness of Weir Mitchell's rest cure for shell-shock patients. Soldiers who were isolated and treated with the rest cure, R. D. Gillespie claimed, did not recover and remained ill throughout the war.[39] Hugh Crichton-Miller protested that rest in bed, nourishment, and encouragement were insufficient to restore masculine self-esteem: "Progressive daily achievement is the only way whereby manhood and self-respect can be regained."[40] Thus instead of the enforced passivity of Virginia Woolf or Charlotte Perkins Gilman, Sassoon was encouraged to resume a life of energetic masculine activity. He was provided with a room of his own, and a place to publish his work. As a poet, he was never deprived of his voice.

Furthermore, he was urged to speak and to write about his war memories and emotions. If Yealland was the worst of the military psychiatrists, Sassoon's therapist, William Halse Rivers Rivers, was unquestionably the best (fig. 26). A Kentishman like Sassoon, he had had a brilliant academic career as a psychologist, neurophysiologist, and anthropologist. He had trained at St. Bartholomew's, writing papers on hysteria, neurasthenia, and delirium, and had worked as clinical assistant at Bethlem under George Savage. In the 1890s he had studied psychology in Germany at Jena and Heidelberg, and had worked with Ludwig Binswanger and Emil Kraepelin.

Rivers was among the first in England to support the discoveries of Freud in the field of psychoneurosis and psychotherapy, and he was one of the most remarkable members of this daring and colorful generation of doctors. Like Ernest Jones, the energetic young neurologist who became Freud's most dedicated English advocate, and David Eder, who brought to his war work the benefits of his contacts with Freud,

Figure 26. W. H. R. Rivers.

Jung, Abraham, and Ferenczi, Rivers had a restless and adventurous mind. He had done ethnological research in Melanesia, and his book on kinship and social organization is still considered a classic in the field. He had participated in the neuropsychologist Henry Head's controversial experiments on the nervous system, and the celebrated psychological laboratory he directed at Cambridge with Charles Myers trained a number of students who later achieved prominence.[41]

Rivers was also a teacher of legendary magnetism and charm. Arnold Bennett, who met him through Sassoon after the war, described his study at St. Johns College, crowded with devoted students:

> His manner to young seekers after wisdom, and to young men who were prepared to teach him a thing or two, was divine. I have sat astride on the sofa and listened to dozens of these interviews. They were touching, in the eager crudity of the visitors, the mature, suave, wide-sweeping sagacity and experience of the Director of Studies, and the fallacious but charming equality which the elder established and maintained between the two.[42]

When Sassoon met him, Rivers was fifty-three. Many of his friends felt that "it was not really until the war that Rivers found himself"; that through his work in treating psychoneuroses he achieved an emotional fulfillment that had been missing in his laboratory research at Cambridge, and even in his teaching and anthropological field work.[43] A stammerer since boyhood, like Sassoon, Rivers was reserved, lonely, and isolated in his private life. He never married, and although his attitudes towards coeducation were progressive, Bennett for one thought he had "almost no interest in women."[44] Rivers's biographer, Richard Slobodin, suggests that in dealing with the suffering of shell-shocked officers, he drew on his own suppressed emotions of love and nurturance.

> A combination of experience, life-view, and manner made Rivers a source of wisdom and security to many shattered young men in the years 1915–19. Langdon-Brown, a wise and compassionate doctor himself, felt that this success was possible "because he had to heal himself that he could heal others"; it might be suggested, conversely, that in healing others, Rivers went far toward healing, that is, helping himself.[45]

Langdon-Brown believed that Rivers's "whole personality expanded as he grew to realize what was his true mission in life." Myers, who was probably Rivers's closest friend, recalled that during the war he "became another and far happier man."[46]

Rivers's name is also associated with the most enlightened, probing, humane, and sensitive studies of wartime neurosis. He recognized the part immobility, powerlessness, and silence played in bringing on neurotic symptoms, and argued in behalf of a psychoanalytic approach to shell shock which would stress the psychic effects of repression of war experience. In his therapeutic practice Rivers relied on what he called autognosis, or self-understanding, which involved the discussion of traumatic experiences; and re-education, in which "the patient is led to understand how his newly acquired knowledge of himself may be utilized . . . and how to turn energy, hitherto morbidly directed, into more healthy channels."[47]

This positive attitude made Rivers a comforting therapist to Sassoon. From the beginning, Rivers established himself as a benign figure, who made Sassoon "feel safe at once" and who understood him "better than I understood myself." The twenty-year difference in their ages made it possible for Rivers to seem like a "father-confessor" helping the fatherless Sassoon through a prolonged adolescence to "mental maturity."[48] But what was mental maturity? For Sassoon it was not recovery from any obvious neurotic symptoms. In the medical report Rivers wrote, he described Sassoon as "a healthy-looking man of good physique . . . perfectly intelligent and rational. . . . There is no evidence of any excitement or depression."[49] As Rivers saw it, Sassoon's problem was "a very strong 'anti-war' complex"[50]

Curing an antiwar complex, even for a therapist as gifted as Rivers, was a matter of time, delicacy, and indirection. Three times a week Rivers and Sassoon had "friendly confabulations" about Sassoon's life, but also about European politicians, German military history, and the dangers of a premature peace. As Sassoon wrote to Lady Ottoline Morrell, Rivers "doesn't *pretend* my nerves are wrong, but regards my attitude as abnormal. I don't know how long he will go on trying to persuade me to modify my views."[51] Soon Sassoon's talking cure had proceeded far enough for him to feel uneasy about the gaps in his information, ashamed of his ignorance next to Rivers, the Cambridge don, and embarrassed that his pacifism was more emotional than intellectual. Other circumstances supported this period of insecurity. The flurry of celebrity that accompanied his gesture of protest had stopped. Meanwhile Sassoon, the force of whose war poetry came from his fierce wish to show all patriotic and complacent civilians the bestial reality of the trenches, found himself overwhelmed by guilt and humiliation at being "dumped down among nurses and nervous wrecks," the women and noncombatants he had always despised. Looking around at his "fellow breakdowns," "160 more or less dotty officers . . . many of them degenerate-looking," he needed to dissociate himself from them and to affirm his own sanity—in a way, his own masculinity.[52] Despite the golf, the horseplay, the incessant round of hearty male activity, the atmosphere of Craiglockhart, like that of other mental institutions, was emasculating.

> Sometimes I had an uncomfortable notion that none of them respected one another; it was as though there were a tacit understanding that we were all failures, and this made me want to reassure myself that I wasn't the same as the others. "After all, I haven't broken down, I've only broken out," I thought one evening.[53]

In September, Rivers had to take a leave of absence because of illness, and Sassoon felt abandoned and uneasy. In the *Memoirs,* Rivers's absence is the occasion of a remarkable trial of Sassoon's pacifist beliefs, an episode so well timed that it is uncannily like a part of the therapy, or a version of Jekyll and Hyde. Sassoon's autobiographical hero, George Sherston, is visited by a stranger, a talkative Ph.D. named Macamble, who congratulates him effusively on his heroic pacifism and invites him to a conspiratorial tea in Edinburgh. At their meeting in the lounge of the Edinburgh Hotel, Macamble unveils a plot to liberate Sherston "from the machinations of that uniformed pathologist," Rivers (the only character called by his real name in the book), who is "a subtly disintegrating influence . . . at work on my Pacifist zealotry." Sherston is to abscond to London, where he will be welcomed by a pacifist committee and taken to an "eminent alienist" who will declare him absolutely sane and responsible. It says a great deal for the efficacy of autognosis and re-education that, given this opportunity to regain his integrity as an objector to the war, Sherston rejects Macamble's proposal, and thinks of it, in fact, as an invitation to "do the dirty on Rivers," to whom his loyalties have now been transferred. Back at the hydro that evening, he is rewarded by a fatherly smile from Rivers, wearily returning from his leave.[54]

It is really as if Macamble is the negative side of Rivers, the evil version of the benevolent authority; and the pacifist plot a test. From this point on, Sassoon's protest became futile in his own eyes. Staying at Craiglockhart made him no better than a coward, and if he continued to do anything outrageous, he wrote Ottoline Morrell, "they would only say I had a relapse and put me in a padded room." The only alternative was to go back to the war. Sassoon's ploy was to refuse to disown his views, but to ask for a return to General Service. Rivers, however, urged him to recant fully, and if he did, promised to help Sassoon "wangle things" with the War Office in order to be sent back to the front.[55]

Yet the subtle process of behavior modification could not completely control the unconscious. As soon as Sassoon let Rivers persuade him and agreed to recant his views, he began, for the first time, to have recurring nightmares about the war. When the day of the Medical Board arrived in October, he was irritable and fed up, and did not appear for his review. It was this final act of unwitting protest that in fact concluded his re-education. Faced with Rivers's stern judgment, Sassoon at last reached the desired state of numbness. He stopped being introspective; he stopped worrying; he felt nothing; and in this condition he passed successfully through a second Medical Board in November, becoming once more "an officer and a gentleman," and bidding farewell to the "Mecca of psychoneuroses."[56]

No one kept follow-up records on the men treated with either disciplinary or analytical therapies and sent back to combat. It was suspected that many of the hysterical patients broke down again or worse when they returned to the trenches. Sassoon, however, seemed to have no further nervous problems. He always maintained that his return to the war was the proper and inevitable choice. And he never turned upon Rivers the corrosive irony that he could employ so tellingly upon other noncombatants. Indeed, the two remained close personal friends until Rivers's unexpected death in 1922. Thirty years later Sassoon still thought of him often, with gratitude and love.[57]

And yet was Rivers's influence so benign, and was Sassoon's pacifism really so "emotional," so "futile," so "immature"? Or was his cure really a regression from maturity and moral courage? Was the man who went back to the front demonstrably saner than the one who entered the hospital?

Some historians blame the change on a neurotic death-wish in Sassoon, something that "courted death, that craved annihilation, that derived a drug-like satisfaction from facing danger unafraid."[58] But this view seems mistaken to me. Without psychiatric intervention, Sassoon might have taken a different road; even with it, he resisted. His therapy was a seduction and a negotiation; his return to France, an acknowledgment of defeat. Obviously it was better for the authorities to have treated his pacifism as an antiwar complex, to have framed his rebellion as nervous breakdown, and to have isolated him in a mental hospital, than to have allowed him to find the political and collective audience for his ideas that might have helped him resist.

It is significant that, for the rest of his life, Sassoon devoted himself to an obsessive revisiting and rewriting of his experiences before and during the war, in a series of six memoirs. He became one for whom, as Paul Fussell has said, "remembering the war became something like a life work."[59] In these memoirs, Sassoon continued the process of autognosis in which Rivers had trained him, conducting a self-analysis whose object was to justify his life as a man. Rivers was installed in his memoirs and in his diary as a kind of superego, a father figure who represented the masculine ideal.

And yet, ironically, Rivers was as changed by Sassoon as Sassoon was by Rivers. Even before Sassoon arrived at Craiglockhart, Rivers had felt some uncertainties about his total support for the war. In March he dreamed of reading a letter reproaching him for his political views; he felt worried about subscribing to the antiwar *Cambridge Magazine*. Later he had pacifist dreams brought on by his discussions with Sassoon. Rivers was well aware of his political obligations as a Royal Army Medical Corps officer; they were symbolized by his uniform. He had also "thought of the situation that would arise if my task of converting a patient from his 'pacifist errors' to the conventional attitude should have as its result my own conversion to his point of view. My attitude throughout the war had been clearly in favor of fighting until Germany recognized defeat, and though the humorous side of the imagined situation struck me more than its serious aspect, there can be little doubt that there was a good opening for conflict and repression."[60]

After the war, mixing with radicals, writers, editors, and politicians he had met through Sassoon, Rivers allowed the questions he had long suppressed to emerge. At the time of his death in 1922, he was a Labour Party candidate for Parliament in the General Election, and his biographer speculates that if he had lived into the 1930s and 1940s, he would have been "the most leftward of leading British anthropologists."[61] In a sense, then, Rivers caught Sassoon's antiwar complex in the process of treating it. Nonetheless, his postwar writing reveals no moral ambivalence, no second thoughts about the immediate effects of his successful therapies, no painful reconsideration of his own service to the state. Ideal military training, he wrote without irony in 1920, "should bring the soldier into such a state that even the utmost horrors and rigours of warfare are hardly noticed, so inured is he to their presence and so absorbed in the immediate task presented by his military duties."[62] This could be a description of Rivers himself, so perfectly conditioned by his education, his class, his sex, and his professional role that he performed his duties—even if his dreams were sometimes a bit troubled and unconventional—with perfect aplomb.

Dr. Farquhar Buzzard had noted in a preface to Yealland's book on hysterical disorders that the war, if it had served no other good purpose, "must surely have stimulated a more universal and keener interest in psychotherapy." Although Rivers would never have adopted Buzzard's words or the tone of bloodthirsty professionalism Yealland used when he congratulated himself "in having at my disposal a wealth of clinical material,"[63] he nonetheless did learn a great deal from working with the officers at Maghull and Craiglockhart. He also had an opportunity to learn from such like-minded colleagues as Elliott Smith, T. H. Pear, and Bernard Hart, and to work in an atmosphere "in which the interpretation of dreams and the discussion of mental conflicts formed the staple subjects of conversation."[64] Rivers was struck by the correspondence between Freudian theory and his clinical practice, and especially by the ideas of the unconscious. As he explained in an essay for *The Lancet*:

> There is hardly a case which this theory does not help us the better to understand—not a day of clinical experience in which Freud's theory may not be of direct practical use in diagnosis and treatment. The terrifying dreams, the sudden gusts of depression or restlessness, the cases of altered personality . . . which are among the most characteristic results of the present war, receive by far their most natural explanation as the result of war experience, which, by some pathological process, often assisted later by conscious activity on the part of the patient, has been either suppressed or is in process of undergoing changes which will lead sooner or later to this result. While the results of warfare provide little evidence in favour of the production

> of functional nervous disorders by the activity of repressed sexual complexes, I believe that they will be found to provide abundant evidence in favour of the validity of Freud's theory of forgetting.

In fact, Rivers concluded, the advent of the war presented psychiatry with an extraordinary demonstration of the validity of Freudian theory in general: "It is a wonderful turn of fate that just as Freud's theory of the unconscious and the method of psycho-analysis founded upon it should be so hotly discussed, there should have occurred events which have produced on an enormous scale just those conditions of paralysis and contracture, phobia and obsession, which the theory was especially designed to explain."[65]

In the burst of creativity that followed his war experience, Rivers was one of the most influential popularizers of Freudian theory in England. Before the war, he acknowledged, Freudian theory had "not merely failed to meet with general acceptance, but was the subject of hostility exceptional even in the history of medicine." This was primarily because of the emphasis on infantile sexuality and sexual trauma as the cause of psychoneuroses. But the war, he wrote in *Instinct and the Unconscious,* had been "a vast crucible in which all our preconceived views concerning human nature have been tested."[66] Rivers proposed a compromise view of psychoneurosis, based on his clinical experience, which seemed to bridge the gap between evolutionist and Freudian theory. In wartime, he argued, sexual disturbances were negligible factors in the production of psychoneuroses; instead, the instincts of danger and self-preservation were put into intolerable conflict with the demands of military duty.

But even if he dismissed Freud's sexual theories, he held to Freudian concepts of the unconscious and repression to explain the process by which moments of terror or disgust were suppressed and converted into physical symptoms; and he defended psychoanalytic techniques of dream interpretation, hypnosis, suggestion, and transference. By minimizing the significance of the sexual drives in Freudian theory, Rivers helped domesticate it for an English audience. In the last essays he wrote before he died, Rivers was thinking too of ways to apply the lessons of the war to industrial psychology as well as to improved military training.[67]

The experience of male hysteria inevitably had a number of effects on English psychiatric practice. It forced a reconsideration of all the positions that Darwinian psychiatry had taken on the causation of mental illness, on male and female roles, and on therapeutic responsibility. The overwhelming allegiance of English psychiatry to organic explanations of mental disorders was breached and subverted by the experience of the war, as it became clear that shell shock had an emotional, not a physical, origin. Psychotherapy and the ideas of Freud, strongly resisted by Darwinian psychiatrists, gained ground despite the hostility to Germany and "Teutonic" science. And new methods of treatment had to be devised to deal with psychological wounds. Under conditions of war, therapeutic practices took on a new urgency, and psychiatrists were granted unprecedented powers of domination, intervention, and control.

Psychiatrists did not anticipate, however, that men's war neurosis would be worse *after* the war. Rivers did not live to see the startling influx of neurasthenic ex-servicemen—about 114,600 in all—who applied for pensions for shell-shock-related disorders between 1919 and 1929, or predict that the insecurities and pathologies about roles generated by the extraordinary conditions of war would not end with the Armistice, but would continue to work themselves out in peacetime, in households and offices as well as in veterans' hospitals. The soldiers who returned looked, as Philip Gibbs noted, "very much like the young men who had gone to business in the peaceful days before August 1914." But they were not the same: "Something had altered in them. They were subject to queer moods and queer tempers, fits of profound depression alternating with a restless desire for pleasure. Many were easily moved to passion where they lost control of themselves, many were bitter in their speech, violent in opinion, frightening."[68]

What had happened to make these men so unstable, so emotional, in a word, so feminine? Women understood the lesson of shell shock better than their male contemporaries: that powerlessness could lead to pathology, that a lasting wound could result when a person lost the sense of being in control, of being "an autonomous actor in a manipulable world."[69]

Immediately after the war, in fact, women novelists appropriated the theme of shell shock, and fixed it in the public mind. They also made explicit connections between psychiatric therapies and the imposition of patriarchal values insensitive to passion, fantasy, and creativity. The historian Eric Leed has speculated that in the decade after the war, male veterans were struggling to repress their war experience, to banish the most painful memories from their minds. For this reason, he suggests, there were very few men's war memoirs or novels published during the 1920s; they did not begin to appear in substantial numbers until the 1930s, after the Depression had "closed the gap between civilian and ex-soldier" by making all abject and powerless.[70] This "latency period" in which male war experience was forgotten may explain in part why the earliest and most vigorous critiques of civilian and psychiatric attitudes towards shell shock came from women writers.

Rebecca West's *The Return of the Soldier* (1918), the first English novel about shell shock, took as its hero an officer who has made a separate peace by escaping into amnesia, or "hysterical fugue." Sent home to recuperate, Chris Baldry does not recognize his glossy estate or his elegant wife, Kitty, and remembers only the intense emotions of his boyhood love for Margaret, a working-class girl, now a worn and shabby matron. Through his passionate dependency on Margaret, who comes back to care for him, he finds a refuge from all the suffocating male roles of his life: Tory landowner, dutiful husband, brave officer. But obviously his family and his society cannot allow him to remain in this private retreat. Kitty summons a Freudian analyst, Dr. Gilbert Anderson, whose chubby face and mild appearance are yet "suggestive of power." Although he knows that he cannot make Chris happy, but only "ordinary," Anderson restores his patient's memory by showing him the toys of his dead son. In the end, the women, including Margaret, collaborate in the therapy because they too feel that they must cherish his rational masculinity: "For if we left him in his magic circle there would come a time when his delusion turned to a senile idiocy. . . . He would not be quite a man." The return of the soldier (he's "every inch a soldier" after the cure) is the return of the male automaton. The cure has replaced passion with a "dreadful decent smile," and protective affection with the yoke of an unwanted embrace. Worst of all, it condemns Baldry not only to his loveless marriage but also to return to "that flooded trench in Flanders . . . that No Man's Land where bullets fall like rain on the rotting faces of the dead."[71]

West goes well beyond even the enlightenment of Rivers in grasping the connections between male hysteria and a whole range of male social obligations. While her account of the psychoanalytic process is simplistic, West's understanding of the unconscious motives and symbolic meanings of shell shock is moving and complex.

The "return of the soldier" as officer and gentleman is also a theme in several of Dorothy Sayers's novels in the 1920s. In *The Unpleasantness at the Bellona Club* (1928), the "indecent neurasthenia" of a shell-shocked veteran is central to the plot and very much part of the postwar atmosphere she portrays—men coming home with small pensions and shaky nerves to face unemployment, the moribund patriotism of elderly clubmen and generals, and the demands of their wives that they reassume a manly control they no longer feel.

The most famous of Sayers's shell-shocked heroes is of course her aristocratic detective, Lord Peter Wimsey, who admits in *Busman's Honeymoon* (1937) that he "has never been really right since the War." For eighteen months after his discharge in 1918, Wimsey had terrible nightmares, was afraid to go to sleep, and could not even give an order to his servants. As his mother observes, "if you've been giving orders for nearly four years to people to go and get blown to pieces," the responsibility of giving orders becomes unbearable. Nursed through the worst of his breakdown by his servant and former sergeant, Bunter, Lord Peter is still having "the old responsibility-dream" nearly twenty years after the war: "Fifteen of us, marching across a prickly desert, and we were all chained together. There was something I had forgotten—to do or tell somebody—but I couldn't stop, because of the chain. . . . When I looked down, I saw the bones of my own feet, and they were black, because we'd been hanged in chains a long time ago and were beginning to come to pieces."[72] Lord Peter's wife, Harriet Vane, must hold him like a child when these nightmares recur.

It remained to Virginia Woolf, however, to connect the shell-shocked veteran with the repressed woman of the man-governed world through their common enemy, the nerve specialist. Woolf knew more about psychiatric power than most noncombatants, and as much as most shell-shock patients. Many of her doctors, having failed to cure her neurasthenia during a decade of effort, had gone on to apply their dubious expertise to war neurosis. Woolf also knew Siegfried Sassoon, and had reviewed his war poems, *The Old Huntsman* and *Counter-Attack,* for the *Times Literary Supplement.* He came to visit her in 1924, while she was writing *Mrs. Dalloway:* "Old S.S. is a nice dear kind sensitive warm-hearted good fellow," she confided to her diary in an uncharacteristic burst of praise.[73] Septimus Smith, the victim of "deferred shell-shock" in *Mrs. Dalloway* (1925), perhaps owes something of his name, his appearance, and his war experience to Sassoon.

More than any other novelist of the period, Woolf perceived and exposed the sadism of nerve therapies that enforced conventional sex roles. Septimus Smith has "developed manliness," which is to say acquired numbness, in the trenches; he has "congratulated himself upon feeling very little and very reasonably," even when his dearest friend Evans is killed beside him. But back in England, this façade of stoic masculinity wears thin; Septimus is appalled at how much he really does feel about the war, and desperately tries to deny it. Yet the more he struggles to repress his war experience, the more hideously it rises up to haunt him. The doctors who try to "cure" Septimus, the stupid general practitioner Holmes and the sinister nerve specialist Sir William Bradshaw, do not want to hear about his memories either. They insist that the way to mental health is conformity and routine. Holmes is a bully who tells Septimus that "health is largely a matter in our own control," and blimpishly advocates bromides, porridge, the music hall, hobbies, and cricket. Bradshaw, who wants Septimus committed to his private rest home, is a tyrant, ruthlessly determined to crush creativity, passion, and imagination.[74]

Cornered by the implacable team of Holmes and Bradshaw, Septimus leaps from a window to escape them. Such cases were not uncommon among returning soldiers. One young officer, regarded as a "perfect soldier," had "enjoyed the fighting hugely and even got indifferent to the burial work. The death of chums saddened him, but he carried on and soon forgot about the incidents." After the war, however, he tried to kill himself.[75] George Savage described the case of another veteran who felt pursued by faceless enemies; when he heard them coming, "he threw himself from the window, and though he lived for a few hours, he died."[76] But suicide, as Woolf makes clear in *Mrs. Dalloway,* was regarded as a final admission of shameful and unmanly weakness; when Septimus leaps to his death, Dr. Holmes cries out, "The coward!" Only Clarissa Dalloway sees that men like Holmes and Bradshaw "make life intolerable," and that suicide can be a heroic act of defiant feeling.[77] Septimus's problem is that he feels too much for a man. His grief and introspection are emotions that are consigned to the feminine. "Belonging to Clarissa's world," as Lee R. Edwards notes, " . . . they must by definition fail to be manly and thus disqualify Septimus from the masculine role assigned him by society, the particular heroism it is prepared to accept from him."[78]

Whereas Sassoon's fictionalized Rivers is a fatherly and saintly figure, his name associated with fresh pastoral scenes, Woolf's physicians are rapacious brutes, indifferent and domineering. Shell shock was the male counterpart of hysteria, a discourse of masculinity addressed to patriarchal thought; but it was scarcely possible for either male patients or male psychiatrists, themselves deeply implicated in patriarchal structures, to see its meanings. Women writers like Woolf and West thus played an important role in explicating the significance of gender and power in therapeutic strategies, and in addressing the ethical and emotional questions raised by the treatment of shell shock.

The Great War was the first and, so far, the last time in the twentieth century that men and the wrongs of men occupied a central position in the history of madness. It is ironically appropriate that in 1930, when Bethlem Hospital moved to new facilities, its former buildings became the Imperial War Museum. Despite the lingering male mental casualties of the postwar period, as soldiers returned to take over their former places as social leaders, women returned to *their* former places as the primary psychiatric patients. The crude faradic battery of the military hospital became the electric-shock machine of modern psychiatry. In this era, psychiatric descendants of both Yealland and Rivers would come to fullest power.

8

WOMEN AND PSYCHIATRIC MODERNISM

The therapies of Rivers and Yealland represented the two modes of English psychiatric modernism which would affect women both inside and outside the asylum from the 1920s to the 1960s: psychoanalysis, which offered the twentieth century's most influential theory of femininity and female sexuality; and traditional medical psychiatry, which made rapid advances in scientific knowledge and technological skill.

In many respects, it seemed as if women had benefitted from the social upheaval of the war. The image of idle middle-class women as the chief clientele for nervous disorders had been substantially modified. In the decade after the war, the incidence of female hysteria dramatically declined. Many believed that women had become stronger and less vulnerable to mental breakdown when they were faced with real crises and when they were given meaningful work. "If the First World War was a clear-cut victory for anything," the historian David Mitchell proclaims, "it was a clear-cut victory for women's emancipation."[1]

Furthermore, the field of psychiatry seemed more open to women's participation, to women's ideas, and to new thinking about female psychology. In 1927, "after much heart-searching" and in view of the large number of female patients, the employment of women doctors in London County mental hospitals was sanctioned by the London County Council, and two women were immediately appointed as assistant medical officers.[2] Over all, forty women members of the Medico-Psychological Association were working in English hospitals by this date.[3]

Within the field of psychoanalysis, the situation was even more promising. Many feminists had been attracted to psychoanalysis from its earliest years, seeing it as a theory that accepted female sexuality and freed women from the shackles of a puritanical Darwinian science. Freudian ideas became immediately popular with the literary avant-garde after the war. "All literary London discovered Freud," the novelist Bryher (Winifred Ellerman) recalled; "the theories were the great subject of conversation wherever one went at that date."[4] As the heiress to an enormous fortune, Bryher herself provided financial support for the psychoanalytic movement in Vienna, helped to found the *Psychoanalytic Review,* and gave money directly to Freud in the 1930s. She and the poet H.D. were among the first to be analyzed themselves. Furthermore, because psychoanalysis was a new field, women found fewer barriers against them within it than in the traditional work of the asylum or consulting room. Among the thirty original members of the British Psychoanalytic Society, six were women: Alix Strachey (1892–1973), Joan Rivière (1883–1962), Sylvia Payne (1880–1976), Barbara Low, Susan Isaacs (1885–1948), and Ella Freeman Sharpe (1875–1947).

Yet the real effect of these changes was disappointing; in cold reality the political or psychic victories women gained during the war were few. By the 1920s, women found themselves with little progress besides the vote (which had, in any case, been won by 1914) to show for their brief period of wartime emancipation. Although women's employment had skyrocketed during the war, returning soldiers took their industrial jobs back from the women who had replaced them. In 1921, the female percentage of the work force was exactly what it had been in 1911—29 percent—and it did not increase significantly during the next thirty years.[5] Sexual behavior and standards also quickly reverted to prewar levels. Illegitimacy rates dropped and divorce rates stabilized in the late 1920s, as women were encouraged by advertising and urged by the government to return to domesticity and chastity. Feminist feeling, which had reached a peak in the suffrage movement, subsided.

Denied their work and coping with emotional loss, many women felt despair at the prospect of returning to shopworn roles and old routines. For them, too, the war continued to be fought in the psyche, and the period of readjustment precipitated psychological problems. By the 1930s, the Tavistock Clinic, founded for the psychoanalytic treatment of functional nervous disorders, reported that 61 percent of its patients were women.[6] And psychoanalysis, for its part, hardened into a discourse that devalued women—despite the presence of women in its ranks.

The failure of women analysts to develop a feminist view of female sexuality and psychology is a fascinating instance of the general collapse of the feminist movement after the war. The turn of the century had been a period in which definitions of both masculinity and femininity were being revised. The postwar period, however, was one of renewed conservatism about sex roles and gender issues. One of the main signs of this conservatism was the erosion of late Victorian institutions formed by and for middle-class women (settlement houses, schools, colleges, and sisterhoods). Another was the shift of feminist interests away from questions of women's independence to questions of women's relationship to men. Both changes affected woman's role in the early years of psychoanalysis.

The story of the Medico-Psychological Clinic in London offers a striking illustration of the way that male professionalism could crush the early experimentation of women in psychoanalysis. Founded in 1913 by two women, Dr. Jessie Margaret Murray and Julia Turner, and funded by the novelist May Sinclair, this was the first public clinic in England to offer psychoanalytic treatment. While not explicitly feminist in theory, the clinic was clearly a practical feminist initiative in the field that might well have become a center for new ideas on the psychology of women. Murray had a medical degree from Durham and had studied with the neurologist Pierre Janet in Paris; she and Turner were well read in a variety of psychotherapeutic fields, including the work of Freud, Jung, Brill, and Breuer. They took an eclectic approach to the treatment of nervous disorders, combining psychoanalysis with diet, exercise, and medical treatment. They also sponsored a training center in which students took a three-year course in applied psychology.

Originally, the clinic served mainly women patients, as was undoubtedly the intention of its founders. During the war, however, Murray and Turner found themselves besieged by male patients discharged from the armed services because of shell shock and nervous disorders.

In order to handle the deluge of cases, they expanded the clinic in Brunswick Square to include a residence for shell-shocked soldiers, and took on a partner, Dr. James Glover, a young doctor interested in psychoanalysis who had been rejected for military service because of the early symptoms of diabetes.

Tragically, Jessie Murray developed cancer in 1919 and died the following year at the age of fifty-three, leaving Glover and Turner in charge of the clinic. Once the war was over, Glover was eager to learn more about psychoanalysis at first hand. In 1920, he had the opportunity to attend the Sixth International Psychoanalytical Congress at The Hague, where he met Karl Abraham; and a few months later, he went to Berlin to undergo a Freudian analysis with Abraham. When Glover returned to London, he had become "a total convert to psychoanalysis. He firmly believed that only psychoanalytic treatment, on proper Freudian lines, should be applied to all patients accepted by the Clinic, and that the eclectic practice which Dr. Jessie Murray had established should be abandoned."[7]

Glover further proposed that the clinic and its program should become affiliated with the new British Psycho-Analytical Society founded by Ernest Jones. When Julia Turner refused to join, Glover left the clinic, taking most of the women students and staff with him. By 1922, Julia Turner was forced to close the clinic and to liquidate its assets to pay her debts. Several of her medical consultants joined the staff of the Tavistock Clinic, opened in 1919 by Dr. Hugh Crichton-Miller; others joined the British Psycho-Analytical Society. Within a few years, the work of Murray and Turner had passed into oblivion.

James Glover's conversion in Berlin and his subsequent "normalization" of the Medico-Psychological Clinic can be seen as a reaction against the feminist leadership of an older generation. Murray and Turner were representatives of the first generation of college-educated women in England. Their relationship was typical of the intimate friendships that for so many pioneering women relieved the pressure of professional careers; and their clinic was modeled on other women's institutions founded at the end of the century. But by the time of the war, both women's friendships and women's institutions were under direct attack, not only in the writings of male sexologists and psychologists such as Havelock Ellis and Freud, but also in sensational novels about lesbian villainy, such as Clemence Dane's *Regiment of Women* (1917). As Martha Vicinus has shown, at a time when "single women were powerful and highly visible leaders in the public sphere," loving friendships between single women were attacked as deviant and perverse.[8]

Glover's takeover of the clinic occurred in the context of this cultural change. Indeed, it was Glover's analyst, Karl Abraham, who had first interpreted the feminist movement of the period as the expression of a "masculinity complex" in neurotic women. In the famous paper he gave at the postwar psychoanalytical congress attended by Glover, "Manifestations of the Female Castration Complex," Abraham described feminists as women who sublimated their wish to be men by "following masculine pursuits of an intellectual and professional nature."[9]

Freud accepted Karl Abraham's view on feminists, praising Abraham's description of the female castration complex as "unsurpassed." In addition to his work on hysteria, Freud formulated his own views about female psychology and sexuality in three brief essays of the late 1920s and early 1930s: "Some Psychological Consequences of the Anatomical Differences Between the Sexes" (1925); "Female Sexuality" (1931); and "Femininity" (1933). In these essays, Freud developed his theory of the girl's anatomical deficiency, or what he called "the fact of her castration," leading to the female version of the Oedipus complex, which comprised penis envy, feelings of inferiority or self-hatred, and contempt for the mother. In coming to terms with her "castration" in early childhood, the girl had three possible paths of psychic development: sexual fear and withdrawal; defiant competition with men, and possibly homosexuality; or the happy resolution in which she switched affection from her mother to her father, changed her libidinal object from female to male, repressed her "masculine, active, clitoral sexuality," and finally accepted an infant, particularly a male infant, as a substitute for the phallus. Freud thus modeled his theory of female sexual identity on the woman's difference from the male. But he did not consider the importance for female identity of the daughter's similarity to the mother. Although in his later work Freud recognized that mother-infant bonding in the pre-Oedipal phase (the term for the period of exclusive attachment to the mother) might have a significant and possibly a determining influence on the construction of femininity, he also believed that this phase was almost impossible to uncover in analytic practice, that it was "grey with age and shadowy," like the buried civilization of the Minoans behind the civilization of Greece.[10]

For a brief period, from about 1925 to 1935, there was an intense debate within the psychoanalytic movement on the question of femininity, female sexuality, and the psychology of women. This came about in part because Freud encouraged female rather than male disciples after 1924. Yet one historian has argued that Freud sought out surrogate daughters because they were "less difficult and competitive" than men.[11] Paradoxically, it was often female analysts, such as Helene Deutsch, Ruth Mack Brunswick, Jeanne Lampl–de Groot, and Marie Bonaparte, who (despite their differences) sided with Freud, while some male analysts, such as Ernest Jones and Carl Muller-Braunschweig, disagreed with Freud's fundamental assumptions about feminine psychology as a defective version of masculine psychic development.

The leading figure in this debate was the German analyst Karen Horney (1885–1952). In a series of powerful papers written between 1926 and 1935, Horney challenged the basic tenets of Freudian psychoanalysis with regard to women. She described psychoanalysis as a male-dominated and androcentric discipline, "the creation of a male genius," in which the psychology of women had necessarily "been considered only from the point of view of men." Horney stressed the sociocultural influence on female psychology, "the actual disadvantages under which women labor in social life"; the role of male fantasy in the construction of feminine "nature" and of "male narcissism" in such psychoanalytic concepts as penis envy.[12] Speaking not only from her psychoanalytic training but also from her experience as the mother of three children, she argued that Freud had overlooked the importance of motherhood in female psychology, and the significance of men's envy of pregnancy, childbirth, suckling, and mothering.

Yet in the 1930s, after she moved from Berlin to the United States, Horney ended her quarrel with Freud; she dropped the subject of feminine psychology and turned to investigating the problems of marriage. The feminist historian Dee Garrison has speculated that the shift was partly Horney's response to problems in her own marriage, and partly her prudence in abandoning a dangerously controversial position. Women analysts, moreover, were handicapped by the absence of a feminist movement that could help them articulate a collective position.[13] As female dissidents were marginalized or converted by the Freudian community, which pressed for internal cohesion and solidarity, the feminist discourse within psychoanalysis collapsed, and was not revived until the 1970s, when important studies of the pre-Oedipal phase and its implications for female development by Nancy Chodorow, Margaret Mahler, and Carol Gilligan, among others, reopened the field to feminist analysis.

The English women analysts, meanwhile, tended to avoid the debate over female psychology altogether. Low, Payne, and Isaacs concentrated on work with children and on the training and teaching of other analysts. Rivière and Strachey took responsibility for translating Freud's work into English, both through the *International Journal of Psychoanalysis* and through the Hogarth Press edition of Freud's collected works. Sharpe, who had been an English teacher before she trained with Jessie Murray's clinic, devoted herself to psychoanalytic readings of literature, especially Shakespeare. The most influential woman in the British Psycho-Analytical Society, Melanie Klein, did break with Freud; but she, too, chose to specialize in an alternative psychoanalysis of children and infants, which ignored the woman question. As Juliet Mitchell has noted, although Klein drew attention to the importance of the mother-child relation and the pre-Oedipal phase, the Kleinian school "avoided contributing anything really new or specific to the understanding of feminine psychology."[14]

Over all, the fields that became the special purview of women psychoanalysts in England during the 1920s and 1930s—child psychiatry, mother-child relations, literary criticism, translation, and pedagogy—can be seen as defenses against orthodox Freudian charges of the "masculinity complex." In a sense, the women analysts in the British Psycho-Analytical Society assumed roles within the discipline and the profession that were extensions of their prewar feminine roles, and that were not a threat to the Society itself—run "in a patriarchal manner," as one woman recalled, by Ernest Jones and Edward Glover.[15]

Just as there were few changes in the theoretical view of female insanity within the profession, so too with regard to the treatment of female insanity in asylums and mental institutions, neither psychoanalysis nor the lessons of the war had much effect. Moreover, the employment of forty women doctors in British mental hospitals was ultimately insignificant. They had little impact on the traditional structure of these institutions.

Octavia Wilberforce (1888–1963), who later became Virginia Woolf's physician, was one of the pioneering English women doctors who worked in mental institutions. With the support of the feminist writer Elizabeth Robins, she had defied her family and qualified as a physician in 1920, and at the beginning of her career she worked for a few weeks at Graylingwell Mental Hospital in Chichester. Wilberforce divided the responsibility for three hundred women patients with one other doctor, and she wrote up reports on six of them each day. As the first woman doctor to work in the hospital, she faced the suspicion of both nurses and patients: "Before I came they were all very agitated and *hated* the thought of a woman Dr." But her enthusiasm, her interest in the patients, and her forthrightness with the nursing staff won them all over.

Despite good intentions, the overworked staff had few resources—intellectual, medical, or psychological—for dealing with withdrawn, or even worse, violent women patients. Because her stay at Graylingwell was brief, Wilberforce did not have time to become discouraged by her work. She found it a challenge to persuade patients to exercise and eat by addressing them politely and treating them like adults. Despite the demands on her time, she listened to the women's worries and talked to them often, urging one to play the piano, another to remember her happy memories. "This place is going to make *me* a very good conversationalist," she noted. Wilberforce also thought about the reasons for the women's behavior. She observed that many were former governesses. "Why should teaching send you dotty? Continual hard work, no future, no ambitions, *bad pay,* eh?" The worst cases seemed to be "the inelastic conservative governesses in *military families*"; and Wilberforce quickly perceived the connection between women's economic dependence and oppression, and mental breakdown: "As you see, I hold the view that it's quite a presentable complaint in *many* instances. Were slaves ever mad? What about its being *mentally unhealthy* to be the underdog? Socialism is needed." Wilberforce interpreted the patients' symptoms too in terms of the restrictions and anxieties of the female role. Among the women were "a good number of folk whose husbands have been unfaithful." Many patients were angry and abusive: "It's interesting, isn't it, that women use worse language and are more obscene than men? Why? 'Cos they've been taught to repress it always." When she left Graylingwell, Wilberforce felt that she had "done *quite good spade work* here for any future women who might like to come," and that being there "was the best thing that could have happened to me."[16] She had bolstered her own self-confidence, won the nurses' respect, and shown them how to handle the women patients with dignity and good humor.

But Wilberforce's optimism was contradicted by the resistance of old-fashioned asylums to applying new ideas to the treatment of female mental patients. In 1922, the novelist Antonia White had a serious mental breakdown and spent ten harrowing months in Bethlem, where she was forcibly fed, heavily drugged, straitjacketed, put in a padded cell, and tied down to her bed. In her novel *Beyond the Glass* (1954), White described her memories of the asylum, which retained its Victorian ambience—"wax flowers under cases, and engravings of Queen Victoria and Balmoral"—as well as its pre-Victorian harshness: "She woke up in a small bare cell. The walls were whitewashed and dirty, and she was lying on a mattress on the floor, without sheets, with only rough, red-striped blankets over her. She was wearing a linen gown, like an old-fashioned nightshirt, and she was bitterly cold."[17] The enlightened thinking that had made Sassoon's stay at Craiglockhart so comfortable did not extend beyond a few privileged institutions.

Many women's inmate narratives contrast the male psychiatrists—uncomprehending, patronizing, hurried, even cruel—with the comforting and maternal woman doctor. But despite official acceptance of women doctors in English mental hospitals, they remained a powerless minority. Thus, Mary Cecil met "a lady doctor, very kind and interested, not so detached as the men," whom everyone on the ward liked and respected. But she was quickly replaced by another man.[18] Moreover, Colney Hatch did not hire even one woman doctor until World War II. As late as 1964, Morag Coate laments in *Beyond All Reason,* "women psychiatrists in mental hospitals are such a rare species that I have scarcely ever met them."[19]

During the postwar period, the female malady, no longer linked to hysteria, assumed a new clinical form: schizophrenia. And whereas psychoanalysis rarely treated schizophrenia, confining itself to the neuroses, traditional medical psychiatry here came into its own.

The psychotic syndrome of schizophrenia was defined around the turn of the century in the work of Emil Kraepelin and Eugen Bleuler. In 1896, Kraepelin's model of "dementia praecox" emphasized the qualities of listlessness, vacancy, and withdrawal in the patient, a "peculiar and fundamental want of any *strong feeling of the impressions of life.*" Typically stricken in late adolescence, the patient rapidly deteriorated through hallucinations and delusions to dementia. In 1911, Kraepelin's theory was modified by Bleuler, who proposed the term "schizophrenia" ("split mind"). He saw the chief issue as the split between thoughts and emotions, and described four symptoms that characterized the schizophrenic disorder: lack of affect, disturbed associations, autism, and ambivalence. Schizophrenics who were untreated eventually lost all emotional responsiveness:

> They sit about the institutions to which they are confined with expressionless faces, hunched-up, the image of indifference. They permit themselves to be dressed and undressed like automatons, to be led from their customary place of inactivity to the messhall, and back again, without expressing any sign of satisfaction or dissatisfaction.[20]

Still the most baffling, controversial, and malignant of the psychoses, schizophrenia has, since Bleuler's time, been extended to cover a vast assortment of odd behaviors, cultural maladjustments, and political deviations, from shabbily dressed bag ladies to Soviet dissident writers. In England, diagnostic criteria have been relatively conservative, following the outline endorsed by the World Health Organization in 1973, which includes auditory hallucinations, delusions, and episodes of passivity in which the individual feels his thoughts or impulses to be under external control. There are disputes over whether schizophrenia is an organic disease, caused by biochemical and genetic disfunctions, or a social disease caused by the breakdown of relationships between an individual and his milieu; but there is a growing consensus that schizophrenia encompasses several different disorders rather than a single phenomenon with a single cause.

Schizophrenia offers a remarkable example of the cultural conflation of femininity and insanity. First of all, unlike hysteria, anorexia nervosa, or depression, schizophrenia is clinically and statistically *not* a predominantly female mental disorder. Most studies seem to show that the incidence is about equal in women and men.[21] Nevertheless, schizophrenia does carry gender-specific meanings. The best-known studies of the inner life of the schizophrenic—Marguerite Sechaye's *Autobiography of a Schizophrenic Girl,* Barbara O'Brien's *Operators and Things,* and Hannah Green's *I Never Promised You a Rose Garden*—have female protagonists.[22] Moreover, the schizophrenic woman has become as central a cultural figure for the twentieth century as the hysteric was for the nineteenth. Modernist literary movements have appropriated the schizophrenic woman as the symbol of linguistic, religious, and sexual breakdown and rebellion. In surrealist texts, such as André Breton's *Nadja* (1928), in

Yeats's "Crazy Jane" poems of the 1930s, and in Jean Giraudoux's *The Madwoman of Chaillot* (1945), psychotic women become the artist's muse, and speak for a revolutionary potential repressed in the society at large. Films such as Ingmar Bergman's *Persona* and *Through a Glass Darkly,* Robert Altman's *Images,* Richard Benner's *Outrageous,* and John Cassavetes' *A Woman Under the Influence* also use the female schizophrenic as symbol.

Most significantly, the treatments for schizophrenia have strong symbolic associations with feminization and with the female role. From the 1930s to the 1950s, the main English treatments for schizophrenia were insulin shock, electroshock, and lobotomy. Although serious questions have been raised about the effectiveness and the ethics of all three, none has been completely discredited, and all are still in active, if diminished, use today. In the case of each, women are both statistically and representationally predominant as patients.

The medical rationale for the shock treatments which were invented in the 1930s originated in the belief that the grand-mal convulsions of epilepsy were biologically antagonistic to schizophrenia, and that one disorder could be prevented or cured by inducing the symptoms of the other. In insulin therapy, developed by the Viennese psychiatrist Manfred Sakel (1900–1957), schizophrenic patients were given injections of insulin to reduce their blood-sugar level and to induce hypoglycemic shock, which produced convulsions or a coma. After twenty minutes to an hour they were revived by the intravenous injection of glucose. A course of treatment involved anywhere from thirty to ninety shocks. Under insulin therapy, patients also gained twenty to sixty pounds, and in this respect for women this prolonged and very controlling treatment seemed to parallel the pseudopregnancy of the rest cure. It also had effects on the patient's memory. Among Sakel's early cases was a schoolteacher who had developed an "obsessive" love for her superintendent. After insulin shock, she briefly forgot her imaginary love affair, but permanently lost her ability to teach.[23]

Insulin-shock treatment was brought to England by a Viennese doctor who worked in a private mental hospital, Moorcraft House. In November 1938, two English psychiatrists, William Sargent and Russell Fraser, began to use insulin shock at the Maudsley Hospital to induce deep comas in schizophrenic patients.[24] Insulin was administered by female nurses on the wards, and had emotional connotations of infantilization. After receiving her injection, the patient was put to bed to wait for the coma. For some, the worst part was waiting for the several days it initially took for the insulin level to produce a reaction, listening to the hoarse animal cries of the other comatose women, knowing they too would slobber or grunt, wet the bed, and become ugly and grotesque; and seeing afterwards in the ward each "flushed or chalky face stamped with a sort of nullity." Being revived from an insulin coma, as Mary Cecil recalls, was a peculiarly slow and humiliating rebirth: "I tried to address a nurse who looked in, and to my horror heard only unintelligible sounds. The bedtable was pushed across and my nightgown handed to me. I changed into it with clumsy movements. It took a long time. I handled the spoon like a baby; it kept going the opposite way on the plate and then missing my mouth. I wept with shame."[25]

There were other aspects of insulin therapy, however, such as the daily hot baths, the personal attention, the diet of sugar and starch, that suggested surrogate mothering; and the infantile regression that Mary Cecil found so degrading was seen by some doctors as part of the cure. William Sargent reports that one hospital unit recommended that nurses with big breasts should have charge of the treatment so that when the patient came out of the coma, "he or she was greeted on rebirth with this invitingly maternal sight."[26]

Electroconvulsive therapy, or ECT, was developed by an Italian researcher, Ugo Cerletti, who did his first experiments on pigs in the Rome slaughterhouse. It was first administered to human subjects in 1938, and over the next two decades became established as the major physical treatment for schizophrenia and depression. Early in 1940, electric shock was introduced to England by two neurologists in Bristol. Shortly after, Drs. E. A. Straus and W. Macphail were treating patients at St. Bartholomew's Hospital in London with their own shock machine. Although the London County Council at first refused to buy electric-shock machines for its hospitals, ECT was soon widely used throughout England. In the early days of ECT, before the advent of muscle-relaxant drugs, the spasms produced by the current were so powerful that nurses had to hold the patient down, and fractures of the spine, arm, pelvis, or leg were not uncommon. At Colney Hatch, the occurrence of fractures among patients doubled in the late 1940s with the introduction of electroconvulsive treatment.[27]

In current practice, a patient receiving ECT does not eat for several hours before the treatment. He "lies on a bed or couch with the pillow removed and the usual precautions (e.g., removal of false teeth, spectacles, etc.) observed. He is then given an intravenous injection of a short-acting anaesthetic . . . and through the same needle, a dose of muscle relaxant. . . ." Respiration is controlled by an anaesthetist with a face mask and a pressure bag. When the patient is unconscious, "two electrodes, dampened with a bicarbonate solution to prevent skin burns at their points of contact, are applied to the anterior temporal areas of the scalp. . . . A gag is inserted in the patient's mouth to prevent him biting his tongue. An electric current, usually eighty volts . . . is given which results in a 'modified' convulsion. . . . After the convulsion, the gag is removed, the patient is turned on his side. . . . Within five to twenty minutes the patient gradually returns to full consciousness although he may feel sleepy. . . ."[28] Among the most frequently noted side effects are short-term and partial amnesias.

Although this clinical description of ECT, taken from a recent text by the psychiatrist Anthony Clare, uses the male pronoun, the available statistical evidence shows that in England and the United States women to this day outnumber men as ECT patients by a ratio of two or even three to one. Peter Breggin, an American doctor who has been a forceful opponent of ECT, argues that women more often receive this treatment because they "are judged to have less need of their brains." Much psychiatric literature on ECT, he maintains, recommends it for the less-skilled persons whose livelihoods are not dependent on the use of memory and intellect; housewives can be seen as excellent candidates on these terms. The "improvement" seen in their behavior after the treatment may simply reflect their greater tractability, or reflect the male bias in the profession that finds "mental incapacity and helpless dependence . . . far more acceptable in women than in men."[29]

The photographic and cinematic representation of ECT, moreover, almost always depicts a female patient. Following the iconographic conventions of the mesmerist and his subject, the vampire and his victim, Charcot and his hysteric, and the prison doctor and his suffragette, the representation of shock treatment too makes use of archetypal patterns of masculine dominance and feminine submission. In the photograph of ECT reproduced, for example, in a history of Cheadle Royal Hospital in Manchester (fig. 27), the anaesthetized woman is covered with a white sheet so that only her calm and beautiful face is seen. Leaning over her with a needle is the male doctor; the two women nurses, both older than the patient, are holding her down and manipulating the ugly arrangement of boxes and tubes. Insofar as gender defines the positions in the scene, the electroshock patient is always "feminine"—that is, even a male patient plays a feminine role.

Lobotomy is the most extreme and irreversible form of medical intervention in schizophrenia. In 1935, the Portuguese neurosurgeon Egas Moniz first developed a method of surgically severing portions of the brain to produce modifications in behavior. Experimenting on social misfits provided by the Portuguese government, Moniz developed a procedure he called "prefrontal lobotomy," which worked especially well on people with "anxiety-tension states" and "obsession syndromes." He believed he had discovered a treatment of revolutionary potential for the management of schizophrenics, alcoholics, homosexuals, and even political dissidents. Moniz, who has become one of Portugal's national heroes, received the Nobel Prize in 1949.[30]

The chief advocate and pioneer of lobotomy in the United States was Dr. Walter Freeman, the head of neurology at George Washington University. "The father of American lobotomy," Freeman developed a simplified surgical technique he called "transorbital lobotomy." The surgeon or psychiatrist entered the patient's brain under the eyelid with an icepicklike instrument, severing the nerves connecting the cortex with the thalamus. The operation could be performed in a few minutes,

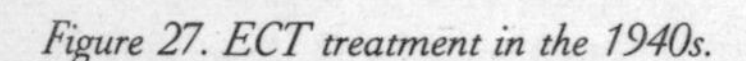

Figure 27. ECT treatment in the 1940s.

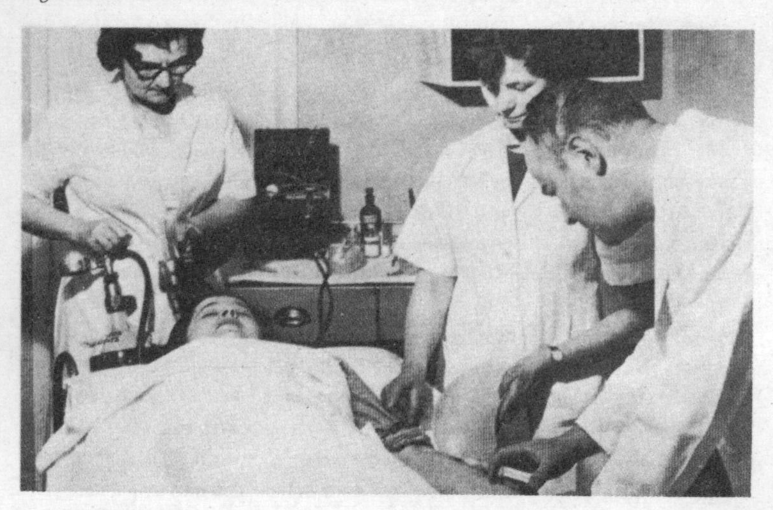

often with local anaesthetics.[31] In the 1940s Freeman traveled extensively in the United States, teaching his surgical method to doctors in state mental institutions and performing mass lobotomies himself. In West Virginia, on one memorable occasion, he lobotomized thirty-five women in one afternoon; in 1948, at Washington State Hospital, he lobotomized thirteen women, probably including the actress Frances Farmer. Although Freeman never confronted the issue of gender, most of the photographs in his textbook *Psychosurgery* show women before and after the operation.[32]

In 1939, William Sargent and Russell Fraser went to see Freeman and his colleague, the neurosurgeon James Watts, and examined three of his postoperative patients: a chronic alcoholic, a chronic depressive, and a chronic schizophrenic. The alcoholic was enthusiastic about the operation; now, he claimed, he could get twice as drunk on half as much whiskey. The depressive was much less inhibited about telling people when she was angry or resentful, and felt remarkably better. The schizophrenic (predictably female) could still hear threatening voices but refused to let them bother her. Sargent and Fraser realized that lobotomy did not cure her schizophrenia, only her anxiety; but they were eager to take it back to England in a modified form, called leucotomy.

For Sargent, a zealous advocate of physical treatment for mental disorder, any medical or governmental effort to prevent his experimentation on patients was a pointless frustration or "irksome restraint" to be circumvented or outwitted. As he triumphantly notes in his memoir, he and Fraser "generally got our own way in the end." In order to perform lobotomies, or leucotomies, which were banned by the London County Council (LCC), he and Eliot Slater collaborated on a ruse to get their patients transferred from Belmont Hospital to St. George's, a teaching hospital where the LCC prohibitions did not apply. Through this trick they were able to perform several leucotomies and to experiment with different forms of the operation.[33] During a sabbatical year in the United States, however, Sargent was outraged when he was prevented by the Veterans' Hospital Administration in Washington from lobotomizing fifty black schizophrenic patients at the Tuskegee Hospital in Alabama as part of another experiment.

Like electroshock, lobotomy is a treatment more frequently recommended for and performed on women. Since 1941 the majority of the 15,000 lobotomies performed in England have been on women: "Psychosurgeons consider that the operation is potentially more effective with women because it is easier for them to assume or resume the role of a housewife."[34] Two-thirds of all patients lobotomized were schizophrenics. At the Glasgow Royal Hospital, when R. D. Laing was psychiatric resident there in the 1950s, chronic female schizophrenics were given baths and electroshock once a week. Every once in a while, Laing has recalled, "a neurosurgeon would turn up . . . patients would line up," and he would perform lobotomies on all of them.[35] Sargent and Slater's widely used English psychiatric textbook published in 1972 recommends psychosurgery for a depressed woman "who may owe her illness to a psychopathic husband who cannot change and will not accept treatment." When separation is ruled out by the patient's religious convictions or by her "financial or emotional dependence" and when antidepressant drugs do not work, the authors suggest that a lobotomy will enable the woman to cope with her marriage.[36]

These cultural and medical associations of schizophrenia and femininity were given a particular interpretation in the very extensive English women's literature dealing with madness, institutionalization, and shock. In scores of literary and journalistic works produced between 1920 and the early 1960s, from inmate narratives protesting against the asylum to autobiographical novels and poems, schizophrenia became the bitter metaphor through which English women defined their cultural situation. Individually and collectively, these narratives provide the woman's witness so marginal or absent in the nineteenth-century discourse on madness; they give us a different perspective on the asylum, on the psychiatrist, and on madness itself; and they transform the experiences of shock, psychosurgery, and chemotherapy into symbolic episodes of punishment for intellectual ambition, domestic defiance, and sexual autonomy.

Beginning with Rachel Grant-Smith's *Experiences of an Asylum Patient* in 1922, most of this literature is set in the female wards of ironically named asylums: Gardenwell, Scott-Haven, Nazareth, Heartbreak House. As Ellen Moers has observed, the insane asylum is the contemporary locale of the female Gothic novel. In these stories, "the asylum itself becomes . . . an elaborated, enclosed, and peculiarly feminine testing ground for survival. There are the large, spreading, mysteriously complicated buildings; the harsh guards and strange rules; the terrifying inmates; the privations, restraints, and interrogations; the well-meant but indubitable torture of electric shock treatment."[37]

Few of the twentieth-century narratives before the 1960s, however, attempt anything like Mary Wollstonecraft's feminist protest against the wrongs of women, except perhaps in the discussion of shock. They are guilt-ridden accounts of institutionalization as a punishment for transgressing the codes of feminine behavior, docility, and affection. Unlike the representation of madwomen in male texts of the same period, they do not romanticize madness. "It is seldom," writes Janet Frame in *Faces in the Water,* "the easy Opheliana recited like the pages of a seed catalog, or the outpouring of Crazy Janes who provide, in fiction, an outlet for poetic abandon. Few of the people who roamed the dayroom would have qualified as acceptable heroines in popular taste."[38]

For women writers, Alice's journey through the looking glass is a more apt analogy than Ophelia's decline for the transition from sanity to schizophrenia, an allusion from the nursery world which the infantilization of the institution brings readily to mind. Mary Cecil called her memoir *Through the Looking Glass.* In Antonia White's *Beyond the Glass,* Clara Batchelor, coming to her senses in a mental hospital she calls the "House of Mirrors," watches several women patients playing a topsy-turvy game of croquet: "Her first thought was 'Alice in Wonderland again. They might as well play with hedgehogs and flamingoes.' But the next moment it came to her. These women were mad. . . . She was imprisoned in a place full of mad people."[39]

The asylums are indeed confusing places, secretive prisons operated on Wonderland logic. Their female inmates are instructed to regard themselves as "naughty girls" who have broken a set of mysterious rules that have to do with feminine conduct. "What *kind* of hospital am I in?" asks Helen in Antonia White's "The House of Clouds." "A hospital for girls who ask too many questions and need to give their brains a rest," the nurse replies; "Now go to sleep." "What shall I do?" cries another woman on a ward called Sixes and Sevens. "I'm wicked . . . I've broken my word . . . I *promised* my husband I'd get better."[40]

In the asylums, the symptoms of schizophrenia reflect specifically female anxieties. In Maude Harrison's novel *Spinner's Lake* (1941), a schizophrenic's voices torment her with her status: "Of course women go mad in far greater numbers than men, especially the unmarried ones, my dear."[41] Within the looking-glass house of the asylum, moreover, the female body, in all of its phases from puberty to senility, is always on display. In the communal bath, women gaze "curiously at one another's bodies, at the pendulous bellies and tired breasts, the faded wisps of body hair, the unwieldy and the supple shapes that form to women the nagging and perpetual 'withness' of their flesh."[42] The "withness" of the flesh, and its proper management, adornment, and disposition, are a crucial and repeated motif in the schizophrenic women's sense of themselves as unoccupied bodies. Feeling that they have no secure identities, the women look to external appearances for confirmation that they exist. Thus they continually look at their faces in the mirror, but out of desperation rather than narcissism.

The abyss that opens between the schizophrenic's body and mind, however, can be seen as an exaggeration of women's "normal" state. The art historian John Berger has suggested that woman's psyche is split in two by her constructed awareness of herself as a visual object and her resulting double role as actor and spectator. "A woman must continually watch herself," Berger says in *Ways of Seeing.*

> She is almost continually accompanied by her own image of herself. Whilst she is walking across a room or whilst she is weeping at the death of her father, she can scarcely avoid watching herself walking or weeping. From earliest childhood she has been taught and persuaded to survey herself continually.
>
> And so she comes to consider the *surveyor* and the *surveyed* within her as the two constituent yet always distinct elements of her identity as a woman.[43]

In the asylums, too, women are encouraged, persuaded, and taught to become surveyors, to "watch themselves being looked at," and to make themselves attractive objects being surveyed. In their make-up from the ward box with its "stump of lipstick," and "box of blossom-pink powder," the patients at one asylum dance, Janet Frame sardonically observes, "looked like stage whores."[44] As in the nineteenth century, female sanity is measured against a detailed standard of grooming and dress. In fact, as one American psychiatrist in the 1930s jovially remarked, "the 'female of the species' never becomes too psychotic to enjoy her visits to the Beauty Shop."[45] Evaluating chronic female schizophrenics in English mental hospitals in the 1960s, J. W. Wing and G. W. Brown noted that although Mapperley Patient No. 5 had "attractively styled hair," she wore too much make-up, had it "slightly smeared on her nose—and her powder was not uniformly applied." As in Victorian asylums, women were also censured for too *much* concern for physical appearance. Veronica A., for example, had appropriate make-up and had learned to style her hair to conceal her lobotomy scars, but her home visits were a failure because it took her three hours to get dressed.[46]

It is not surprising that in the female narrative the hectoring spirit of the auditory hallucination, the loquacious demon who jeers, judges, commands, and controls schizophrenics, is almost invariably male. He delivers the running critique of appearance and performance that the woman has grown up with as a part of her stream of consciousness; but in psychosis, the assessing voice of the surveyor becomes the voice of the Other, an actual voice that she no longer recognizes as part of herself. Frequently, too, the dictatorial voice of the "surveyor" is echoed by that of the male therapist. Having wrestled with the nagging, wheedling, abusing spirit she calls her "resident," for example, Mary Cecil meets an equally hostile psychiatrist: " 'Been behaving very oddly indeed, haven't you?' he thundered contemptuously in exactly the jargon of my resident who was now joining in."[47] The doctors, the demons, and the fathers begin to sound alike; their voices merge in a chorus of condemnation.

As this example suggests, schizophrenic symptoms of passivity, depersonalization, disembodiment, and fragmentation have parallels in the social situation of women. Some feminist critics have maintained that schizophrenia is the perfect literary metaphor for the female condition, expressive of women's lack of confidence, dependency on external, often masculine, definitions of the self, split between the body as sexual object and the mind as subject, and vulnerability to conflicting social messages about femininity and maturity.[48]

These parallels between schizophrenia and female identity were developed most fully in three important women's autobiographical novels of the 1960s: Jennifer Dawson's *The Ha-Ha* (1961), Janet Frame's *Faces in the Water* (1961), and Sylvia Plath's *The Bell Jar* (1963). While the earlier novels did not question the idea that madness was the woman's own fault, these novels place the blame for women's schizophrenic breakdowns on the limited and oppressive roles offered to women in modern society, and deal very specifically with institutionalization and shock treatment as metaphors for the social control of women.

Jennifer Dawson's *The Ha-Ha* is a moving and neglected novel that criticizes the marginal social roles of educated women in England in the mid-1950s. The narrator, Josephine Traughton, is an intelligent and imaginative Oxford scholarship student with an eccentric, overprotective mother. Stifled by the fusty decorum her widowed mother imposes on their household, Josephine has always been a lonely outsider. At Oxford, she is painfully aware that she is wearing the wrong clothes, that she does not know the social rules, that she cannot play the required conversational games. And while she is absorbed in books, her women classmates seem to be marking time until they can marry and vegetate. "Tony says I'm almost a cabbage already," says one with a pleased and happy look. "So much for the higher education of women."[49] As Dawson commented in 1985, "*The Ha-Ha* was written during another lull . . . in the feminist movement." For many young women, Oxford "was still a superior kind of finishing school. Others were there on sufferance, guiltily in a house that had been the man's for nearly eight hundred years."[50] Unable to adapt to the social codes of femininity in this patriarchal world, Josephine invents a world of her own to which she can retreat, populated by exotic and comic animals. When her mother dies suddenly, Josephine has a breakdown and is committed to a mental hospital, "Gardenwell Park," where the insane are kindly herded like the zoo animals of her fantasies.

Diagnosed as a schizophrenic, Josephine is treated with insulin and befriended by the motherly ward nurse. But dependence on controlling maternal figures is one of her problems. She is finally shocked into maturity and a kind of sanity when she is seduced and then abandoned by another patient, an ex-medical student with a history of impotence and bad relationships with women. Alisdair demands that she recognize repressed hatred for her mother, and relief at her mother's death, as the source of her illness. His prescription for her schizophrenia is sex, which conveniently cures his "performance anxiety" and does him "lots of good." Josephine, however, feels "slightly sick": "It did not surprise me that I did not enjoy it. I had not expected pleasure, only some contact with the real world, and that I had found. Only my head felt odd, as though it were not mine, and the world seemed farther, not nearer."[51]

When Alisdair deserts her with only a thank-you note, Josephine runs away from the hospital and lets herself be picked up by a variety of men. But she is brought back by the police under certificate and given ECT, which she regards as a punishment for her sexual experimentation. Her sexuality is as much of a problem as her intelligence; both must be managed according to the rules of the hospital, which are like the rules of middle-class society. In order to get out of the hospital, Josephine realizes, she must learn all "the rules of what to do and what to say," to have "the corners rubbed off." This means joining in the sing-song around the ward piano, knitting sweaters in occupational therapy, playing cards with the other women, keeping a bright smile for the superintendent, and growing fat and dull. Looking into the mirror, Josephine sees that she has become a grotesque image of female passivity: "There was the grey skirt and pink jumper strapped about me, and the shoes bolted on. And above them was the face, heavy, puffy, quilted; the eyes too small and almost sealed down in the eyelids; the expression blank and shut-down. . . . I could only giggle and eat too much and knit cardigans and follow the routine of little things that kept the momentous things out." Rather than remain a rule-follower all her life and become "a rubberized old woman, immune to all hope and fear and illusion," Josephine decides to escape and to take her chances with madness. The novel ends with her climbing over the hospital wall and running "until I knew for certain that I had not been extinguished, and that my existence had been saved."[52]

While *The Ha-Ha* anticipated the feminist movement in seeing mental institutions as environments in which deviants from conventional feminine roles were forced to conform, Dawson does not romanticize madness as prophetic insight. "I was lucky to have written *The Ha-Ha* before being influenced by the ideas of the mid-sixties," she wrote. Indeed, in 1961, Dawson recalled, "very few people thought that mental disturbance had any social meaning, or political, as opposed to cultural, interest. It was [not] associated with . . . women with bad feet on the assembly line or in the home. Here it was something to be kept hidden; to keep quiet about. A few pained and painful letters which I later received from women made me surprised at the damp cellar of guilt."[53]

In her autobiography *An Angel at My Table* (1984), the novelist Janet Frame has explained how in her early twenties, as a lonely, imaginative university student, she was diagnosed as schizophrenic; how she read up on the disease and consciously played the role of schizophrenic, inventing hallucinations and fantasies in order to win the attention of a young male professor who was fascinated by psychology and art; and how she was finally committed to a series of mental institutions in which she spent eight years of her life, underwent over two hundred electroshock treatments, and nearly had a lobotomy. Unable to escape from the asylum, she was released only when she published a book of poems that won a literary award.[54]

These events are recounted in Frame's novel *Faces in the Water,* structured around the experience of shock treatment, which she, like Dawson, connects with the enforcement of feminine conformity. Her heroine, Istina Mavet, sees ECT as "the new and fashionable means of quieting people and of making them realize that orders are to be obeyed and floors are to be polished without anyone protesting and faces are made to be fixed into smiles and weeping is a crime."[55]

An anomaly in her family, stubbornly intellectual and unfeminine, resistant even to shock treatment in the asylum, Istina is finally told that her "personality [has] been condemned, like a slum dwelling." The lobotomy, she is assured, will make her a happier and more successful woman. "With your personality changed," she is told, "no one will dream you were what you were." She will be able to leave the hospital and get a job selling hats or working in an office; she can wear a lobotomy scarf on her head, with a butterfly bow at the top, and she "will never regret having had a lobotomy." Frame's asylums are only too clearly places where thinking women are executed and replaced by clockwork dolls, their minds "cut and tailored to the ways of the world."[56]

Of all these novels, Sylvia Plath's *The Bell Jar* offers the most complex account of schizophrenia as a protest against the feminine mystique of the 1950s. In the first part of the novel, Plath's autobiographical heroine, Esther Greenwood, is spending the summer of 1953 in New York as a college guest editor for a fashionable women's magazine. A brilliant student and an aspiring poet, Esther feels lost and displaced among the sexual sophisticates, prom queens, and future homemakers who are her fellow editors. She enters a depressive spiral in which none of the alternatives available to educated women seems satisfactory. Career women, like her editor-in-chief or the professors at her college, seem sexless and even freakish. Housewives, like her boyfriend's mother, seem defeated and servile. Esther feels most keenly that she is trapped by her sexuality, that if she experiments she will be trapped by marriage and children. Motherhood and writing, she believes, are incompatible. Esther's sense of an absolute division between her creativity and her femininity is the basis of her schizophrenia. And her frustration precisely reflects the values endorsed even by liberals for intellectual women in the mid-1950s. At Sylvia Plath's Smith graduation in 1955, for example, Adlai Stevenson exhorted her class to write "laundry lists" rather than poems.[57]

While Esther Greenwood is a less accomplished and forceful person than Plath herself was at twenty, the novel goes on to follow the events of the summer in which Plath attempted suicide and then spent several months in a private mental hospital where she was treated with insulin and ECT. For several years after, Plath had tried to bury her memories of breakdown, institutionalization, and shock treatment. From the perspective of her family, especially her widowed mother, these experiences were shameful and should be forgotten. But in terms of her identity as a poet, Plath came more and more to view her recovery from madness through shock treatment as a poetic rebirth in which the split between the feminine and the creative selves was resolved. In her journals in the late 1950s, she wrote detailed descriptions of her shock treatment, describing "the deadly sleep of her madness, and . . . waking to a new world, with no name, being born again, and not of woman."[58] In her poetry, Plath mythologized ECT as a possession by a male god who is also the Muse. "By the roots of my hair some god got hold of me," she wrote in "The Hanging Man"; "I sizzled in his blue volts like a desert prophet." To be seized by this electric god was to be born again only of *man,* fathered rather than mothered, and thus, in Plath's imagination, purged of the inheritance of feminine vulnerability. The woman artist achieves her freedom and sanity, Plath seems to argue, by transcending ordinary womanhood not just through madness but also through the terrifying and redemptive ordeal of ECT.

Why should Plath have identified this act of purgation and rebirth with electroshock treatment? First of all, ECT has the trappings of a powerful religious ritual, conducted by a priestly masculine figure. The procedure itself, as Joseph Berke has pointed out, is "invested with magic and fantasy. The apparatus of anaesthesia, the small black box covered with dials and buttons, the electrodes attached to the head, everything is charged with significance for both patients and professional staff." Furthermore, the magic of ECT, according to Berke, comes from its imitation of a death and rebirth ceremony. For the patient it represents a rite of passage in which the doctor kills off the "bad" crazy self, and resurrects the "good" self. For this reason, suicidal patients are often comforted by ECT; upon awakening, they feel that in a sense they have died and been born again, with the hated parts of the self annihilated—literally, electrocuted.[59]

The Bell Jar makes a number of metaphorical connections between electricity and death, but Plath also connects this theme to female sexuality and creativity. The novel begins in "the summer they electrocuted the Rosenbergs"; political dissidence and sexual dissidence both will be punished electrically. And while shock treatment may lead to renewal, it is also painful and controlled by men. In this respect, it is like sex. When a man first touches Esther's hair, "a little electric shock" flares through her; her first experience of intercourse produces "a sharp, startlingly bad pain." Childbirth too is like electrotherapy; Esther watches a drugged woman give birth "on a bed like some awful torture table, with . . . all sorts of instruments and wires and tubes." Women have become passive objects in these rituals; as a medical student remarks in the delivery room, "They oughtn't to let women watch."

In order to become creative, active, and free in a social milieu that denies these options to women, Esther must symbolically destroy the female side of her psyche, the side controlled by sexual need, maternal pieties, and social conventions. The paradox of the novel, then, is that a woman can free herself from the constraints of schizophrenic womanhood only by denying her solidarity and emotional bonds with other women. We see this process dramatized in *The Bell Jar.* After her first insulin shock treatment, Esther tells her psychiatrist that she hates her mother. After her first electroshock treatment in the hospital, she looks coldly upon her women friends in the ward, noting that they are too ugly and sour to hold a man's interest. Although she often feels closer to women than to men, when she accidentally walks in on two women in bed together, Esther is disgusted and harshly condemning. On the eve of her discharge from the hospital, Joan, the lesbian who is Esther's alter ego in the novel, kills herself. Esther's graduation from the asylum thus comes at the price of her feminist double's death. Although she is reborn at the end of the book, "born twice—patched, retreaded, and approved for the road," she is certainly not reborn of woman.[60]

It is only fair to note that in the early 1960s, shock treatment was also a metaphor in men's writing. Yet the male literature of shock, such as Harold Pinter's *The Caretaker* (1960), Anthony Burgess's *A Clockwork Orange* (1962), and Ken Kesey's *One Flew over the Cuckoo's Nest* (1962), makes an instructive contrast to these female condemnations of psychiatric power. All of them represent shock treatment as a feminizing therapy. In Pinter's play, it turns the violent Aston into a slow-thinking, passive man who describes his accumulation of disjointed memories as "interior decoration."

Anthony Burgess's version of shock treatment is an Orwellian brainwashing called the Ludovico technique, a sadistic aversion therapy designed to restrain psychopathic aggression in young men. But the reconditioning of Burgess's teen-age hoodlum Alex becomes a political issue, and the government is forced by the public uproar against tampering with man's existential freedom to reverse the procedure and to re-educate Alex in robbery, rape, and the old ultra-violence. And in Ken Kesey's *One Flew over the Cuckoo's Nest* the social forces that are out to shock and tame the amoral, violent, sexually aggressive male are represented as feminine, embodied in the figure of Big Nurse. Kesey's novel, and the movie version in which Jack Nicholson gave another brilliant performance of the woman-hating man he has played in many films, might seem to be just a reversal of the women's narratives. But whereas women's accounts of institutionalization and treatment reflect their powerlessness in patriarchal institutions, Kesey's novel (and to some degree, Burgess's) is a disquieting fantasy of sexual violence against women, a fantasy rationalized by the fiction that women push the buttons and call the shots.

By the early 1960s, then, a very powerful female literature had grown up outside the medical journals and the psychiatric institutes, which presented schizophrenia and institutionalization as extremes of typical female experiences of passivity and confinement. The literature of schizophrenia would have a double impact. The feminist aspects were important in the early years of the women's liberation movement, which, in its reclamation of female "victims," made Plath, among others, a heroine. And the fascination with psychotic experience would influence the valorization of schizophrenia by R. D. Laing and the antipsychiatry movement.

9

WOMEN, MADNESS, AND THE FAMILY

R. D. Laing and the Culture of Antipsychiatry

Lucie Blair was a chronic schizophrenic who had spent twelve of her thirty-eight years in a mental hospital. She suffered from "vague and woolly thoughts," and from auditory hallucinations in which "people put unpleasant sexual ideas into her head." She was puzzled about the meaning of life and felt "tormented and torn to pieces." After giving birth to an illegitimate daughter, she had been sterilized. As a girl Lucie had wanted to be a professional musician, but her father had ridiculed her, and warned her that if she went out alone "she would be kidnapped, raped, or murdered." When she brought her friends home, her father made fun of them. "Women nowadays had got ideas about being independent, according to Mr. Blair. His daughter was made to be a gentlewoman. There had always been a place for her at home." He wanted his daughter to be "a pure, virginal, spinster."[1]

Lucie's story might have come from a novel by Antonia White or Sylvia Plath, but in fact it is the second case study in Aaron Esterson and R. D. Laing's *Sanity, Madness, and the Family* (1964). Esterson and Laing had chosen to study women between the ages of fifteen and forty who had been hospitalized as chronic schizophrenics, who had not had brain surgery, and who had "not received more than fifty electro-shocks in the year before the investigation and not more than one hundred and fifty in all."[2] They came up with only eleven cases.

These dramatized female plots, composed of taped interviews with the women and their families, demonstrated that the signs and symptoms of schizophrenia could be caused by the patient's unlivable situation in the home, as the parents (but more often the mother) contradicted and fought their daughter's efforts to achieve independence and autonomy. Laing and Esterson concluded that schizophrenia was not an organic disease to be treated with psychosurgery, drugs, and shock, but a social process that was comprehensible as a response to family "transactions" and "interactions." In transferring the onus of inadequacy from the schizophrenic to the family, Laing and Esterson announced a shift that had "historical significance no less radical than the shift from a demonological to a clinical viewpoint three hundred years ago."[3] And since the failed struggles of these sick women to free themselves from the puritanism and hypocrisy of their families was only an exaggeration of the crisis faced by normal daughters when they tried to separate from their families, *Sanity, Madness, and the Family* struck many women readers, not just as an exploration of schizophrenia, but as the story of their own lives.

David Cooper, a colleague of Laing's who named the new movement "antipsychiatry," connected it with an attack on psychiatric power in institutions, on the hierarchical authority structure of the doctor-patient relationship, on psychosurgery and shock treatment. Over all, he explained, antipsychiatry was an attempt to reverse the rules of the "psychiatric game," countering "medical power as embodied in the diagnosis . . . the secret dossier . . . [and] the system of compulsory detention" with "attentive non-interference aimed at the opening up of experience rather than its closing down."[4] According to the antipsychiatrists, mental illness had to be examined in terms of its social contexts: the emotional dynamics of the family and the institution of psychiatry itself.

The antipsychiatry movement was not limited to England. Laing's first books, appearing at the same time as Michel Foucault's *Histoire de la folie* in Paris and Erving Goffman's *Asylums* in the United States, were part of an international trend of renewed interest in the history of madness and the social institutions of psychiatry. The new views of madness as a social construct and of the asylum as a "total institution" —an enclosed, encompassing, regimented setting—were as much influenced by European structuralism and American communications research as by British psychiatric practice. One important source was the labeling theory of deviance proposed by the American sociologist Thomas Scheff, who held that the symptoms of mental illness were primarily "offenses against implicit understandings of particular cultures," forms of "residual rule-breaking" that, in being labeled as madness, were stabilized and fixed, launching the offender on a career as mental patient.[5] Nevertheless, London rather than Paris, Palo Alto, or New York became the center of psychopolitics. As Clancy Sigal exclaimed in his novel *Zone of the Interior*, "London was where it was all happening. London was the Vienna of the 1960s, the Havana of the schizophrenic revolution."[6]

For women, antipsychiatry seemed to offer important new ways of conceptualizing the relationship between madness and femininity. Labeling theory provided a way of looking at female insanity as the violation of sex-role expectations. Laingian theory interpreted female schizophrenia as the product of women's repression and oppression within the family. Madness itself became intelligible as a strategy, a form of communication in response to the contradictory messages and demands about femininity women faced in patriarchal society. Finally, schizophrenia could be seen as a form of protest against the female role. Laingian therapy not only listened to the woman's words, as psychoanalysis had done, but also attended to her social circumstances. And the brilliant and moving case studies in *Sanity, Madness, and the Family* promised a psychiatry responsive to the nuances of silence as well as to the systems of language.

But for all its promise, did radical antipsychiatry finally have any more to offer women than its predecessors, and did R. D. Laing, after his extraordinary debut, fulfill the expectations his studies had created? According to Juliet Mitchell, Laing's early work "helped to introduce a new phase of radical humanism to which the women's movement is heir."[7] Although he never directly discussed the connection of sex roles and schizophrenia, Laing's exposé of the assumptions about feminine dependence, passivity, chastity, dutifulness, obedience, and docility that governed the behavior of his eleven families towards their daughters gave feminists important ammunition in their analysis of women's oppression. But what of the therapy itself? And what of the personality and ideology of its central figure? What happens if we look at antipsychiatry from a feminist perspective?

The charismatic leadership of R. D. Laing gave English antipsychiatry a powerful spokesman; as one of his sharpest and most perceptive critics, Peter Sedgwick, has pointed out, "amid the succession of psychiatric prophets who compelled attention during the sixties and early seventies it was R. D. Laing who dominated the scene longest, as arch-seer and prophet-in-chief."[8] Like Conolly, Maudsley, and Rivers, Laing exemplified in his attitudes and in his career the psychiatric ideologies of his generation. With the publication of *The Divided Self* in 1960, he became the mentor of the counterculture in all of its political, psychedelic, mystical, and especially artistic manifestations. His books provided texts for the New Left, the drug culture, and the Eastern religious revival, as well as for the nascent women's movement. Laingian concepts of madness and sanity, the self, and the Other pervade some of the most important English writing of the decade. As Doris Lessing explained, Laing had become the "key authority figure" educated people looked to as a "law giver."[9] Lecturing in New York in 1972, Laing himself described his life as culturally representative: "It's just the story of a mid-twentieth century intellectual. I suppose I'm *one of the symptoms of the times.*"[10]

While Laing's insistence on the intelligibility of madness, his reformist attitudes, and his fascination with literature are reminiscent of Conolly, he especially admired Maudsley, and considered him the most brilliant of the English psychiatrists.[11] Like both Conolly and Maudsley, Laing has had a controversial career. No one who has written on Laing seems to know much about his life beyond the book jacket blurbs and publicity releases that make his professional training sound conventional and bland, and his career a series of abrupt and unmotivated conversions. Part of the problem, of course, is Laing's vagueness about his own past. "The first family to interest me was my own," he has remarked. "I still know less about it than I know about my other families."[12] His readers too know less about the Laings than about the Blairs, the Churches, the Danzigs, or any of the other families whose sanity and madness he so intimately revealed.

Yet piecing together the information scattered in different sources, we can reconstruct a fairly continuous story. Laing was born in 1927 in the Gorbals, the roughest, darkest, and most depressed district of Glasgow. Mysterious, even miraculous circumstances surrounded his birth, as he explains in his memoir *The Facts of Life* (1976). His parents were astonished that it occurred at all, since they slept in separate rooms, had long since ceased to have sexual intercourse, and swore they did not know how the child had been conceived. Laing's father kept the birth a secret for several days. His mother went into a "decline," and like Conolly and Maudsley, Laing was separated from her as a child. During infancy he was cared for by nurses who turned out to be drunken sluts. (Laing believes that the asthma from which he suffered all his life derives from this unpropitious infant experience.[13]) However, anyone who has read Otto Rank's *Myth of the Birth of the Hero,* a book from which Laing frequently quotes, will recognize that this miraculous story of a secret, even virgin, birth also places him in exalted company, with such heroes as Moses and Jesus. In Laing's personal version of the family romance, he was clearly destined for heroic action from the start.

To grow up in Glasgow in the 1930s, however, was to suffer the drab mixture of sexual repression, sodden respectability, and masculine violence made familiar by the working-class novels of Alan Sillitoe and John Wain. Laing remembers being beaten, "smashed to pieces" by his father when he was three; to escape his feelings of terror and rage, he practiced a naive form of meditation or mental withdrawal, which became an important psychological resource. Sex was shrouded in Victorian secrecy and taboo; his father gave him a tract on "self-abuse" and urged him to lead a clean life; his mother (whose bedroom he shared) told him that babies came from heaven, and fainted dead away when he innocently said "fucking" in her presence. Laing finally learned about sex from a book on venereal disease when he was sixteen.[14]

This childhood fraught with miscommunication, obfuscation, and denial might have made Laing a perfect case study for one of his own books. But unlike the sensitive victims of maddening families and binding environments he would later study, Laing assessed his talents and interests, formed (as Peter Mezan puts it) "a single-minded project to become a famous intellectual," and pursued it "with an indomitable tenacity."[15] He read the *Dictionary of National Biography* for models, taking special interest in the career of Havelock Ellis and vowing to publish his own first book, like Ellis, by the age of thirty. He learned to play the piano and even the clavichord so well that the family considered whether he might become a concert performer. He passed quickly through an adolescent religious conversion to a passionate agnosticism; by fourteen he defined his major interests as psychology, philosophy, and theology. A voracious reader of the Bible, Voltaire, Darwin, Mill, and Huxley at home, he had the advantages of an English classical education at school; by the time he was seventeen he was fluent in Greek and had read Plato, Aeschylus, Homer, and Sophocles. Few of Laing's contemporaries in any field could claim to be more literate or cultivated.

After attending the University of Glasgow—"largely a waste of time"—Laing decided on medical school because he thought it would give him "access to birth and death."[16] The experiences of those years —mystical as well as medical—are frequently cited in his books, and they show Laing's constant predilection for extreme experiences through which he could test his capacities for heroism. Like John Conolly (who also studied in Glasgow), Laing never felt comfortable with traditional medicine; medical training, he felt, was fragmented and hobbled by its efforts to achieve distance and scientific objectivity. During his psychiatric internship, Laing took physical and psychological risks in an effort to overcome distance from his patients. He mentally "tried on" the different psychoses "to see how they worked and felt." Another time he buried himself naked in the snow on a freezing night to see how far he could push his senses. He deliberately sought the sharp edge of mortality in dangerous mountain-climbing trips. Initially, psychoanalysis—rather than medical psychiatry—seemed to promise some genuine enlightenment: it was "the first lifting of the veil—the first detachment from the objects of consciousness to look at consciousness itself."[17] Freud became another in his pantheon of epic heroes who had descended to the Underworld, this time in the psyche, carrying with him "his theory as a Medusa's head which turned these terrors to stone." Laing's project, however, would be even more daring: to survive "without using a theory that is in some measure an instrument of defence."[18]

The most perilous area of psychiatric work was the world of the schizophrenic. From 1951 to 1956, first in an army hospital, then in Glasgow, Laing began to study schizophrenic patients. At Glasgow Royal Hospital, the same hospital where Conolly had begun, Laing worked with chronic female schizophrenics on the intractable ward.

These women were allowed "no personal possessions of any kind—no underwear, no stockings, no cosmetics, no books."[19] They wore cotton uniform dresses, were bathed and given ECT once a week, and received sporadic and impersonal medical attention. Laing decided to experiment with the twelve most hopeless patients on the wards, creating a special environment for them, and attempting to reach them through personalized therapy. All the patients improved so dramatically that they were released to their families—but within a year they were all back in the hospital.

This experience made him aware of the role played by the family network in the establishment of schizophrenia. He also realized the importance of the human bond, a kinship between "sane" therapist and "mad" patient which an institutionalized psychiatry too often replaced by power relations. In his contacts with American sociologists like Goffman who had studied asylums as total institutions, Laing began fully to understand how effective a force for social control benevolent institutionalization could be.

In the 1950s some English therapists were beginning to investigate the social contexts of psychosis. Laing's efforts to understand schizophrenic experience, to render it intelligible, and to rescue it from surgery and shock brought him to the attention of the psychiatric profession, and in 1956 he joined the staff of the Tavistock Clinic. There he worked with D. W. Winnicott, Melanie Klein, and Susan Isaacs, entered analysis with Charles Rycroft, and carried out research with Aaron Esterson. By the time Laing was in private therapeutic practice, he had also established a reputation with the radical community of London as a "good" psychiatrist, a working-class Marxist who was especially helpful to writers, because he would not interfere in his therapy with the strange knots, tangles, and binds that writers needed in order to create.[20]

Laing's works further established him as the psychiatric spokesman for intellectuals, artists, and radicals. His first book, *The Divided Self,* used the techniques and ideas of modernist literature and criticism to define a new theory of schizophrenia; its basic purpose, he wrote in the preface to the original edition in 1960, "is to make madness and the process of going mad, comprehensible."[21] While Laing soon regarded the book as too conventional (by 1964, he described it as the academic work of "an old young man," and by 1972, he thought it could be "filed away in a phenomenological museum as examples of how people were thinking in the Fifties"), *The Divided Self* contained all the basic themes upon which he would work his harmonies and variations.[22] Although prominent intellectuals like Philip Toynbee and John Bowlby to whom Laing submitted the manuscript of *The Divided Self* had serious reservations about it, and eight publishers rejected it, it eventually became one of the best-known works of the decade, selling 380,000 copies in the British paperback alone.[23]

Laing took his title from the eighth lecture of William James's *Varieties of Religious Experience,* in which James suggested a psychological explanation for mystical experience. According to James, mystics and saints were divided selves responding not to God but to their own repressed guilt. Laing offers a rational explanation for schizophrenic experience.[24] For Laing, psychosis was the intensification of the divisions within the self that mirrored the compartmentalization and fragmentation of modern society. The sense of reality and substantiality, he argues, depends on the sense of "embodiment," of unity between body and mind, of temporal continuity, and on the sense of relatedness to other persons. In psychosis, however, the person experiences an acute division between the body and mind; the inner or "true" self is relegated to a disembodied mind, which becomes the detached spectator of the behavior of the "false self" located in an unfeeling, mechanized body. Even the well-intentioned actions of others, including the therapist, may seem threatening or devastating to this disembodied self, which protects its perilous autonomy by cutting itself off from relation to others, and which functions primarily through observation and fantasy. The behavior of the schizophrenic, a behavior that includes his deteriorated language or "schizophrenese," becomes a text to be decoded with the psychiatrist's full resources of knowledge, understanding, and empathy. The act of interpretation is an act of risk which pulls the analyst into a human relationship with his patient, as he draws upon his own psychotic potentiality to enter the patient's strange and alien world. "The mad things said and done by the schizophrenic," Laing writes, "will remain a closed book if one does not understand their existential context." But the existential context cannot be mastered by intellect alone; it demands that the therapist transcend the barriers created by his professional *persona* and by the institution of psychiatry; he must survive his encounter with the patient as *person* only—without the shield of reification, without the armor of theory, without the sword of status.[25]

The paradoxical project of articulating a "science of persons," of becoming the "Linnaeus of human bondage," took Laing out of the positivist school of psychiatry in which he had been trained and back to the realm of his earlier interests—art, literature, and philosophy. He was struck by the similarity between problems physicians diagnosed as pathological and the permanent and profound human dilemmas of alienation expressed in existentialist and modernist writing. He drew repeatedly on his rich literary and philosophical background, mixing his psychiatric observations with quotations from Blake, Beckett, Kafka, Dostoevsky, Genet, Strindberg, Tillich, and Sartre. Laing developed an original style that is poetic, fresh, powerfully evocative, and nuanced. Take, for example, his depiction of the loneliness that accompanies recognition of separateness:

> We may remember how, in childhood, adults at first were able to look right through us, and into us, and what an accomplishment it was, when we, in fear and trembling, could tell our first lie, and make, for ourselves, the discovery that we are irredeemably alone in certain respects, and know that within the territory of ourselves there can be only our footprints.[26]

The subtle play of implication here, the unemphatic allusions to Kierkegaard and Defoe, and the cadence of subordination and climax, show a gift for language equaled by only a very few social critics of the time. These are the qualities Robert Coles has in mind when he reminds us that Laing is "a writer and a poet, an aphorist, a symbolist. . . . As a writer Laing etches out things, draws out things, emphasizes, points up as artists always do, and makes larger than life so that we will be somehow responsive to qualities in people and situations that we might ordinarily miss."[27]

For all its innovations, Laing's work to this point could be regarded as a humanizing reform of psychiatric practice. In the mid-sixties, however, he went significantly further in what could be seen either as a daring break from the stultifying conventions of professional psychiatric behavior or a bizarre departure from its professional standards and responsibilities. For by this time, Laing had come to believe that schizophrenia was merely a sociological label applied to those who had not adapted to a mad society by those who had, and that psychiatry was not merely detached but pathological. The fear of nuclear war, a powerful political force in the Campaign for Nuclear Disarmament and the

Aldermaston peace marches, shows up in Laing's writing of the 1960s, along with protests against American involvement in Vietnam. The really dangerous lunatics, he argued, were those who supported the mad policies of global destruction. Thus, "the perfectly adjusted bomber pilot may be a greater threat to species survival than the hospitalized schizophrenic deluded that the bomb is inside him."[28]

While *The Divided Self* (1960) was a smoothly written and carefully organized work in a familiar and even fashionable intellectual tradition, *The Politics of Experience* (1967), published at the height of 1960s utopian euphoria in the same year as *Sergeant Pepper's Lonely Hearts Club Band* and Laing's own political carnival, the Dialectics of Liberation Congress, was an emotionally charged and surrealistic collection of essays that came as a shock and an affront to other psychiatrists. Here Laing argued that far from being a form of mental illness, schizophrenia was a mode of insight and prophecy. Rumors spread that Laing himself was a suitable case for treatment, mad, wasted by acid, violent, hospitalized. Yet the book, too, reached a sizable general audience and became one of the best-known texts of the decade. Ten years later, Laing was still getting letters from people who claimed to carry *The Politics of Experience* around with them, and who believed that it had changed their lives.

In accordance with his new view of schizophrenia as religious vision and spiritual quest, Laing maintained that in a properly supportive environment, the schizophrenic would eventually pass safely through the acute phases of his journey. Shock treatments and surgery would only disrupt a natural healing process. This concept had many sources: clinical accounts of schizophrenic remission, shamanism and initiation rituals, hallucinogenic drug experiences, and the widespread sixties fascination with "trips." From Laing's Glaswegian contemporary Alexander Trocchi, who had declared his mission as "the cosmonaut of inner space," to the Beatles in *The Yellow Submarine,* everyone had become a traveler in psychic climes. The most direct source for Laing, however, was neither cultural tradition nor clinical observation, but a theory derived from the autobiography of a Victorian schizophrenic, John Perceval. In the introduction to his edition of *Perceval's Narrative* (1961), Gregory Bateson interpreted Perceval's psychotic experience as an extraordinary voyage into the self:

> It would appear that once precipitated into psychosis the patient has a course to run. He is, as it were, embarked upon a voyage of discov-

> ery which is only completed by his return to the normal world, to which he comes back with insights different from those of the inhabitants who never embarked on such a voyage.[29]

At this point, however, Laing's only contact with a schizophrenic journey was his friend Jesse Watkins's account of a psychotic episode he had twenty-seven years before. Watkins recounted how he had regressed in time to a primitive stage of animal life, then awakened in a higher religious sphere, and finally willed a return to normalcy when the intensity of his mystical visions became unbearable. Laing imposed his own terminology of spiritual death and rebirth on Watkins's narrative, and added his own interpretation of the role of the "physician-priest" who accompanies the patient. The proper function of the therapist "in a truly sane society," he maintained, is to act as the patient's guide in a metanoiac, or transforming, journey that is archetypally epic, heroic, and masculine, a psychic pilgrimage more exotic and perilous than the voyages of Ulysses or Kurtz.

> We do not regard it as pathologically deviant to explore a jungle or to climb Mount Everest. We feel that Columbus was entitled to be mistaken in his construction of what he discovered when he came to the New World. . . . We respect the voyager, the explorer, the climber, the space man. It makes far more sense to me as a valid project—indeed as a desperately and urgently required project for our time—to explore the inner space and time of consciousness.[30]

The metaphors of heroic adventure and conquest so prominent in Laing's writing of the mid-1960s were put into practice in the communal world he created with other members of the Philadelphia Association (a group dedicated to reforming the treatment of mental illness). The group included David Cooper, Aaron Esterson, and Clancy Sigal, an American writer who had come to England to escape the blacklist, and who became Laing's patient, friend, and enthusiastic co-worker. In 1965, the Philadelphia Association established a therapeutic community at Kingsley Hall in East London to put the theories of antipsychiatry into practice, and to test the belief that people who were lost and "mad" might be healed if, instead of going to a mental hospital, "a re-servicing factory for human breakdown," they could "be guided with full social encouragement and sanction into inner space and time."[31] The high point of the Kingsley Hall day was its sacramental late dinner and "lunatics' ball," over which Laing sacerdotally presided. At nine-thirty staff and guests gathered at a long table garlanded with flowers. In candlelight Laing expounded on philosophy, medicine, religion, or mysticism. About midnight, the table was pushed back, and "impromptu, unrestrained, free-form dancing to flamenco or the Rolling Stones continued until dawn."[32]

Kingsley Hall became the center of countercultural activity in London, swarming with rock groups, experimental drama groups, artists, poets, anti-university students, and hip celebrities. Most staff members were renegades from American medical schools. Many visitors wrote about Kingsley Hall; indeed, in addition to its therapeutic function it was often a kind of schizophrenic Yaddo, where nearly everyone was writing a book. Clancy Sigal kept a journal that would lead to his novel *Zone of the Interior,* Morton Schatzman was planning his study of Schreber and paranoia, and David Cooper and Aaron Esterson were engaged in their own psychomystical researches.

In antipsychiatry, too, the typical patient—the misunderstood or mislabeled "schizophrenic"—was female, and the woman's role remained that of patient rather than doctor. In Laing's early work, the majority of case studies describe women struggling with conflicting messages about femininity from their family and the society, but these potential theories of gender are not developed in the studies themselves. In *The Divided Self,* for example, Laing analyzed the situation of Mrs. R., a twenty-eight-year-old agoraphobic, as a "lack of ontological autonomy," although to a feminist reader, her infantilization and dependence on male approval seem more immediately relevant. Similarly, Mrs. D., a forty-year-old woman in an acute anxiety state, was treated coldly by Laing, who argued that in withholding comfort, he gave her the existential freedom to take responsibility for her life. But Mrs. D.'s main symptom was intense anger toward her husband, an anger Laing calls "unaccountable" and never takes seriously. Marie, a twenty-year-old college student, strongly identified with the victimized girl in the film *La Strada,* but Laing never comments on this paradigmatic figure of female oppression. Two other young schizophrenic women, Julie and Joan, had parents who had wanted them to be boys—but Laing does not consider the social and psychological effects of this preference. Even Ophelia turns up in *The Divided Self* as "undoubtedly a schizophrenic" without an identity: "There is no integral selfhood expressed through her actions or utterances."[33] No mention of her being a woman is made.

At Kingsley Hall, too, Laing's model patient was a woman. While he may have been hoping for a Sylvia Plath or an Antonin Artaud to guide through the void into hypersanity, only Mary Barnes, a Catholic nurse in her forties, showed up at Kingsley Hall to take the round trip. A veteran of several stints in mental institutions, shock treatment, and drugs, she was already well launched on her career as a psychiatric patient when she joined Laing's therapeutic community. Mary Barnes is in fact Laing's only complete case study, his Augustine, his Dora, his Anna O.

Unlike these other famous female patients, however, Mary Barnes ran her own show. She had read *The Divided Self* and had selected Laing as someone who would understand schizophrenic women. As Joseph Berke puts it in the book he wrote with Barnes about her treatment, "Mary had elected herself to the position of head guinea pig. . . . Mary had her trip all worked out years before she had ever heard of Laing." Possessive and demanding, she made herself the center of community life; residents had to take turns feeding, bathing, and nursing her as she "went down," or regressed to passive infancy. There were frightening times when she refused to eat and became emaciated and weak. Her erotic transference to Berke, who became her primary therapist at Kingsley Hall, was forthright, even clamorous. In her infantile episodes, she played, sculpted, and painted with her shit, at one point noisomely accosting Berke in the game room like "the creature from the black lagoon," at another creating such a stench with her murals that a major board meeting had to be called on the question of her "smell-space." Berke thought she smeared "with the skill of a Zen calligrapher," but other residents were less impressed.[34] After her discharge from Kingsley Hall, Barnes had a one-woman show of painting smeared in oil on canvas (fig. 28).

Like so many other English women in the twentieth century, Mary Barnes also wrote a narrative of her sickness and treatment. It is a particularly interesting narrative, in fact, because it is combined with an account by her therapist, Joseph Berke. Reading these "two accounts of a journey through madness," we can compare the female patient's description of her experience with the male psychiatrist's interpretation of her illness. We can understand exactly what is left out when the mad woman's story is mediated through the male voice.

Figure 28. Mary Barnes and one of her paintings, 1971.

As Mary Barnes tells her own story, we see many expressions of her frustration with the sexual, intellectual, and vocational limits imposed on her by the female role; indeed, she often seems like a contemporary sister of Florence Nightingale's Cassandra. Mary's mother had withheld sexual information from her, and told her horror stories about the pain and danger of childbirth. When she reached puberty, Mary was disgusted by the changes in her body and tried to deny them, refusing to wear a brassiere. Guilt over masturbation remained a problem well into her adult life. She wanted desperately to be a boy like her brother, who had fewer restrictions on his activities and who had passed his exams for grammar school. Mary herself trained to be a nurse because it was one of the very few occupations open to girls of her class.

But nursing proved another trap—the lack of independence, the drudgery, the emphasis on obedience rather than curiosity. For an English woman in the 1950s, marriage and motherhood were the only routes out of this career impasse. But Mary's ambivalence about her sexuality, her sense of "pretending to be feminine," and her conscious avoidance of male domination made her prefer to stay single. She did want to have a baby, and began to think seriously about going to Russia where, she had heard, women "with babies and no husbands were quite accepted." In Russia, too, it was rumored, women had more career opportunities: "You could carry on studying from being a nurse to become a doctor. I felt ashamed that I wanted to be a doctor. I knew this shame was bound up with the enormous guilt I had in connection with my desire to be a boy. Anything masculine in myself must be hidden, buried in secret, hardly admitted."[35]

Instead of pursuing these secret wishes, she took the opposite tack, converting to Catholicism and even entering a convent. It was then that she had her first complete breakdown, during which she became completely withdrawn, unable to eat, urinate, or talk. Through the help of a sympathetic doctor, who advised her to stay away from the church, Mary recovered from this breakdown, and entered a training course in nursing education. But her problems did not go away, and in the early 1960s, after failing to persuade Anna Freud to take her on as a patient, she settled on Laing as the only man who could help her. Mary's role in Kingsley Hall allowed her, in a sense, to resolve her conflicting desires about ambition. In asserting her position as a key figure in the community's life, she acted out her longing to become a "doctor," an authority figure, but within a suitable, even classically feminine, role as "patient." The community of male doctors became her nurses; unable to have a baby of her own, Mary became one herself.

There might be many ways of "reading" Mary's symptoms that would take her feelings about being a woman into account. But what is remarkable is that neither Berke, in his part of the narrative, nor Laing, in his many discussions of Mary Barnes, makes reference to any of the explicit sex-role issues raised in her narrative. In fitting her into their model of the successful schizophrenic voyage, they have ceased to hear or see the woman herself.

In all fairness, it has to be said that Mary Barnes made enormous demands on Berke's patience and understanding. She wanted to be with him all the time, whined and cried when he tried to go out, was ferociously jealous of his wife, and once urinated in their bed. He must have sometimes felt like Rochester dealing with a monstrous Bertha Mason, and indeed, Berke ruefully notes, he often asked himself, "Why the hell did you ever get involved with a woman like Mary?"[36] Berke's section of the narrative reveals his honesty, warmth, and commitment to the ideals of Kingsley Hall.

Yet Berke also brought to his turbulent interaction with Mary Barnes a number of narrow psychoanalytic ideas about femininity and female sexuality. He describes Mary as "a hotbed of sexual desire and frustration," filled with anger and guilt because of her incestuous feelings for her father and brother and her resentment of her mother. Her withdrawal into infancy, according to Berke, was a way to integrate the different aspects of her psyche, and "to come to terms with herself as a woman."[37]

But although he had gotten her started on her painting, encouraged her to study, taken her to galleries, and introduced her to artists, Berke does not seem to relate Mary's psychological improvement to the approval, attention, and visibility she received as a painter. He sees her primary drives and desires as sexual rather than vocational, and does not comment on the powerful ambitions she had repressed and defined as "masculine." What Berke sees as Mary's penis envy was rather her envy of male mobility, status, and independence. Ironically, Mary first achieved the success she craved by becoming the "Queen of the Schizophrenics" at Kingsley Hall, the main attraction of a psychiatric theater much like Charcot's at the Salpêtrière.

Although Laing made the most of Mary Barnes's "recovery," I suspect that her voyage was disappointingly unlike his expectations. It was one thing to relive the dangerous exhilaration of his mountain-climbing experiences in Scotland, and to be the manly physician-priest leading another explorer to the heart of darkness, or the top of Everest, five days in and five days out. It was quite another to spend three years changing diapers, giving bottles, and generally wiping up after a noisy, jealous, smelly, middle-aged woman. The image of the schizophrenic voyage that Laing had created drew upon his own heroic fantasies; it was a male adventure of exploration and conquest—scarcely the reality of Mary Barnes's experience. Faced with the obligation to play mother on the psychic journey, Laing seems to have lost enthusiasm for it.

The Mary Barnes story, however, appealed strongly to the playwright David Edgar, who saw Laing as a representative figure of 1960s culture, and the case as a way to engage audiences on the side of antipsychiatry. Edgar's play, *Mary Barnes,* was produced at the Birmingham Rep in 1977 and then transferred to the Royal Court. A fictionalized and stylized version of the Barnes-Berke narrative, it makes the story of Mary Barnes the story of antipsychiatry. Mary's madness becomes the myth of Kingsley Hall; she is its heroine and its symbolic ideal. On the opening night of the play, however, the impact of Laing's theories was significantly undermined, for those who could look away from the image to the reality, by the presence of the real Mary Barnes, a lisping, bouncing, and giggling fifty-five-year-old woman, who acted in a "beguiling child-like way," and who admitted to a reporter from *The Guardian* that she was still wrestling with acute attacks of depression and withdrawal.[38]

An even more important dramatist of Laingian theory was David Mercer. Laing acted as official consultant for Mercer's television play *In Two Minds* (1967), a drab, documentarylike demonstration of Laing's theory of schizophrenia and the schizophrenogenic family. Although Mercer denied that he had a particular Laingian case in mind, his heroine, Kate Winter, seems to be a composite of several cases in *Sanity, Madness, and the Family,* especially Maya and June. In 1972, Mercer, in collaboration with Laing, adapted *In Two Minds* for the screen in a film called *Family Life* (*Wednesday's Child* in the United States). The film was naturalistic in style; the action and dialogue were improvised within the framework provided by the script. Some hospital scenes were shot unrehearsed with the Philadelphia Association's North London community of sixteen people; and amateurs played several of the leading roles.

Like the women in Laing's case studies, the heroine, Janice, is caught in a double bind. She is alternately threatened and discredited by her parents, who demand that she be "good" on their terms—sexless, dependent, and docile—while expressing dissatisfaction with her lack of autonomy and maturity. When she becomes pregnant and wants to have the baby, they insist upon an abortion. They also insist upon mental hospitalization, and require that the doctors provide "discipline" and "control." When Janice, still a voluntary patient, attempts to leave the hospital with her boyfriend, the parents intervene to have her committed under a special provision of the Mental Health Act. By the end of the film, she is indeed broken and "mad"—a person who has given up trying to have a self.

Family Life makes brilliant use of visual techniques to bring out the political implications that Mercer particularly admired in Laing's work. The film uses images of mass transit, mass production, and mass medicine to capture the sense of social alienation. Janice first breaks down on the Tube; she is an Underground Woman watching people rush back and forth on their way to meaningless jobs. Her own job is in a candy factory, where chocolates rush by on a conveyor belt like commuters, and plunge into boxes of various sizes and shapes. As in similar scenes in Chaplin's *Modern Times,* or Peter Sellers's *I'm All Right, Jack* (1959), the assembly line becomes a metaphor for the mechanization and depersonalization of human beings. The identical houses in Janice's neat working-class community, endless rows of interchangeable roofs, chimneys, and little gardens, reproduce the mental conformity of insecure men and women, locked into a system of values as tidy, uniform, and banal as their homes. When Janice and her art-student lover spray-paint the family's garden blue, gnomes and all, they threaten the safe familiarity of material objects that has its parallel in rigid views of decency, marriage, and filial obligation.

The therapeutic community that Janice enters is an alternative to this dehumanizing sameness. The highly individualized young patients support each other, and are supported by the Laingian psychiatrist Mike, in finding the strength to confront their families and to go their own way. But the hospital board decides to discontinue the experiment. In a devastating scene, we see Janice herded with a group of other women mental patients to be processed for ECT. Protesting the whole time, she is anaesthetized, shocked by a male doctor, and with a wooden gag in her mouth, rolled into a ward full of unconscious shocked women, all with their mouths plugged, like infants or (in an allusion to Cerletti's original experiments) suckling pigs. The parallel is clear between the rows of women, the rows of houses, and the rows of chocolates—mute, processed, identical objects.

For all the sensitive staging of what is basically a woman's story, Mercer, like Laing, never explicitly confronts the relationship of sex roles and schizophrenia. He does not question the Laingian assumption that Janice's problems are caused mainly by her mother, or raise the issues of feminine social conditioning in the group-therapy sessions. *Family Life* ends, however, by bringing the viewer into the debate. Janice is exhibited as a case to an amphitheater of staring young male medical students, whose perspective we are made to share. By now totally numb, hopeless, and withdrawn, she sits huddled on a chair while the male psychiatrist describes her "symptoms," concluding that there is no connection between her behavior and her environment (fig. 29). The last line of the film, spoken directly to the audience, is "Do you have any questions?"

The questions about Laingian women left unanswered in the narratives, plays, and films of these male psychiatrists and playwrights come closer to being resolved in the novels of Doris Lessing. In London in the late 1950s, Lessing, Laing, and Clancy Sigal "formed a circle of almost incestuous mutual influence."[39] But Lessing had had a lifelong interest in madness and in the unconscious. "I have spent nearly thirty years in close contact with mental illness," she wrote in 1972, "first through various brands of analyst and therapist and psychiatrist, and then through people who were 'mad' in various ways, and with whom I had very close contact. . . . I have always been close to crazy people."[40]

The evolution of Lessing's fiction in the 1960s parallels Laing's movement from an interpretation of schizophrenia as an intelligible and potentially healing response to conflicting social demands, to a view of madness as a form of rebellion, and the schizophrenic as the sanest person in a mad society.

In her earlier novels, Lessing poses the problem of madness in feminist as well as Laingian terms, using schizophrenia as a metaphor for female consciousness. In *The Golden Notebook* (1962), the writer Anna Wulf (the name recalls the case of Anna O.) is unable to reconcile and integrate the divided selves that make up her difficult position as a "free woman" of the twentieth century—her Marxism, her literary ambition,

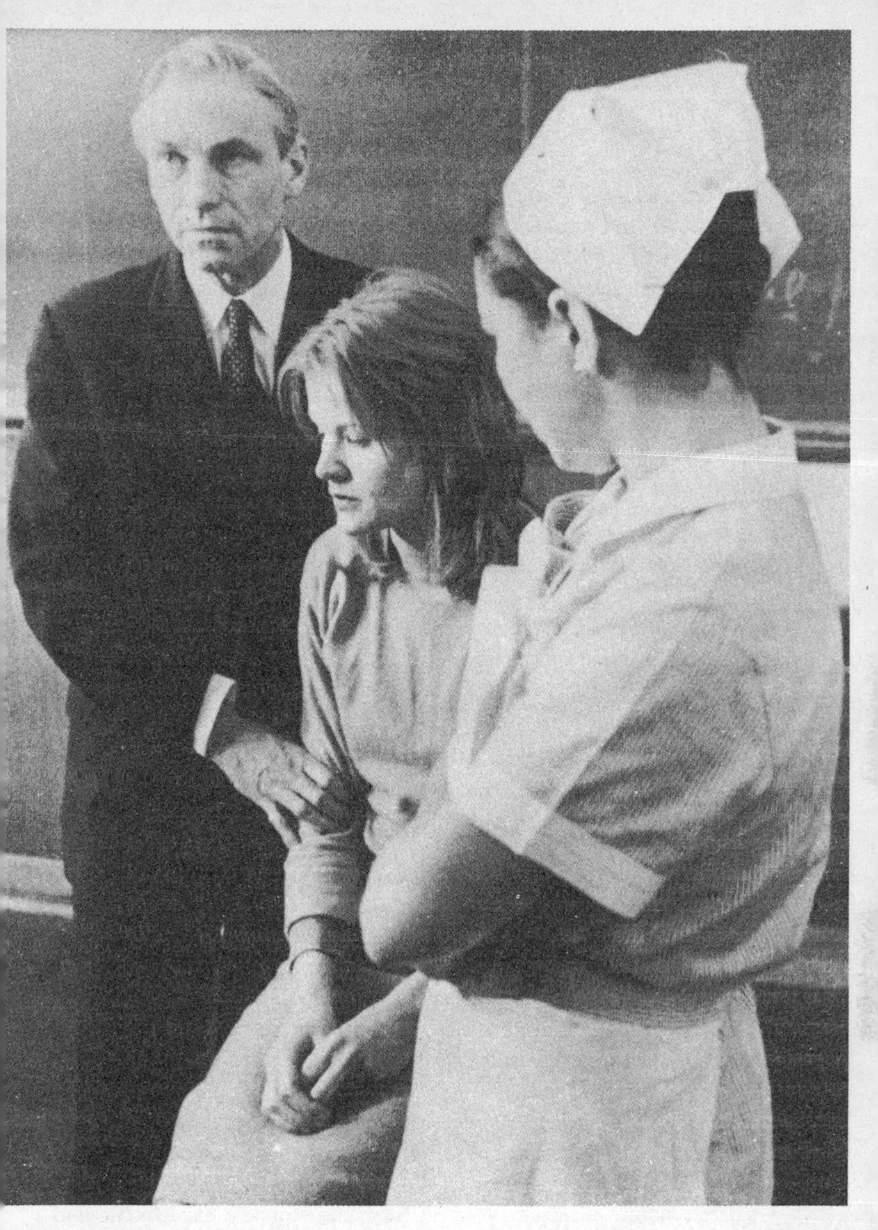

Figure 29. Janice's case being demonstrated to the medical students, in Family Life, *1973.*

her sexuality, her maternal feelings, her relationships with other women. She attempts to control this chaotic fragmentation by keeping several notebooks for each aspect of her personality. But the notebooks reach a dead end of confusion and frustration. Unable to write her novel, Anna is reduced to outlining plots for possible stories, plots that sound like Laing's scenarios of sanity, madness, and the family. At the end of the novel, Anna and her American lover, Saul Green (a character based on Clancy Sigal), "break down" into each other in a *folie à deux* that is unifying and redemptive for both. Madness, Lessing suggests, is a way of learning, of getting around or breaking through the paralyzing impasses of contemporary life. In accepting the authenticity of all her roles, Anna is able to begin to write both the Golden Notebook in which the boundaries between male and female, madness and sanity, are broken down, and then the novel itself.

In *The Four-Gated City* (1969), however, "schizophrenia" is no longer a comprehensible reaction to conflicting feminine roles and rules, but rather a higher capacity of the female mind which has been suppressed by a ruthless psychiatric power. This novel is a much harsher polemic against the psychiatric establishment than *The Golden Notebook,* several of whose important male and female characters are therapists. Lessing's Lynda Coldridge is a telepathic who has been diagnosed as schizophrenic; she is shocked, given insulin treatments, and institutionalized until she is psychologically crippled and nearly destroyed by her doctors. Lessing suggests that what the psychiatrists call "schizophrenia" is a form of extrasensory perception, a gift that can be cultivated or suppressed. Lynda's experience is representative of the victimization of psychologically advanced members of society:

> When they stopped torturing and killing witches, they locked people with certain capacities into lunatic asylums and told them they were freaks, and forced them into conformity by varieties of torture which included electric shocks, solitary confinement, ice baths, and forcible feeding. They used every kind of degradation, moral and physical. As the methods of society for control and manipulation became more refined, it was discovered that the extremities of physical violence were less effective than drugs which deprived the victims of their moral stamina and ability to fight back; and more effective than the drugs were techniques of persuasion and brainwashing. By these means the members of the population with capacities above normal

> ... were systematically destroyed, either by fear ... or by classing them with the congenitally defective.[41]

Women, Lessing argues, were more vulnerable to such labeling and incarceration. *Briefing for a Descent into Hell* (1971), however, the most Laingian of Lessing's novels, does not make connections between female powerlessness and schizophrenia. Entirely focused on the schizophrenic experience as voyage into a more authentic world, it describes the breakdown of a male classics professor named Charles Watkins. (The similarity to Laing's Jesse Watkins, according to Lessing, was entirely coincidental since she had not read *The Politics of Experience.*[42]) The novel alternates between documents about Watkins's treatment with Librium, Tofronil, and other antipsychotic drugs by Doctors X and Y in the Central Intake Hospital, and a first-person narrative of his mystical trip into first a primitive and then a mythic world. Like Rebecca West's shell-shocked Chris Baldry, Watkins has forgotten his wife, family, and job. Finally he consents to have electroshock (although "there was no method of treatment that caused more emotion in the wards, more fear"), which "cures" him and sends him back into a normality that is drab, unfeeling, and unreal. By this point, however, Lessing's novels were no longer at all concerned with the schizophrenic journey as a woman's exploration of the self; and Watkins's male adventure story is less interesting and complex than Anna Wulf's memories, dreams, and fictions.

The problems of Laingian therapy for schizophrenic women are most disturbingly set out in *Anna* (1977), an account of the breakdown and eventual suicide of a young German woman, told in the form of a diary by her English husband under the pseudonym "David Reed." The case history of Anna is a patchwork of allusions to other female mental patients; Anna O., Anna Wulf, Sylvia Plath, and Mary Barnes can all be glimpsed in her story. Like Anna O., Anna was caught between two languages, German and English, struggling to write about female experience in the words of her fatherland or her husband's land. Like Anna Wulf, she tried to order her feelings of fragmentation by filling "notebook after notebook with jottings." In these notebooks, discovered by her husband after her death, Anna wrote about "everything from her own schizophrenia to penis envy and infantile sexuality, from bombing in Hanover to IRA bombs in London."[43] Here too she wrote poems modeled on those of Sylvia Plath, whom she regarded as her heroine and precursor. And like Mary Barnes, Anna had a long history of breakdowns, suicide attempts, hospitalization, shock treatments, and psychotherapy. In 1969 she too consulted Laing, who was unable to treat her but recommended one of his disciples to be her therapist. In 1971, she wrote to Laing again. As she described her dilemma: "More therapy has been suggested to me to cure my 'excessive jealousy' of my husband, his former mistress, and his work (writing). But I do not want to be a patient any longer."[44]

But the circumstances of her life, and particularly her marriage, made it difficult for Anna to be other than a patient. While she raised their two sons, David put his energies into teaching and writing, and then into an extramarital affair. During one of her breakdowns, Anna jealously cried out to him, "Yes, you are a writer, and I am not creative, not grateful." In 1971, she and David were planning to collaborate at last, on a biography of two European writers who were brothers. Anna felt that the project was "a unique chance for both of us," certainly her chance to stop being a patient. But they disagreed over which brother was to be the focus of the biography, and although Anna did enormous amounts of research for it, the book, David notes, "slipped into my domain." He would not even have dedicated it to her, but she insisted on at least this recognition.[45]

Within a month after David completed the biography, in May 1973, Anna had a serious breakdown, and tried to kill one of her children. This time, David, who had been reading *The Divided Self* and was profoundly impressed by it, decided to care for his wife at home, to refuse permission for ECT, and to follow a Laingian therapeutic model. Laing himself came as a consultant, smartly dressed in a velvet jacket, but with "rings of suffering around his eyes."[46] After talking with Anna, he gave the opinion that her psychosis was nearly over, and that she could be guided through the schizophrenic experience without ECT.

The Reeds had many handicaps, however, in attempting to follow Laing's advice. They were not part of a therapeutic community, and the responsibilities for watchfulness and protection, of the children as well as of Anna, fell entirely on David. At one point they visited a run-down satellite Laingian community in an old house in London; but here David was put off by the squalor and disorganization, and Anna, totally ignored, eventually wandered off into the streets. After six weeks of acute psychosis, however, Anna seemed to make a sudden dramatic recovery, brought on by watching the film *To Have and Have Not* on television. (These recoveries through seeing the self reflected in a film seemed to be a characteristic of Laingian women; in *The Divided Self,* Marie was "cured" after seeing Fellini's *La Strada,* and another patient, Morag Coate, was much better after she had seen *David and Lisa.*[47]) But Mary Barnes, who came to visit the Reeds—by this time a "thin, frail" saintly creature, who drank only warm milk with honey—warned David that Anna's recovery was too abrupt. That night Anna set fire to herself, and burned 75 percent of her body. She died five weeks later, after an agonizing interval in which the hospital staff tried against hopeless odds to save her.

Vivian Gornick, comparing *Anna* to Gilman's "The Yellow Wallpaper," pointed to the presence in both books of decent men who, "standing on the edge, suffer intensely as they gaze down into the pit that has swallowed the women they love."[48] Gornick suggests that men speaking for women—even with love—may stifle their language and being. Anna speaks to us only posthumously, through a male interpreter, to the end. Unlike Anna O., she did not find a Josef Breuer to listen to her, to help her find her voice. Over and over again, Laing's women, the women of antipsychiatry, appear as latter-day Ophelias and Cassandras whose voices are silenced and whose prophecies go unheeded. Indeed, the series of female cases begin to seem interchangeable rather than unique. David Edgar's "Mary," David Mercer's "Janice," and David Reed's "Anna" are fictionalized and stylized figures of female insanity which effectively mute the significance of the gender structures of psychiatric power even as the authors sympathize with—but finally appropriate—the suffering of their originals.

The successes of antipsychiatry did not outlast the 1960s. The Kingsley Hall community broke up by 1971; Cooper, Esterson, and Laing were at odds, and Joseph Berke and Morton Schatzman left Laing to form another therapeutic community for mental patients, the Arbours Association. In the 1970s, too, Doris Lessing began to back away from her endorsement of Laingian ideas, and her response to critics pressing her about Laing became increasingly impatient. "My view of Laing," she told an interviewer in 1977, "is that at an appropriate time in Britain, he challenged extreme rigidities in psychiatry with alternate viewpoints, and made other attitudes than the official ones possible. That is what he did. No more and no less."[49]

Laing's demotion, David Edgar explained, was part of the general erosion of the beliefs of the 1960s:

> Laing has been undermined, since it is now much clearer that there is a chemical causative effect to schizophrenia. Chomsky has been undermined. Marcuse's theories have been shown just not to have been true, and the Black Power Movement has withered on the vine. The generation that was never going to be assimilated *has* been assimilated.[50]

Those who had always thought Laing was a huckster and an opportunist congratulated themselves for having guessed right. Worse still, like Conolly in Reade's *Hard Cash,* the post-sixties Laing also became the prototype for satirical and even comic fictional characters. In Erica Jong's *Fear of Flying* (1971) "Adrian Goodlove" is a charismatic but impotent English antipsychiatrist, who "idealized madness in typical Laingian fashion. Schizophrenics were the true poets. Every raving lunatic was Rilke."

The sharpest, cleverest, and most hilarious satire on the psychopolitics of madness is Clancy Sigal's *Zone of the Interior* (1976), which takes its American leftwing hero, Sid Bell, on an odyssey into the macho world of the Scottish guru of schizophrenia, Dr. Willie Last. Sigal and Laing had been close friends and associates since the early 1960s when Sigal, suffering from a writing block, had begun "a perfectly conventional analysis" with Laing. Their personalities clicked. Sigal became deeply involved in antipsychiatric projects from David Cooper's experimental open ward for schizophrenics, Villa 21, to Laing's Philadelphia Association; Laing, for his part, showed Sigal drafts of his own writing and revealed to him his impatience with the whole medical side of his life.[51] But as the decade wore on, Sigal became increasingly disillusioned with psychopolitics and more and more worried by the seductive presentation of schizophrenia as superior consciousness. *Zone of the Interior,* which draws on this experience, has never found an English publisher willing to risk the libel laws in bringing it out.

Dr. Willie Last, author of a successful book about the families of schizophrenic children, *The Unhealed Heart,* believes that schizophrenics are "existential guerillas," while mental hospitals are "Auschwitzes of the soul." Joining Last and his collaborators, Sid Bell gives up leftwing politics, volunteers at "Conolly House," an experimental open ward for schizophrenics, and helps found Meditation Manor, a house in Brixton where rich schizophrenics can be guided on their spiritual journeys. But gradually Bell begins to realize that the "schizophrenic" patients are temperamental prima donnas, that the doctors are on ego trips of their own, and that Last is promoting himself as a "Highland Jesus Christ."[52]

Bell also catches on to the male sexual competition and role-playing at Meditation Manor. The doctors' wives are resentful outsiders (by the end of the novel all have been replaced by younger mistresses); other women are either "exalted Light Bringers or slightly subnormal Earth Mothers."[53] The star patient, a schizophrenic predictably named Anna who believes she's a fish, lives in a corrugated tin tank in the cellar, where she is cleaned, fed, nursed, and regularly hosed down by the volunteers. The doctors battle for possession of the sexy young schizophrenic patients. All these antics begin to resemble farce, a version of *Carry On, Schizophrenia*; but a more serious note is sounded in the suicide of Bell's German lover, Lena, a patient rejected by Last.

Despite his growing disillusionment with Meditation Manor, Bell is still obsessed with Last's charismatic presence. In a desperate effort to impress Last, Bell decides to starve and drug himself into a psychotic trip. Cleansed by a diet of nuts and berries, and fortified by massive doses of LSD, he takes flight in the midst of Last's admiring associates. But the seraphs Bell meets in the Great Breakthrough are not demons or mythic divinities. They are polemical and didactic angels, including I. F. Stone, Clarence Darrow, Emma Goldman, and Edmund Wilson, who argue among themselves but agree that Bell must "stop romanticizing the heroic in life and politics."[54] At the end of the voyage, Bell lands in the lap of the divinity; but the divinity wears overalls and a sweat-stained bandanna, has the face of Eugene V. Debs, and wears as his only religious emblem an IWW button on his frayed work shirt. The divine revelation of Bell's metanoiac voyage is that he has given up his soul to a Movement geek, that, in the language of his Chicago past, he must "get his ass out of this creep joint." His rebirth is also a bust-out.

Eventually even Laing became an anti-Laingian in the 1970s, nervously separating from leftwing politics, drugs, mysticism, attacks on the family, even antipsychiatry. Just at the point in 1970 when Marshall Berman declared in a front-page essay in the *New York Times Book Review* that Laing's work "has shaken just about everyone and everything it has touched,"[55] the man himself dropped out of sight, first taking a long sabbatical to Sri Lanka, India, and Japan, then re-emerging to a post-sixties world in which everything was utterly changed.

On the eve of his first public lecture in the seventies, Laing told an interviewer for *The Times* that he was "singing a new song." He "never called himself an anti-psychiatrist," was "never an apostle of the drug experience," "never meant to imply that madness is superior to true sanity," and would "never recommend madness." Laing's new tune also included a testimonial to the family and a good word for electric-shock treatment.[56] In 1973 he confessed to David Reed, the troubled husband of "Anna," that he knew less about how people came back from schizophrenic journeys than he did "twenty years ago as a young doctor."[57]

Since then, Laing has moved with the conservative spirit, making quiet appearances in books of conversations with his children or sonnets to his second wife, as the advocate of yoga, a vegetable diet, and the Leboyer obstetric method. This determined exit from all the political positions he had claimed in the 1960s came as a shock to Laing's supporters and critics both. Peter Sedgwick scorned him as laundered, sanitized, cool, and safe, a trimmer who moved with the times. Laing's "ultimate inability to connect himself with any really radical social critique," wrote Joel Kovel, left his insights "adrift on an existential sea."[58]

The same could be said about Laing's contribution to the understanding of women and madness. It is impossible to write as a feminist about R. D. Laing without acknowledging the importance of his analysis of madness as a female strategy within the family. For a whole generation of women, Laing's work was a significant validation of perceptions that found little social support elsewhere. In the academy, too, Laing's work has been important to feminist critics, his theory of "ontological insecurity" providing a valuable method for understanding the *representation* of women from Clarissa Harlowe to Millie Theale.[59]

Yet, in retrospect, it seems clear that despite vivid representations of women's suffering, antipsychiatry had no coherent analysis to offer women. As Simone de Beauvoir maintained in 1979, "At bottom antipsychiatry is still psychiatry. And it doesn't really address itself to women's problems."[60] Like other radical movements of the 1960s, antipsychiatry in practice was male-dominated, yet unaware of its own sexism. The movement never produced a woman theorist of Laing's stature and power; moreover, it came perilously close to exploiting its women patients. David Cooper, who was the most politically radical of the Kingsley Hall group, exemplified the combination of charisma in the male therapist and infantilism in the female patient which Peter Sedgwick sees as the fundamental antipsychiatric constellation. In *The Grammar of Living,* Cooper advocates sex with patients, which he calls "bed therapy," as a useful way to establish contact. Not only does he have a Reichian faith in orgasm as the ultimate in self-expression and self-knowledge, but he also is confident that he can detect the "non-orgasmic personality" (predictably female) by "minute ocular deflections and by sentences spoken to one that fail to connect because they are never properly ended." Cooper seems blind, however, to the ethical issues involved when he picks up a beautiful twenty-year-old schizophrenic Dutch woman named Marja, a mute whom he takes home, feeds, and "makes love with."[61] Here the promises of antipsychiatry for women are pitifully betrayed, and we seem to have returned to a Victorian saga of the wrongs of women comparable to the rape of asylum patients by their keepers. As Laing himself had discovered, the elimination of shock treatments, psychosurgery, and drugs does not in itself guarantee a restructuring of the forces of social control: "In the best places, where straitjackets are abolished, doors are unlocked, leucotomies largely forgotten, these can be replaced by more subtle lobotomies and tranquillizers that place the bars of Bedlam and the locked doors *inside* the patient."[62]

Epilogue

MADNESS AND THE RIGHTS OF WOMEN

Laing politicized madness just at the point when statistics showed that English institutionalization rates had begun to decline; like syphilitic insanity at the *fin de siècle,* schizophrenia seemed to become a symbolic illness just when it lost some of its virulence. In 1954, the mental hospital population in England peaked at 148,000, a rate of 33.45 per 10,000 people. Reliance on tranquilizers and antipsychotic drugs such as Librium, Largactil, and the phenothiazines, and the government's commitment to a policy of community treatment are credited with the subsequent steady decline in the number of institutionalized patients. In 1961, Enoch Powell, then minister of health, predicted that during the next fifteen years "the acute population of mental hospitals . . . [would] drop by half . . . and the long-stay population ultimately dwindle to zero."[1] Madness entered the mainstream as patients were transferred from asylums to the psychiatric wards of general hospitals, or released into the community. By 1971, the government's report "Hospital Services for the Mentally Ill" could confidently predict "the complete abolition of the mental hospital system," and Sir Keith Joseph, the minister of health, declared that "the treatment of psychoses, neuroses, and schizophrenia has been entirely changed by the drug revolution. People go into hospital with mental disorders and they are cured."[2] In 1977, a report of the Camden and Islington Health Authority recommended that Friern Hospital—the modern name of Colney Hatch Asylum—should be reduced in size and maintained only as a small hospital for elderly long-term patients.[3] It seemed that the long era of the English malady had finally come to a close.

What, then, about the long history of the female malady? It would be foolish to deny that advances in the medical management of mental illness have made reasonably normal lives possible for thousands of women who might earlier have been institutionalized. Yet, like previous cycles of therapeutic optimism, this period of decarceration too has its problems. Women have now become the primary clientele for psychotropic drugs; in the late 1970s, studies showed that 21 percent of the women in the patient population, as compared to 9.7 percent of the men, received such medication.[4] Decarceration is a woman's issue in yet another sense: the sharp cuts in government funds to support decarceration have placed the burden of what is euphemistically called "family" and "community" care on women, tying them, as Peter Sedgwick points out, to "traditional servicing roles for their disabled kinfolk . . . [and loosening] the tyranny of the mental institution by reinforcing an archaic sexual division of labour."[5] As long as women are overrepresented among mental patients and family caretakers and underrepresented among psychiatrists, administrators, and politicians, their lives will continue to be unhappily affected by decisions in which they take no part.

Furthermore, new treatments of mental illness and deinstitutionalization seem to have little effect on the cultural image of women as mental patients. In the 1980s, Ophelia is a pretty schizophrenic girl; she takes pills that keep her from hearing voices. Crazy Jane is a depressed young mother in a housing project in Camberwell. She has an illegitimate child, no work outside her home, and no friends. She cries a lot and takes tranquilizers.[6] Lucia is a West Indian immigrant whose husband beats her; sometimes she has murderous thoughts about her child.[7] In contemporary practice, medical management has replaced moral management as a way of containing women's suffering without confronting its causes. We can predict that if "depression" is soon viewed as a meaningless catchall category, another female malady will appear to take its place for another generation.

The best hope for the future is the feminist therapy movement. In the 1970s, for the first time, women came together to challenge both the psychoanalytic and the medical categories of traditional psychiatry, to propose alternatives like feminist psychotherapy, women's self-help groups, and political activism. A new feminist psychology of women has found its starting point in the analysis of the mother-daughter relation. It is beyond the scope of this book to trace out the history of the feminist therapy movement, but its work is essential to the future understanding of women, madness, and culture, and to the development of a psychiatric theory and practice that, by empowering women, offers a real possibility of change. Throughout the history of psychiatry, there have been many male liberators—Pinel, Conolly, Charcot, Freud, Laing—who claimed to free madwomen from the chains of their confinement to obtuse and misogynistic medical practice. Yet when women are spoken for but do not speak for themselves, such dramas of liberation become only the opening scenes of the next drama of confinement. Until women break them for themselves, the chains that make madness a female malady, like Blake's "mind-forg'd manacles," will simply forge themselves anew.

NOTES

INTRODUCTION. THE FEMALE MALADY

1. Mary Wollstonecraft, *Maria; or, The Wrongs of Woman* (New York: W. W. Norton, 1975), pp. 21, 23, 27.
2. See the discussion of this painting in Sander L. Gilman, *Seeing the Insane: A Cultural History of Psychiatric Illustration* (New York: Brunner-Mazel, 1982), pp. 212–13. Tony Robert-Fleury may have been representing some of his own attitudes towards women. He taught women artists in Paris at the Académie Julian, where his students described him as Byronic, domineering, magnetic; "his eyes . . . smouldered with burnt-out fires." See Germaine Greer, *The Obstacle Race: The Fortunes of Women Painters and Their Work* (London: Secker & Warburg, 1979), pp. 317–18. On other representations of women in nineteenth-century science and medicine, see Ludmilla Jordanova, "Natural Facts: A Historical Perspective on Science and Sexuality," in *Nature, Culture, and Gender,* ed. Carol MacCormack and Marilyn Strathern (Cambridge: Cambridge University Press, 1980), p. 54.
3. For a comprehensive study of data and theory, see Elizabeth Howell and Marjorie Bayes, eds., *Women and Mental Health* (New York: Basic Books, 1981). Other useful sources are John Archer and Barbara Lloyd, *Sex and Gender* (Harmondsworth: Penguin Books, 1982); Susan Lipshitz, "Women and Psychiatry," in *The Sex-Role System: Psychological and Sociological Per-*

spectives, ed. Jane Chetwynd and Oonagh Hartnett (London: Routledge & Kegan Paul, 1978), pp. 93–108; P. Susan Penfold and Gillian A. Walker, *Women and the Psychiatric Paradox* (Montreal and London: Eden Press, 1983); and Ludmilla Jordanova, "Mental Illness, Mental Health: Changing Norms and Expectations," in Cambridge Women's Study Group, *Women in Society: Interdisciplinary Essays* (London: Virago Press, 1981), pp. 95–114.

4. Michael MacDonald, *Mystical Bedlam: Madness, Anxiety, and Healing in Seventeenth-Century England* (Cambridge: Cambridge University Press, 1981), pp. 36–40.
5. See Walter Gove and J. F. Tudor, "Adult Sex Roles and Mental Illness," *American Journal of Sociology* 78 (1973): 812–35, cited in Howell and Bayes, *Women and Mental Health*, p. 155.
6. MacDonald, *Mystical Bedlam*, p. 74.
7. See, for example, Shoshana Felman, "Woman and Madness: The Critical Phallacy," *Diacritics* 5 (1975): 2–10; and Genevieve Lloyd, *The Man of Reason: "Male" and "Female" in Western Philosophy* (Minneapolis: University of Minnesota Press, 1984), especially pp. 1–17.
8. Felman, "Woman and Madness," p. 7.
9. Sandra M. Gilbert and Susan Gubar, *The Madwoman in the Attic: The Woman Writer and the Nineteenth-Century Literary Imagination* (New Haven, Conn.: Yale University Press, 1979), p. 85.
10. Phyllis Chesler, *Women and Madness* (Garden City, N.Y.: Doubleday, 1972), pp. 31, 16.
11. See Charles Bernheimer and Claire Kahane, eds., *In Dora's Case: Freud, Hysteria, Feminism* (New York: Columbia University Press, 1985), especially pp. 1–32.
12. Felman, "Woman and Madness," p. 2. On the historical contexts of hysteria, see Juliet Mitchell, *Women: The Longest Revolution* (New York: Pantheon Books, 1984), pp. 115–24.
13. See Vieda Skultans, "The English Malady," *English Madness: Ideas on Insanity, 1580-1890* (London: Routledge & Kegan Paul, 1978), pp. 26–51; Cecil A. Moore, "The English Malady," in his *Backgrounds of English Literature, 1700–1760* (Minneapolis: University of Minnesota Press, 1953), pp. 179–235; and Roy Porter, "The Rage of Party: A Glorious Revolution in English Psychiatry?" *Medical History* 27 (1983): 35--50.
14. George Cheyne, *The English Malady; or, A Treatise on Nervous Disorders of All Kinds* (London: Strahan & Leake, 1733), p. 54.
15. Henry Maudsley, *The Pathology of Mind: A Study of Its Distempers, Deformities, and Disorders* (London and New York: Macmillan, 1895), p. 461.
16. See Patricia Allderidge, *Cibber's Figures from the Gates of Bedlam*, Victoria and Albert Museum Masterpieces, no. 14 (London, 1977); and Ronald Paulson, *Hogarth: His Life, Art, and Times*, 2 vols. (New Haven, Conn.: Yale University Press, 1971), 1: 326–27.
17. On the attitudes of Augustan poets towards gender and madness, see Max

Byrd, *Visits to Bedlam: Madness and Literature in the Eighteenth Century* (Columbia: University of South Carolina Press, 1974), pp. 42–43, 67–69; and Byrd, "The Madhouse, the Whorehouse, and the Convent," *Partisan Review* 44 (1977): 269–72.

18. See Andrew T. Scull, *Museums of Madness: The Social Organization of Insanity in Nineteenth-Century England* (Harmondsworth: Penguin Books, 1982), pp. 67–68, 73–75, 81; and Anne Digby, *Madness, Morality and Medicine: A History of the York Retreat* (Cambridge: Cambridge University Press, 1985). The most publicized individual case, however, was the caged lunatic James Norris at Bethlem in 1814.
19. See Byrd, *Visits to Bedlam,* pp. 92–93. See also Michael V. DePorte, *Nightmares and Hobbyhorses: Swift, Sterne, and Augustan Ideas of Madness* (San Marino, Calif.: Huntington Library, 1974).
20. Allderidge, *Cibber's Figures.*
21. George Dyer, "Written in Bedlam: On Seeing a Beautiful Young Female Maniac," *Poems* (London: Longman & Rees, 1801).
22. See Gilman, *Seeing the Insane,* p. 126. For a fuller discussion of Ophelia, see Elaine Showalter, "Representing Ophelia," in *Shakespeare and the Question of Theory,* ed. Patricia Parker and Geoffrey Hartman (London and New York: Methuen, 1985).
23. See Maurice and Hanna Charney, "The Language of Shakespeare's Madwomen," *Signs* 3 (1977): 452–53, 457; and Allan Dessen, *Elizabethan Stage Conventions and Modern Interpreters* (Cambridge; Cambridge University Press, 1984), pp. 36–38.
24. See Margery Garber, *Coming of Age in Shakespeare* (London: Methuen, 1981), pp. 155–57; and Bridget G. Lyons, "The Iconography of Ophelia," *English Literary History* 44 (1977): 65, 70–72.
25. See Carroll Camden, "On Ophelia's Madness," *Shakespeare Quarterly* 15 (1964): 254; and Gaston Bachelard on the "Ophelia complex" in *L'Eau et les rêves* (Paris: Librairie Jose Corti, 1942), pp. 109–25.
26. See Peter Raby, *Fair Ophelia: Harriet Smithson Berlioz* (Cambridge: Cambridge University Press, 1982).
27. See Ole Munch-Pedersen, "Crazy Jane: A Cycle of Popular Literature," *Eire-Ireland* 14 (1979): 56–73.
28. There is a useful discussion of these paintings in Gilman, *Seeing the Insane,* pp. 126–32.
29. Alexander Morison, *The Physiognomy of Mental Diseases* (1843; reprint ed., New York: Arno Press, 1976), p. 79.
30. Sir Walter Scott, *The Bride of Lammermoor* (London: J. M. Dent, 1964), p. 323.
31. See Ellen H. Bleiler, introduction to Gaetano Donizetti, *Lucia Di Lammermoor,* ed. Bleiler (New York: Dover Publications, 1972), pp. 1–44.
32. Donal Henahan, "Why They Were Crazy About Mad Scenes," *New York Times,* Sunday, 21 September 1980.

33. Gustave Flaubert, *Madame Bovary,* trans. Eleanor Marx Aveling (New York: Holt, Rinehart & Winston, 1962), p. 233.
34. The term "psychiatric Darwinism" comes from Vieda Skultans, *Madness and Morals: Ideas on Insanity in the Nineteenth Century* (London and Boston: Routledge & Kegan Paul, 1975), p. 203. She calls the phase of moral management "psychiatric Romanticism" because of its emphasis on the individual will; I have chosen instead to emphasize the parallels with Victorian social history and values.
35. The term "second psychiatric revolution" comes from Gregory Zilboorg, *A History of Medical Psychology* (New York: W. W. Norton, 1941), pp. 479 ff.

CHAPTER 1. DOMESTICATING INSANITY: JOHN CONOLLY AND MORAL MANAGEMENT

1. Richard Hunter and Ida Macalpine, *Psychiatry for the Poor: 1851 Colney Hatch Asylum–Friern Hospital 1973* (London: Dawsons, 1974), pp. 25–29; Andrew Wynter, "Lunatic Asylums," *Quarterly Review* 101 (1857): 364, 367. Wynter (1819–1876) looked at Colney Hatch, Hanwell, and Bethlem for his essay. For his later work, see chapter 4. On the Great Exhibition, see David Thomson, *England in the Nineteenth Century* (Harmondsworth: Penguin Books, 1961), p. 100.
2. Hunter and Macalpine, *Psychiatry for the Poor,* p. 29.
3. Andrew Halliday, *A General View of the Present State of Lunatics and Lunatic Asylums in Great Britain and Ireland* (London: Underwood, 1828), pp. 79–80.
4. Quoted in Peter Gay, *The Education of the Senses: The Bourgeois Experience—Victoria to Freud,* vol. 1 (New York and Oxford: Oxford University Press, 1984), p. 61.
5. John Hawkes, "On the Increase in Insanity," *Journal of Psychological Medicine and Mental Pathology* 10 (1857): 509, quoted in George Rosen, *Madness in Society: Chapters in the Historical Sociology of Mental Illness* (New York: Harper & Row, 1968), p. 187.
6. Wynter, "Lunatic Asylums," p. 390.
7. J. C. Bucknill, *The Psychology of Shakespeare* (1859; reprint ed., New York: AMS Press, 1970), pp. 96–97. Bucknill (1817–1896) was also medical superintendent of the Devon County Lunatic Asylum from 1844 to 1862. See *Dictionary of National Biography,* 1st supp., 1: 331–32.
8. John Conolly, *Treatment of the Insane Without Mechanical Restraints* (1856; reprint ed., London: Dawsons, 1973), pp. 32–33.
9. John Arlidge, *On the State of Lunacy and the Legal Protection for the Insane* (London: John Churchill, 1859), p. 32.
10. Wynter, "Lunatic Asylums," p. 353.

11. Andrew T. Scull, *Museums of Madness,* pp. 226, 233, 242–44. See also Denis Leigh, *The Historical Development of British Psychiatry* (London: Pergamon Press, 1961).
12. Edgar Sheppard, "The Modern Teachings of Insanity," *Journal of Mental Science* 17 (1872): 510. Sheppard was medical superintendent of the male department at Colney Hatch from 1862 to 1881.
13. E. T. Conolly, "Suggestions for the Amendment of the Laws Relating to Private Lunatic Asylums" (1858), quoted in William Parry-Jones, *The Trade in Lunacy: A Study of Private Madhouses in England in the Eighteenth and Nineteenth Centuries* (London: Routledge & Kegan Paul, 1972), p. 33; and Thomas Mulock, *British Lunatic Asylums: Public and Private* (Stafford: Hill & Haldon, 1858), p. 4. See also Scull, "The Social History of Psychiatry in the Victorian Era," in *Madhouses, Mad-Doctors, and Madmen: The Social History of Psychiatry in the Victorian Era,* ed. Andrew T. Scull (Philadelphia: University of Pennsylvania Press, 1981), p. 6. Throughout this book, I have used the terms "madness" and "psychiatry" in their most general sense, to describe manifestations of mental disorder and the medical specialty devoted to them.
14. See Andrew T. Scull, "The Domestication Of Madness," *Medical History* 27 (1983): 233–48, for a general discussion of these issues.
15. Daniel Hack Tuke, *Reform in the Treatment of the Insane* (London: John Churchill, 1892), p. 153. Hack Tuke (1827–1895) had been visiting physician at the York Retreat and coeditor of the *Journal of Mental Science.* On his life and work, see Gregory Zilboorg, *The History of Medical Psychology,* pp. 422–31.
16. Nathaniel Bingham, *Observations on the Religious Delusions of Insane Persons* (London: Hatchard, 1841), p. 105.
17. John Conolly, *The Construction and Government of Lunatic Asylums and Hospitals for the Insane* (1847; reprint ed., London: Dawsons, 1968), p. 144.
18. G. H. Lewes, "Dickens in Relation to Criticism," *Literary Criticism of George Henry Lewes,* ed. Alice R. Kaminsky (Lincoln: University of Nebraska Press, 1964), p. 96.
19. J. C. Bucknill and Daniel Hack Tuke, *A Manual of Psychological Medicine* (1858; reprint ed.; New York and London: Hafner, 1968), p. 78.
20. Eric T. Carlson and Norman Dain, "The Meaning of Moral Insanity," *Bulletin of the History of Medicine* 36 (1962): 131. See also Michael Donnelly, *Managing the Mind: A Study of Medical Psychology in Early Nineteenth-Century Britain* (London and New York: Tavistock Publications, 1983), pp. 137–40; and Vieda Skultans, *Madness and Morals,* pp. 180–200.
21. Hunter and Macalpine, *Psychiatry for the Poor,* p. 198; and Donnelly, *Managing the Mind,* pp. 136–37.
22. Hunter and Macalpine, *Psychiatry for the Poor,* p. 199
23. J. Mortimer Granville, *The Care and Cure of the Insane,* 2 vols. (London: Hardwicke & Bogue, 1877), 1: 48.

24. Hunter and Macalpine, *Psychiatry for the Poor,* p. 195.
25. John Barlow, *Man's Power over Himself to Prevent or Control Insanity* (London: William Pickering, 1843), p. 24, quoted in Skultans, *Madness and Morals,* p. 163.
26. William Tuke and Samuel Tuke, quoted in Scull, *Museums of Madness,* p. 69.
27. Daniel Hack Tuke, *Chapters in the History of the Insane in the British Isles* (1882; reprint ed., Amsterdam: E. J. B. Bunset, 1968), p. 256. See also Andrew T. Scull, "Humanitarianism or Control? Some Observations on the Historiography of Anglo-American Psychiatry," *Rice University Studies* 67 (1981): 33–34; and Robert Gardiner Hill, *Lunacy: Its Past and Present* (London: Longmans, Green, Reader & Dyer, 1870).
28. John Haslam, *Considerations on the Moral Management of the Insane* (London: R. Hunter, 1817), pp. 30–32.
29. For the history of nonrestraint, see Samuel Tuke, *A Description of the Retreat* (1813; reprint ed., London: Dawsons, 1964); William Charles Ellis, *A Treatise on the Nature, Symptoms, Causes, and Treatment of Insanity* (1838; reprint ed., New York: Arno Press, 1976); and Robert Gardiner Hill, *Total Abolition of Personal Restraint in the Treatment of the Insane* (London: Simpkin, Marshall, 1838).
30. Henry Maudsley, "Memoir of the Late John Conolly, M.D.," *Journal of Mental Science* 12 (July 1866): 170. For Maudsley, see chapter 4.
31. Benjamin Ward Richardson, "Medicine Under Queen Victoria: The First Advancement: The Treatment of the Insane," *Asclepiad* 4 (1877), quoted in Andrew T. Scull, "A Brilliant Career? John Conolly and Victorian Psychiatry," *Victorian Studies* 27 (1984): 203.
32. Conolly, *Construction,* p. 143.
33. See Donnelly, *Managing the Mind,* p. vii.
34. Conolly, *Construction,* pp. 26–44.
35. Granville, *Care and Cure,* 1:79.
36. Lenore Davidoff, Jean L'Esperance, and Howard Newby, "Landscape with Figures: Home and Community in English Society," in *The Rights and Wrongs of Women,* ed. Juliet Mitchell and Ann Oakley (Harmondsworth: Penguin Books, 1976), pp. 139–75.
37. William Stark, "On the Construction of Public Hospitals for the Cure of Mental Derangement" (1807), quoted in Richard Hunter and Ida Macalpine, *Three Hundred Years of Psychiatry, 1535–1860* (London: Oxford University Press, 1963), p. 629.
38. Donnelly, *Managing the Mind,* p. 67.
39. Ibid., pp. 31, 40.
40. Conolly, *Construction,* p. 8.
41. Isaac Ray, "Observations of the Principal Hospitals for the Insane in Great Britain, France, and Germany," *American Journal of Insanity* 2 (1846): 309–10. On the Victorian landscape, see George Levine, *The Realistic Imagina-*

tion: English Fiction from Frankenstein to Lady Chatterley (Chicago: University of Chicago Press, 1982), pp. 204–26.

42. Ray, "Observations," p. 312.
43. William Gilbert, "A Visit to a Convict Lunatic Asylum," *Cornhill Magazine* 10 (1864): 457. Gilbert, a surgeon, journalist, and novelist, was the father of the composer W. S. Gilbert.
44. W. A. F. Browne, "The Moral Treatment of the Insane," *Journal of Mental Science* 10 (1864): 313.
45. Ray, "Observations," p. 327.
46. John Conolly, "Lunatic Asylums of Paris," *British and Foreign Medical Review,* January 1845, quoted in Ray, "Observations," p. 326.
47. Wynter, "Lunatic Asylums," p. 365.
48. John Conolly, *Letter to Benjamin Rotch . . . on the Plan and Government of the Additional Lunatic Asylum for the County of Middlesex, about to be Erected at Colney Hatch,* quoted in "J.R.," "Colney Hatch Asylum," *Westminster Review* 48 (1848): 122–23.
49. Granville, *Care and Cure,* 2: 350.
50. Hunter and Macalpine, *Psychiatry for the Poor,* pp. 41, 44.
51. Edward Palmer, "Lincolnshire County Lunatic Asylum," *Journal of Mental Science* 13 (1867): 369.
52. See Klaus Doerner, *Madmen and the Bourgeoisie: A Social History of Insanity and Psychiatry,* trans. Joachim Naugroschel and Jean Steinberg (Oxford: Basil Blackwell, 1981), p. 216; Granville, *Care and Cure,* 1:190.
53. Hunter and Macalpine, *Psychiatry for the Poor,* p. 44; Wynter, "Lunatic Asylums," p. 372; Scull, *Museums of Madness,* p. 207.
54. Browne, "Moral Treatment," pp. 317–18.
55. Wynter, "Lunatic Asylums," pp. 372–73; and Gilbert, "Visit," p. 454.
56. *Illustrated Times,* 29 December 1859, quoted in Anthony Masters, *Bedlam* (London: Michael Joseph, 1977), p. 163; and Wynter, "Lunatic Asylums," p. 354.
57. Gilbert, "Visit," pp. 448, 449–50.
58. "Autobiography of the Insane," *Journal of Psychological Medicine and Mental Pathology* 8 (1855): 349.
59. "New Year's Eve in a Pauper Lunatic Asylum," *Athenaeum* (1842): 65–66.
60. Wynter, "Lunatic Asylums," p. 375.
61. W. A. F. Browne, *What Asylums Were, Are, and Ought to Be* (1837; reprint ed., New York: Arno Press, 1976), pp. 93–94.
62. John Arlidge, "An Examination of the Practice of Bloodletting in Mental Disorders, by Pliny Earle," *Asylum Journal of Mental Science* 2 (1856), quoted in Scull, *Museums of Madness,* p. 177.
63. Wynter, "Lunatic Asylums," p. 372.
64. Hunter and Macalpine, *Psychiatry for the Poor,* pp. 18–19.
65. Browne, *What Asylums Were,* pp. 229–30.

66. "J.R.," "Colney Hatch Asylum," pp. 127–28.
67. G. E. Paget, *The Harveian Oration* (Cambridge: Deighton, Bell, 1866), pp. 34–35, quoted in Andrew Wynter, *The Borderlands of Insanity,* 2nd ed. (London: Robert Hardwicke, 1875), p. 112.
68. Hunter and Macalpine, introduction to Conolly, *Construction,* p. 7. For Conolly's life and work, the best sources are the introductions by Hunter and Macalpine to Conolly's three books, and Andrew Scull's essay "A Brilliant Career?" pp. 203–35.
69. Andrew Wynter, "Non-Restraint in the Treatment of the Insane," *Edinburgh Review* 131 (1870): 83.
70. See Doerner, *Madmen and the Bourgeoisie,* p. 94.
71. See Sir James Clark, *A Memoir of John Conolly* (London: John Murray, 1869), p. 120.
72. Ibid., p. 46.
73. Maudsley, "Memoir," p. 167.
74. Scull, "A Brilliant Career?" p. 216, n. 32.
75. John Conolly, "Recollection of the Varieties of Insanity," *Medical Times and Gazette* 1 (1860): 9; and Hunter and Macalpine, introduction to Conolly, *Construction,* p. 23.
76. John Conolly to Leigh Hunt, 1861, in Clark, *Memoir,* p. 6.
77. Barbara Taylor, *Eve and the New Jerusalem: Socialism and Feminism in the Nineteenth Century* (New York: Pantheon Books, 1983), pp. 152–53.
78. Conolly, *Treatment,* pp. 250–51.
79. Ibid., pp. 172–73. See also the section on the medical superintendent in *Construction,* pp. 140–42.
80. Maudsley, "Memoir," p. 172.
81. Scull, "A Brilliant Career?" pp. 219–21.
82. John Conolly, *A Remonstrance with the Lord Chief Baron Touching the Case Nottidge versus Ripley,* 3rd ed. (London: John Churchill, 1849), p. 3, quoted in Scull, "A Brilliant Career?" p. 229.
83. See Hunter and Macalpine, introduction to Conolly, *Treatment,* p. xl; and Scull, "A Brilliant Career?" p. 230.
84. Charles Reade, *Hard Cash: A Matter-of-Fact Romance* (London: Ward, Lock, 1864). For the scandal over Reade's novel, see Richard Hunter and Ida Macalpine, "Dickens and Conolly: An Embarrassed Editor's Disclaimer," *Times Literary Supplement,* 11 August 1961, pp. 534–35.
85. Maudsley, "Memoir," p. 168.
86. Ray, "Observations," p. 347. On the history of American mental institutions, see David J. Rothman, *The Discovery of the Asylum: Social Order and Disorder in the New Republic* (Boston: Little, Brown, 1971).
87. For example, Thomas Mulock, *British Lunatic Asylums,* p. 5. Mulock, father of the novelist Dinah Maria Mulock, was a dissenting minister who had been an inmate of Stafford Asylum.
88. Arlidge, *On the State of Lunacy,* p. 102.

89. Janot, quoted in "Popular Psychological Literature," *Journal of Psychological Medicine* 10 (1857): 551.
90. *Illustrated Times,* quoted in Masters, *Bedlam,* pp. 165–66.
91. Wynter, "Lunatic Asylums," p. 376.
92. Michael Ignatieff, *A Just Measure of Pain: The Penitentiary in the Industrial Revolution* (New York: Pantheon Books, 1978), p. 214.
93. David Roberts, *Paternalism in Early Victorian England,* (New Brunswick, N.J.: Rutgers University Press, 1979), pp. 4–5.
94. Ibid., p. 5.

CHAPTER 2. THE RISE OF THE VICTORIAN MADWOMAN

1. Charles Dickens with W. H. Wills, "A Curious Dance Round a Curious Tree," 17 January 1852, in *Charles Dickens: Uncollected Writings from "Household Words," 1850–1859,* ed. Harry Stone, 2 vols. (Bloomington: Indiana University Press, 1968), 2: 387–88.
2. John Thurnam, *Observations and Essays on the Statistics of Lunacy,* quoted in William Parry-Jones, *The Trade in Lunacy,* pp. 49–50.
3. For statistics, see J. Mortimer Granville, *The Care and Cure of the Insane,* 1: 142 and 2: 230. In the general population in 1871 there were 1,056 women for every 1,000 men.
4. Parry-Jones, *The Trade in Lunacy,* p. 50.
5. Charles Lamb to S. T. Coleridge, 3 October 1796, *The Letters of Charles and Mary Lamb,* ed. Edwin W. Marrs, Jr., 3 vols. (Ithaca, N.Y.: Cornell University Press, 1975–78), 1: 49. Since Mary Lamb had killed her mother, who, according to Charles Lamb, had always been cold and rejecting, this care by a mother surrogate may have been therapeutic.
6. William Thackeray to his mother, September 1842, *The Letters and Private Papers of William Makepeace Thackeray,* ed. Gordon N. Ray, 4 vols. (London: Oxford University Press, 1945), 2: 81.
7. J. C. Bucknill, "Tenth Report of the Commissioners in Lunacy to the Lord Chancellor," *Asylum Journal of Mental Science* 3 (1857): 19–20, quoted in Parry-Jones, *The Trade in Lunacy,* p. 81.
8. See Lyttleton Winslow, *Manual of Lunacy* (London: Smith, Elder, 1874), pp. 77–81.
9. For a discussion of the medicalization of the care of the insane, see Scull, *Museums of Madness,* p. 163.
10. See C. N. French, *The Story of St. Luke's Hospital* (London: William Heineman, 1951), p. 79.
11. At Colney Hatch in 1852, for example, female attendants were paid £15 a year, with board, lodging, and laundry; male attendants received £25 with the same benefits. Asylum nursing was not regarded as a respectable occupation for women, although there were efforts to upgrade it. Female

attendants at Colney Hatch were not given uniforms until the matron petitioned the committee of visitors. Until 1968, at Colney Hatch–Friern, female nurses took care only of female patients. See Hunter and Macalpine, *Psychiatry for the Poor,* pp. 92–95, 102.

12. John Arlidge, *On the State of Lunacy and the Legal Provision for the Insane,* p. 113; and Conolly, *Construction,* pp. 136–37. Conolly further argued that matrons were often harsh to patients and nurses and resistant to the non-restraint method.
13. The theory of an accumulation of female incurables was argued by Edgar Sheppard in *Lectures on Madness in Its Medical, Legal, and Social Aspects* (London: John Churchill, 1873), pp. 3–5. See also Conolly, *Construction,* pp. 146–50.
14. See Scull, *Museums of Madness,* pp. 241–45; and Pat Thane, "Women and the Poor Law in Victorian and Edwardian England," *History Workshop Journal* 6 (1979): 29.
15. Hunter and Macalpine, *Psychiatry for the Poor,* pp. 63–64.
16. French, *St. Luke's Hospital,* p. 43; and W. A. F. Browne, *What Asylums Were, Are, and Ought to Be,* p. 184.
17. See Scull, *Museums of Madness,* pp. 245–53.
18. John Millingen, *Aphorisms on Insanity* (1840), quoted in Richard Hunter and Ida Macalpine, *Three Hundred Years of Psychiatry,* p. 902.
19. Horatio R. Storer, *The Causation, Course, and Treatment of Reflex Insanity in Women* (1871; reprint ed., New York: Arno Press, 1972), p. 78.
20. G. Fielding Blandford, *Insanity and Its Treatment* (Philadelphia: Henry C. Lea, 1871), p. 69. Blandford (1829–1911) was the resident medical officer at Blacklands House, a private asylum for men, from 1859 to 1863, and later had a private practice in the treatment of mental illness. He wrote widely on insanity, and in 1894 became president of the psychiatric section of the British Medical Association.
21. George Man Burrows, *Commentaries on Insanity* (1828), quoted in Vieda Skultans, *Madness and Morals,* p. 224.
22. See Carroll Smith-Rosenberg, "Puberty to Menopause," in her book *Disorderly Conduct: Visions of Gender in Victorian America* (New York: Alfred A. Knopf, 1985), pp. 188–203. See also Vieda Skultans, *Madness and Morals,* p. 12; James Sheppard, *Observations of the Proximate Causes of Insanity* (London: Longman, Brown, Green & Longmans, 1844), quoted in *Madness and Morals,* pp. 52–53; Parry-Jones, *The Trade in Lunacy,* p. 106; John Millar, *Hints on Insanity* (London: Henry Renshaw, 1861), quoted in *Madness and Morals,* p. 230; and L. Forbes Winslow, *On the Obscure Diseases of the Brain and Disorders of the Mind,* 4th ed. (London: John Churchill, 1851), p. 31.
23. "Woman in her Psychological Relations," *Journal of Psychological Medicine and Mental Pathology* 4 (1851): 34.
24. Edward J. Tilt, *The Change of Life in Health and Disease* (London: John Churchill, 1887), p. 265.

25. Smith-Rosenberg, *Disorderly Conduct,* p. 194.
26. Edward J. Tilt, *On the Preservation of the Health of Women at the Critical Periods of Life* (London: John Churchill, 1851), pp. 19–20.
27. See Leonore Davidoff, *The Best Circles: Society, Etiquette, and the Season* (London: Croom Helm, 1973), pp. 51, 87; and Deborah Gorham, *The Victorian Girl and the Feminine Ideal* (Bloomington: Indiana University Press, 1982), pp. 85–99.
28. Edward J. Tilt, *The Elements of Health, and Principles of Female Hygiene* (London: Henry G. Bohn, 1852), p. 173.
29. T. S. Clouston, *Clinical Lectures on Mental Diseases,* 5th ed. (London: J. & A. Churchill, 1898), pp. 531, 157.
30. J. C. Bucknill and Daniel Hack Tuke, *A Manual of Psychological Medicine,* pp. 238–39. See also John Reid, "On the Causes, Symptoms, and Treatment of Puerperal Insanity," *Journal of Psychological Medicine* 1 (1848): 128–51; and J. Batty Tuke, "On the Statistics of Puerperal Insanity as Observed in the Royal Edinburgh Asylum, Morningside," *Edinburgh Medical Journal* 10 (1865): 1013–28.
31. John Conolly, *Treatment of the Insane,* p. 107.
32. Henry Maudsley, *Body and Mind*, 2nd ed. (London: Macmillan, 1873), p. 91.
33. Bucknill and Tuke, *Manual of Psychological Medicine,* p. 273.
34. Ibid. For a thorough discussion of puerperal insanity in the contexts of Victorian legal views on madness and responsibility, see Roger Smith, *Trial by Medicine: Insanity and Responsibility in Victorian Trials* (Edinburgh: Edinburgh University Press, 1981), pp. 143–60.
35. J. B. Tuke, "On the Statistics of Puerperal Insanity," p. 1015.
36. John Conolly, "The Physiognomy of Insanity" (1858), in *The Face of Madness: Hugh W. Diamond and the Origin of Psychiatric Photography*, ed. Sander L. Gilman (New York: Brunner-Mazel, 1976), p. 45.
37. See R. Smith, *Trial by Medicine,* p. 154.
38. W. Tyler Smith, "The Climacteric Disease of Women," *London Journal of Medicine* 1 (1848): 601.
39. Maudsley, *Body and Mind,* p. 90.
40. Ibid.
41. See Smith-Rosenberg, *Disorderly Conduct,* pp. 198–99, for doctors' views that menopause ought to be considered the beginning of old age and that postmenopausal women should lead retiring lives.
42. William Moseley, *Eleven Chapters on Nervous and Mental Complaints* (1838), quoted in Skultans, *Madness and Morals,* p. 43.
43. Browne, *What Asylums Were,* p. 68.
44. Conolly, *Treatment of the Insane,* p. 161.
45. Samuel Tuke, *Description of the Retreat* (1813; reprint ed., London: Dawsons, 1964), pp. 151–52. See also Roy Porter, "Being Mad in Georgian England," *History Today* 31 (December 1981): 46.

46. Dinah Mulock Craik, "On Sisterhoods," *About Money and Other Things* (New York: Harper & Brothers, 1887), pp. 147–48.
47. Florence Nightingale, *Suggestions for Thought to Searchers After Religious Truth,* 3 vols. (privately printed, London: Eyre & Spottiswoode, 1860), 2: 220. For a full discussion of the sources of this book, see Elaine Showalter, "Florence Nightingale's Feminist Complaint," *Signs* 6 (1981): 395–412.
48. Nightingale, *Suggestions for Thought,* 2: 58.
49. Cecil Woodham-Smith, *Florence Nightingale* (New York: McGraw-Hill, 1951), p. 6. See also Donald R. Allen, "Florence Nightingale: Towards a Psychohistorical Interpretation," *Journal of Interdisciplinary History* 8 (1975): 23–45.
50. Woodham-Smith, *Florence Nightingale,* pp. 51–58.
51. Nightingale, *Suggestions for Thought,* 2:197.
52. The most accurate text of *Cassandra* is in vol. 2 of *Suggestions for Thought,* but this privately printed edition is difficult to obtain. There are copies at the British Library, the London Library, the New York Public Library, and the Yale Medical School Library. I have taken the following quotations from the best available edition, *Florence Nightingale's "Cassandra,"* ed. Myra Stark (Old Westbury, N.Y.: Feminist Press, 1979). An English edition is forthcoming from Virago Press, as well as an edition of Nightingale's letters prepared by Martha Vicinus.
53. *The Life and Letters of Benjamin Jowett,* ed. Evelyn Abbott and Lewis Campbell (London: John Murray, 1899), pp. 159–60.
54. Andrew Wynter, *The Borderlands of Insanity* (1875), p. 52.
55. Charlotte Brontë to W. S. Williams, 4 January 1848, in Clement Shorter, *The Brontës: Life and Letters,* 2 vols. (London: Hodder & Stoughton, 1908), 1: 383.
56. Conolly, *Treatment of the Insane,* pp. 149–50.
57. Sandra M. Gilbert and Susan Gubar, *The Madwoman in the Attic,* pp. 359–62.
58. Michael Ignatieff, *A Just Measure of Pain,* p. 198.
59. Ibid., pp. 198–200.
60. Conolly, "Physiognomy of Insanity," p. 55.
61. Mary E. Braddon, *Lady Audley's Secret* (New York: Dover Publishers, 1974). Subsequent references are given parenthetically in the text. For fuller discussion of this novel, see Elaine Showalter, *A Literature of Their Own: British Novelists from Brontë to Lessing* (Princeton, N.J.: Princeton University Press, 1977), pp. 163–68.

CHAPTER 3. MANAGING WOMEN'S MINDS

1. "A Sane Patient," *My Experiences in a Lunatic Asylum* (London: Chatto & Windus, 1879), p. 149.

2. John Millar, *Hints on Insanity,* quoted in Vieda Skultans, *Madness and Morals,* p. 59.
3. Henry Maudsley, *Body and Mind,* pp. 82–83.
4. Edward J. Tilt, *On the Preservation of the Health of Women at the Critical Periods of Life,* p. 31.
5. W. Tyler Smith, "The Climacteric Disease in Women," p. 607.
6. Isaac Baker Brown, *On the Curability of Certain Forms of Insanity, Epilepsy, Catalepsy, and Hysteria in Females* (London: Robert Hardwicke, 1866), pp. 14–15.
7. Ibid., p. 70.
8. Ibid., p. 73.
9. Ibid., pp. 37, 84. On the significance of clitoridectomy, see Gayatri C. Spivak, "French Feminism in an International Frame," *Yale French Studies,* no. 62 (1981), pp. 154–84.
10. Charles Routh, *British Medical Journal,* 1866, p. 673; T. Hawkes Tanner and Henry Maudsley, *British Medical Journal,* 1866, pp. 705–6; Wynn Williams, *British Medical Journal,* 1866, p. 673. For full transcripts of the debate, see "The Obstetrical Society Meeting to Consider the Proposition of the Council for the Removal of Mr. I. B. Brown," *British Medical Journal,* 1866, pp. 705–8, 728–30; 1867, pp. 18–19, 395–410. On the controversy over clitoridectomy, see also *The Lancet* 1 (1866): 699, 718–19; 2 (1866): 51–52, 114, 495, 560–61, 616–17, 639, 667–79, 678–79, 697–98, 709–11; (1867): 427–41.
11. "Obstetrical Society Meeting," *British Medical Journal,* 1867, p. 396.
12. Conolly, *Treatment of the Insane,* pp. 129, 114, 115–16, 122. During Conolly's tenure at Hanwell, there were approximately 567 women patients and 418 men. By the 1870s, women residents at Hanwell exceeded men by 36 percent. See Conolly, *Construction,* p. 148; and Granville, *Care and Cure,* 1: 142. Women patients at the Pennsylvania Hospital in the nineteenth century also became strongly attached to the medical superintendent, Dr. Thomas Kirkbride. In 1866, he married a former patient. On these "transference problems" in American asylums, see Nancy Tomes, *A Generous Confidence: Thomas Story Kirkbride and the Art of Asylum Keeping, 1840–1883* (Cambridge and New York: Cambridge University Press, 1984), pp. 226–34 and 336, n. 75.
13. Conolly, *Treatment of the Insane,* pp. 127–28.
14. Great Britain, *Parliamentary Papers,* vol. 4 (*Reports,* vol. 2), Select Committee Report, "Care and Treatment of Lunatics," 1859, pp. 20–21. The Alleged Lunatics' Friend Society, formed in 1845, was a small organization chiefly concerned with wrongful confinement in private asylums.
15. Robert Gardiner Hill, *Lunacy: Its Past and Present,* p. 4.
16. See C. T. Andrews, *The Dark Awakening: A History of St. Lawrence's Hospital* (London: Cox & Wyman, 1978), pp. 77–78; and Hunter and Macalpine, *Psychiatry for the Poor,* pp. 98–99.

17. Wynter, "Lunatic Asylums," pp. 358–59.
18. Conolly, *Treatment of the Insane,* p. 107; Granville, *Care and Cure,* 1:180.
19. Hunter and Macalpine, *Psychiatry for the Poor,* p. 113; *The Philosophy of Insanity,* by an inmate of the Glasgow Royal Asylum, ed. Frieda Fromm-Reichmann (1860; reprint ed., London: Fireside Press, 1947), p. 84. In prisons, too, the violent resistance of female convicts to their routines amazed wardens, who expected even criminals to abide by "the code of female docility." See Michael Ignatieff, *A Just Measure of Pain,* p. 203.
20. Hunter and Macalpine, *Psychiatry for the Poor,* p. 91; and Granville, *Care and Cure,* 1:184. At the Hanwell Asylum, however, Mr. Peeke Richards successfully calmed excitable women patients by allowing them to move around and visit other wards. The treatment of women in Bethlem is from testimony of Dr. W. Ward to the Select Committee, Commissioners in Lunacy on Bethlem Hospital, 7 July 1851, in Great Britain, *Parliamentary Papers,* 6: 271.
21. Andrew T. Scull, "Museums of Madness," Ph.D. dissertation, Princeton University, 1976, 2: 425; and Hunter and Macalpine, *Psychiatry for the Poor,* pp. 45, 76, 88.
22. Conolly, *Treatment of the Insane,* p. 58.
23. Granville, *Care and Cure,* 2: 177.
24. Erich Neumann, *Amor and Psyche: The Psychic Development of the Feminine* (Princeton, N.J.: Princeton University Press, 1956), pp. 41, 94–96.
25. Isaac Ray, "Observations of the Principal Hospitals for the Insane in Great Britain, France, and Germany," p. 350.
26. Wynter, "Lunatic Asylums," p. 353.
27. Harriet Martineau, "The Hanwell Lunatic Asylum" (1834), *Miscellanies,* 2 vols. (Boston: Hilliard, Gray, 1834), 1: 232.
28. John Conolly, *An Inquiry Concerning the Indications of Insanity* (1830; reprint ed., London: Dawsons, 1964), p. 52.
29. "Report of the Commissioners for Scotland," *Journal of Mental Science,* January 1882, quoted in Daniel Hack Tuke, *Chapters in the History of the Insane,* p. 384.
30. Francis Scott, "English County Asylums," *Fortnightly Review* 32 (1879): 131–32.
31. Granville, *Care and Cure,* 2: 176–77. See Judith R. Walkowitz, *Prostitution and Victorian Society: Women, Class, and the State* (London: Cambridge University Press, 1980), p. 221, for a discussion of laundry work in the reform of prostitutes.
32. Ray, "Observations," p. 359; Scott, "English County Asylums," pp. 124–25.
33. Conolly, *Construction,* p. 61; and Sir James Clark, *A Memoir of John Conolly,* p. 41.
34 Granville, *Care and Cure,* 1: 53.
35. For an account of James Crichton Browne's photography, see Sander L. Gilman, *Seeing the Insane,* pp. 179–81. Crichton Browne (1840–1938) was

the editor of the *West Riding Lunatic Asylum Medical Reports,* and later coeditor of *Brain.*

36. Quoted in Sander L. Gilman, *The Face of Madness,* p. 9.
37. Hugh Diamond, "On the Application of Photography to the Physiognomy and Mental Phenomena of Insanity," in Gilman, *The Face of Madness,* pp. 19–20, 24.
38. John Ruskin, "Of Queens' Gardens," *Sesame and Lilies* (1864; reprint ed., London: Dent, 1970), p. 52.
39. For an account of nineteenth-century paintings of Ophelia, see George Landow, *Images of Crisis: Literary Iconography 1750 to the Present* (London: Routledge & Kegan Paul, 1982), pp. 214–15.
40. Michael Donnelly, *Managing the Mind,* pp. 122–23. For a description of Ophelia as a Victorian heroine, see Nina Auerbach, *Woman and the Demon: The Life of a Victorian Myth* (Cambridge, Mass.: Harvard University Press, 1982), pp. 94–96.
41. J. C. Bucknill, *The Psychology of Shakespeare,* p. 110.
42. John Conolly, *A Study of Hamlet* (London: E. Moxon, 1863), pp. 177–78. See also Henry Maudsley, *The Pathology of Mind* (1895), p. 239.
43. Gilman, *Seeing the Insane,* p. 118; and Donnelly, *Managing the Mind,* p. 122.
44. Conolly, *Study of Hamlet,* pp. 180, 178.
45. Ellen Terry, *The Story of My Life* (New York: Schocken Books, 1982), p. 98. For other accounts of Victorian actresses playing Ophelia, see Elaine Showalter, "Representing Ophelia," in Parker and Hartmann, *Shakespeare and the Question of Theory;* and Nina Auerbach, "Ellen Terry's Victorian Marriage," *Romantic Imprisonment: Women and Other Glorified Outcasts* (New York: Columbia University Press, 1985).
46. Diamond, "On the Application of Photography," p. 21.
47. John Conolly, "The Physiognomy of Insanity," pp. 49, 67–70, 71.
48. Ibid., pp. 29–32.
49. Susan Sontag, *On Photography* (Harmondsworth: Penguin Books, 1977), pp. 5, 21.
50. Charles Dickens and W. H. Wills, "A Curious Dance Round a Curious Tree," pp. 382, 388–89.
51. Conolly, *Treatment of the Insane,* p. 116.
52. T. S. Clouston, *Clinical Lectures on Mental Diseases,* pp. 530–31.

CHAPTER 4. ON THE BORDERLAND: HENRY MAUDSLEY AND PSYCHIATRIC DARWINISM

1. Hunter and Macalpine, *Psychiatry for the Poor,* pp. 30ff.
2. Granville, *Care and Cure,* 1: 75.
3. Andrew Wynter, *The Borderlands of Insanity* (1875), pp. 124–25.
4. See John Arlidge, *On the State of Lunacy,* p. 102; Hunter and Macalpine, *Psychiatry for the Poor,* p. 87; Scull, *Museums of Madness,* pp. 222–26.

5. Scull, *Museums of Madness,* pp. 201–4.
6. Wynter, "Lunatic Asylums," p. 364.
7. "Autobiography of the Insane," *Journal of Psychological Medicine and Mental Pathology* 8 (1855): 353.
8. Scull, *Museums of Madness,* p. 182.
9. Granville, *Care and Cure,* 1: 99.
10. G. Fielding Blandford, *Insanity and Its Treatment,* p. iv.
11. Henry Maudsley, *Responsibility in Mental Disease,* 2nd ed. (London: Kegan Paul, 1874), p. 28.
12. These observations depend on the fullest discussion of the theories of late Victorian psychiatry, Michael Clark, "Victorian Psychiatry and the Concept of Morbid Introspection," unpublished paper, Oxford University, 1981. I am indebted to Michael Clark for sharing this work with me.
13. Wynter, *Borderlands of Insanity,* pp. 45–46; Maudsley, *Responsibility in Mental Disease,* p. 40; and George M. Beard, *Sexual Neurasthenia: Its Hygiene, Causes, Symptoms, and Treatment,* ed. A. D. Rockwell (New York: Treat, 1884).
14. Wynter, *Borderlands of Insanity,* p. 31.
15. J. Mortimer Granville, in Wynter, *The Borderlands of Insanity,* 2nd ed., (London: Henry Renshaw, 1877), p. 276. Granville contributed five chapters to this edition.
16. Henry Maudsley, *Body and Mind* (London: Macmillan, 1870), p. 154.
17. Daniel Hack Tuke, *Prichard and Symonds in Especial Relations to Mental Science, with Chapters on Moral Science* (1894), quoted in Peter Cominos, "Late Victorian Sexual Respectability and the Social System," *International Review of Social History* 8 (1963): 236–37.
18. Charles Mercier, "Vice, Crime, and Insanity," in *A System of Medicine,* ed. Thomas Clifford Allbutt and Humphrey Davy Rolleston, 2nd ed., 9 vols. (London: Macmillan, 1910), 7: 851.
19. Sander L. Gilman, *Seeing the Insane,* p. 188.
20. Maudsley, *Responsibility in Mental Disease,* p. 276; *Body and Mind,* pp. 58–59.
21. Henry Maudsley, *The Pathology of Mind* (1895), p. 536.
22. L. Forbes Winslow, *The Insanity of Passion and Crime* (London: John Ousely, 1912), pp. 287, 288–89.
23. Judith R. Walkowitz, "Jack the Ripper's London," unpublished paper, Rutgers University, 1982. I am indebted to Judith Walkowitz for sharing this material from her forthcoming book on sexuality and violence in late Victorian England. For L. Forbes Winslow's life, see his autobiography, *Recollections of Forty Years* (London: John Ousely, 1910).
24. Furneaux Jordan, *Character as Seen in Body and Parentage* (London: Kegan Paul, Trench & Trubner, 1886), pp. 1–5.
25. Charles Mercier, *A Textbook of Insanity,* 2nd ed. (London: George Allen & Unwin, 1914), p. 17.

26. Daniel Hack Tuke, *Insanity in Ancient and Modern Life, with Chapters on Its Prevention* (London: Macmillan, 1878), pp. 98, 91–92.
27. Wynter, "Lunatic Asylums," p. 392.
28. Maudsley, *Pathology of Mind* (1895), p. 30.
29. George Henry Savage, "Mental Diseases: An Introduction," in Allbutt and Rolleston, *A System of Medicine,* 7: 832. Savage (1842–1921) was knighted in 1912. He was physician superintendent at Bethlem Hospital, president of the Medico-Psychological Association of Great Britain, and editor of the *Journal of Mental Science.* His textbook *Insanity and Allied Neuroses* (1884) was frequently reprinted and cited. On Savage's career and ideas, see Stephen Trombley, *All That Summer She Was Mad: Virginia Woolf and Her Doctors* (London: Junction Books, 1981), pp. 107–58.
30. See Leonore Davidoff, "Class and Gender in Victorian England," *Feminist Studies* 5 (1979): 88–89.
31. See Geoffrey Pearson, *The Deviant Imagination: Psychiatry, Social Work, and Social Change* (London: Macmillan, 1975), p. 162; Gertrude Himmelfarb, "Mayhew's Poor: A Problem of Identity," *Victorian Studies* 14 (1971): 320; and Judith R. Walkowitz, *Prostitution and Victorian Society*, p. 4.
32. Gareth Stedman Jones, *Outcast London: A Study in the Relationship Between Classes in Victorian Society* (Harmondsworth: Penguin Books, 1971), p. 290.
33. See Judith R. Walkowitz, "Jack the Ripper and the Myth of Male Violence," *Feminist Studies* 8 (1982): 545.
34. Arnold White, "The Nomad Poor of London," *Contemporary Review* 47 (May 1885): 715; Alfred Marshall, *Industrial Remuneration Conference* (1885), p. 198, quoted in Stedman Jones, *Outcast London,* pp. 287, 288–89.
35. George Henry Savage and Edwin Goodall, *Insanity and Allied Neuroses,* 4th ed. (London: Cassell, 1907), p. 44.
36. Frederick W. Mott, "Heredity and Insanity," *The Lancet,* 1911, pp. 1259, 1251.
37. T. B. Hyslop, *The Borderland* (London: P. Allan, 1924), p. 240. For Hyslop's career and ideas, see Trombley, *All That Summer She Was Mad,* pp. 239–40.
38 Hunter and Macalpine, *Psychiatry for the Poor,* p. 201.
39. Thomas Austin, *A Practical Account of General Paralysis* (1859; reprint ed., New York: Arno Press, 1976), pp. 23, 24.
40. W. Julius Mickle, "General Paralysis of the Insane," in *Dictionary of Psychological Medicine,* ed. Daniel Hack Tuke (Philadelphia: P. Blakiston, 1892), p. 521.
41. Maudsley, *Responsibility in Mental Disease,* p. 74.
42. Richard von Krafft-Ebing, cited in George Rosen, *Madness in Society,* p. 247.
43. See C. F. Marshall, *Syphilology and Venereal Disease* (New York: William Wood, 1906), p. 216; and George Savage, "GPI," in Allbutt and Rolleston, *A System of Medicine,* 8: 349. For a fuller account of syphilitic insanity and

late Victorian culture, see Elaine Showalter, "Syphilis, Sexuality, and the Fin de Siècle," in *Sex, Politics, and Science in the Nineteenth-Century Novel: Essays from the English Institute,* ed. Ruth Yeazell and Neil Hertz (Baltimore: Johns Hopkins University Press, forthcoming 1986).

44. On Maudsley, see Sir Aubrey Lewis, "Henry Maudsley: His Work and Influence," *The State of Psychiatry* (New York: Science House, 1967), pp. 29–48; and Michael J. Clark, biographical appendix to "Late Victorian Psychiatry," D. Phil. dissertation, Oxford University, 1982, pp. 341–43.
45. Lewis, "Henry Maudsley," pp. 37, 38.
46. Henry Maudsley, *The Pathology of Mind* (London: Macmillan, 1879), p. 88.
47. Lewis, "Henry Maudsley," pp. 30. 37.
48. Ibid., p. 30.
49. Ibid., p. 31.
50. Nesta Roberts, *Cheadle Royal Hospital: A Bicentenary History* (Altrincham: John Sherratt & Son, 1967), pp. 87–95.
51. Henry Maudsley, *The Physiology and Pathology of Mind* (New York: D. Appleton, 1867), p. 430.
52. Henry Maudsley, "Memoir of the Late John Conolly, M.D.," p. 160.
53. Maudsley, *Physiology and Pathology of Mind,* pp. 253, 256, 257.
54. Maudsley, *Responsibility in Mental Disease,* p. 109; quoted in Vieda Skultans, *Madness and Morals,* p. 210. I have been unable to locate this quotation in Maudsley's text.
55. Maudsley, "Memoir," p. 173.
56. Mercier, "Vice, Crime, and Insanity," p. 852. L. Forbes Winslow thought that the English "love of athletic sports" would counteract the tendency to neurasthenia; "American Nervousness," *Journal of Psychological Medicine* n.s. (1881): 118. The idea that exercise may combat stress and produce a sense of mental well-being is, of course, popular in the 1980s as well. Nineteenth-century nerve specialists, however, did not prescribe vigorous physical activity for women. For biographies of Maudsley, Bucknill, Blandford, and Mercier, see G. H. Brown, comp., *Lives of the Fellows of the Royal College of Physicians of London, 1826–1925* (London: Royal College of Physicians, 1955), continuation of William Munk, *The Roll of the Royal College of Physicians of London; Comprising Biographical Sketches of All the Eminent Physicians* (1878).
57. Clark, "Morbid Introspection," p. 22.
58. Lewis, "Henry Maudsley," p. 40.
59. Maudsley, *Responsibility in Mental Disease,* pp. 22, 25, 30, 33.
60. Maudsley, *Pathology of Mind* (1895), p. 61.
61. Henry Maudsley, *Body and Will* (London: Kegan Paul, Trench, 1883), p. 237.
62. Clark, biographical appendix to "Late Victorian Psychiatry," p. 342.
63. Lewis, "Henry Maudsley," p. 48.
64. Clark, biographical appendix, p. 342.

65. Henry Maudsley, "Insanity in Relation to Criminal Responsibility," *Alienist and Neurologist,* 17 April 1896, p. 175.
66. Maudsley, *Pathology of Mind* (1895) p. 563.
67. Savage and Goodall, *Insanity and Allied Neuroses,* p. 14.

CHAPTER 5. NERVOUS WOMEN: SEX ROLES AND SICK ROLES

1. Thomas Clifford Allbutt, "Nervous Diseases and Modern Life," *Contemporary Review* 67 (1895): 217. Allbutt (1836–1925) was a Commissioner in Lunacy from 1889 to 1892, and then became Regius Professor at Cambridge.
2. Charles Darwin, *The Descent of Man* (1871; reprint ed., Princeton, N.J.: Princeton University Press, 1981), pp. 326–27.
3. For important studies of the effects of Darwinian theory on women and feminism, see Flavia Ayala, "Victorian Science and the 'Genius' of Woman," *Journal of the History of Ideas* 38 (1977): 261–80; Jill Conway, "Stereotypes of Femininity in a Theory of Sexual Evolution," in *Suffer and Be Still: Women in the Victorian Age,* ed. Martha Vicinus (Bloomington: Indiana University Press, 1972), pp. 140–54; Carol Dyhouse, *Girls Growing Up in Late Victorian and Edwardian England* (London: Routledge & Kegan Paul, 1981), pp. 151–55; and Lorna Duffin, "Prisoners of Progress: Women and Evolution," in *The Nineteenth-Century Woman: Her Cultural and Physical World,* ed. Sara Delamont and Lorna Duffin (London: Croom Helm, 1978), pp. 57–91.
4. Henry Maudsley, "Sex in Mind and in Education," *Fortnightly Review* 15 (1874): 468.
5. T. S. Clouston, *Female Education from a Medical Point of View* (Edinburgh: Macniven & Wallace, 1882), p. 41. Clouston (1840–1915) was medical superintendent at Morningside Asylum in Edinburgh and lecturer on mental diseases at the University of Edinburgh.
6. Maudsley, "Sex in Mind," p. 472.
7. Clouston, *Female Education,* p. 20.
8. Maudsley, "Sex in Mind," p. 471.
9. T. S. Clouston, "The Psychological Dangers to Women in Modern Social Development" in *The Position of Women: Actual and Ideal,* ed. Sir Oliver Lodge (London: James Nisbet, 1911), pp. 109–10; George Henry Savage and Edwin Goodall, *Insanity and Allied Neuroses,* pp. 26–27; and Wynter, *Borderlands of Insanity,* p. 52.
10. Henry Maudsley, *The Pathology of Mind* (1895), p. 389.
11. Maudsley, "Sex in Mind," p. 482.
12. Michel Foucault, *The History of Sexuality,* trans. Robert Hurley (New York: Vintage Books, 1980), p. 104.
13. See Maudsley, "Sex in Mind," pp. 466–83, and also Clouston, *Female Education,* pp. 8–9. The best account of the controversy is Joan N. Burstyn,

Victorian Education and the Ideal of Womanhood (London: Croom Helm, 1980), pp. 84–98.

14. Daniel Hack Tuke, *Insanity in Ancient and Modern Life,* pp. 109–10; George Henry Savage and Edwin Goodall, *Insanity and Allied Neuroses,* p. 22; and T. S. Clouston, *Clinical Lectures on Mental Diseases,* p. 582. See also Clouston, *Female Education,* pp. 16, 18; and his essay "The Psychological Dangers to Women in Modern Social Development," in Lodge, *Position of Women.*
15. Louisa Lowe, "Quis Custodiet Ipsos Custodes?" *The Bastilles of England; or, The Lunacy Laws at Work* (London: Crookenden, 1883), p. 137. See also E. P. W. Packard, *Modern Persecution; or, Insane Asylums Unveiled* (1873; reprint ed., New York: Arno Press, 1973); and the accounts of legal cases in D. J. Mellett, "Bureaucracy and Mental Illness: the Commissioners in Lunacy, 1845–1890," *Medical History* 25 (1981): 241–42, and Peter McCandless, "Liberty and Lunacy: The Victorians and Wrongful Confinement," in Scull, *Madhouses, Mad-Doctors, and Madmen,* pp. 339–62.
16. Letter from Dr. Alexander Walk, Royal College of Psychiatrists, November 26, 1981. See also Charlotte Mackenzie, "Women and Psychiatric Professionalization, 1780–1914," in London Feminist History Group, *The Sexual Dynamics of History* (London: Pluto Press, 1985), pp. 107–19. The situation was different in the United States, where nearly two hundred women physicians were employed in mental institutions from 1870 to 1900. Despite their numbers, however, they failed to develop a distinctly feminist position as administrators or theorists. See Constance M. McGovern, "Doctors or Ladies? Women Physicians in Psychiatric Institutions, 1872–1900," in *Women and Health in America,* ed. Judith Walzer Leavitt (Madison: University of Wisconsin Press, 1984), pp. 438–52; and Gerald Grob, *Mental Illness and American Society, 1875–1940* (Princeton, N.J.: Princeton University Press, 1983), pp. 65–66.
17. W. W. Gull, "Anorexia Nervosa," *Transactions of the Clinical Society of London* 7 (1874): 22–28, quoted in R. L. Palmer, *Anorexia Nervosa* (Harmondsworth: Penguin Books, 1980), p. 8. See also Hilde Bruch, *Eating Disorders: Obesity, Anorexia Nervosa, and the Person Within* (New York: Basic Books, 1973), pp. 211–14; and Sheila MacLeod, *The Art of Starvation* (London: Virago Press, 1981).
18. Quoted in Palmer, *Anorexia Nervosa,* pp. 8–9.
19. See Joan Jacobs Brumberg, " 'Fasting Girls': Nineteenth-Century Medicine and the Public Debate Over Anorexy," paper read at Berkshire Conference on the History of Women, June 1984. I am indebted to Joan Brumberg, of Cornell University, for sharing this material from her forthcoming book *Fasting Girls: A Social and Cultural History of Anorexia Nervosa* (Cambridge, Mass.: Harvard University Press).
20. Nightingale, *Cassandra,* pp. 41–42.
21. Thomas Clifford Allbutt, "Neuroses of the Stomach," in *A System of Medi-*

cine, ed. Thomas Clifford Allbutt and Humphrey Davy Rolleston, 2nd ed., 9 vols. (London: Macmillan, 1910), 3: 398–99.

22. See Joan Jacobs Brumberg, "Chlorotic Girls, 1870–1920: A Historical Perspective on Female Adolescence," in Leavitt, *Women and Health in America,* p. 191.
23. Jan Goldstein, "The Hysteria Diagnosis and the Politics of Anticlericalism in Late Nineteenth-Century France," *Journal of Modern History* 54 (1982): 210.
24. Stephen Heath, *The Sexual Fix* (London: Macmillan, 1982), pp. 25–27.
25. Edward J. Tilt, *A Handbook of Uterine Therapeutics and of Diseases of Women,* 4th ed. (New York: William Wood, 1881), p. 85.
26. S. Weir Mitchell, quoted in Barbara Sicherman, "The Uses of a Diagnosis: Doctors, Patients, and Neurasthenia," *Journal of the History of Medicine* 32 (1977): 41.
27. Henry Maudsley, *The Pathology of Mind* (1879), p. 450. In the 1895 version of the book, Maudsley elaborated on this idea. See pp. 388–89.
28. Charles Mercier, *Sanity and Insanity* (New York: Scribner & Welford, 1890), p. 213.
29. See Ruth First and Ann Scott, *Olive Schreiner* (New York: Schocken Books, 1980), pp. 150, 145, 157–58; Yvonne Kapp, *Eleanor Marx,* 2 vols. (London: Virago Press, 1979), 1: 222.
30. H. B. Donkin, "Hysteria," in D. H. Tuke, *Dictionary of Psychological Medicine,* pp. 619, 620. For a historical overview, see Ilza Veith, *Hysteria: The History of a Disease* (Chicago: University of Chicago Press, 1965).
31. Robert Brudenell Carter, *On the Pathology and Treatment of Hysteria* (London: John Churchill, 1853), pp. 21, 32.
32. F. C. Skey, *Hysteria,* 2nd ed. (London: Longmans, Green, Reader & Dyer, 1867), pp. 77–84. Skey was a former president of the Royal College of Surgeons.
33. Carroll Smith-Rosenberg, "The Hysterical Woman," *Disorderly Conduct,* pp. 215–16.
34. Donkin, "Hysteria," p. 621. See also Mercier, who maintained that the most serious manifestation of hysteria, the appetite for "giving pain and annoyance to others," could end in murder. *Sanity and Insanity,* p. 215.
35. Maudsley, *Pathology of Mind* (1895), pp. 397–98; see also Maudsley, *Body and Will,* p. 257.
36. Donkin, "Hysteria," p. 623.
37. T. S. Clouston, *Hygiene of Mind* (London: Methuen, 1906), p. 69.
38. G. Fielding Blandford, *Insanity and Its Treatment,* p. 408.
39. Savage, *Insanity and Allied Neuroses,* pp. 96–97.
40. S. Weir Mitchell, "Rest in Nervous Disease: Its Use and Abuse," in *A Series of American Clinical Lectures,* ed. W. Sequin (1875), p. 94; see also Sicherman, "Uses of a Diagnosis," p. 41, and W. S. Playfair, "Functional Neuroses," in D. H. Tuke, *Dictionary of Psychological Medicine,* p. 851.

41. George Miller Beard, *Sexual Neurasthenia,* p. 36. See also Beard, *American Nervousness: Its Causes and Consequences* (1881; reprint ed., New York: Arno Press, 1972). On Beard, see Charles D. Rosenberg, "The Place of George M. Beard in Nineteenth-Century British Psychiatry," *Bulletin of the History of Medicine* 36 (1962): 245–59.
42. Beard, *Sexual Neurasthenia,* pp. 204, 59, 60; and Beard, *A Practical Treatise on Nervous Exhaustion,* ed. A. D. Rockwell (1905; reprint ed., New York: Kraus Reprint, 1971), p. 255. Maudsley too felt that the madness of a European would be as different from that of an aborigine as "the ruins of a palace must be vaster and more varied than the ruins of a log hut" (*Physiology and Pathology of Mind,* pp. 250–51).
43. Herbert Spencer, quoted in Howard M. Feinstein, "The Use and Abuse of Illness in the James Family Circle," in *Ourselves, Our Past: Psychological Approaches to American History,* ed. Robert J. Brugger (Baltimore: Johns Hopkins University Press, 1981), p. 230.
44. On Margaret Cleaves, see Sicherman, "Uses of a Diagnosis"; Suzanne Poirier, "The Weir Mitchell Rest Cure: Doctors and Patients," *Women's Studies* 10 (1983): 28–29; and McGovern, "Doctors or Ladies?" pp. 442–43.
45. Rudolph Arndt, "Neurasthenia," in D. H. Tuke, *Dictionary of Psychological Medicine,* pp. 841, 848.
46. Lorna Duffin, "The Conspicuous Consumptive: Woman as an Invalid," in Delamont and Duffin, *Nineteenth-Century Woman,* pp. 37–38; Allbutt, "Neurasthenia," in Allbutt and Rolleston, *A System of Medicine,* 8: 748; Savage, "Mental Diseases," in *A System of Medicine,* 7: 835.
47. See Martha Vicinus, " 'One Life to Stand Beside Me': Emotional Conflicts in First-Generation College Women in England," *Feminist Studies* 8 (1982): 608. For a fascinating description of one such case of New Womanly neurasthenia, also associated with nursing a dying father, see Deborah Epstein Nord, *The Apprenticeship of Beatrice Webb* (Amherst: University of Massachusetts Press, 1985), pp. 45–46, 100–103.
48. Michael J. Clark, "The Rejection of Psychological Approaches to Mental Disorder in Late Nineteenth-Century British Psychiatry," in Scull, *Madhouses, Mad-doctors, and Madmen,* p. 295.
49. Allbutt, "Neuroses of the Stomach," p. 398; Lasegue, quoted in Palmer, *Anorexia Nervosa,* p. 9.
50. Sarah Grand, *The Heavenly Twins* (London: George Heinemann, 1893), p. 594.
51. Carter, *Pathology and Treatment of Hysteria,* p. 108; Allbutt, "Neurasthenia," p. 777; Donkin, "Hysteria," p. 626; Mercier, *Sanity and Insanity,* pp. 229–30.
52. J. A. Ormerod, "Hysteria," in Allbutt and Rolleston, *A System of Medicine,* 8: 724.
53. Skey, *Hysteria,* p. 60.

54. F. Cecily Steadman, *In the Days of Miss Beale,* quoted in Janet Horowitz Murray, *Strong-Minded Women and Other Lost Voices of Nineteenth-Century England* (New York: Pantheon Books, 1982), pp. 205–6.
55. S. Weir Mitchell, *Fat and Blood and How to Make Them* (Philadelphia: J. B. Lippincott, 1877), pp. 7, 41.
56. Sicherman, "Uses of a Diagnosis," p. 50.
57. Ann D. Wood, "The Fashionable Diseases: Women's Complaints and Their Treatment in Nineteenth-Century America," in *Clio's Consciousness Raised: New Perspectives on the History of Women,* ed. Mary Hartman and Lois W. Banner (New York: Harper & Row, 1971), p. 9; G. Barker-Benfield, *The Horrors of the Half-Known Life* (New York: Harper Colophon, 1976), p. 130; Jean Strouse, *Alice James* (New York: Houghton Mifflin, 1980), pp. 103–6.
58. W. S. Playfair, *The Systematic Treatment of Nerve Prostration and Hysteria* (Philadelphia: Henry Lea, 1883), p. 89.
59. Ibid., pp. 20, 76.
60. "Why I Wrote 'The Yellow Wallpaper,' " in *The Charlotte Perkins Gilman Reader,* ed. Ann J. Lane (New York: Pantheon Books, 1980), pp. 19–20.
61. Sandra M. Gilbert and Susan Gubar, *The Madwoman in the Attic,* p. 89.
62. Elaine Hedges, "Afterword," in Charlotte Perkins Gilman, *The Yellow Wallpaper* (New York: Feminist Press, 1973), p. 39.
63. Wood, "Fashionable Diseases," pp. 10–12.
64. *The Letters of Virginia Woolf,* ed. Nigel Nicolson and Joanne Trautmann, 6 vols. (New York: Harcourt Brace Jovanovich, 1975–82), 1: 190. Woolf reviewed *A Dark Lantern* in *The Guardian,* 24 May 1905.
65. *Letters of Virginia Woolf,* 1: 147–48.
66. *The Diary of Alice James,* ed. Leon Edel (New York: Dodd, Mead, 1964), p. 142.
67. "George Egerton" (Mary Chavelita Dunne), *Keynotes* (1894; reprint ed., London: Virago Press, 1983), p. 57.

CHAPTER 6. FEMINISM AND HYSTERIA: THE DAUGHTER'S DISEASE

1. F. C. Skey, *Hysteria,* p. 55.
2. Henry Maudsley, "Sex in Mind," p. 482. By the end of the century, sexologists were redefining the rebellious New Woman as an "invert" or lesbian. See Carroll Smith-Rosenberg, *Disorderly Conduct,* pp. 272–89.
3. Henry James, *The Bostonians* (1886; reprint ed., New York: Modern Library, 1956), chap. 34; *The Times* (London), 21 April 1891, quoted in Michael Egan, *Ibsen: The Critical Heritage* (London: Routledge & Kegan Paul, 1972), p. 218; Margaret Oliphant, "The Anti-Marriage League," *Blackwood's* 159 (1896): 136–49.

4. On Edith Lanchester, see Hal Sears, *The Sex Radicals: Free Love in Victorian America* (Lawrence: Regents Press of Kansas, 1977), p. 87; Yvonne Kapp, *Eleanor Marx,* 2: 621; and Elsa Lanchester, *Herself* (New York: St. Martin's Press, 1983), pp. 1–5.
5. The description of hysteria as the "daughter's disease" is from Juliet Mitchell, "The Question of Femininity and the Theory of Psychoanalysis," *Women: The Longest Revolution,* p. 308. For psychoanalysis as the child of the hysterical woman, see Smith-Rosenberg, *Disorderly Conduct,* p. 204.
6. Sigmund Freud, "Charcot," *Collected Papers*, ed. Ernest Jones, 5 vols. (London: Hogarth Press, 1948), 1: 18.
7. Axel Munthe, *The Story of San Michele* (London: John Murray, 1930), pp. 296, 302–3. On Blanche Wittmann, see A. R. G. Owen, *Hysteria, Hypnosis, and Healing: The Work of J.-M. Charcot* (London: Dennis Dobson, 1971), pp. 186–90.
8. Review of vol. 1 of *Iconographie* in *Progrès médical* 7 (1879): 331; quoted in Jan Goldstein, "The Hysteria Diagnosis," p. 215.
9. See Georges Didi-Huberman, *Invention de l'hystérie: Charcot et l'iconographie photographique de la Salpêtrière* (Paris: Macula, 1982), pp. 32–68.
10. Freud, "Charcot," pp. 10–11.
11. See Hippolyte Bernheim, "L'Hypnotisme de la Salpêtrière est un produit artificiel, la conséquence d'un apprentissage," *Le Temps,* 1891, discussed in George Frederick Drinker, *The Birth of Neurosis: Myth, Malady, and the Victorians* (New York: Simon & Schuster, 1984), pp. 144–48.
12. See Goldstein, "The Hysteria Diagnosis," pp. 209–10.
13. Charcot, quoted in Didi-Huberman, *Invention de l'hystérie,* p. 32.
14. Albert Londe, quoted in Didi-Huberman, *Invention de l'hystérie,* p. 35.
15. On "Augustine," also called "Louise" and "X," "L," and "G" in the *Iconographie,* see Didi-Huberman, *Invention de l'hystérie,* and Drinker, *Birth of Neurosis.*
16. Stephen Heath, *The Sexual Fix*, pp. 36–37.
17. See Didi-Huberman, *Invention de l'hystérie,* pp. 108, 269. Other famous hysterics at the Salpêtrière had similarly dramatic experiences. "Genevieve" ran away twice with medical students; Blanche Wittmann stayed on in the hospital as a radiology technician, and developed cancer from radiation. In her last months, her limbs were amputated one by one. See Drinker, *Birth of Neurosis,* pp. 93–96, 150.
18. See Didi-Huberman, *Invention de l'hystérie,* p. 134.
19. J.-M. Charcot, *L'Hystérie,* ed. E. Trillat (Toulouse: Eduoard Privat, 1971), p. 119.
20. Robert Brudenell Carter, *Pathology and Treatment of Hysteria,* p. 43.
21. For the life of Bertha Pappenheim, see Dora Edinger, *Bertha Pappenheim—Freud's Anna O.* (Highland Park, Ill.: Congregation Solel, 1968); Lucy Freeman, *The Story of Anna O.* (New York: Walker, 1972); and Max Rosenbaum and Melvin Muroff, eds., *Anna O.: Fourteen Contemporary Reinterpretations* (New York and London: Free Press, 1984).

22. Sigmund Freud and Joseph Breuer, "Fraülein Anna O.," *Studies on Hysteria* (New York: Avon Books, 1966), pp. 55–56, 59, 76.
23. Ibid., p. 64.
24. Mitchell, *Women: The Longest Revolution,* p. 298.
25. Dianne Hunter, "Hysteria, Psychoanalysis, and Feminism: The Case of Anna O.," *Feminist Studies* 9 (1983): 474.
26. Ibid., pp. 474–75.
27. Ibid., p. 484.
28. Freud and Breuer, *Studies on Hysteria,* pp. 48, 282.
29. Ibid., pp. 141, 202, 22.
30. Sigmund Freud, *Dora: An Analysis of a Case of Hysteria* (New York: Collier Books, 1964), pp. 74, 37, 34, 52.
31. Ibid., pp. 50, 34, 38.
32. Ibid., p. 37. On Dora's subsequent life, see Felix Deutsch, "A Footnote to Freud's Fragment of an Analysis of a Case of Hysteria," *Psychoanalytic Quarterly* 26 (1957): 159–67.
33. Freud, *Dora,* p. 37.
34. Claire Kahane, Introduction to Charles Bernheimer and Claire Kahane, *In Dora's Case,* p. 31.
35. Jane Gallop, "Nurse Freud: Class Struggle in the Family," unpublished paper, Miami University, 1983. For other important feminist treatments of Dora, see especially the essays by Maria Ramas, Toril Moi, and Madelon Sprengnether in Bernheimer and Kahane, *In Dora's Case*; and Janet Malcolm, *Psychoanalysis: The Impossible Profession* (New York: Vintage Books, 1982), pp. 93–101.
36. Hélène Cixous, "Castration or Decapitation?" trans. Annette Kuhn, *Signs* 7 (1981): 49; and *Portrait de Dora* (Paris: Editions des femmes, 1976).
37. Hélène Cixous and Catherine Clément, *La Jeune Née* (Paris: Union Générale d'Editions, 1975), pp. 271–96.
38. See *La Jeune Née* and Catherine Clément, "Enclave Esclave," trans. Marilyn R. Schuster, in *New French Feminisms,* ed. Isabelle de Courtivron and Elaine Marks (Amherst: University of Massachusetts Press, 1981), p. 133. The exchange between Cixous and Clément is analyzed by Jane Gallop in *The Daughter's Seduction: Feminism and Psychoanalysis* (Ithaca, N.Y.: Cornell University Press, 1982), pp. 132–50.
39. J. A. Ormerod, "Hysteria," in Allbutt and Rolleston, *A System of Medicine,* 8: 693.
40. Allbutt, "Neurasthenia," in *A System of Medicine,* 8: 760; see also Michael J. Clark, "The Rejection of Psychological Approaches to Mental Disorder in Late Nineteenth-Century British Psychiatry," in Scull, *Madhouses, Mad-doctors, and Madmen,* pp. 298–300.
41. Jeffrey Weeks, *Sex, Politics, and Society* (London: Longman, 1981), p. 142.
42. On David Eder, see Claude Girard, "La Psychanalyse en Grande-Bretagne," *Histoire de la psychanalyse,* ed. Roland Jacquard (Paris: Hachette, 1982), p. 319.

43. McKenna made this admission in a debate in the House of Commons on June 11, 1914. See Midge Mackenzie, ed., *Shoulder to Shoulder* (New York: Alfred A. Knopf, 1975), p. 277. Some hunger strikers feared mental breakdown from the combination of physical and emotional strain. See Martha Vicinus, *Independent Women: Work and Community for Single Women, 1850–1920* (Chicago: University of Chicago Press, 1985), p. 272.
44. Leonard Woolf, *Beginning Again: An Autobiography of the Years 1911 to 1918* (New York: Harcourt Brace Jovanovich, 1972), p. 76.

CHAPTER 7. MALE HYSTERIA: W. H. R. RIVERS AND THE LESSONS OF SHELL SHOCK

1. Charles S. Myers, *Shell-Shock in France* (Cambridge: Cambridge University Press, 1940) pp. 25, 37, 26.
2. Martin Stone, "Shellshock and the Psychologists," in *The Anatomy of Madness,* ed. W. F. Bynum, Roy Porter, and Michael Shepherd (London: Tavistock, forthcoming 1985).
3. Thomas W. Salmon, *The Care and Treatment of Mental Diseases and War Neuroses ("Shell Shock") in the British Army* (New York: War Work Committee of the National Committee for Mental Hygiene, 1917), p. 88. Salmon was an American public-health campaigner, editor of the *American Journal of Mental Hygiene,* who had become director of American army neuropsychiatry in France in 1917.
4. Paul Fussell, *The Great War and Modern Memory* (New York and London: Oxford University Press, 1975), pp. 22ff.
5. Ernest Jones, "War and Individual Psychology," *Sociological Review,* 1915, p. 180. Thanks to Judith Johnston for this reference. See also Ernest Jones, "War Shock and Freud's Theory of the Neuroses" (1918), *Papers on Psychoanalysis,* 3rd ed. (New York: William Wood, 1923).
6. H. C. Marr, *Psychoses of the War* (London: Henry Froude, 1919), pp. 60–73.
7. André Léri, *Shell-Shock, Commotional and Emotional Aspects* (London: University of London Press, 1919), p. 118.
8. Myers, *Shell-Shock,* pp. 38–39.
9. Salmon, *Care and Treatment,* p. 30.
10. Myers, *Shell-Shock,* pp. 24–25.
11. Salmon, *Care and Treatment,* p. 31.
12. Elliott Smith and T. H. Pear *Shell-Shock and Its Lessons* (London: Longmans Green, 1917), p. 7.
13. Jones, "War and Individual Psychology," p. 177.
14. Fussell, *The Great War and Modern Memory,* pp. 273–74.
15. Richard Fein, quoted in *The Great War and Modern Memory,* p. 280.

16. See chapter 6.
17. Robert Brudenell Carter, *On the Pathology and Treatment of Hysteria,* p. 33.
18. Karl Abraham, in *Psycho-analysis and the War Neuroses,* ed. Sandor Ferenczi (London: International Psycho-Analytical Press, 1921), p. 24. I am indebted to Judith Johnston for this reference. The Freudian theory of psychosexual etiology for shell shock infuriated the older generation of Darwinian psychiatrists. See the heated correspondence between Charles Mercier, David Forsyth, Ernest Jones, Elliott Smith, and others in *The Lancet,* 25 December 1915, 15 January 1916, 22 January 1916, 19 February 1916, and throughout the spring of 1916.
19. Eric Leed, *No Man's Land: Combat and Identity in World War I* (Cambridge: Cambridge University Press, 1979), pp. 183–84. Much of my analysis in this chapter is influenced by Leed's important work.
20. Sandra M. Gilbert, "Soldier's Heart: Literary Men, Literary Women, and the Great War," *Signs* 8 (1983): 423.
21. Richard Aldington, *Death of a Hero* (London: Chatto & Windus, 1929), p. 387.
22. Ford Madox Ford, *Parade's End* (London: Bodley Head, 1980), 4: 23.
23. T. S. Eliot, "Hysteria," *Collected Poems, 1909–1962.* See Gilbert, "Soldier's Heart," for a brilliant discussion of the "sexual anger" against women in World War I writing.
24. Erving Goffman, cited in Carroll Smith-Rosenberg, *Disorderly Conduct,* p. 340 n. 5.
25. Gilbert, "Soldier's Heart," pp. 447–48.
26. Reprinted in Paul Fussell, *Siegfried Sassoon's Long Journey* (New York and London: Oxford University Press, 1983), p. 39. For statistics on officers, see Salmon, *Care and Treatment,* pp. 13, 29.
27. Myers, *Shell-Shock,* p. 40. See also Frederick W. Mott, *War Neuroses and Shell Shock* (London: Hodder & Stoughton, 1919), p. 95; and Robert Graves, *Goodbye to All That* (Harmondsworth: Penguin Books, 1973), p. 144.
28. W. H. R. Rivers, *Instinct and the Unconscious,* 2nd ed. (Cambridge: Cambridge University Press, 1922), pp. 210, 209, 218, 225.
29. W. N. Maxwell, *A Psychological Retrospective of the Great War* (London: George Allen & Unwin, 1923), p. 149.
30. Ernst Simmel, *Psychoanalysis and the War Neuroses,* cited in Leed, *No Man's Land,* p. 167.
31. Lewis R. Yealland, *Hysterical Disorders of Warfare* (London: Macmillan, 1918), pp. 7–10. For another discussion of this case, see Leed, *No Man's Land,* pp. 174–75. The term "disciplinary therapy" comes from Leed, pp. 170–76.
32. Yealland, *Hysterical Disorders,* pp. 92, 197.
33. Siegfried Sassoon, *Memoirs of an Infantry Officer,* in *The Memoirs of George Sherston* (New York: Doubleday, 1936), p. 319.

34. E. C. Southard, *Shell-Shock and Other Neuro-Psychiatric Problems* (Boston: W. M. Leonard, 1919), p. 60.
35. Sassoon, *Memoirs of an Infantry Officer,* p. 322. In later years, Sassoon and Graves had bitter quarrels over the version of this episode in Graves's *Goodbye to All That.* See the exchange of letters in *In Broken Images: Selected Letters of Robert Graves, 1914–1946*, ed. Paul O'Prey (London: Hutchinson, 1982), pp. 196–208.
36. Jon Stallworthy, *Wilfred Owen* (London: Oxford University Press and Chatto & Windus, 1974), p. 191.
37. A. G. Macdonnell, *England, Their England* (London: Macmillan, 1936), pp. 17–18.
38. Siegfried Sassoon, *Siegfried's Journey* (London: Faber & Faber, 1945), p. 64. See also Sassoon, *Diaries, 1915–1918,* ed. Rupert Hart-Davis (London: Faber & Faber, 1983), p. 189.
39. R. D. Gillespie, cited in Stone, "Shellshock and the Psychologists."
40. Hugh Crichton-Miller, quoted in Salmon, *Care and Treatment,* p. 40. See also Smith and Pear, *Shell-Shock and Its Lessons,* pp. 32–33.
41. On Rivers, see the biography by Richard Slobodin, *W. H. R. Rivers* (New York: Columbia University Press, 1978), on which my discussion of his life heavily depends. Rivers did not leave much personal material for the biographer; Slobodin remarks that at times he felt that he was "investigating a minor notable of the seventh century" (p. vii).
42. Arnold Bennett, *New Statesman,* 17 June 1922, p. 290.
43. Walter Langdon-Brown, "To a Very Wise Man," *St. Barts Hospital Journal,* November 1936, p. 30.
44. Arnold Bennett, quoted in Slobodin, *W. H. R. Rivers,* p. 40.
45. Slobodin, *W. H. R. Rivers,* p. 59.
46. Langdon-Brown, "To a Very Wise Man," p. 30, and Charles Myers, "The Influence of the Late W. H. R. Rivers," in Rivers, *Psychology and Politics* (London: Kegan Paul, Trench & Trubner, 1923), p. 168.
47. Rivers, "Psycho-therapeutics," in *Encyclopedia of Religion and Ethics,* ed. James Hastings, 13 vols. (Edinburgh: T. & T. Clark, 1918), 10: 440.
48. Siegfried Sassoon, *Sherston's Progress,* (New York: Doubleday, Doran, 1936), pp. 4, 45, 32.
49. Medical Case Sheet, Craiglockhart War Hospital, 23/7/17; Imperial War Museum. I am indebted to Paul Fussell for sharing this and other details of Sassoon's medical history with me. Rivers's report is reproduced in Fussell, *Sassoon's Long Journey,* pp. 134–35.
50. Sassoon, *Sherston's Progress,* p. 5.
51. Ibid., p. 4; Sassoon to Ottoline Morrell, 30 July 1917, in *Diaries, 1915–1918,* pp. 183–84.
52. Sassoon, *Sherston's Progress,* p. 13; *Diaries, 1915–1918,* p. 183.

53. Sassoon, *Sherston's Progress,* p. 14.
54. Ibid., pp. 29, 30. There is nothing about such a visitor in Sassoon's letters from this period.
55. See Sassoon's letters to Ottoline Morrell in *Diaries, 1915–1918,* pp. 190–94.
56. Sassoon, *Sherston's Progress,* p. 48. Sassoon told Robert Graves that before the board he had insisted that he had not changed his views. Sassoon to Graves, 7 December 1917, in *Diaries, 1915–1918,* p. 196.
57. Sassoon, *Siegfried's Journey,* p. 47. See also Sassoon, *Diaries 1920–1922,* ed. Rupert Hart-Davis (London: Faber & Faber, 1981), pp. 163–65, especially the account of Rivers's funeral, at which Sassoon was overcome with grief (pp. 166–69).
58. Robert Wohl, *The Generation of 1914* (Cambridge, Mass.: Harvard University Press, 1979), p. 100.
59. Fussell, *The Great War and Modern Memory,* p. 92.
60. W. H. R. Rivers, *Conflict and Dream* (London: Kegan Paul, Trench & Trubner, 1923), pp. 118, 168.
61. Slobodin, *W. H. R. Rivers,* p. 3.
62. Rivers, *Instinct and the Unconscious,* p. 210.
63. Yealland, *Hysterical Disorders,* pp. vii, ix.
64. Elliott Smith, quoted in Slobodin, *W. H. R. Rivers,* p. 55.
65. W. H. R. Rivers, "Freud's Psychology of the Unconscious," *The Lancet,* June 16, 1917, in *Instinct and the Unconscious,* pp. 166, 164.
66. Ibid., p. 252.
67. See the essays by Rivers in the posthumously published *Psychology and Politics* (1923).
68. Philip Hamilton Gibbs, *Now It Can Be Told* (New York, 1920), pp. 547–48, quoted in Leed, *No Man's Land,* p. 187.
69. Ibid., p. 186.
70. Ibid., pp. 191–92.
71. Rebecca West, *The Return of the Soldier* (1918; reprint ed., London: Virago Press, 1979), pp. 150, 183, 187.
72. Dorothy Sayers, *Busman's Honeymoon* (1937; reprint ed., New York: Avon Books, 1968), pp. 316, 304, 260.
73. Virginia Woolf, 20 January 1924, *The Diaries of Virginia Woolf,* ed. Anne Olivier Bell (London: Hogarth Press, 1978), 2: 287.
74. Virginia Woolf, *Mrs. Dalloway* (New York: Harcourt, Brace & World, 1925), pp. 130, 136.
75. Ibid., p. 138.
76. Quoted in Jane Marcus, "On Dr. George Savage," *Virginia Woolf Newsletter,* no. 17 (Fall 1981), p. 4.
77. Woolf, *Mrs. Dalloway,* p. 281.
78. Lee R. Edwards, *Psyche as Hero: Female Heroism and Fictional Form* (Middletown, Conn.,:Wesleyan University Press, 1984), p. 264.

CHAPTER 8. WOMEN AND PSYCHIATRIC MODERNISM

1. See Roberta Salow, "Where Has All the Hysteria Gone?" *Psychoanalytic Review* 66 (1979–80): 463–78; David Mitchell, *Women on the Warpath* (London: Jonathan Cape, 1966), p. 389.
2. Hunter and Macalpine, *Psychiatry for the Poor,* p. 84.
3. Letter from Dr. Alexander Walk, Royal College of Psychiatrists, 26 November 1981; and Charlotte Mackenzie, "Women and Psychiatric Professionalization, 1780–1914," pp. 117–19.
4. Susan Stanford Friedman, *Psyche Reborn: The Emergence of H.D.* (Bloomington: Indiana University Press, 1981), p. 18.
5. Paul Thompson, *The Edwardians: The Remaking of British Society* (London: Paladin, 1977), p. 270. See also Renate Bridenthal, "Something Old, Something New: Women Between the Two World Wars," in *Becoming Visible: Women in European History,* ed. Renate Bridenthal and Claudia Koonz (Boston: Houghton Mifflin, 1977), pp. 422–44.
6. H. V. Dicks, *Fifty Years of the Tavistock Clinic* (London: Routledge & Kegan Paul, 1970).
7. On the history of the clinic and its founders, see Theophilus E. M. Boll, "May Sinclair and the Medico-Psychological Clinic of London," *Proceedings of the American Philosophical Society* 106 (1962): 320. I am indebted to Carol Barash, Princeton University, for bringing this important article to my attention.
8. Martha Vicinus, " 'One Life to Stand Beside Me,' " p. 624.
9. Karl Abraham, "Manifestations," *International Journal of Psycho-Analysis* 3 (March 1922): 2.
10. Sigmund Freud, "Female Sexuality," *Sexuality and the Psychology of Love,* ed. Philip Rieff (New York: Collier Books, 1970), p. 195.
11. Paul Roazen, *Freud and His Followers* (New York: Alfred A. Knopf, 1975), p. 420. On Freud's psychoanalytic "daughters," see Roazen on Brunswick, pp. 420–36, and Bonaparte, pp. 448–51. See also Paul Roazen, *Helene Deutsch: A Psychoanalyst's Life* (New York: Anchor Press, 1985). Freud's real-life daughter, Anna, also became a psychoanalyst.
12. See Karen Horney, "The Flight from Womanhood" (1926), "Inhibited Femininity" (1926), "The Dread of Woman" (1932), and "The Denial of the Vagina" (1933), *Feminine Psychology,* ed. Harold Kelman (New York: W. W. Norton, 1973), pp. 54, 56, 69, 136.
13. Dee Garrison, "Karen Horney and Feminism," *Signs* 6 (1981): 680, 688.
14. Claude Girard, "La Psychanalyse en Grande-Bretagne," pp. 333–34. See also Elyse Levy, "Susan Isaacs: An Intellectual Biography," Ph.D. dissertation, Claremont Graduate School and University Center, 1977; Carol Netzer, "Annals of Psychoanalysis: Ella Freeman Sharpe," *Psychoanalytic Review* 69 (Summer 1982); Charles William Wahl, "Ella Freeman Sharpe," in *Psychoanalytic Pioneers,* ed. Franz Alexander, Samuel Eisenstein, and Marin Grotjahn (New York: Basic Books, 1966), pp. 265–71; Juliet Mitch-

ell, *Women: The Longest Revolution,* pp. 270–73; Hanna Segal, *Melanie Klein* (Harmondsworth: Penguin Books, 1981).

15. Melitta Schmideberg, "A Contribution to the History of the Psycho-Analytic Movement in Britain," *British Journal of Psychiatry* 118 (1971): 62.
16. Dr. Octavia Wilberforce had no psychiatric training, and Graylingwell was her only experience in a mental hospital. She went into private practice in Brighton, and in 1940–1941 was the family physician to Leonard and Virginia Woolf. It was Wilberforce who treated Virginia Woolf during her last suicidal breakdown. Details of their relationship can be found in *The Letters of Virginia Woolf,* ed. Nicolson and Trautmann, 6: 103, 335, 446, 450, 454, 456, 462, 465, 477, 479, 481. Woolf wrote of her: "That's the sort of woman I most admire—the reticence, the quiet, the power" (letter to Elizabeth Robins, 13 March 1941, p. 479).

    Wilberforce's letters to Elizabeth Robins about Graylingwell cover the period 12 December–31 December 1920. They were transcribed from the originals by her executor, Mrs. Mabel Smith of Wimbledon, England, who has kindly granted me permission to quote from them. I am especially grateful to Maxine Berry of Vancouver, British Columbia, who received copies of the Wilberforce letters in the course of her work on Virginia Woolf, generously brought them to my attention, and arranged for me to use them. All Wilberforce references are to these eighteen pages of typed letters.
17. Antonia White, *Beyond the Glass* (London: Virago Press, 1979), pp. 211, 207.
18. Mary Cecil, "Through the Looking Glass," *Encounter,* December 1956, reprinted in *The Inner World of Mental Illness,* ed. Bert Kaplan (New York and London: Harper & Row, 1964), p. 224.
19. Morag Coate, *Beyond All Reason* (London: Constable, 1964), p. 196.
20. Emil Kraepelin, *Lectures on Clinical Psychology,* ed. Thomas Johnstone (London: Balliere, Tindall & Cox, 1913), p. 4; Eugen Bleuler, *Dementia Praecox, or the Group of Schizophrenics,* trans. Joseph Zinkin (New York: International Universities Press, 1950), p. 40.
21. See J. W. Wing, *Reasoning About Madness* (London: Oxford University Press, 1978), p. 113; Florence Schumer, "Gender and Schizophrenia," in *Gender and Disordered Behavior: Sex Differences in Psychopathology,* ed. Edith S. Gomberg and Violet Franks (New York: Brunner-Mazel, 1979), pp. 321–53; Ihsan Al-Issa, "Gender and Schizophrenia," in *Gender and Psychopathology,* ed. Ihsan Al-Issa (New York: Academic Press, 1982); and Helen Block Lewis, *Psychic War in Men and Women* (New York: New York University Press, 1976), pp. 286–98. On schizophrenia in married women having difficulties in separating from their families, see Harold Sampson, Sheldon L. Messinger, and Robert D. Towne, *Schizophrenic Women: Studies in Marital Crisis* (New York: Atherton, 1964).
22. For some other important works, see Emma Santos, *La Malcastrée* (Paris: Editions des femmes, 1976), and Susan Sheehan, *Is There No Place on Earth*

for Me? (New York: Vintage Books, 1983). Among the well-known American novels dealing with female schizophrenia and confinement are Mary Jane Ward's *The Snake Pit* (1948) and Marge Piercy's *Woman on the Edge of Time* (1976).

23. See Manfred Sakel, *Schizophrenia* (New York: Philosophical Library, 1958), pp. 187–236, 331. In the United States, insulin therapy, and the related metrazol therapy, became widespread in the late 1930s. See Gerald Grob, *Mental Illness and American Society,* pp. 296–304.
24. William Sargent, *The Unquiet Mind* (Boston: Little, Brown, 1967).
25. Cecil, "Through the Looking Glass," p. 222.
26. Sargent, *The Unquiet Mind,* p. 55.
27. Hunter and Macalpine, *Psychiatry for the Poor,* p. 187.
28. Anthony Clare, *Psychiatry in Dissent* (London: Tavistock Publications, 1976), pp. 228–29.
29. Peter R. Breggin, *Electroshock: Its Brain-Disabling Effects* (New York: Springer Publishing, 1979), pp. 8, 126–27. At one large American state mental hospital, records showed 80 percent of ECT patients to be women (information from a study in progress by Andrew Scull). Psychiatrists respond to these figures by arguing that the majority of *depressed* patients, the group most likely to be treated with ECT, are women. Here again, gender issues enter into diagnosis and treatment. In his study of this process of psychiatric residency in the United States, Donald Light suggests that while psychiatrists are perturbed by administering ECT, they do not acknowledge their conflicts "because it is unmanly and unprofessional to feel upset." When he himself first observed ECT, he felt faint. See *Becoming Psychiatrists* (New York: W. W. Norton, 1980), p. 368. In one celebrated American case, Natalie Parker was unable to resume her professional career because of the massive retrograde amnesia following a course of ECT. This case was described in an essay by the medical journalist Burton Roueché, "As Empty as Eve," *New Yorker,* 9 September 1974, pp. 84–100.
30. See William Arnold, *Shadowland* (New York: Jove, 1978), pp. 158–59.
31. See Walter Freeman and James Watts, *Psychosurgery* (Springfield, Ill.: Charles C. Thomas, 1942). Dedicated to Egas Moniz, "who first conceived and executed a valid operation for mental disorder," it describes the way that "partial separation of the frontal lobes from the rest of the brain results in reduction of disagreeable self-consciousness, abolition of obsessive thinking, and satisfaction with performance, even though the performance is inferior in quality" (p. vii).
32. See ibid., tables 5, 6, 7, and 8; Arnold, *Shadowland,* p. 160.
33. Sargent, *The Unquiet Mind,* pp. 78, 85.
34. Berke, *I Haven't Had to Go Mad Here,* p. 96; see also Sydney Smith, "The Treatment of Anxiety, Depression, and Obsessionality," *Psychosurgery and Society,* ed. Sydney Smith and L. G. Kiloh (London: Pergamon Press, 1977), p. 29.

35. Peter Mezan, "After Freud and Jung, Now Comes R. D. Laing," *Esquire,* January 1972, pp. 92–97, 160–78.
36. Clare, *Psychiatry in Dissent,* p. 306.
37. Ellen Moers, *Literary Women: The Great Writers* (Garden City, N.Y.: Doubleday, 1976), p. 133. Among the interesting works about madness by English women which I do not discuss specifically in this chapter are Anna Kavan, *Asylum Piece* (1940), Isabella Morrison, *A Tale Told by a Lunatic* (1956), Jane Simpson, *The Lost Days of My Life* (1958), Ella Hales [pseud.], *Like a Lamb* (1958), and Penelope Mortimer, *The Pumpkin Eater* (1962).
38. Janet Frame, *Faces in the Water* (1961; reprint ed., London: Women's Press, 1980), p. 112.
39. White, *Beyond the Glass,* p. 243.
40. Antonia White, "The House of Clouds" (1928), *Strangers* (London: Virago Books, 1981), p. 59; and Alyssa Wingfield, *The Inside of the Cup* (London: Angus & Robertson, 1958), p. 34.
41. Maude Harrison, *Spinners Lake* (London: Bodley Head, 1941), p. 35.
42. Frame, *Faces in the Water,* p. 41.
43. John Berger, *Ways of Seeing* (Harmondsworth: Penguin Books, 1972), pp. 46–47. For fascinating descriptions of the shifting sense of appearance in schizophrenia, see Antonia White, *Beyond the Glass,* and *As Once in May: The Early Autobiography of Antonia White,* ed. Susan Chitty (London: Virago Books, 1983), p. 67.
44. Frame, *Faces in the Water,* p. 186.
45. Charles W. Mayos, *Poetry of the Insane* (Peoria, Kans.: n.p., 1933), p. 57. Thanks to Gerry Grob for this reference.
46. J. W. Wing and G. W. Brown, *Institutionalization and Schizophrenia* (Cambridge: Cambridge University Press, 1970), p. 113.
47. Cecil, "Through the Looking Glass," p. 217.
48. Elizabeth Abel, "Women and Schizophrenia: The Fiction of Jean Rhys," *Contemporary Literature* 20 (1979): 155–77; Judith Kegan Gardiner, "Good Morning, Midnight; Good Night, Modernism," *Boundary* 2 (1983): 233–51; Barbara Hill Rigney, *Madness and Sexual Politics in the Feminist Novel* (Madison: University of Wisconsin Press, 1978).
49. Jennifer Dawson, *The Ha-Ha* (1961; reprint ed., London: Virago Press, 1985), p. 49.
50. Ibid., p. 181.
51. Ibid., p. 122.
52. Ibid., pp. 152, 166–67, 169, 179.
53. Ibid., p. 178–79, 180.
54. Janet Frame, *An Angel at My Table: An Autobiography,* vol. 2 (New York: George Braziller, 1984), pp. 73, 76, 82–83, 98–99.
55. Frame, *Faces in the Water,* p. 24.
56. Ibid., pp. 23, 56, 100.
57. Adlai Stevenson, quoted in Linda Huf, *A Portrait of the Artist as a Young Woman* (New York: Frederick Ungar, 1983), p. 128.

58. *The Journals of Sylvia Plath,* ed. Ted Hughes and Frances McCullough (New York: Dial Press, 1982), p. 318.
59. Berke, *I Haven't Had to Go Mad Here,* pp. 71–72. See also Michael Shepherd, *People Not Psychiatry* (London: George Allen & Unwin, 1973), p. 45.
60. Sylvia Plath, *The Bell Jar* (London: Faber & Faber, 1963), pp. 6, 101, 171, 272, 226, 67, 230–31, 290.

CHAPTER 9. WOMEN, MADNESS, AND THE FAMILY: R. D. LAING AND THE CULTURE OF ANTIPSYCHIATRY

1. Aaron Esterson and R. D. Laing, "The Blairs," *Sanity, Madness, and the Family* (Harmondsworth: Penguin Books, 1970), pp. 51–74.
2. Esterson and Laing, *Sanity, Madness, and the Family,* p. 15.
3. Ibid., p. 27.
4. David Cooper, *The Language of Madness* (Harmondsworth: Penguin Books, 1980), pp. 130–31. See also Cooper's *Psychiatry and Anti-Psychiatry* (New York: Ballantine Books, 1967) and *The Death of the Family* (New York: Vintage Books, 1971).
5. Thomas Scheff, *Labeling Madness* (Englewood, N.J.: Prentice-Hall, 1975), pp. 7, 10.
6. Clancy Sigal, *Zone of the Interior* (New York: Thomas Y. Crowell, 1976), p. 143.
7. Juliet Mitchell, *Psychoanalysis and Feminism* (New York: Pantheon Books, 1974), p. xviii. Mitchell's view is that Laing gave the women's movement a "vocabulary of protest" and a theoretical analysis of the nuclear family. She also makes the interesting comment that the ideal Laingian therapist is a "good *mother*" (p. 291) who substitutes for the bad mother of the psychotic. In view of the extreme sexism of Laingian therapy in its later phases, this appropriation of the feminine seems to have been superficial.
8. Peter Sedgwick, *Psycho Politics* (London: Pluto Press, 1982), p. 67.
9. Doris Lessing, 1972, quoted in Nancy Shields Hardin, "Doris Lessing and the Sufi Way," in *Doris Lessing: Critical Studies,* ed. Annis Pratt and L. S. Dembo (Madison: University of Wisconsin Press, 1974), pp. 154–55.
10. Peter Mezan, "R. D. Laing: Portrait of a Twentieth-Century Skeptic, in *R. D. Laing: The Man and His Ideas,* ed. Richard I. Evans (New York: E. P. Dutton, 1976), p. lxxv.
11. See Michael Clark, biographical appendix to "Late Victorian Psychiatry," p. 342.
12. R. D. Laing, *The Politics of the Family and Other Essays* (New York: Vintage Books, 1972), p. 67. Laing has recently published a memoir, but it is more a series of impressions than an autobiography, and adds little information to the record. See R. D. Laing, *Wisdom, Madness and Folly: The Making of a Psychiatrist, 1927–1957* (London: Macmillan, 1985).

13. R. D. Laing, *The Facts of Life* (New York: Ballantine Books, 1976), p. 1; and Peter Mezan, "After Freud and Jung, Now Comes R. D. Laing," *Esquire,* January 1972, p. 174.
14. Laing, *The Facts of Life,* pp. 72–73.
15. Mezan, "After Freud and Jung," p. 166.
16. Ibid., p. 165.
17. Ibid.
18. R. D. Laing, *The Divided Self* (Harmondsworth: Penguin Books, 1976), p. 25.
19. Mezan, "After Freud and Jung," p. 167.
20. Clancy Sigal, interview with the author, August 1978.
21. Laing, *The Divided Self,* p. iv.
22. Mezan, "After Freud and Jung," p. 92.
23. Victoria Brittain, "An End to Fashionable Madness," *The Times* (London), October 9, 1972, p. 9.
24. On Laing's debt to James, see Mezan, "After Freud and Jung," p. 171.
25. Laing, *The Divided Self,* p. 1.
26. Ibid., p. 37.
27. Robert Coles, "An R. D. Laing Symposium," in *R. D. Laing and Anti-Psychiatry,* ed. Robert Boyers and Robert Orrill (New York: Harper & Row, 1971), p. 228.
28. R. D. Laing, *The Politics of Experience* (New York: Ballantine Books, 1967), p. 120.
29. Gregory Bateson, ed., *Perceval's Narrative: A Patient's Account of his Psychosis, 1830–32* (New York: William Morrow, 1974), p. xiv.
30. Laing, *Politics of Experience,* pp. 126–27.
31. Mary Barnes and Joseph Berke, *Mary Barnes: Two Accounts of a Journey Through Madness* (New York: Harcourt Brace Jovanovich, 1971), p. 221.
32. Ibid., pp. 257–63. See also James S. Gordon, "Who is Mad? Who Is Sane? R. D. Laing in Search of a New Psychiatry," in *Going Crazy,* ed. Hendrik W. Ruitenbeek (New York: Bantam Books, 1972), pp. 65–102; and Morton Schatzman, "Madness and Morals," in Boyers and Orrill, *R. D. Laing and Anti-Psychiatry,* pp. 235–72. For a view of Kingsley Hall goings-on from the perspective of the East London community, see Lylie Valentine, *Two Sisters and the Cockney Kids* (London: Club Row Press, 1978). Thanks to Martha Vicinus for this reference.
33. Laing, *The Divided Self,* pp. 59, 155–56, 176, 179, 195n., 204.
34. Berke, *Mary Barnes,* pp. 221, 236.
35. Ibid., pp. 39, 40.
36. Ibid., p. 220. For a different kind of critique of this case, see Félix Guattari "Mary Barnes, or Oedipus in Anti-Psychiatry," *Molecular Revolution: Psychiatry and Politics,* trans. Rosemary Sheed (Harmondsworth: Penguin Books, 1984), pp. 51–59.

37. Berke, *Mary Barnes,* pp. 254, 346–47, 78.
38. David Edgar, *Mary Barnes* (London: Eyre Methuen, 1979); and Angela Neustatter, *The Guardian,* 5 January 1979, p. 9.
39. Lesley Hazleton, "Doris Lessing on Feminism, Communism, and 'Space Fiction,'" *New York Times Magazine,* July 25, 1982, p. 27.
40. Lessing to Roberta Rubenstein, 17 November 1972, quoted in Rubenstein, *The Novelistic Vision of Doris Lessing* (Urbana: University of Illinois Press, 1979), p. 197.
41. Doris Lessing, *The Four-Gated City* (New York: Bantam Books, 1970), pp. 524–25.
42. Lessing to Roberta Rubenstein, 28 March 1977, quoted in Rubenstein, *The Novelistic Vision,* pp. 196–97.
43. David Reed, *Anna* (Harmondsworth: Penguin Books, 1979), pp. 112–13, 115.
44. Ibid., p. 119. She later felt that "R. D. Laing would have let me write" (p. 120).
45. Ibid., pp. 115, 123–126.
46. Ibid., pp. 36, 45–46.
47. Ibid., p. 87; Laing, *The Divided Self,* p. 155; Morag Coate, *Beyond All Reason,* p. 119.
48. Vivian Gornick, "Twice Told Tales," *The Nation,* 23 September 1978, p. 287.
49. Lessing to Roberta Rubenstein, 28 March 1977, quoted in *The Novelistic Vision,* p. 199.
50. Interview with David Edgar in *New Theatre Voices of the Seventies,* ed. Simon Trussler (London: Eyre Methuen, 1981), p. 163.
51. Clancy Sigal, interview with the author, August 1978.
52. Sigal, *Zone of the Interior,* p. 220.
53. Ibid., pp. 165, 166.
54. Ibid., pp. 222, 268.
55. Marshall Berman, *New York Times Book Review,* 22 February 1970, p. 1.
56. Brittain, "An End to Fashionable Madness," p. 9.
57. Reed, *Anna,* p. 69.
58. Joel Kovel, "The American Mental Health Industry," in *Critical Psychiatry,* ed. David Ingleby (New York: Pantheon Books, 1980), p. 99; Sedgwick, *Psycho Politics,* p. 103.
59. See, for example, Barbara Hill Rigney, *Madness and Sexual Politics in the Feminist Novel;* Virginia C. Fowler, "Millie Theale's Malady of Self," *Novel* 14 (1980): 57–74; Elizabeth Abel, "Women and Schizophrenia: The Fiction of Jean Rhys," pp. 155–77; Marion Vlastos, "Doris Lessing and R. D. Laing: Psychopolitics and Prophecy," *PMLA* 91 (1976): 245–57.
60. Simone de Beauvoir, interview by Alice Jardine, *Signs* 5 (1979): 228.
61. David Cooper, *The Grammar of Living: An Examination of Political Acts* (Harmondsworth: Penguin Books, 1974), pp. 41, 98–100, 115.
62. Laing, *The Divided Self,* p. 12.

EPILOGUE. MADNESS AND THE RIGHTS OF WOMEN

1. Andrew T. Scull, *Decarceration: Community Treatment of the Deviant* (Englewood Cliffs, N.J.: Prentice-Hall, 1977), p. 65.
2. Ibid., pp. 69, 81.
3. *The Guardian,* 18 November 1977, p. 26.
4. Ann Oakley, *Subject Women* (New York: Pantheon Books, 1981), p. 79. See also Ivan Reid and Eileen Warmald, *Sex Differences in Britain* (London: Grant McIntyre, 1982), pp. 37, 40, 44, 48, for statistics on women and mental health.
5. Peter Sedgwick, *Psycho Politics,* p. 241.
6. See George W. Brown and Tirril Harris, *The Social Origins of Depression: A Study of Psychiatric Disorder in Women* (London: Tavistock Publications, 1978).
7. See Roland Littlewood and Maurice Lipsedge, *Aliens and Alienists: Ethnic Minorities and Psychiatry* (Harmondsworth: Penguin Books, 1982).

BIBLIOGRAPHY

Alexander, Franz, Samuel Eisenstein, and Martin Grotjahn, eds. *Psychoanalytic Pioneers.* New York: Basic Books, 1966.

Al-Issa, Ihsan, ed. *Gender and Psychopathy.* New York: Academic Press, 1982.

Allbutt, Thomas Clifford. "Nervous Diseases and Modern Life." *Contemporary Review* 67 (1895): 210–31.

Allbutt, Thomas Clifford, and Humphrey Davy Rolleston, eds. *A System of Medicine.* 9 vols. 1898. 2nd ed. London: Macmillan, 1910.

Allen, Donald R. "Florence Nightingale: Towards a Psychohistorical Interpretation." *Journal of Interdisciplinary History* 8 (1975): 23–45.

Andrews, C. T. *The Dark Awakening: A History of St. Lawrence's Hospital.* London: Cox & Wyman, 1978.

Archer, John, and Barbara Lloyd. *Sex and Gender.* Harmondwsorth: Penguin Books, 1982.

Arlidge, John. *On the State of Lunacy and the Legal Protection for the Insane.* London: John Churchill, 1859.

Austin, Thomas. *A Practical Account of General Paralysis.* 1859. Reprint. New York: Arno Press, 1976.

"Autobiography of the Insane." *Journal of Psychological Medicine and Mental Pathology* 8 (1855): 338–53.

Ayala, Flavia. "Victorian Science and the 'Genius' of Woman." *Journal of the History of Ideas* 38 (1977): 261–80.

Barker-Benfield, G. *The Horrors of the Half-Known Life.* New York: Harper Colophon, 1976.

Barlow, John. *Man's Power Over Himself to Prevent or Control Insanity.* London: William Pickering, 1843.

Barnes, Mary, and Joseph Berke. *Mary Barnes: Two Accounts of a Journey Through Madness.* Harmondsworth: Penguin Books, 1973.

Bateson, Gregory, ed. *Perceval's Narrative: A Patient's Account of His Psychosis, 1830–1832.* New York: William Morrow, 1974.

Beard, George M. *American Nervousness: Its Causes and Consequences.* 1881. Reprint. New York: Arno Press, 1972.

———. *A Practical Treatise on Nervous Exhaustion.* Edited by A. D. Rockwell. 1905. Reprint. New York: Kraus, Reprint 1971.

———. *Sexual Neurasthenia: Its Hygiene, Causes, Symptoms, and Treatment.* Edited by A. D. Rockwell. New York: Treat, 1884.

Berke, Joseph H. *I Haven't Had to Go Mad Here.* Harmondsworth: Penguin Books, 1979.

Bernheimer, Charles, and Claire Kahane, eds. *In Dora's Case: Freud, Hysteria, Feminism.* London: Virago Press, 1985.

Bingham, Nathaniel. *Observations on the Religious Delusions of Insane Persons.* London: Hatchard, 1841.

Blandford, G. Fielding. *Insanity and Its Treatment.* Philadelphia: Henry C. Lea, 1871.

Bleuler, Eugen. *Dementia Praecox, or the Group of Schizophrenias.* Translated by Joseph Zinkin. New York: International Universities Press, 1950.

Boll, Theophilus E. M. "May Sinclair and the Medico-Psychological Clinic of London." *Proceedings of the American Philosophical Society* 106 (1962): 310–26.

Boyers, Robert, and Robert Orrill, eds. *R. D. Laing and Anti-Psychiatry.* New York: Harper & Row, 1971.

Breggin, Peter R. *Electroshock: Its Brain-Disabling Effects.* New York: Springer Publishing, 1979.

Brown, G. H., comp. *Lives of the Fellows of the Royal College of Physicians of London, 1826–1925.* London: Royal College of Physicians, 1955. Continuation of *The Roll of the Royal College of Physicians of London, Comprising Biographical Sketches of All the Eminent Physicians,* by William Munk. London: Royal College of Physicians, 1878.

Brown, George W., and Tirril Harris. *The Social Origins of Depression: A Study of Psychiatric Disorder in Women.* London: Tavistock Publications, 1978.

Brown, Isaac Baker. *On the Curability of Certain Forms of Insanity, Epilepsy, Catalepsy, and Hysteria in Females.* London: Robert Hardwicke, 1866.

Browne, W. A. F. "The Moral Treatment of the Insane." *Journal of Mental Science* 10 (1864): 309–37.

———. *What Asylums Were, Are, and Ought to Be.* 1837. Reprint. New York: Arno Press, 1976.

Bruche, Hilde. *Eating Disorders: Obesity, Anorexia Nervosa, and the Person Within.* New York: Basic Books, 1973.

Brugger, Robert J., ed. *Ourselves, Our Past: Psychological Approaches to American History.* Baltimore: Johns Hopkins University Press, 1981.

Brumberg, Joan Jacobs. "Chlorotic Girls, 1870–1920: A Historical Perspective on Female Adolescence." In *Women and Health in America,* edited by Judith Walzer Leavitt, pp. 186–95. Madison: University of Wisconsin Press, 1984.

Bucknill, J. C. *The Psychology of Shakespeare.* 1859. Reprint. New York: AMS Press, 1970.

Bucknill, J. C., and Daniel Hack Tuke. *A Manual of Psychological Medicine.* London: John Churchill, 1858. Reprint. New York and London: Hafner, 1968.

Burstyn, Joan N. *Victorian Education and the Ideal of Womanhood.* London: Croom Helm, 1980.

Bynum, W. F., Roy Porter, and Michael Shepherd, *The Anatomy of Madness.* 2 vols. London: Tavistock, 1985.

Byrd, Max. *Visits to Bedlam: Madness and Literature in the Eighteenth Century.* Columbia: University of South Carolina Press, 1974.

Carter, Robert Brudenell. *On the Pathology and Treatment of Hysteria.* London: John Churchill, 1853.

Charcot, J.-M. *L'Hystérie.* Edited by E. Trillat. Toulouse: Edouard Privat, 1971.

Chesler, Phyllis. *Women and Madness.* Harmondsworth: Penguin Books, 1979.

Chetwynd, Jane, and Oonagh Hartnett, eds. *The Sex-Role System: Psychological and Sociological Perspectives.* London: Routledge & Kegan Paul, 1978.

Cheyne, George. *The English Malady; or, A Treatise on Nervous Disorders of All Kinds.* London: Strahan & Leake, 1733.

Cixous, Hélène. "Castration or Decapitation?" Translated by Annette Kuhn. *Signs* 7 (1981): 41–55.

———. *Portrait de Dora.* Paris: Editions des femmes, 1976.

Cixous, Hélène, and Catherine Clément. *La Jeune Née.* Paris: Union Générale d'Editions, 1975.

Clare, Anthony. *Psychiatry in Dissent.* London: Tavistock Publications, 1976.

Clark, Sir James, *A Memoir of John Conolly.* London: John Murray, 1869.

Clark, Michael J. "Late Victorian Psychiatry." D. Phil. dissertation, Oxford University, 1982.

Clouston, T. S. *Clinical Lectures on Mental Diseases.* 5th ed. London: J. & A. Churchill, 1898.

———. *Female Education from a Medical Point of View.* Edinburgh: Macniven & Wallace, 1882.

———. *Hygiene of Mind.* London: Methuen, 1906.

———. "The Psychological Dangers to Women in Modern Social Development." In *The Position of Women: Actual and Ideal,* edited by Sir Oliver Lodge, pp. 103–17. London: James Nisbet, 1911.

Coate, Morag. *Beyond All Reason.* London: Constable, 1964.

Conolly, John. *The Construction and Government of Lunatic Asylums and Hospitals for the Insane.* 1847. Reprint. London: Dawsons, 1968.

———. *An Inquiry Concerning the Indications of Insanity.* 1830. Reprint. London: Dawsons, 1964.

———. *A Study of Hamlet.* London: E. Moxon, 1863. Reprint. New York: AMS Press, 1973.

———. *Treatment of the Insane Without Mechanical Restraints.* 1856. Reprint. London: Dawsons, 1973.

Conway, Jill. "Stereotypes of Femininity in a Theory of Sexual Evolution." In *Suffer and Be Still: Women in the Victorian Age,* edited by Martha Vicinus, pp. 140–54. London: Methuen, 1980.

Cooper, David. *The Death of the Family.* Harmondsworth: Penguin Books, 1972.

———. *The Grammar of Living: An Examination of Political Acts.* Harmondsworth: Penguin Books, 1974.

———. *The Language of Madness.* Harmondsworth: Penguin Books, 1980.

———. *Psychiatry and Anti-Psychiatry.* New York: Ballantine Books, 1967.

Courtivron, Isabelle de, and Elaine Marks, eds. *New French Feminisms.* Sussex: Harvester Press, 1981.

Dain, Norman. *Concepts of Insanity in the United States, 1789–1865.* New Brunswick, N.J.: Rutgers University Press, 1964.

Darwin, Charles. *The Descent of Man.* 1871. Reprint. Princeton, N.J.: Princeton University Press, 1981.

Davidoff, Leonore. *The Best Circles: Society, Etiquette, and the Season.* London: Croom Helm, 1973.

———. "Class and Gender in Victorian England." *Feminist Studies* 5 (1979): 87–141.

Delamont, Sara, and Lorna Duffin, eds. *The Nineteenth-Century Woman: Her Cultural and Physical World.* London: Croom Helm, 1978.

DePorte, Michael V. *Nightmares and Hobbyhorses: Swift, Sterne, and Augustan Ideas of Madness.* San Marino, Calif.: Huntington Library, 1974.

Deutsch, Felix. "A Footnote to Freud's Fragment of an Analysis of a Case of Hysteria." *Psychoanalytic Quarterly* 26 (1957): 159–67.

Dickens, Charles. *Uncollected Writings from "Household Words," 1850–1859.* Edited by Harry Stone. 2 vols. Bloomington: Indiana University Press, 1968.

Dicks, H. V. *Fifty Years of the Tavistock Clinic.* London: Routledge & Kegan Paul, 1970.

Didi-Huberman, Georges. *Invention de l'hystérie: Charcot et l'iconographie photographique de la Salpêtrière.* Paris: Macula, 1982.

Doerner, Klaus. *Madmen and the Bourgeoisie: A Social History of Insanity and Psychiatry.* Translated by Joachim Naugroschel and Jean Steinberg. Oxford: Basil Blackwell, 1981.

Donnelly, Michael. *Managing the Mind: A Study of Medical Psychology in Early Nineteenth-Century Britain.* London and New York: Tavistock Publications, 1983.

Doughty, Oswald. "The English Malady of the Eighteenth Century." *Review of English Studies* 2 (1926): 257–69.

Drinker, George Frederick. *The Birth of Neurosis: Myth, Malady, and the Victorians.* New York: Simon & Schuster, 1984.

Duffin, Lorna. "Prisoners of Progress: Women and Evolution." In *The Nineteenth-Century Woman: Her Cultural and Physical World,* edited by Sara Delamont and Lorna Duffin, pp. 57–91. London: Croom Helm, 1978.

Dyhouse, Carol. *Girls Growing Up in Late Victorian and Edwardian England.* London: Routledge & Kegan Paul, 1981.

Edgar, David. *Mary Barnes.* London: Eyre Methuen, 1979.

Edinger, Dora. *Bertha Pappenheim—Freud's Anna O.* Highland Park, Ill.: Congregation Solel, 1968.

Ellenberger, Henri F. *The Discovery of the Unconscious.* London: Basic Books, 1981.

Ellis, William Charles. *A Treatise on the Nature, Symptoms, Causes, and Treatment of Insanity.* 1838. Reprint. New York: Arno Press, 1976.

Esterson, Aaron, and R. D. Laing. *Sanity, Madness, and the Family.* Harmondsworth: Penguin Books, 1970.

Evans, Richard I., ed. *R. D. Laing: The Man and His Ideas.* New York: E. P. Dutton, 1976.

Ferenczi, Sandor, ed. *Psycho-Analysis and the War Neuroses.* London: International Psycho-Analytical Press, 1921.

First, Ruth, and Ann Scott. *Olive Schreiner.* London: Andre Deutsch, 1980.

Foucault, Michel. *The History of Sexuality.* Translated by Robert Hurley. Harmondsworth: Penguin Books, 1981.

Frame, Janet. *Faces in the Water.* 1961. Reprint. London: Women's Press, 1980.

Freeman, Lucy. *The Story of Anna O.* New York: Walker, 1972.

Freeman, Walter, and James Watts. *Psychosurgery.* Springfield, Ill.: Charles C. Thomas, 1942.

French, C. N. *The Story of St. Luke's Hospital.* London: William Heinemann, 1951.

Freud, Sigmund. *Collected Papers.* Edited by Ernest Jones. 5 vols. London: Hogarth Press, 1948.

———. *Dora: An Analysis of a Case of Hysteria.* New York: Collier Books, 1964.

———. "Female Sexuality" (1931). In *Sexuality and the Psychology of Love,* edited by Philip Rieff, pp. 194–211. New York: Collier Books, 1970.

Freud, Sigmund, and Josef Breuer. *Studies on Hysteria.* Harmondsworth: Penguin Books, 1974.

Fromm-Reichmann, Frieda, ed. *The Philosophy of Insanity.* By an inmate of the Glasgow Royal Asylum. 1860. Reprint. London: Fireside, 1947.

Fussell, Paul. *The Great War and Modern Memory.* New York and London: Oxford University Press, 1975.

———. *Siegfried Sassoon's Long Journey.* New York and London: Oxford University Press, 1983.

Gallop, Jane. *The Daughter's Seduction: Feminism and Psychoanalysis.* London: Macmillan Press, 1982.

Garrison, Dee. "Karen Horney and Feminism." *Signs* 6 (1981): 672–91.

Gilbert, Sandra M. "Soldier's Heart: Literary Men, Literary Women, and the Great War." *Signs* 8 (1983): 422–50.

Gilbert, Sandra M., and Susan Gubar. *The Madwoman in the Attic: The Woman Writer and the Nineteenth-Century Literary Imagination.* New Haven, Conn.: Yale University Press, 1978.

Gilbert, William. *Shirley Hall Asylum; or, The Memoirs of a Monomania.* London: William Freeman, 1863.

———. "A Visit to a Convict Lunatic Asylum." *Cornhill Magazine* 10 (1864): 448–60.

Gilman, Charlotte Perkins. "Why I Wrote 'The Yellow Wallpaper.' " In *The Charlotte Perkins Gilman Reader,* edited by Ann J. Lane, pp. 19–20. London: The Women's Press, 1981.

———. *The Yellow Wallpaper.* London: Virago Press, 1981.

Gilman, Sander L. *Seeing the Insane: A Cultural History of Psychiatric Illustration.* London: Wiley, 1985.

Gilman, Sander L., ed. *The Face of Madness: Hugh W. Diamond and the Origins of Psychiatric Photography.* New York: Brunner-Mazel, 1976.

Girard, Claude. "La Psychanalyse en Grande-Bretagne." In *Histoire de la psychanalyse,* edited by Roland Jacquard, pp. 313–61. Paris: Hachette, 1982.

Goffman, Erving. *Asylums: Essays on the Social Situation of Asylum Patients and Other Inmates.* Harmondsworth: Penguin Books, 1970.

Goldstein, Jan. "The Hysteria Diagnosis and the Politics of Anticlericalism in Late Nineteenth-Century France." *Journal of Modern History* 54 (1982): 209–39.

Gomberg, Edith S., and Violet Franks, eds. *Gender and Disordered Behavior: Sex Differences in Psychopathology.* New York: Brunner-Mazel, 1979.

Gordon, James S. "Who Is Mad? Who Is Sane? R. D. Laing in Search of a New Psychiatry." In *Going Crazy,* edited by Hendrik W. Ruitenbeek, pp. 65–102. New York: Bantam Books, 1972.

Gorham, Deborah. *The Victorian Girl and the Feminine Ideal.* London: Croom Helm, 1982.

Granville, J. Mortimer. *The Care and Cure of the Insane.* 2 vols. London: Hardwicke & Bogue, 1877.

Graves, Robert, *Good-bye to All That.* Harmondsworth: Penguin Books, 1973.

Grob, Gerald. *Mental Illness and American Society, 1875–1940.* Princeton, N.J.: Princeton University Press, 1983.

Guattari, Félix. "Mary Barnes, or Oedipus in Anti-Psychiatry." In *Molecular Revolution: Psychiatry and Politics,* translated by Rosemary Sheed, pp. 51–59. Harmondsworth: Penguin Books, 1984.

Halliday, Andrew. *A General View of the Present State of Lunatics and Lunatic Asylums in Great Britain and Ireland.* London: Underwood, 1828.

Haslam, John. *Considerations on the Moral Management of the Insane.* London: R. Hunter, 1817.

Heath, Stephen. *The Sexual Fix.* London: Macmillan, 1982.

Hill, Robert Gardiner. *Lunacy: Its Past and Present.* London: Longmans, Green, Reader & Dyer, 1870.

———. *Total Abolition of Personal Restraint in the Treatment of the Insane.* London: Simpkin, Marshall, 1838.

Horney, Karen. *Feminine Psychology.* Edited by Harold Kelman. London: W. W. Norton, 1980.

Howell, Elizabeth, and Marjorie Bayes, eds. *Women and Mental Health.* London: Basic Books, 1982.

Hunter, Dianne. "Hysteria, Psychoanalysis, and Feminism: The Case of Anna O." *Feminist Studies* 9 (1983): 465–88.

Hunter, Richard, and Ida Macalpine. "Dickens and Conolly: An Embarrassed Editor's Disclaimer." *Times Literary Supplement,* 11 August 1961, pp. 534–35.

———. *Psychiatry for the Poor: 1851 Colney Hatch Asylum–Friern Hospital 1973.* London: Dawsons, 1974.

———. *Three Hundred Years of Psychiatry, 1535–1860.* London: Oxford University Press, 1963.

Hyslop, T. B. *The Borderland.* London: P. Allan, 1924.

Ignatieff, Michael. *A Just Measure of Pain: The Penitentiary in the Industrial Revolution.* London: Macmillan Press, 1979.

Ingleby, David, ed. *Critical Psychiatry: The Politics of the Mental State.* Harmondsworth: Penguin Books, 1981.

"Inside Bedlam." *Timsley's Magazine* 3 (1869): 456–63.

Israël, L. *L'Hystérique, le sexe, et le médecin.* Paris: Masson, 1983.

Jones, Ernest. "War and Individual Psychology." *Sociological Review,* 1915.

Jones, Kathleen. *A History of the Mental Health Services.* London: Routledge & Kegan Paul, 1972.

———. *Lunacy, Law, and Conscience, 1744–1845: The Social History of the Care of the Insane.* London: Routledge & Kegan Paul, 1955.

———. *Mental Health and Social Policy, 1845–1959.* London: Routledge & Kegan Paul, 1960.

———. *Mental Hospitals at Work.* London: Routledge & Kegan Paul, 1962.

Jordan, Furneaux. *Character as Seen in Body and Parentage.* London: Kegan Paul, Trench & Trubner, 1886.

Kaplan, Bert, ed. *The Inner World of Mental Illness.* New York and London: Harper & Row, 1964.

Kapp, Yvonne. *Eleanor Marx.* 2 vols. London: Virago Press, 1976.

Kovel, Joel. "The American Mental Health Industry." In *Critical Psychiatry,* edited by David Ingleby, pp. 72–101. New York: Pantheon Books, 1980.

Kraepelin, Emil. *Lectures on Clinical Psychology.* Edited by Thomas Johnstone. London: Balliere, Tindall & Cox, 1913.

Laing, R. D. *The Divided Self.* Harmondsworth: Penguin Books, 1976.

———. *The Facts of Life.* Harmondsworth: Penguin Books, 1977.

———. *The Politics of Experience.* Harmondsworth: Penguin Books, 1984.

———. *The Politics of the Family and Other Essays.* New York: Vintage Books, 1972.

———. *Wisdom, Madness and Folly: The Making of a Psychiatrist, 1927–1957.* London: Macmillan, 1985.

Leavitt, Judith Walzer, ed. *Women and Health in America.* Madison and London: University of Wisconsin Press, 1984.

Leed, Eric. *No Man's Land: Combat and Identity in World War I.* Cambridge: Cambridge University Press, 1979.

Leigh, Denis. *The Historical Development of British Psychiatry.* London: Pergamon Press, 1961.

Léri, André. *Shell-Shock, Commotional and Emotional Aspects.* London: University of London Press, 1919.

Lewis, Sir Aubrey. "Henry Maudsley: His Work and Influence." In *The State of Psychiatry,* vol. 1 of *Essays and Addresses.* New York: Science House, 1967.

Lewis, Helen Block. *Psychic War in Men and Women.* New York: New York University Press, 1976.

Littlewood, Roland, and Maurice Lipsedge. *Aliens and Alienists: Ethnic Minorities and Psychiatry.* Harmondsworth: Penguin Books, 1982.

Lloyd, Genevieve. *The Man of Reason: "Male" and "Female" in Western Philosophy.* Minneapolis: University of Minnesota Press, 1984.

London Feminist History Group. *The Sexual Dynamics of History.* London: Pluto Press, 1985.

Lowe, Louisa. *The Bastilles of England; or, The Lunacy Laws at Work.* London: Crookenden, 1883.

MacCormack, Carol, and Marilyn Strathern, eds. *Nature, Culture, and Gender.* Cambridge: Cambridge University Press, 1980.

MacDonald, Michael. *Mystical Bedlam: Madness, Anxiety, and Healing in Seventeenth-Century England.* Cambridge: Cambridge University Press, 1981.

Mackenzie, Charlotte. "Women and Psychiatric Professionalization, 1780–1914." In *The Sexual Dynamics of History,* by the London Feminist History Group. London: Pluto Press, 1985.

MacLeod, Sheila. *The Art of Starvation.* London: Virago Press, 1981.

Marr, H. C. *Psychoses of the War.* London: Henry Froude, 1919.

Marshall, C. F. *Syphilology and Venereal Disease.* New York: William Wood, 1906.

Martineau, Harriet. *Miscellanies.* 2 vols. Boston: Hilliard, Gray, 1834.

Masters, Anthony. *Bedlam.* London: Michael Joseph, 1977.
Maudsley, Henry. *Body and Mind.* London: Macmillan, 1870.
———. *Body and Mind.* 2nd ed. London: Macmillan, 1873.
———. *Body and Will.* London: Kegan Paul, Trench, 1883.
———. "Memoir of the Late John Conolly, M.D." *Journal of Mental Science* 12 (1866): 151–74.
———. *The Pathology of Mind.* London: Macmillan, 1879.
———. *The Pathology of Mind: A Study of Its Distempers, Deformities, and Disorders.* London and New York: Macmillan, 1895.
———. *The Physiology and Pathology of Mind.* New York: D. Appleton, 1867.
———. *Responsibility in Mental Disease.* 2nd ed. London: Kegan Paul, 1874.
———. "Sex in Mind and in Education." *Fortnightly Review* 15 (1874): 466–83.
Maxwell, W. N. *A Psychological Retrospective of the Great War.* London: George Allen & Unwin, 1923.
Mayos, Charles W. *Poetry of the Insane.* Peoria, Kans.: n.p., 1933.
McGovern, Constance M. "Doctors or Ladies? Women Physicians in Psychiatric Institutions, 1872-1900." In *Women and Health in America,* edited by Judith Walzer Leavitt, pp. 438–52. Madison: University of Wisconsin Press, 1984.
Mellett, D. J. "Bureaucracy and Mental Illness: The Commissioners in Lunacy, 1845–1890." *Medical History* 25 (1981): 221–50.
Mercier, Charles. *Sanity and Insanity.* New York: Scribner & Welford, 1890.
———. *A Textbook of Insanity.* 2nd ed. London: George Allen & Unwin, 1914.
Mezan, Peter. "After Freud and Jung, Now Comes R. D. Laing." *Esquire,* January 1972, pp. 92–97, 160–78.
———. "R. D. Laing: Portrait of a Twentieth-Century Skeptic." In *R. D. Laing: The Man and His Ideas,* edited by Richard I. Evans, pp. xxii–xxv. New York: E. P. Dutton, 1976.
Millar, John. *Hints on Insanity.* London: Henry Renshaw, 1861.
Mitchell, Juliet. *Psychoanalysis and Feminism.* Harmondsworth: Penguin Books, 1974.
———. *Women: The Longest Revolution.* London: Virago Press, 1984.
Mitchell, Juliet, and Ann Oakley, eds. *The Rights and Wrongs of Women.* Harmondsworth: Penguin Books, 1976.
Mitchell, S. Weir. *Fat and Blood and How to Make Them.* Philadelphia: J. B. Lippincott, 1877.
Moers, Ellen. *Literary Women: The Great Writers.* London: The Women's Press, 1984.
Moore, Cecil A. "The English Malady." In *Backgrounds of English Literature, 1700–1760,* pp. 179–235. Minneapolis: University of Minnesota Press, 1953.
Morison, Alexander. *The Physiognomy of Mental Diseases.* 1843. Reprint. New York: Arno Press, 1976.
Mott, Frederick W. *War Neuroses and Shell Shock.* London: Hodder & Stoughton, 1919.

Mulock, Thomas. *British Lunatic Asylums: Public and Private.* Stafford: Hill & Haldon, 1858.

Munthe, Axel. *The Story of San Michele.* London: John Murray, 1930.

My Experience in a Lunatic Asylum. By "A Sane Patient." London: Chatto & Windus, 1879.

Myers, Charles S. *Shell-Shock in France.* Cambridge: Cambridge University Press, 1940.

Neumann, Erich. *Amor and Psyche: The Psychic Development of the Feminine.* Princeton, N. J.: Princeton University Press, 1956.

Nightingale, Florence. *Cassandra.* Edited by Myra Stark. Old Westbury, N. Y.: Feminist Press, 1979.

———. *Suggestions for Thought to Searchers After Religious Truth.* 3 vols. Privately printed. London: Eyre & Spottiswoode, 1860.

Oakley, Ann. *Subject Women.* London: Fontana Press, 1985.

O'Prey, Paul, ed. *In Broken Images: Selected Letters of Robert Graves, 1914–1946.* London: Hutchinson, 1982.

Owen, A. R. G. *Hysteria, Hypnosis, and Healing: The Work of J.-M. Charcot.* London: Dennis Dobson, 1971.

Packard, E. P. W. *Modern Persecution; or, Insane Asylums Unveiled.* 1873. Reprint. New York: Arno Press, 1973.

Palmer, R. L. *Anorexia Nervosa.* Harmondsworth: Penguin Books, 1980.

Parry-Jones, William. *The Trade in Lunacy: A Study of Private Madhouses in England in the Eighteenth and Nineteenth Centuries.* London: Routledge & Kegan Paul, 1972.

Pearson, Geoffrey. *The Deviant Imagination: Psychiatry, Social Work, and Social Change.* London: Macmillan, 1975.

Penfold, P. Susan, and Gillian A. Walker. *Women and the Psychiatric Paradox.* Montreal and London: Eden Press, 1983.

Playfair, W. S. *The Systematic Treatment of Nerve Prostration and Hysteria.* Philadelphia: Henry Lea, 1883.

Poirier, Suzanne. "The Weir Mitchell Rest Cure: Doctors and Patients." *Women's Studies* 10 (1983): 15–40.

"Popular Psychological Literature." *Journal of Psychological Medicine* 10 (1857): 548–64.

Porter, Roy. "Being Mad in Georgian England." *History Today* 31 (1981): 42–48.

Raby, Peter. *Fair Ophelia: Harriet Smithson Berlioz.* Cambridge: Cambridge University Press, 1982.

Ramon, Shulamit. *Psychiatry in Britain: Meaning and Policy.* London: Croom Helm, 1985.

Reade, Charles. *Hard Cash: A Matter-of-Fact Romance.* London: Ward, Lock, 1864.

Reed, David. *Anna.* Harmondsworth: Penguin Books, 1979.

Reid, Ivan, and Eileen Warmald. *Sex Differences in Britain.* London: Grant McIntyre, 1982.

Reid, John. "On the Causes, Symptoms, and Treatment of Puerperal Insanity." *Journal of Psychological Medicine* 1 (1848): 128–51.

Rivers, W. H. R. *Instinct and the Unconscious.* 2nd ed. Cambridge: Cambridge University Press, 1922.

———. *Psychology and Politics.* London: Kegan Paul, Trench & Trubner, 1923.

Roazen, Paul. *Freud and His Followers.* Harmondsworth: Penguin Books, 1979.

———. *Helene Deutsch: A Psychoanalyst's Life.* New York: Anchor Press, 1985.

Roberts, Nesta. *Cheadle Royal Hospital; A Bicentenary History.* Altringham: John Sherratt & Son, 1967.

Rosen, George. *Madness in Society: Chapters in the Historical Sociology of Mental Illness.* New York: Harper & Row, 1968.

Rosenbaum, Max, and Melvin Muroff, eds. *Anna O.: Fourteen Contemporary Reinterpretations.* New York and London: Free Press, 1984.

Rosenberg, Charles D. "The Place of George M. Beard in Nineteenth-Century British Psychiatry." *Bulletin of the History of Medicine* 36 (1962): 245–59.

Roueché, Burton. "As Empty as Eve." *New Yorker,* 9 September 1974, pp. 84–100.

Ruitenbeek, Hendrik W., ed. *Going Crazy.* New York: Bantam Books, 1972.

Sakel, Manfred. *Schizophrenia.* New York: Philosophical Library, 1958.

Salmon, Thomas W. *The Care and Treatment of Mental Diseases and War Neuroses ("Shell Shock") in the British Army.* New York: War Work Committee of the National Committee for Mental Hygiene, 1917.

Salow, Roberta. "Where Has All the Hysteria Gone?" *Psychoanalytic Review* 66 (1979–80): 463–78.

Sampson, Harold, Sheldon L. Messinger, and Robert D. Towne. *Schizophrenic Women: Studies in Marital Crisis.* New York: Atherton, 1964.

"A Sane Patient." See *My Experience in a Lunatic Asylum.*

Sargent, William. *The Unquiet Mind.* Boston: Little, Brown, 1967.

Sassoon, Siegfried. *Diaries, 1915–1918.* Edited by Rupert Hart-Davis. London: Faber & Faber, 1983.

———. *Diaries, 1920–1922.* Edited by Rupert Hart-Davis. London: Faber & Faber, 1981.

———. *Memoirs of an Infantry Officer.* London: Faber & Faber, 1965.

———. *Sherston's Progress.* London: Faber & Faber, 1983.

———. *Siegfried's Journey.* London: Faber & Faber, 1982.

Savage, George Henry, and Edwin Goodall. *Insanity and Allied Neuroses.* 4th ed. London: Cassell, 1907.

Schatzman, Morton. "Madness and Morals." In *R. D. Laing and Anti-Psychiatry,* edited by Robert Boyers and Robert Orrill, pp. 235–72. New York: Harper & Row, 1971.

Scheff, Thomas, *Labeling Madness.* London: Prentice-Hall, 1975.

Schmideberg, Melitta. "A Contribution to the History of the Psycho-Analytic Movement in Britain." *British Journal of Psychiatry* 118 (1971): 66-68.

Schumer, Florence. "Gender and Schizophrenia." In *Gender and Disordered Behavior: Sex Differences in Psychopathology,* edited by Edith S. Gomberg and Violet Franks, pp. 321–53. New York: Brunner-Mazel, 1979.

Scott, Francis. "English County Asylums." *Fortnightly Review* 32 (1879): 114–43.

Scull, Andrew T. "A Brilliant Career? John Conolly and Victorian Psychiatry." *Victorian Studies* 27 (1984): 203–35.

———. *Decarceration: Community Treatment of the Deviant.* London: Polity Press, 1984.

———. "The Domestication of Madness." *Medical History* 27 (1983): 233–48.

———. *Museums of Madness: The Social Organization of Insanity in Nineteenth-Century England.* New York: St. Martin's Press, 1979. Harmondsworth: Penguin Books, 1982.

———. ed. *Madhouses, Mad-Doctors, and Madmen: The Social History of Psychiatry in the Victorian Era.* London: Athlone Press, 1981.

Sedgwick, Peter. *Psycho Politics.* London: Pluto Press, 1982.

Shepherd, Michael. *People Not Psychiatry.* London: George Allen & Unwin, 1973.

Sheppard, Edgar. *Lectures on Madness in Its Medical, Legal, and Social Aspects.* London: John Churchill, 1873.

Sheppard, James. *Observations of the Proximate Causes of Insanity.* London: Longman, Brown, Green & Longmans, 1944.

Showalter, Elaine. "Florence Nightingale's Feminist Complaint." *Signs* 6 (1981): 395–412.

———. *A Literature of Their Own: British Women Novelists from Brontë to Lessing.* London: Virago Press, 1978.

———. "Syphilis, Sexuality, and the Fin de Siècle." In *Sex, Politics, and Science in the Nineteenth-Century Novel: Essays from the English Institute,* edited by Ruth Yeazell and Neil Hertz. Baltimore: Johns Hopkins University Press, forthcoming 1986.

Sicherman, Barbara. "The Uses of a Diagnosis: Doctors, Patients, and Neurasthenia." *Journal of the History of Medicine* 32 (1977): 33–54.

Sigal, Clancy. *Zone of the Interior.* New York: Thomas Y. Crowell, 1976.

Skey, F. C. *Hysteria.* 2nd ed. London: Longmans, Green, Reader & Dyer, 1867.

Skultans, Vieda. *English Madness: Ideas on Insanity, 1580-1890.* London: Routledge & Kegan Paul, 1978.

———. *Madness and Morals: Ideas on Insanity in the Nineteenth Century.* London and Boston: Routledge & Kegan Paul, 1975.

Slobodin, Richard. *W. H. R. Rivers.* New York: Columbia University Press, 1978.

Smith, Elliott, and T. H. Pear. *Shell-Shock and Its Lessons.* London: Longmans Green, 1917.

Smith, Roger, *Trial by Medicine: Insanity and Responsibility in Victorian Trials.* Edinburgh: Edinburgh University Press, 1981.

Smith, W. Tyler. "The Climacteric Disease in Women." *London Journal of Medicine* 1 (1848): 601–609.

Smith-Rosenberg, Carroll. *Disorderly Conduct: Visions of Gender in Victorian America.* New York: Alfred A. Knopf, 1985.

Southard, E. C. *Shell-Shock and Other Neuro-Psychiatric Problems.* Boston: W. M. Leonard, 1919.

Spivak, Gayatri C. "French Feminism in an International Frame." *Yale French Studies,* no. 62 (1981): 154–84.

Stallworthy, Jon. *Wilfred Owen.* London: Oxford University Press and Chatto & Windus, 1974.

Stedman Jones, Gareth. *Outcast London: A Study in the Relationship Between Classes in Victorian Society.* Harmondsworth: Penguin Books, 1971. New York: Pantheon Books, 1984.

Storer, Horatio R. *The Causation, Course, and Treatment of Reflex Insanity in Women.* 1871. Reprint. New York: Arno Press, 1972.

Strouse, Jean. *Alice James: A Biography.* London: Cape, 1981.

Tilt, Edward J. *The Change of Life in Health and Disease.* London: John Churchill, 1887

———. *The Elements of Health, and Principles of Female Hygiene.* London: Henry G. Bohn, 1852.

———. *A Handbook of Uterine Therapeutics and of Diseases of Women.* 4th ed. New York: William Wood, 1881.

———. *On the Preservation of the Health of Women at the Critical Periods of Life.* London: John Churchill, 1851.

Tomes, Nancy. *A Generous Confidence: Thomas Story Kirkbride and the Art of Asylum Keeping, 1840–1883.* Cambridge and New York: Cambridge University Press, 1984.

Trombley, Stephen. *All That Summer She Was Mad: Virginia Woolf and Her Doctors.* London: Junction Books, 1981.

Tuke, Daniel Hack. *Chapters in the History of the Insane in the British Isles.* 1882. Reprint. Amsterdam: E. J. B. Bunset, 1968.

———. *Insanity in Ancient and Modern Life, with Chapters on Its Prevention.* London: Macmillan, 1878.

———. *Reform in the Treatment of the Insane.* London: John Churchill, 1892.

Tuke, Daniel Hack, ed. *Dictionary of Psychological Medicine.* Philadelphia: P. Blakiston, 1892.

Tuke, J. Batty. "On the Statistics of Puerperal Insanity as Observed in the Royal Edinburgh Asylum, Morningside." *Edinburgh Medical Journal* 10 (1865): 1013–28

Tuke, Samuel. *A Description of the Retreat.* 1813. Reprint. London: Dawsons, 1964.

Veith, Ilza. *Hysteria: The History of a Disease.* Chicago: University of Chicago Press, 1965.

Vicinus, Martha. *Independent Women: Work and Community for Single Women, 1850–1920.* London: Virago Press, 1985.

———. "'One Life to Stand Beside Me': Emotional Conflicts in First-Generation College Women in England." *Feminist Studies* 8 (1982): 603–28.

Wahl, Charles William. "Ella Freeman Sharpe." In *Psychoanalytic Pioneers,* edited by Franz Alexander et al., pp. 265–71. New York: Basic Books, 1966.

Walkowitz, Judith R. *Prostitution and Victorian Society: Women, Class, and the State.* London: Cambridge University Press, 1980.

———. "Jack the Ripper and the Myth of Male Violence." *Feminist Studies* 8 (1982): 543–74.

Weeks, Jeffrey. *Sex, Politics, and Society.* London: Longman, 1981.

White, Antonia. *As Once in May: The Early Autobiography of Antonia White.* Edited by Susan Chitty. London: Virago Press, 1983.

———. *Beyond the Glass.* London: Virago Press, 1979.

Wing, J. W. *Reasoning About Madness.* London: Oxford University Press, 1978.

Wing, J. W., and G. W. Brown. *Institutionalization and Schizophrenia.* Cambridge: Cambridge University Press, 1970.

Winslow, L. Forbes. *The Insanity of Passion and Crime.* London: John Ousely, 1912.

———. *On the Obscure Diseases of the Brain and Disorders of the Mind.* 4th ed. London: John Churchill, 1851.

———. *Recollections of Forty Years.* London: John Ousely, 1910.

Winslow, Lyttleton. *Manual of Lunacy.* London: Smith, Elder, 1874.

Wohl, Robert. *The Generation of 1914.* Cambridge, Mass.: Harvard University Press, 1979.

Wollstonecraft, Mary. *Mary,* and *The Wrongs of Woman.* London: Oxford University Press, 1980.

"Woman in Her Psychological Relations." *Journal of Psychological Medicine and Mental Pathology* 4 (1851): 18–50.

Women in Society: Interdisciplinary Essays. By the Cambridge Women's Study Group. London: Virago Press, 1981.

Wood, Ann D. "The Fashionable Diseases: Women's Complaints and Their Treatment in Nineteenth-Century America." In *Clio's Consciousness Raised,* edited by Mary Hartman and Lois W. Banner, pp. 1–22. New York: Harper & Row, 1971.

Woodham-Smith, Cecil. *Florence Nightingale.* New York: McGraw-Hill, 1951.

Woodward, John, and David Richards, eds. *Health Care and Popular Medicine in Nineteenth-Century England.* London: Croom Helm, 1977.

Woolf, Virginia. *The Diary.* 5 vols. Edited by Anne Olivier Bell. London: Hogarth Press, 1978–84.

———. *The Letters.* 6 vols. Edited by Nigel Nicolson and Joanne Trautmann. London: Hogarth Press, 1975–80.

Wynter, Andrew. *The Borderlands of Insanity*. 2nd ed. London: Robert Hardwicke, 1875.
———. "Lunatic Asylums." *Quarterly Review* 101 (1857): 353–93.
Yealland, Lewis R. *Hysterical Disorders of Warfare*. London: Macmillan, 1918.
Zilboorg, Gregory. *A History of Medical Psychology*. New York: W. W. Norton, 1941.

INDEX